The Power of Human Imagination
New Methods in Psychotherapy

EMOTIONS, PERSONALITY, AND PSYCHOTHERAPY

Series Editors:
Carroll E. Izard • *University of Delaware, Newark, Delaware*
and
Jerome L. Singer • *Yale University, New Haven, Connecticut*

HUMAN EMOTIONS
Carroll E. Izard

THE PERSONAL EXPERIENCE OF TIME
Bernard S. Gorman and Alden E. Wessman, eds.

THE STREAM OF CONSCIOUSNESS: Scientific Investigations into the
Flow of Human Experience
Kenneth S. Pope and Jerome L. Singer, eds.

THE POWER OF HUMAN IMAGINATION: New Methods in Psychotherapy
Jerome L. Singer and Kenneth S. Pope, eds.

EMOTIONS IN PERSONALITY AND PSYCHOPATHOLOGY
Carroll E. Izard, ed.

A Continuation Order Plan is available for this series. A continuation order will bring delivery of each new volume immediately upon publication. Volumes are billed only upon actual shipment. For further information please contact the publisher.

The Power of Human Imagination
New Methods in Psychotherapy

Edited by
Jerome L. Singer
Yale University

and

Kenneth S. Pope
Brentwood Veterans Administration Hospital
Los Angeles, California

PLENUM PRESS · NEW YORK AND LONDON

Library of Congress Cataloging in Publication Data

Main entry under title:

The Power of human imagination.

(Emotions, personality, and psychotherapy)
Includes bibliographical references and index.
1. Fantasy – Therapeutic use – Addresses, essays, lectures. I. Singer, Jerome L. II. Pope, Kenneth S. III. Series.
RC489.F35P68   616.8'914   78-15392
ISBN-13: 978-1-4613-3943-4   e-ISBN-13: 978-1-4613-3941-0
DOI: 10.1007/978-1-4613-3941-0

© 1978 Plenum Press, New York
Softcover reprint of the hardcover 1st edition 1978
A Division of Plenum Publishing Corporation
227 West 17th Street, New York, N.Y. 10011

All rights reserved

No part of this book may be reproduced, stored in a retrieval system, or transmitted, in any form or by any means, electronic, mechanical, photocopying, microfilming, recording, or otherwise, without written permission from the Publisher

To our patients

from whom we have learned so much about
the human capacity for imagination

Contributors

Joseph R. Cautela • Department of Psychology, Boston College, Boston, Massachusetts

Susan J. Frank • Department of Psychology, University of Maryland, College Park, Maryland

Jesse D. Geller • Department of Psychiatry, Yale University School of Medicine, New Haven, Connecticut

Eric Greenleaf • Private practice, Berkeley, California

Mardi J. Horowitz • Department of Psychiatry, University of California School of Medicine, San Francisco, California

Alan E. Kazdin • Department of Psychology, The Pennsylvania State University, University Park, Pennsylvania

Hanscarl Leuner • Department of Psychiatry, University of Göttingen, Göttingen, West Germany

Leigh McCullough • Department of Psychology, Boston College, Boston, Massachusetts

Donald Meichenbaum • Department of Psychology, University of Waterloo, Waterloo, Ontario, Canada

Kenneth S. Pope • Brentwood Veterans Administration Hospital, Los Angeles, California

Joseph Reyher • Department of Psychology, Michigan State University, East Lansing, Michigan

K. David Schultz • Division of Psychiatry, Waterbury Hospital Health Center, Waterbury, Connecticut

Anees A. Sheikh • Department of Psychology, Marquette University, Milwaukee, Wisconsin

Joseph E. Shorr • Institute for Psycho-Imagination Therapy, Los Angeles, California

Jerome L. Singer • Psychology Department, Yale University, New Haven, Connecticut

Preface

For at least half of the twentieth century, psychology and the other mental health professions all but ignored the significant adaptive possibilities of the human gift of imagery. Our capacity seemingly to duplicate sights, sounds, and other sensory experiences through some form of central brain process continues to remain a mysterious, almost miraculous skill. Because imagery is so much a private experience, experimental psychologists found it hard to measure and turned their attention to observable behaviors that could easily be studied in animals as well as in humans. Psychoanalysts and others working with the emotionally disturbed continued to take imagery information seriously in the form of dream reports, transference fantasies, and as indications of hallucinations or delusions. On the whole, however, they emphasized the maladaptive aspects of the phenomena, the distortions and defensiveness or the "regressive" qualities of daydreams and sequences of images.

The present volume grows out of a long series of investigations by the senior author that have suggested that daydreaming and the stream of consciousness are not simply manifestations in adult life of persisting phenomena of childhood. Rather, the data suggest that imagery sequences represent a major system of encoding and transforming information, a basic human capacity that is inevitably part of the brain's storage process and one that has enormous potential for adaptive utility. A companion volume, *The Stream of Consciousness*, edited by Kenneth S. Pope and Jerome L. Singer (New York: Plenum Press, 1978) presents some of the basic theory and experimental research to providing a systematic scientific understanding of the nature of imagery sequences as a part of the flow of experience.

This volume emphasizes a major new turn in the clinical application of our understanding of imagery and related fantasy or daydream activities. While some of the methods can, of course, be traced to early experimental uses by Freud (imagery association), Jung (active imagination), and Schultz (autogenic training), most of the procedures emphasized in this volume have evolved as systematic treatment procedures within the past fifteen or twenty years. An earlier work (Singer, J. L., *Imagery and Daydream Methods in Psychotherapy and Behavior Modification*, New York: Academic Press, 1974) pointed to the coexistence of imagery uses in a wide variety of treatment modalities from psychoanalysis through the European mental imagery approaches and the American and British emphasis on behavior modification. The present volume brings together leading practitioners and theorists of these methods for the first time. It provides a forum for presenting, under one cover, systematic examples of practical clinical applications of imagery and fantasy methods within psychoanalytic, cognitive, and behaviorist orientations and the mental imagery approaches that have been thriving in Europe. While it may be premature to attempt a systematic integration of these diverse uses of imagery for clinical purposes, the unifying principle of this volume is that imagery or the sequences of images that we call daydreams or fantasies have tremendous adaptive possibilities for treatment of emotional disorders or for self-development in general.

The book is organized into six sections. The first consists of a chapter by the editors reviewing the range of clinical uses of imagery and relating imagery and fantasy to basic processes in psychology. There is, at least, a signpost toward possible convergences of the differing paths. The second section brings together uses of imagery that relate closest to psychoanalytic or psychodynamic orientations in psychotherapy. The third section reflects the developments influenced by Jung, Schultz, and Desoille in Europe of the mental imagery or guided daydream techniques and also provides examples of treatment in which imagery is the core of the therapeutic strategy. The fourth section provides examples of how leading American behaviorists view the value of imagery in treatments with more precisely specified focal points and with stronger emphasis on evaluative research. The fifth section provides broader applications of imagery use, its potential for hospital treatment, for preventative application, and for ties to humanistic or body-oriented self-development approaches. This section also provides in greater detail examples of very specific research to suggest new directions for systematic evaluations of the possibilities of imagery use in a variety of treatment or preventive systems. The final section presents an attempt, from the standpoint of the newly evolving field of cognitive behavior modification, to point to possible bases for why imagery methods in so many different theoretical systems of psychotherapy do produce personality change. Extensive bibliographies are

Preface

provided by each contributor to permit clinicians and researchers in imagery or psychotherapy opportunities to explore in more detail basic theoretical or empirical studies that underlie the particular approaches included herein.

Some of the material of this volume was developed while Kenneth Pope held fellowships from the National Institute of Mental Health. The translation of the chapter by Professor Hanscarl Leuner was provided by Augusta Arthur of Yale University, who would like to acknowledge the assistance of Kevyn Arthur and Jeffrey Blum in some phases of the work. Valuable aid in typing or retyping portions of the manuscript was provided by Judith McBride, Lisa Rosenberg, Muriel Jarmak, and Virginia Hurd. Bibliographic assistance was also provided the editors by Lawrence Rosenberg and John Caldeira.

JEROME L. SINGER
KENNETH S. POPE

Contents

Part I • Introduction and Overview 1

Chapter 1
The Use of Imagery and Fantasy Techniques in Psychotherapy
Jerome L. Singer and Kenneth S. Pope

1. Introduction 3
2. The Stunted Growth of Psychology and Psychotherapy: A Bias toward Verbal and Directed Thought 5
3. Therapy and Imagination 7
4. Dimensions of Cognition and Expression 8
5. Psychoanalysis and Related Psychodynamic Approaches .. 14
6. More Direct Forms of Clinical Intervention 23
7. Self-Efficacy and Imagery 26
8. Some Preventive and Constructive Uses of Our Imagery Capacities 28
   8.1. Imagery and Adaptive Escapism 29
   8.2. Imagery Uses for Self-Awareness 29
   8.3. Imagery for Self-Regulation and Biofeedback 30
   8.4. Imagery for Creativity and Aesthetic Experience .. 31
   References 32

Part II • Psychoanalytically Oriented Uses of Imagery .. 35

Chapter 2
Controls of Visual Imagery and Therapist Intervention
Mardi J. Horowitz

1. Introduction 37

2. Image Formation as a Mode of Representation 38
3. Utility of the Visual Image System 40
4. A Model of the Image System 41
5. Defenses and the Process of Working-Through 43
6. Techniques to Alter Inhibitory Operations 43
7. Facilitations and Inhibitory Failures 46
8. More Complex Defensive Operations 46
9. Summary 48
   References 48

Chapter 3
Emergent Uncovering Psychotherapy: The Use of Imagoic and Linguistic Vehicles in Objectifying Psychodynamic Processes
Joseph Reyher

1. Introduction 51
2. Procedures for Objectifying and Differentiating Awareness and Interpersonal Behavior 53
   2.1. Self-Disclosure 53
   2.2. Entrée Points: The Exploration of Self-Awareness 54
   2.3. Eyes Closed Free Association 57
   2.4. The Verbalization of Suppressed and Dissociated Material: A Clinical Illustration 59
   2.5. Relevant Laboratory Investigations 62
3. Objectifying Repression and Repressed Drive-Related Impulses 64
4. Modes of Information Processing 67
5. Relevant Clinical Illustrations 69
6. Laboratory Investigations of Drive Intensification 72
7. A Conceptual Integration 73
   7.1. Intrapsychic Drives 74
   7.2. Dissociation 78
   7.3. Security Operations and Defenses against Impulses .. 81
   7.4. Endopsychic Drives 83
   7.5. Free Imagery: The Mechanisms of Image Retrieval ... 84
   7.6. Uncovering: Pathogenesis and Therapeutics 86
8. Conclusions and Wider Implications 88
   8.1. Domains of Phenomena 88
   8.2. Can Spontaneous Visual Imagery Be Symbolic? 89
   8.3. Creativity 90
   8.4. Implications for Freudian and Sullivanian Theory 91
   References 92

Chapter 4
Clinical Use of Categories of Therapeutic Imagery
Joseph E. Shorr

1. Introduction: The Function of Imagery 95
2. The Technique of Psycho-Imagination Therapy 97
3. Spontaneous Imagery 99
4. Directed Imagery 101
5. Self-Image Imagery 101
6. Dual Imagery 102
7. Body Imagery 105
8. Sexual Imagery 106
9. Predicting Imagery 108
10. Task Imagery 109
11. Cathartic Imagery 111
12. Depth Imagery 111
13. General Imagery 112
14. Detection of Resistance in Imagery Production 113
15. Group Therapy Imagery 115
16. Current Research 119
    References 120

Part III • Mental Imagery Therapies 123

Chapter 5
Basic Principles and Therapeutic Efficacy of Guided Affective Imagery (GAI)
Hanscarl Leuner

1. Introduction 125
2. Theoretical Foundations 126
3. Mobile Projection 127
    3.1. Diagnostic Aspect 128
    3.2. Spontaneous Projection 129
    3.3. Synchronic Transformation 130
4. Bringing Core Conflicts into Focus 130
5. Standard Themes 132
    5.1. Standard Motifs of GAI 132
6. Therapeutic Techniques 139
    6.1. Specific Techniques and Strategies 139
7. Management Models in Symbolic Drama (Symbolic Operation) 143

	7.1. Two Examples	143
	7.2. Theoretical Excursus	144
	7.3. Elementary Level	146
	7.4. Intermediate Level	146
	7.5. Advanced Level	147
8.	Investigative Findings	148
	8.1. Literature	148
	8.2. Statistical Studies	149
	8.3. Case Histories	154
	8.4. Didactic Possibilities	157
9.	Some Theoretical Reflections on GAI	158
	9.1. The General Psychodynamic Concept	158
	9.2. What Is Therapeutically Effective in GAI?	158
	9.3. The Nature of Transference Relationships in GAI	159
	9.4. Symbolic Concepts	161
10.	Indications	162
11.	Summary	162
	References	163

Chapter 6
Active Imagining
Eric Greenleaf

1. Introduction	167
2. Dream Action and Dream Meanings	168
3. Human Competence	171
4. Realism in Dreamwork	173
5. Modalities of Experience	176
6. The Structure of Healing	179
7. Archetype and Image	183
8. Images and the Structure of Thought	186
9. Structure Abstracted	191
References	195

Chapter 7
Eidetic Psychotherapy
Anees A. Sheikh

1. Introduction	197
2. Mental Images and Their Classification	198
2.1. After-Images	200

	2.2. Eidetic Images	200
	2.3. Memory Images	200
	2.4. Imagination Images	201
3.	Ahsen's Eidetic Image: The ISM	201
	3.1. Visiosomatic Fixation and Dessociation	203
	3.2. Bipolar Configurations	204
	3.3. The Magical Laws of the Psyche	204
4.	Eidetics and Electrically Evoked Recollections	205
5.	The ISM Theory of Personality	207
6.	Diagnostic and Therapeutic Procedures	210
	6.1. The Age Projection Test	211
	6.2. Eidetic Parents Test	212
7.	A Case History	219
8.	Concluding Remarks	220
	References	222

Part IV • Behavior-Therapy Uses of Imagery 225

Chapter 8
Covert Conditioning: A Learning-Theory Perspective on Imagery
Joseph R. Cautela and Leigh McCullough

1.	Introduction	227
2.	Covert Conditioning Assumptions and Procedures	228
	2.1. A Learning-Theory Basis for Covert Conditioning	228
	2.2. Covert Conditioning Procedures	230
3.	Imagery Development	234
	3.1. Construction of Covert Scenes	234
	3.2. Development of Imagery Capacity	235
	3.3. Training to Enhance Vividness and Controllability	236
	3.4. Imagery Practice	238
	3.5. Assessment of Imagery	239
4.	Application of Covert Processes to Overall Functioning	239
	4.1. Covert Processes and Maladaptive Behavior	240
	4.2. Behavioral Hygiene and Therapeutic Measures	241
5.	Application of Covert Processes to Specific Classes of Behavior	243
	5.1. Covert Behavior and Daydreaming	243
	5.2. Covert Behavior of Nocturnal Dreaming	246
	5.3. The Use of Covert Conditioning in the Modification of Organic Dysfunction	248
	References	250

Chapter 9
Covert Modeling: The Therapeutic Application of Imagined Rehearsal
Alan E. Kazdin

1. Introduction	255
2. Background and Implication of Covert Modeling	256
3. Efficacy of Covert Modeling	259
4. Important Parameters of Covert Modeling	261
4.1. Model–Client Similarity	261
4.2. Model Identity	263
4.3. Multiple Models	263
4.4. Model Consequences	264
4.5. Unexplored Parameters	265
5. Assessment of Imagery and the Mechanisms of Behavior Change	267
6. Imagery-Based Techniques versus Overt Behavior Rehearsal	270
7. Conclusions and Implications	273
References	275

Part V • Broader Applications of Imagery 279

Chapter 10
Imagery and the Control of Depression
K. David Schultz

1. Introduction	281
2. Imagery in the Treatment of Depression: A Research Strategy	282
2.1. Methodology	283
2.2. Results	284
2.3. Discussion	288
2.4. Directedness of Imagery	289
2.5. Interpersonal Significance of Imagery	290
3. Alternative Models	291
4. Patterns of Depressive Experiences	295
5. Daydreaming Patterns	297
6. Conclusions	298
7. The Nature of the Psychotherapeutic Process	299
8. Imagery, Daydreaming, and a Cognitive Theory of Self-Control	299

9. The Conscious Control of Consciousness: The Use of Imagery in Alleviating Depression 300
10. Psychotherapeutic Uses of Imagery 303
    10.1. Clinical Illustrations 303
    10.2. An Overview 305
    References 305

Chapter 11
Just Imagine How I Feel: How to Improve Empathy Through Training in Imagination
Susan J. Frank

1. Introduction 309
2. Theoretical Background: Three Levels of Empathy 310
    2.1. The Behavioral Level of Empathy 310
    2.2. The Subjective Level of Empathy 311
    2.3. The Psychoanalytic Notion of Empathy 314
    2.4. The Cognitive-Structural Level of Empathy 314
    2.5. Implications for Empathy Training 317
3. Research Procedures 318
    3.1. Overview of the Research Plan 318
    3.2. Hypotheses 318
    3.3. Empathy Training Conditions 320
    3.4. Outcome Measures 322
4. Results of the Study 325
    4.1. Major Findings 326
    4.2. Additional Findings 331
5. Discussion 336
    5.1. Review of the Findings: Some "Ifs," "Ands," and "Buts" 336
    5.2. Further Implications for Research and Practice 341
    5.3. Theoretical Implications: The Fourth Level of Empathy 342
    References 344

Chapter 12
The Body, Expressive Movement, and Physical Contact in Psychotherapy
Jesse D. Geller

1. Introduction 347

2. The Democratization of the Relationship of the Mind and
    the Body 350
 3. The Romantic Vision of the Body-Movement Therapies ... 352
 4. Obstacles to the Development of Body-Awareness 353
 5. Communication in Psychotherapy 354
 6. Form and Content in Psychotherapy 356
 7. The Role of Language in Psychoanalytic Therapy 357
 8. The Search for Meaning 360
 9. The Unconscious in the Body-Movement Therapies 361
10. Movements Are Expressive 363
11. Against Interpretation 366
12. Overcoming Resistances: The Reichian Influence 368
13. Styles of Exercising Authority 371
14. Changing Conceptions of Countertransference 373
    References 375

Part VI • Conclusion 379

Chapter 13
Why Does Using Imagery in Psychotherapy Lead to Change?
Donald Meichenbaum

1. The Need for an Integrative Orientation 381
2. Imagery and the Context of Psychotherapy 383
3. Cognitive Theory of Behavior Change 383
   3.1. Self-Awareness 384
   3.2. Generating Adaptive New Thoughts and Responses .. 385
   3.3. *In Vivo* Practice 386
4. Imagery-Based Therapies 386
5. Psychological Processes Underlying Imagery-Based
   Therapies 387
   References 393

Author Index 395

Subject Index 401

PART I

Introduction and Overview

1

The Use of Imagery and Fantasy Techniques in Psychotherapy

Jerome L. Singer and Kenneth S. Pope

1. Introduction

Psychology has displayed much more prudishness about the stream of consciousness than it ever did about sex. The Victorians went so far as to cover the legs of the piano to avoid, when speaking of furniture, mentioning the words "leg" or "foot" so as not to raise sexual connotations. This strikes most of us as pretty silly today, and yet, as we study the literature of psychology, psychiatry, and psychotherapy for the last 70 odd years, we find a strange reluctance to acknowledge, to describe, or to study seriously that ever-changing constellation of memories, sense-data, anticipations, fantasies, rational thoughts, and images that constitute our moment-to-moment awareness as we go about our lives. To anyone but a psychologist it would seem amazing indeed that textbooks on thinking (Bourne, Ekstrand, and Dominowski, 1971; Johnson, 1955) can omit reference to the stream of consciousness and daydreaming, that introductions to personality (Mischel, 1971) or adolescence (Seidman, 1960) can ignore imagination or fantasy. Yet, until recently, psychology's overemphasis on "public" or observable behavior barred almost any serious reference to the stream of consciousness except perhaps for such distancing, cleansing, socially acceptable code words as "epiphenomenon."

Jerome L. Singer • Psychology Department, Yale University, New Haven, Connecticut 06520. **Kenneth S. Pope** • Brentwood Veterans Administration Hospital, Los Angeles, California 90073.

The repression is no longer total and absolute. Aspects of the stream of consciousness are now legitimate topics of research. Imagery, for instance, has attracted scientists interested in its role in areas as diverse as memory (Paivio, 1971), voluntary control of heart rate (Schwartz, 1973), improvement of athletic performance (Suinn, 1976), and the treatment of cancer (Simonton and Simonton, 1975). Ongoing thought in all its rich diversity and complexity, the topic proposed for study by William James (1890/1952), remains, however, relatively neglected and primarily the domain of the fine artist.

Indeed, it was the writer, the painter, and the filmmaker who responded with enthusiasm to James's challenge. The excitement engendered in the early decade of this century by the efforts of James Joyce to produce what Edmund Wilson called "perhaps the most faithful X-ray ever taken of the ordinary human consciousness" (Wilson, 1922) reflected the seriousness with which writers accepted James's insights. The artistic literature immediately prior to that time, much like the psychological literature of the first half of this century, lacked a crucial dimension of human experience and therefore did not connect up with life as it is lived. Virginia Woolf wrote plaintively:

> But sometimes, more and more often as time goes by, we suspect a momentary doubt, a spasm of rebellion, as the pages fill themselves in the customary way. Is life like this? (Woolf, 1925/1953, p. 154)

She expressed vividly this denied aspect of life, not only in her fiction, but also in the following prose passage:

> Examine for a moment an ordinary mind on an ordinary day. The mind received a myriad of impressions—trivial, fantastic, evanescent, or engraved with the sharpness of steel. From all sides they come, an incessant shower of innumerable atoms; and as they fall, as they shape themselves into the life of Monday or Tuesday, the accent falls differently of old . . . . Life is not a series of gig lamps symmetrically arranged; but a luminous halo, a semi-transparent envelope surrounding us from the beginning of consciousness to the end . . . . Let us record the atoms as they fall upon the mind in the order in which they fall, let us trace the pattern, however disconnected and incoherent in appearance, which each sight or incident scores upon the consciousness. (Woolf, 1925/1953, pp. 154–155)

As the poets were searching for literary techniques to convey the stream of consciousness, filmmakers such as Sergei Eisenstein perceived an opportunity in moving pictures to present the flow of subjective experience. Through such techniques as the montage and the partial representation, Eisenstein (1942) hoped to evoke in the viewer the same ongoing thought experience that occurred in the mind of the artist or of one of the characters in the film.

2. The Stunted Growth of Psychology and Psychotherapy: A Bias toward Verbal and Directed Thought

Those behavioral scientists who have ventured beyond the realm of public, directly observable phenomena have not enjoyed the artist's freedom from the constraints of a scientific method. Numerous studies focus on outcome products of specific directed thinking tasks or individual features of thought such as the vividness of images, the mental rotation of blocks, and the strategies of memorizing pairs of nonsense syllables. This work has great value in furthering our understanding of mental processes, but taken as a whole and compared to our subjective experience of the flow of consciousness leads us to echo Virginia Woolf's question: "Is life like this?"

Our valued methods of experimental design have encouraged a tendency to study the structured, directed, or "rational" aspects of thought, particularly those aspects that are readily apparent in the accomplishment of discrete, simple, easily measured laboratory tasks. It is as if the human mind were constructed to handle the subtests of the Wechsler Adult Intelligence Scale, and all other activities were intrusion, distraction, pathology, or "noise in the system." It has only been in the most recent years that we have ventured into the careful scientific study of the private judgments we make about our human relationships, of our ethical and moral thinking, of the more "everyday" experiences of humor, art, and athletics. Yet, even these researches are often framed within the format of rational problem solution in a very structured fashion.

Psychoanalysis, while drawing our attention toward the "underside" of thought—the irrational, wishful, and "selfish" aspects of private experience—nevertheless fails to address fully the flow of our experience. Freud, so conscious of the way magical, childlike, fantasy-laden material intrudes into adult mental processes, still tended to assume that the well-analyzed adult would rely mainly on secondary process thinking. The adaptive, pleasurable, or enriching quality of wishful, imagery-laden thinking was downplayed in favor of directed, logical thought.

One of the many debts we owe to Freud is for his elaborate effort to create a comprehensive view of mental progress (Rapaport, 1951, 1960). Yet, the various structural characteristics of the theory—id, ego, superego; unconscious, preconscious, conscious; primary and secondary processes—were developed at different times and don't really fit together (Gill, 1963). Perhaps it is for the best that Freud did not leave us with a frozen, ready-made theory, and we may move forward more easily, treasuring his willingness to look at the human mind rather than clinging to his specific understanding.

One psychoanalyst who sought to move beyond this excessively rational view of human thought was Ernst Kris (1951) who proposed that, at least in the case of creative thought, one might benefit from "regression in the service of the ego." Yet, even here the bias toward rational, directed thought is apparent: Any reliance on fantasies, images, or primary process thinking is "regressive," a throwback to a more primitive form of thinking. How sad it is that we categorize the poet who illuminates our private experiences through vivid images, creative word combinations, and a sensitive ear for the tone of a phrase as relying on a "regressed" human capacity. The fact that we conceptualize the minds of Beethoven and Schubert, teeming with melodies, of Bergman and Altman, alive with the interplay of images, as representing a somehow more primitive style of thought than a mathematician mentally solving albegra problems or a lawyer working his way through the complex reasonings of his legal case perhaps reflects more the weakness of our theories than the weakness of imagery, fantasy, and creative imagination.

There are encouraging signs of change. The recent heightened awareness of the differential processing capacities of the brain and its functional assymetry for verbal-quantitative and imagery-spatial representational capacities suggests that the process of effective thought is far more complex than previously realized (Bogen, 1969; Gazzaniga, 1967; Sperry, 1968; Schwartz, Davidson, and Maer, 1975; Rodin and Singer, 1977). There is research that suggests that the flow of our subjective experience may in fact often have greater recourse to distant memories, fleeting images, irrelevant imaginings, and fanciful anticipations than to the more structured, rational processes of attention to the situation at hand (Pope, 1977). Elsewhere, we have presented attempts to bring together work that gives due to both verbal and nonverbal thought, to both what has been termed "primary process" and "secondary process" mental activities, to both ideation in service of a specific task and that which seemingly serves us indirectly or not at all. We have sought to outline a comprehensive, systematic theory of the flow of human experience (Pope and Singer, 1978a; Pope and Singer, 1978; Singer, 1977). A companion volume (Pope and Singer, 1978c) presents the current works of some who are studying scientifically the stream of consciousness. In this volume, we are concerned with how the astoundingly rich, varied complexities of human experience—particularly the oft-neglected capacities for imagery, imagination, and fantasy—can be attended to, appreciated, evaluated, and effectively included in the psychotherapeutic process. It is to this concern that we now turn.

3. Therapy and Imagination

Increasingly, and from some of the most unlikely quarters, therapists attend to the human being as a creature who can not only behave, feel, and think rationally, but also imagine. The psychoanalytic therapist, frustrated with the verbal juggling of an obsessional patient, skillfully attends to a seemingly unrelated visual scene imagined by the patient (see the account of this therapy in Horowitz's chapter in this volume). Therapists whose prime focus is the posture and movement of the body (discussed in the chapter by Geller), may ask the patient to create and perform an imaginative dance. The biofeedback therapists have learned from their patients that the imagining of a peaceful scene is an effective method of increasing alpha, slowing the heart rate, and lowering blood pressure. In treating physiological complaints with such "thinking" techniques, we should give credit to Satchel Paige who long ago in his "Six Rules for a Long Life" prescribed: "If your stomach disputes you, lie down and pacify it with cool thoughts." Even the behavior therapist (see Kazdin's chapter in this volume), who in theory has traditionally resisted attending to anything but overt, publicly observable behavior, may show great reliance on the imaginative capacity of the client. The treatment of a phobia through systematic desensitization, often conceputalized as a classical conditioning procedure, may proceed by asking the client to imagine, with gradually increasing degress of immediacy, the feared object or situation. Alternatively, operant procedures may be employed to increase the frequency of a specific behavior by asking the client to imagine performing the desired behavior and immediately after to imagine a favorable, rewarding consequence (see chapter by Cautela and McCullough).

The diverse uses of imagination—in classical and neo-Freudian psychoanalysis, in the newer European guided daydream psychotherapies such as Desoille's *Le Rêve Eveillé Dirigé*, in various behavior-modification techniques—seem to provide a basis for linking the heterogeneous approaches that characterize modern psychotherapy (Singer, 1974). A careful analysis of how the human imagination is employed, of the modalities through which it finds expression, and of its relationship to other human capacities may provide us with a common basis for understanding what various psychotherapies have in common with respect not only to technique, but also to objective.

4. Dimensions of Cognition and Expression

We may distinguish three main modalities, which Horowitz in his chapter names *enactive*, *image*, and *lexical*. The enactive dimension embraces the motoric sphere of our lives. Presumably, it is associated with the cortical motor areas and the limbic system. Geller discusses this area at length in his chapter; however, it is important to note at this point that the physical, nonverbal activity that occurs through this modality was thought by Freud to be less under conscious control than speech, rendering us less able to control or conceal it. It thus provides a source of information in therapy concerning material that the patient is unable or unwilling to provide otherwise. Geller quotes Freud (1905/1960): "He that has eyes to see and ears to hear may convince himself that no mortal can keep a secret. If his lips are silent, he chatters with his fingertips; betrayal oozes out of him at every pore" (p. 94).*

The image dimension appears to be associated with the right hemisphere of the brain, whose functions include visual and auditory imagery, spatial representation, pure melodic thought, fantasy, and emotional components of ongoing thought. As Horowitz points out, image thought allows continued information processing after perception and, in such phenomena as dreams and daydreams, is able to lend a sensory configuration to emergent ideas and feelings. As a coding system, imagery or spatial representation operates by parallel (rather than sequential) processing; e.g., we imagine the face of a friend in one instantaneous configuration (Paivio, 1971; Singer, 1974).

The lexical system is largely coordinated through the left hemisphere of the brain, and its chief functions include language and grammatical organization, conceptualization, reasoning, and abstract generalizations. This verbal or linguistic system functions sequentially; e.g., it takes time for a sentence to be presented. The lexical dimension with its abstract, analytic properties is especially efficient for integrating tremendously diverse phenomena into one language label or formula that allows extremely rapid retrieval later on. Consider the range of objects that the verbal label "vehicle" embraces or the heterogeneous phenomena summarized in the formula "$E=MC^2$."

While most behavior involves complex combinations of these systems, there are important differences among them in implication. The

---

* The recent publication of Julian Jaynes's *The Origin of Consciousness in the Breakdown of the Bicameral Mind* (Jaynes, 1977) suggests a sweeping and imaginative hypothesis that the development of the human sense of private experience and personal thought occurred relatively late in evolution (c. 1400 B.C.) when the right half of the brain no longer was the source of the "hallucinatory voices" believed by men to be direct communications from the gods.

lexical system, for instance, enables us to abstract them through such linguistic forms as "if . . . then," "not this, but that," "not this, until that," "both this and that, but not the other," "first this, then that." However, as events are encoded into language (whether verbal or mathematical) they become abstracted and lose their immediate impact on our experience; as such they become less emotional events, make less cogent demands, tend not to present the vivid here-and-now challenge for processing stimulation, which Tomkins (1962, 1963) argues is the basis for affects. As Bruner puts it: "once language becomes a medium for the translation of experience, there is a progressive release from immediacy" (Bruner, 1968, p. 407).

The great mathematician and physicist, S. M. Ulam (a member of the Los Alamos team and inventor of the Monte Carlo methods for studying problems too complex to be fully defined and explained only by a complete system of equations), presents this particular difference between the lexical and image systems quite clearly. He differentiates mathematical (lexical) from physics-related (image) thinking:

> The feeling for problems in physics is quite different from purely theoretical mathematical thinking. It is hard to describe the kind of imagination that enables one to guess at or gauge the behavior of physical phenomena. Very few mathematicians seem to possess it to any great degree. (Ulam, 1976, p. 147)

He goes on to present the immediacy and impact of the visual imagination involved in thinking about physics:

> Very soon I discovered that if one gets a feeling for no more than a dozen other radiation and nuclear constants, one can imagine the subatomic world almost tangibly, and manipulate the picture dimensionally and qualitatively, before calculating the more precise relationships. (Ulam, 1976, p. 148)

The translation of these movements into lexical (linguistic or mathematical) mode involves a considerable miniaturization, distancing, and loss of emotional impact:

> . . . and [I] remarked to him about my surprise that $E = MC^2$—which I of course believed in theoretically but somehow did not really "feel"—was, in fact, the basis of the whole thing and would bring about a bomb. What the whole Project was working on depended on those few little signs on paper. (Ulam, 1976, p. 157)

We are contending in this chapter that is is important not to view the enactive and image systems as early developmental forms that must be superseded by the verbal or lexical system, but rather that all three systems, in their complex interrelationships, are of equal importance. We need not, for instance, view imagery, daydreaming, and fantasy as "regressive" phenomena or manifestations of a "primary" or immature process as some psychoanalytic lore suggests. As Schachtel (1959) observes, the socialization of the individual often involves increased reliance on "empty" verbal clichés or abstractions with a sad loss of the direct contact with experience implicit in the concrete modality-specific imagery system. We respond to great writers because they reawaken in us the possibilities of direct experience through their detailed reconstruction of specific sights, sounds, or smells. Keats's closing lines of the "Ode on a Grecian Urn," "Beauty is truth, truth beauty," might leave us cold or puzzled had he not preceded that abstraction by vivid images and fantasies about the figures depicted on the amphora. Shakespeare, who excelled his contemporaries not only in the number of specific images he employed in his plays and poems but also in the range of sensory modalities involved, pulls our face right up to what he wants us to experience. Falstaff is that "old tub of guts." Hamlet describes his uncle as a "mildewed ear" and tells the Danish courtiers seeking to locate the hidden body of murdered Polonius, ". . . if you find him not within this month, you shall nose him as you go up the stairs into the lobby."

In therapy, similarly, these three modalities—enactive, image, and lexical—are of equal importance. A patient may come in and draw on both the lexical and image modalities to recount a long and ghastly narrative of tragedy after tragedy in vivid detail, culminating with the statement: "I feel horrible." The therapist, however, may attend not only to these spheres but also the flow of enactive thoughts manifested in unmistakable smiles, a posture suggesting "Victory!," and subtle, brief gestures that the therapist might find difficult to translate into either image or lexical thought but that just do not seem consistent with "feeling horrible." Another patient might have a firm, sure, knowledgeable grasp of the lexical mode, and say during the first interview: "I guess I had a typical Oedipal family—you know, a doting mother and a strong father who made me feel very inadequate. I really loved my mother and I really hated my father. Really!" The therapist might view such an abstract, distancing statement as not very useful unless it can be hooked up to the vivid particulars of the patient's life, unless the patient produces a specific memory image portraying in vivid detail an interaction between the child and parents or perhaps experiences the content of the sentence in the enactive/physical/motor sphere, e.g., a tensing of the stomach muscles, clenching his fists at the thought of his father, or weeping at the thought of his mother.

In what way does reference to these three modalities provide a common ground for understanding what various therapies have in common concerning approach, technique, and objective? Table I, based on previous work by Horowitz (1970, 1975) and Singer (1974), presents in briefest form the relationships between various therapies in regard to how their methods and objectives are expressed through the enactive, image, and lexical modes.

Representatives of the various schools will take quick offense if they feel that their approaches represent much more complex aims and methods. However, it does seem likely that there are some valid differences between psychotherapies that are highlighted here. For example, the classical psychoanalytic method aims at a comprehensive reorganization of the total personality. It seems to rely, to a large extent, on assisting the patient to translate the many forms of interior monologue, verbal free associations, and awareness of tentative enactive movements into more concrete manifestations of imagery. Countless obstacles can arise in this process. One patient may cling relentlessly to the lexical level, filling the hour with abstract words. Another may "act out" emergent feelings that are too painful to be experienced at present in another mode. Still another may be aware of fleeting visual images but be unable to "see" them clearly or recognize them. The psychoanalytic method then works with these elaborated, concrete manifestations of imagery, attempting to provide more differentiated and adequate labeling systems for such concrete experiences that will enhance subsequent effective, integrated use of the enactive, image, and lexical methods in normal thought and cognitive appraisal.

By contrast, many of the European mental imagery methods emphasize the translation of verbal experience into imagery as the core of the method and do not attempt in any systematic way to reformulate the imagery experiences into verbal labels or linguistic shorthand. In effect, a change is sought in the undercurrent of ongoing symbolic representations that are part of human experience, with the belief that such changes will lead to efficacious modifications, not only in experience, but also in behavior or interpersonal relationships. A minimum of emphasis is placed, therefore, on verbal encoding and lexical formulation of the "imagery trips" that characterize the procedure.

The Gestalt therapy approach, at least as formulated in action by Perls in his weekend demonstration groups (Perls, 1970), attempts to translate body postures, which may in a sense be called frozen forms of enactive memory, back into an image modality, often with associated memories from early childhood as well as from recent experience. The systematic retranslation of such images into a verbal encoding system is often minimized, however, since the goal of the treatment is formulated in terms of enhancing direct experience rather than intellectual understanding or linguistic encoding.

In the present chapter, we attempt to focus primarily upon specific practical uses of imagery, imagination, body awareness, the flow of

Table I. Technical Variations in the Psychotherapeutic Uses of Imagery[a]

Encoding systems

1. Verbal-sequential (Horowitz's lexical) (left hemisphere function)
2. Motor-kinesthetic (Horowitz's enactive) (limbic-motor areas, etc.)
3. Imagery (visual, auditory, spatial)—parallel (Horowitz's image)[b] (right hemisphere functioning)

Therapeutic orientation	Objective or symptom focus	Direction of system shift or "technique"
1. Hypnosis	Symptom-relief or improved recall	Intense concentration on each encoding system individually. Motor verbal imagery
2. Psychoanalysis (a) Dream interpretation (b) Transference analysis	Insight and *ego* expansion (a) Overcome resistance—enhance affect ideational integrative (b) Identify unlabeled childhood parental memories and fantasies (c) Sharpen interpersonal discrimination from treatment to daily life	Imagery → verbal-sequential Imagery → verbal sequential → joint verbal-imagery integration

3. Reich's character analysis Perls' Gestalt therapy	Freeing and redirecting energy	Motor-kinesthetic → imagery → motor
4. European mental imagery approaches (Desoille's guided daydream)	Resymbolization, symptom relief	Verbal-sequential → imagery or imagery (1) → imagery (2)
5. Gendlin's focusing (Rogerian)	Expanded self-awareness	Verbal or motor → imagery-affective
6. Kelly's personal construct therapy	Improved role-discrimination and role-enactment	Verbal → imagery → verbal → motor
7. Wolpe's systematic desensitization	Relief of phobic symptoms	Motor → imagery → motor
8. Covert aversive conditioning (behavior mod.)	Symptom-relief, control of compulsions, unwanted thoughts or behaviors	Imagery → motor → imagery (1) kinesthetic (2)
9. Bandura's symbolic mediation	Symptom relief and self-regulation	(Perception) → imagery → motor
10. Ellis's rational-emotive or cognitive theories	Symptom relief, self-regulation, self-assertiveness	Verbal → imagery-affect → Verbal (1) (2)

[a] From Singer (1974).
[b] Imagery system ordinarily more closely tied to affect expression and experience.

enactive thoughts, daydreams, and fantasies, which are available to the psychotherapist and by extension, ultimately useful in daily life, perhaps as a form of self-development or prevention of disturbance. These approaches, drawn from a variety of psychotherapies, are not intended to be comprehensive but rather suggestive of how far one can indeed go through systematic analysis of the enactive and imagery—as well as lexical—capacities we all seem to possess.

5. Psychoanalysis and Related Psychodynamic Approaches

Freud's use of an imagery-association method grew out of his early employment of hypnosis (Singer, 1974). Indeed, in the period before the appearance of *The Interpretation of Dreams*, Freud was placing considerably greater emphasis on an imagery-association system, holding the patient's head and encouraging a stream of visual pictures. This approach later shifted toward the rule of verbal free association, and it can be argued that Freud may have lost some of the power of the method in his allowing the patient the freedom of a more verbal associative pattern (Reyher, 1963; Singer, 1974). It is possible that Freud was somewhat suspicious of pure imagery and, with his own great emphasis on rationality, tended to view the visual or purely auditory imagery that characterized dreams and fantasies as regressive phenomena that needed ultimately to be translated into verbal formulations. It was clear to Freud that one could only reach the unconscious through concrete manifestations of imagery as represented in dreams or in the analysis of transference fantasies. It is possible, however, that he underestimated seriously the adaptive power of the human imagery capacity, as this led to the relative slowness and often considerable redundancy that characterizes the modern psychoanalytic method as a clinical intervention procedure.

Individual psychotherapists and psychoanalysts have always relied on the patient's capacity to produce imagery to circumvent obvious defensiveness or resistance. Ferenczi (1950) was extremely sensitive in his clinical work to inhibitions of motor activity that he was able to show often could, when translated into imagery, yield important insights about longstanding fantasies or irrational fears of particular patients. Indeed, he would have a patient who showed a mannerism such as foot-swinging while seated inhibit that movement, and then found that an image occurred to the patient, often revealing important recurring fantasies. This translation of motor activity into imagery was, of course, also adopted by Reich (1945) and has become much more a regular feature of the Gestalt approach to psychotherapy.

A simple example from the clinical experience of one of the authors may indicate how a shift from a verbal pattern to an imagery system may turn out to be extremely useful in opening the way to greater understanding by the patient as well as an indication within the therapeutic session. The patient, a woman in her early fifties, began a session by recurrent comments that she could think of nothing to say, that nothing seemed to be coming to her mind, and that she was simply feeling uncomfortable because there seemed to be no way of getting started. She agreed to lean back for a moment, shut her eyes, allow whatever image occurred to develop as fully as possible, and then to report it. Her report is as follows: "I see a very clear picture of Siamese twins—the funny part of it is that they are not babies, but clearly an image of two men attached at the sides to each other—one is an old man and the other is a younger man."

The oddness of this image, so implausible in reality, evoked laughter from both therapist and patient. To the therapist, this image related directly to the material she had presented at the end of her last session. The patient sat in silence a few minutes, replaying the image in her mind. Suddenly, and without prompting, the same connection occurred to her that had occurred to the therapist. It happened that she had been increasingly uncomfortable in recent months about the fact that her grown son and her husband, who had now joined together in a business venture, were becoming closer to each other than they had ever been before, often excluding her from much of the rapport they shared, not only around work, but around interests in sporting events. The vividness and clarity of the image helped her suddenly to realize the extent to which she was feeling more and more like an outsider in her family, and led her to begin to think about finding resources within herself that would not enhance this experience, but rather free her from her dependence on both husband and son.

This vignette demonstrates the crystallizing potential of our imagery capacity. In effect, the woman produced a kind of waking dream that represented a dramatic metaphor for her experience of increased isolation and for her envy of the increased "attachment" between father and son. She was able to formulate this into a verbal system as well, and recognize that resentment of the closeness between father and son was pointless. Rather, this rapport could be welcomed as a natural development for the two men and did not automatically exclude her from full participation in the pleasures of family life. It did point up the necessity for her to develop a new sense of her own identity as an individual and also within the reconstructed family unit that would be appropriate to a present stage of life.

Another of the authors' patients became blocked in the course of therapy after making substantial progress. Session after session, this young man in his twenties would come in and punctuate long stretches of silence with vague, rambling accounts of rather general discontents. His hands were constantly in motion, generally in service of his chain-smoking. He fidgeted around in his chair, and at particular times he would busy himself adjusting the chair, fiddling with his clothes, or reaching out to adjust the window. The therapist made the following suggestion: "The next time you feel like doing something—reaching for a cigarette, shifting your position, whatever—you may wish to refrain from carrying it out, then see what happens." The patient berated the therapist for paying too much attention "to all this physical stuff," but finally decided to give it a try. He giggled self-consciously once or twice as he tried to remain motionless and to resist what felt to him like an overwhelming urge to reach for a cigarette. Then he grew silent for some time and began to cry. Later he was able to translate some of his experience into words. As he remained motionless, he said he felt initially like lighting up a cigarette. As he refrained from smoking, he began to feel more and more as if he had to run from the room as fast as possible. It was with the greatest difficulty that he was able to keep from acting on this impulse. He then began to see himself, in his mind's eye, running out of the room. To his surprise, in this reverie, the therapist did not follow. The patient then imagined himself running into a large darkness that swallowed him up. No one was with him; no one came looking for him; he was absolutely alone. This lonely feeling—with its attendant sadness, panic, and terror—welled up in him and led to his crying.

In the above account, material originally unavailable through the lexical or image systems finds it way into the therapy through the enactive system. The young man's constant motion was attended to and clarified. He began to experience his bodily activity more directly as nervous efforts to get out of the chair and head toward the door. He was able to clarify it further by drawing on his imagery capacities, letting images play themselves across his mind's eye. Finally, he was able to avail himself more fruitfully of his lexical abilities, through discussion of what he had been experiencing.

It is worth noting here the use classical psychoanalysis makes of the couch, and the ways in which this use influences the enactive, image, and lexical systems. Research by Pope (1977) indicates that posture tends to affect the flow of consciousness as follows. When a person is lying down, the mind is generally more focused on distant memories, anticipations, fantasies, and imaginary images than when the person is seated. Furthermore, reveries and daydreams have a greater tendency to play themselves out and we are less attendant to the "here and now," to the sights and sounds of the environment that constantly bombard us. Reclining on the couch, then, tends to maximize the likelihood that unlabeled but stored visual and auditory images can be retrieved. Certain memories and associations stored primarily in the enactive system may be evoked. When an adult reclines in the presence of another adult who is seated, it recreates a psychological situation that has similarities to the early childhood behavior when, for example, the child was put to bed and perhaps even told a story by an adult seated nearby. The very nature of the social situation established in a classical psychoanalysis brings about a context with the support of emphasis on imagery components such as the recall of dreams or fantasies that enhances the likelihood of the patient recreating childlike memories and attitudes as reflected in the occurrence of the transference (Singer, 1974).

Reyher (1963) has carried the imagery association method much further within a psychoanalytic framework than any other recent clinician. He has urged the value of much more extensive periods of pure imagery association, and has provided considerable research data to indicate that not only are verbalizations freer of defensiveness during such imagery-association sessions, but also that physiological indices of emotional arousal, as well as behavioral indices, support the greater "involvement" of the patient when such methods are employed. Reyher's "emergent uncovering" technique deserves more serious consideration as a regular part of ongoing psychodynamic therapies as a method for avoiding the often excessively prolonged verbal rationalization and defensiveness that characterize so much of the undirected psychoanalytic session.

One of the major functions of the imagery system is that it permits a directness of communication between people often free of the excessive abstraction of verbal formulations. The so-called hovering or free-floating attention that was the stance Freud advocated for the psychoanalyst during a session seems to involve, at its best, an attempt to translate into images the experiences described by the patient. We believe that when the therapist is translating material from the patient into verbal formulations such as "a typical ego-superego conflict" or "obviously an early displacement of oral conflict," the therapist may be losing contact with the reality of the patient's experience. Rather, it seems much more useful for the therapist's orientation to be one of producing images that attempt, as much as possible, to concretize what it is the patient is describing. If the patient is presenting an account of a walk on the beach with an intimate friend, then the therapist's imagery ought to be in effect reproducing that walk and, in some degree, empathizing with the patient's presentation of the experience as closely as possible. Here, of course, there is the danger that the therapist, since he or she draws obviously on a different set of memories to reproduce these images, will inevitably fail to capture the patient's experience. Tauber and Green (1959) examined this issue at some length and with considerable perceptiveness. While recognizing the dangers of countertransference and of foisting upon the patient one's own personal experiences, they also call attention to the fact that the private images of the therapist may clarify the experiences going on between patient and therapist.

In one instance as a patient of one of the authors recounted an early childhood scene, the therapist tried to picture the group seated around the table. The therapist suddenly realized from the woman's presentation that there was a discrepancy between the number of children seated with the parents and her original account of how many siblings she had. One of the children was missing. When asked about this she became flustered and, trying to count the children in the visual image she was describing, came up with two different enumerations in two tries. After the session, which was just ending, she went home and rethought the whole episode, experiencing a cathartic and dramatic emergence of a whole series of memories about a brother who had died. While he had been lying very sick, she had been playing with her ball against the side of her house and her grandmother had emerged from the back door to shout angrily, "Do you want to be the death of your brother?"

In some instances, as Tauber and Green have pointed out, the therapist may generate a completely original fantasy or daydream that may be in itself revealing of something the patient is implicitly communicating, or of a difficulty in the interaction between patient and therapist. In one instance, as a patient was engaged in free association, one of the authors became aware of a vivid image in his own mind of a Galápagos Island tortoise lumbering along a sandy shore. After thinking about the image for a little while, he finally interrupted the patient to convey this to him, and between themselves they quickly recognized that the patient had been extremely defensive during the earlier part of the session, and was trying to avoid coming to grips with a particularly difficult and embarrassing situation that had occurred recently.

Attention to the therapist's spontaneous fantasies may be of immeasurable value in dealing with countertransference and other situations in which the therapist's defensiveness may inhibit the therapeutic process. One of the authors was engaged in psychoanalytically oriented play therapy with a seven-year-old boy. The boy's exuberant displays of affection, enjoyment of the session, and imaginative play made the sessions a delight for the therapist and he was constantly aware of his affection for the patient. Nevertheless the treatment was stalled. During one session, the boy found a cup in the wastebasket, went to the sink, filled the cup with water, and began drinking. The therapist, who rarely interfered with the boy's free play, almost did in this case. There was no telling what could have been in the cup before it had been discarded—paint thinner, cleaning fluid, some other poison? The therapist then had a momentary visual fantasy of the boy dying from poison in the cup. He then reflected on the fact that he was—regardless of whatever danger there may or may not have been in the child's drinking from a discarded cup—fantasizing about the boy's death. This led him to become aware of the anger and aggressive feelings he had toward the boy, feelings that he had been defending against as "unacceptable," particularly when they were "aimed" at such an attractive, vulnerable young child. In this situation, the therapist was able to introduce some of his own feelings into the therapy through the image system, feelings that were unavailable to him otherwise. The beneficial result was two-fold. First, he was able to acknowledge and deal with some difficult countertransference issues. Second, he was able to focus effectively on how the boy's behavior subtly elicited or provoked angry feelings from others.

The imagery system, as we suggested earlier, is also closely related to artistic and often humorous expression. Within the psychoanalytic session, a more direct use of imagery may help not only the therapist, but also the patient to recognize the creative potential that we all share in this medium. As a matter of fact, patients have often remarked about the fact that, despite the belief they hold at the outset that they rarely dream, once encouraged to do so by a psychoanalyst they are surprised at how many dreams do occur and at how interesting they turn out to be. If anything, one of the real dangers of psychoanalysis as a form of clinical intervention is the fact that the inherent, somewhat narcissistic interest we all take in our own dreams and fantasies can become the basis for a continuously reinforcing experience in its own right. Thus, people will continue to attend psychoanalytic treatment for years and years, finding the sessions themselves worthwhile and enjoyable even though there is very little evidence that they have made important gains in the form of improved interpersonal relationships or major symptom relief outside the sessions.

There are periods in the treatment process where the occurrence of a vivid image can help both therapist and patient reexamine their relationship and move to a newer level of mutual understanding. In one instance, a patient of one of the authors had spent quite a number of sessions talking on and on, producing boring material. The therapist experienced the sessions, as he thought about them, much like someone who has no investments must experience the daily news report of stock exchange transactions. It seemed it might be useful for the patient to discontinue this approach for a while and instead attempt to produce a series of interrelated images. The therapist had little hope that this extremely pedestrian and boring individual would do anything. It was fascinating that almost immediately the patient began to unreel a series of images that included some rather vivid scenes of Japanese samurai warriors engaged in combat. When therapist and patient examined these images further it become clear that this man actually had a much more elaborate and vivid imagery capacity than either of them had realized. Of crucial importance, of course, was the direct emergence of suppressed anger and the desire for a more heroic life. But equally important was the fact that suddenly both patient and therapist became more interested in the transaction between them, and the patient became more excited about his own inner life, as a resource.

In still another instance, a woman who had a fairly extended psychotherapy history over the years kept talking at great length about a whole series of physical symptoms. Session after session involved her describing her various frustrations in getting appropriate specialists to take her descriptions of the symptoms seriously. One of the authors suggested to this young woman that they try a form of the European imagery trip, imagining oneself in a field or in a forest and producing a whole series of images one after another, from such a beginning. To the surprise of the therapist, once she had practiced this a little through the use of Jacobsen progressive relaxation technique and through some other imagery exercises as a kind of "warm-up," she suddenly launched on an extremely elaborated series of images. As she did so, it became clear that she was a person who had a highly refined and sensitive awareness of nature, of colors, shapes and sounds, and indeed a fine aesthetic sense that carried over to artistic appreciation as well. This experience greatly enlivened the interaction between patient and therapist, for each now saw how much personal richness and potential was being suppressed by her defensive preoccupation with symptomatology.

It should be apparent that we are in this chapter stressing the structural characteristics of imagery and their relation to broader self-awareness, empathy, and positive affect. Of course, psychoanalytic approaches have traditionally emphasized the content implications of the images produced, that is to say, their relation to dynamics of early childhood conflicts, and so on. Without minimizing the importance of some of these findings, what we are trying to stress is that the image and enactive systems are too easily overlooked as major ego functions and resources for effective coping. While the working-through process in psychoanalysis has often in effect helped patients to develop their imagery and enactive capacities, this has rarely been recognized systematically by writers on psychoanalytic technique (see, however, the combination of psychodynamic and pure imagery approaches in the chapter by Sheikh). It could be argued that psychoanalysis in its very method provides a form of training so that the patient eventually can carry on the following kind of process:

A young man walks into a crowded room and suddenly finds himself feeling extremely uncomfortable and particularly annoyed at one of the people who seem to be holding forth in a small group. Whereas in the past he might have either left the room at once, or perhaps gotten into the group and ended up in an argument with this man, he has now learned instead to carry out, in effect, an "instant replay" of his series of perceptions and thoughts as he walked into the room. By doing so, he is able to recognize that his feeling of distress was occasioned by a superficial resemblance between the other man and his own stepfather who had recurrently humiliated him about his intellectual attainments when he was a boy. He now had a system for coping with a variety of sudden irrational feelings that in the past had erupted into impulsive action that he would later regret.

We wish to stress the fact that imagery and enactive thought can often become a part of a more general set of private cognitions and coping skills. Psychoanalysts often notice that patients in a sense adopt the therapist as a kind of imaginary companion, someone to whom they talk privately in their minds when confronted with difficult situations. This pattern of behavior need not be viewed necessarily as an instance of excessive attachment or dependency. Often it is a natural phase of a new learning procedure in which the patient is gradually assimilating what in effect the analyst has been teaching him about a process of self-examination and heightened self-awareness. In the successful analysis, the image of the therapist should gradually fade and the function of self-examination become much more automatic and ego-syntonic. If we recognize that naturalness of this process, we need not be afraid to suggest it actively from time to time in order to help the patient use his or her power of imagination to deal with potentially threatening or frightening situations. In some instances we have encouraged patients with particular sets of fears or anxieties about particular encounters or travel to imagine that the therapist was along with them, or that they were writing the therapist a letter describing a set of events. This method turned out to be useful not only in helping them deal with the stress as it occurred, but also in helping them formulate some of the nature of the difficulty and suggest some alternative strategies for dealing with the situation.

This orientation, while it has come out of more psychodynamically oriented treatment procedures, bears comparison with the newer developments in what has been called cognitive behavior modification, and the recent emphasis on shorter-term intervention procedures oriented toward self-regulation and self-control (see Meichenbaum's chapter in this volume; Schwartz and Shapiro, 1976). In Meichenbaum's chapter in this volume, which he devotes to addressing the question, "Why does using imagery in psychotherapy lead to change?" Meichenbaum proposes that imagery-based therapists produce change

> because they (1) "seduce," convince, teach the client to entertain the notion that his imagery contributes to his maladaptive behavior; (2) teach the client to become aware of and monitor his images and note their occurrence within the maladaptive behavioral chain, with the consequence of interrupting the maladaptive chain; and (3) alter what the client says to himself, and does, when he experiences images. The consequence of these processes is that they convey to the client a sense of control over his images and "inner life" and in turn over interperonsal behavior.

There remain important differences in objectives between the psychodynamic approaches that place considerable emphasis on early origin and on a dynamic causal analysis for adult emotional problems, and the newer cognitive behavior modification methods that focus primarily on a more immediate analysis of maladaptive behavioral patterns. Still, it is important to see that both approaches are making increased use of imagery in helping to formulate information about the nature of the dilemma the patient brings, and also in providing some clearcut tools to the therapist for, in effect, retraining the patient's capacity for coping as well as self-understanding.

There seems to be increasing room within the psychodynamic tradition for more active use of imagery approaches. In Shorr's chapter in this book, he presents a series of ingenious imagery "assignments" to help the patient to concretize an array of interpersonal dilemmas and also to identify existential difficulties. Another contributor, Leuner, has made use of the guided imagery method in a systematic fashion to uncover major motivational difficulties. By having a patient engage in an imagery trip with respect to climbing a mountain, one can get clues to problems in relation to ambitions, power strivings, and so on. By having the patient engage in an imagery trip related to following a stream to its source, one can often gain important clues through imagery about the relation of child to mother and some sense of important early experiences of attachment. In effect, the range of uses of the power of human imagination is almost unlimited, once the patient comes to accept this dimension as an adaptive resource, and not simply as a form of regressive experience.

6. More Direct Forms of Clinical Intervention

It is intriguing that the many forms of short-term clinical intervention that have developed in the last 15 years largely as reactions against the length and limited application of psychoanalysis, or other personality-change psychodynamic therapies, have increasingly relied, however, upon private experience as a critical feature of the treatment. Wolpe's systematic desensitization, perhaps the most effective and certainly the most thoroughly researched of current behavior therapy approaches, turns out eventually to rely primarily on the patient's production of private imagery rather than on the overt behavior of the patient. Thus, behaviorism, which grew up as a reaction against the introspective orientation of psychology at the turn of the century, has led back again to considerable concern with the nature of human imagination rather than directly observable stimulus-response connections. Indeed, the recent reviews of basic literature on the technique of systematic desensitization have made it clear that the critical factor in treatment is not so much the hierarchy with its ordering of least-to-most phobic situations, or the use of the progressive relaxation. Rather, the most significant feature again and again turns out to be the imagery used by the patient (Singer, 1974). What is becoming increasingly clear is that for many phobias—the symptom for which systematic desensitization is most effective—the thought of fear about the situation prevents the individual from ever coming anywhere near the phobic object or situation, and therefore ever finding out that it can indeed be tolerated. Once one can, through a series of images, gradually attend to the situation, try it out in a variety of settings created by the imagination, then an actual real-life approach becomes much more possible with the frequent consequence that the phobia disappears rather quickly.

Kazdin's chapter in this volume points out the fact that we still do not fully understand the critical "ingredient" in the effectiveness of a technique such as systematic desensitization. At least some studies that have used credible placebo or "bogus therapeutic" strategies have obtained equally good results. Again, such findings suggest that a critical factor in such a treatment is not the conditioning effect, but much more likely, a change in the private anticipations, in the images, self-communication, and daydreams that the patient holds with respect to the critical situations for which treatment has been sought.

Behavior modifiers and cognitive behavior therapists are making increasing use also of aversive control techniques. The patient imagines extremely noxious and unpleasant outcomes for certain situations and rehearses these again and again so that when the thought of engaging in an unwanted or antisocial action comes to mind, the patient quickly introduces the unpleasant consequences of such an act, and often is deterred from engaging in it. If a set of instructive alternative images are also provided for the patient, with his or her gaining some support through experiencing rewards in imagery for such behavior, a considerable flexibility can be generated.

In one instance, one of the authors' patients was attempting to control a personally unacceptable tendency toward anonymous homosexual pickups. By the use of a variety of extremely noxious images, he gradually, but rather quickly, gave up this long-term compulsive pattern. He also rewarded himself mentally by imagining successful encounters of a more longlasting nature with women. Eventually, and rather rapidly considering his long history of anonymous homosexual behavior, he moved into a much more complex, enduring, and satisfying heterosexual relationship that led to a satisfactory marriage. In this instance, while the therapist explored with him at some length through more traditional analytic methods the possible dynamics underlying this behavior that the patient experienced as unwanted and aversive, the patient reported no favorable change until the introduction of the systematic aversive imagery procedure (Singer, 1974).

There is also a very extensive and carefully researched literature on what might be called vicarious, covert, or symbolic modeling, which Kazdin evaluates and discusses in his chapter, "Covert Modeling: The Therapeutic Application of Imagined Rehearsal." The patient imagines other persons engaging successfully in acts either of freedom from phobia or acts of self-control from impulsive behavior. Again, one sees the possibility that all too often individuals have developed longstanding patterns of self-defeating action and have not, because of their anxiety or often because of limited actual experience, been able to anticipate alternative approaches to coping with these behaviors. Indeed, Meichenbaum and Turk (1976) have pointed out that often, even when patients do prove capable of imagining alternative successful coping behaviors, they lack a systematic set of self-instructions that will sustain them as they engage in the activity. Meichenbaum (1974) has developed a whole set of self-instruction techniques designed for what he calls "stress innoculation." These methods use a combination of verbal self-statements as well as images designed to help a person get through particularly stressful situations, or, anticipating these situations, to carry out what Janis (1968) has called the "work of worrying" to establish an effective coping strategy. Within these procedures, considerable emphasis is placed upon the individual's ability to use imagery to distract oneself, to shift attention, or also, to generate very strong experiences that might be capable of psychophysiological counteraction. Thus, in a series of ingenious studies by Turk (1977), it has been possible to show that individuals can sustain a remarkable amount of pain by the use of images, amongst other kinds of self-cogitations, that provide alternative "contexts," or may actually lead to biofeedback that inhibits the pain response.

The effectiveness of imagery in a host of self-regulation procedures is gaining increased recognition. The authors have frequently found it therapeutic to encourage patients who seem to be caught in moderate depressive cycles to use images of peaceful nature scenes or related positive events to see if these could change the mood, at least temporarily, and therefore permit the patient to engage in more effective behavior that could break up the snowballing effect of the depressing affect. In his chapter in this book, Schultz presents his extensive research, which demonstrates that severely depressed, hospitalized male patients who engage either in self-esteem-enhancing imagery or in imagery of positive nature scenes, were able to reduce the amount of depression and actually prove more capable of laughter and positive emotion. It is of interest to note that the imagery methods were also differentially effective depending on the patient's depressive style. For those patients who had depressive symptomatology apparently related more to early experiences of loss of love and lowered self-esteem, the self-esteem-enhancing imagery was more effective. For patients whose depression was more related to superego kinds of conflicts, the focus on positive imagery as a distractor turned out to be more useful. Contrary to theories that depression is an introjected aggression, aggressive fantasies themselves did not necessarily reduce the depression for the superego conflict. Rather, it seemed to be the distraction and positive affect associated with peaceful nature scenes that was more effective.

Imagery has, of course, been increasingly used to enhance sexual arousal. Despite early beliefs that fantasy and daydreaming represented forms of drive reduction, it is increasingly clear that imagery provides a context for increasing sexual arousal, and that this can be especially effective in helping individuals overcome particular types of sexual difficulties (Singer, 1975; Hariton and Singer, 1974; Kaplan, 1974). It should be noted that in the newly evolving multimodal therapeutic orientation of Lazarus (1976), in Ellis's rational-emotive therapy (1973), as well as in other recent short-term intervention techniques, there have been increasing emphases on systematic training of patients in awareness and use of their own imagery for dealing with a variety of interpersonal behaviors, as well as sexuality.

The work presented in the chapter by Frank demonstrates rather clearly that young adults, given opportunities to become more aware of their ongoing imagery capacities through maintaining logs of night dreams and through sharing with each other (*without interpretation*) their night and daydreams, became increasingly more empathetic as measured by a variety of objective procedures. That is, they were subsequently (in comparison with various control groups) more capable of identifying the implicit meanings in others' communications, in recognizing emotions expressed through facial and verbal gestures by others, and in general becoming more sensitive to the affective dimension of human experience.

In general, there is a growing body of evidence to indicate that systematic application of imagery methods can be effective for treatment of a variety of established neurotic conditions, for improving interpersonal behavior such as lack of assertiveness or shyness, treatment of sexual difficulties, for helping individuals control weight, and for socially undesirable behaviors such as excessive drinking or antisocial activities and impulsivity. We are still at the beginning in this area in terms of identifying specific facets of imagery that are more or less effective, identifying those individuals who are more or less capable of different degrees of imagery, and developing techniques for enhancing imagery capacities (Singer, 1975).

7. Self-Efficacy and Imagery

One of the major recurring themes in all uses of imagery in psychotherapy or behavior modification is that of the sense of self-control the patient gains since imagery is so private (Singer, 1974). Recently Bandura (1976, 1977a,b) in developing his powerful theory of social learning has emphasized cognitive processes and the importance of *self-efficacy* for producing ultimate behavior change. He has argued that psychological procedures such as the various psychotherapies as well as other approaches involving persuasion or placebo-suggestion essentially provide the individual with means of strengthening private imagery of "expectations of self-efficacy" (Bandura, 1977). Translating Bandura's formal language, our projections into the future involve expectations of what outcomes we can expect from certain actions and also our images or self-verbalizations of whether we can successfully carry out the necessary actions to produce such outcomes. This approach represents a revival of Lewin's (1935) early emphasis on "means-end cognizance," a concept employed long ago to analyze fantasy projections of various social class or pathological groups (Singer and Sugarman, 1955). Self-efficacy cognitions in the form of imagery, fantasies, or self-communications in some form determine whether we will initiate certain types of behavior and, once engaged in them, how long we will persist or how much effort we will expend. The private image that one *can* cope will help one stick it out in situations that are believed to be dangerous, embarrassing, or otherwise aversive. Such persistence often pays off in the sense that frequently one finds one can indeed handle such situations and therefore strengthens a sense of self-efficacy.

One can see in the increased emphasis on self-constructs in social learning and cognitive style theories (Witkin and Goodenough, 1976) some potential integration with psychodynamic theories. In psychoanalysis, for example, the concept of introjected parental figures or ego-ideals serves as a key to a kind of private self-reinforcement or symbolic modeling that steers our behavior. Bandura's approach carries these notions a step or two further along toward an operation formulation of the components of private experience that contribute to self-efficacy or self-reinforcement (Bandura, 1976, 1977a,b). We need to be able to assess systematically the magnitude, generality, and strength of our expectations of how well we can cope with situations.

Our expectations themselves are based on what we actually have accomplished and our observations of how well others we know have done in similar situations, e.g., our parents or siblings. They also depend on suggestions from others that are more or less persuasive, e.g., a placebo effect that leads us to believe in our images of the future that the addition of a certain drug to our body's armamentarium or the completion of a particular type of psychotherapy will make us more capable of coping with hitherto frightening or difficult circumstances. Indeed, verbal persuasion may also operate to change our attitude when we perceive logical fallacies in our own beliefs, a principle central to Ellis's rational-emotional psychotherapy. Such effects are also evident in psychoanalysis where "insight" often means a patient's recognition that a long-standing belief or behavior pattern represented a persistence into adult life of a childhood misunderstanding, inept parental "suggestion," or immature fantasy. An insight of such a type may lead to a change in the patient's image of potential future coping capacities. In transactional terms the patient may be able to say, "I no longer have to play the buffoon or *shclemiel* to get along with the others at work—I can get their interest and respect by just doing my work well."

The feedback effects of emotional arousal must also be considered in a theory of self-efficacy. Actual participation in frightening or unpleasant situations leaves a memory of the negative affect experience. Sometimes even without an actual aversive or failure experience a person's lack of belief in coping skills for dealing with such situations may lead to strong negative affect just in imagining such situations. Methods such as systematic desensitization, implosive therapy, or symbolic effective modeling often help people to recognize that they can reduce the negative affect associated with imagined situations and provide them with an additional sense that they have coping skills if they confront such situations in reality.

One's self-efficacy orientation is strongly related to chronic affective conditions such as depression. The research and intervention strategies of Beck (1967) and Seligman (1975) emphasize the long-term sense of helplessness or the beliefs that one lacks any efficacy for coping. Very likely we can become depressed if we have experienced a series of failures (or if our parents have early in life convinced us that we have) and thus cannot generate imagery of any positive outcome in our lives. Starker and Singer (1975) found that depressed mental patients also had fewer daydreams of a pleasant, wishful character than did other psychiatric patients. A recent study by Rizley (1976) also suggested that depressed college students were more likely to be precise in attending to their actual failures or limited attainments while nondepressed individuals tended to somewhat overestimate their achievements or possibilities. Hope and fantasied efficacy, if not too unrealistic, may sustain performance and avoid the debilitating effects of depressive mood.

It seems likely that our capacity for considering multiple possibilities through imagery may be strengthened by certain types of psychotherapy. Having learned to use imagery we can now add it to our repertory of coping skills. The awareness of these skills adds further to the specific sense of efficacy we experience in relation to particular upcoming situations. It remains to be seen whether one can talk of a generalized sense of personal efficacy, a position Bandura would question. At least can we differentiate between individuals in terms of the range of likely situations they are to confront and their personal sense of possessing coping skills for each of these—a kind of quantitative measure of ego-strength?

8. Some Preventive and Constructive Uses of Our Imagery Capacities

We will conclude by briefly pointing to some of the preventive or constructive day-to-day implications of imagery, as we see them. Here we have to move somewhat further away from extensive research evidence, although there is mounting support from systematic studies for many of the points we will make.

8.1. Imagery and Adaptive Escapism

Too often our tendencies to daydreaming and fantasy have been labeled as harmful because they have served as forms of escape from the rigors of day-to-day life or from the challenge of direct interpersonal interaction. There seems no question that many of us do indeed use our images or fantasies for such maladaptive escapist purposes. But that recognition has often led people to an excessive concern with the more negative aspects of their daydreaming or imaginative capacities (Singer, 1975). As a matter of fact, there are many situations in which a kind of healthy escapism may be the most useful method of dealing with the reality that faces us. On a long train ride, in a waiting room situation, in a variety of social settings in which we are powerless to act to change our situation, the shift of attention from the dangers or rigors of the immediate setting or its boredom, for that matter, may actually help pass the time and may avoid our developing emotional and, indeed, psychophysiological reactions (Schwartz and Shapiro, 1976) that could be self-defeating.

Some people are suffering from insomina because of concerns about actions they need to take the following day, but which they are powerless to accomplish the night before. Probably the best way of getting to sleep is to develop a recurring and moderately elaborate make-believe fantasy that is sufficiently interesting to distract one from the unfinished business of one's life, and yet not so engrossing as to prevent the natural sleep processes from occurring. Some people have found that imagining themselves engaging in ballet dancing or in sports activities has worked especially effectively from this standpoint. Thus, we can find a great many simple uses for our capacity to engage in attitudes toward the possible, or even the impossible, with impunity via our imagery modality.

8.2. Imagery Uses for Self-Awareness

Perhaps more than any other human process, imagery is uniquely our own. In this sense we can use our capacities for playful shifts of focus for combinations of characters, for recall of pleasant vacations or anticipation of pleasant trips in the future, to help us not only to escape, but also to learn something more about the things that seemed to be of special value. Keeping a log of one's night dreams or one's daydreams, and then examining these for recurring themes such as interest in power, achievement, sexual fulfillment, concern for others, understanding others or understanding nature, avoiding frightening situations, can provide us eventually with a kind of patterning of our own major motivational structure. Even beyond this we can begin to find out more and more what range of roles we might like to play.

We may also gain an awareness about the nature of creativity or inner playfulness itself. To what extent can we, in reading a book, become so immersed in the set of events that we find ourselves almost unable to switch back our attention? This kind of absorption, which in many ways is closely related to the intense imagery that characterizes the hypnotic state, may also tell us a good deal about our desires for deeper experience and for freeing ourselves from some of the superficialities of day-to-day interchange.

It is obvious, of course, that our fantasies will also reveal many of our more petty or less socially desirable tendencies: our jealousies, our envies of the success of others, our hatreds and prejudices. Here again, recognizing the strengths and limitations of one's imagery dimension can help one cope with these. Most white people in our society will quickly recognize, whether through dreams or daydream images, some of their latent prejudice against colored minorities. We may surprise ourselves sometimes, despite our liberal front, by noticing such tendencies. But at the same time we need not be overwhelmed by guilt. We are, after all, reflecting a tremendous range of cultural experience in our thoughts and fantasies. The awareness of such tendencies may alert us more effectively to the way in which such prejudices might eventually work their way into behavior, and we could then avoid such actions more effectively.

8.3. Imagery for Self-Regulation and Biofeedback

It is increasingly clear that a major dimension of human variation has to do with the degree to which individuals have learned a variety of skills for what might be called self-regulation or self-control. Indeed, Strupp (1970) has argued that the major implication of the various forms of psychotherapy has to do with the degree to which individuals learn to control their emotions or their impulsive activity. In many ways the use of our imagery turns out to be a major form for self-control. By trying out in imagery actions that we might undertake in the future, we can learn the possibilities and limitations of such actions. We can use imagery as has been suggested above to control negative affects, or to enhance positive experiences or sexual enjoyment. Imagery is something that is very much within our control and no one else's, and in this sense it has special advantages. In addition, we are increasingly clear that our own images are integrally related to ongoing bodily processes and, indeed, may have feedback consequences, as the work of Schwartz and Shapiro (1976) suggests. There is an increasing body of research in the field of behavioral medicine that suggests that important approaches to the treatment of physical disease, such as hypertension, will involve systematic use of imagery and related techniques for reducing blood pressure or modifying other physically maladaptive behaviors.

Imagery thus has a tremendous range of possibilities in the area of self-control and development. There is increasing work being carried out in the field of sports that suggests that systematic mental practice through visualization and fantasy may actually lead to improved functioning in actual athletic contests. Football players such as O. J. Simpson (1977) report that they made important gains in their own play style through the use of mental anticipation. A series of researches by Richardson (1969) and by Suinn (1976) have also indicated clear advantages for athletes of mental practice. We have probably not carried this far enough in the area of social role rehearsal. Increasing concern about enhancing our ability for effective social interaction, techniques of assertiveness training, techniques of more effective role-sharing in men and women, are involving anticipatory imagery. We need not be afraid of the future so much if we allow ourselves to play out a variety of scenarios, and then gradually choose the one that seems most reasonable, keeping in mind that with each actual experience, we can reexamine our options.

8.4. Imagery for Creativity and Aesthetic Experience

The dimension of imagery as we have suggested many times is close to the highest levels of human achievement in the arts. When we read a story, our ability to immerse ourselves almost totally in the framework of the author and to travel with him or her in the far-off country provides us with a whole series of images and pictures that we will enjoy not only in the reading itself, but that will continue to be played and replayed in our minds. It is not only the actual aesthetic experience, but the memory of it, and then the anticipation that enhances the value of our art. If the television medium is to be faulted from an aesthetic standpoint, it is largely because its rapidity of presentation and power holds one's attention almost completley on the set, and leaves little room for imagery and fantasy. Reading, radio, or the theater allow more leeway in this respect.

Our ability to immerse ourselves in characters of other people gives us, in an odd way, a chance to lead many lives in the short space of our own limited journey on this planet. We need not be afraid that we will be turned into schizophrenics if we can develop a set of alter-egos from literature or art or the opera. Rather, we can enhance the flexibility and fluidity of our life. Naturally, one cannot withdraw from day-to-day meaningful social encounter in such experiences. But there are many times that we can draw on these alternate dimensions to sustain us or to enlarge our perspective on the meaning of our own lives. In its own way because of its range of possibilities, fantasy is also close to humor. We can stand situations on their heads and startle ourselves from time to time with the novelty of our inventiveness. In doing so, we can get a laugh as we realize this novelty still remains our own private fiction. Indeed, as we allow ourselves this range of fantasy possibility, we can also appreciate the outlandish humor of a Donald Barthelme or a Woody Allen.

Religion, prayer, and philosophy can be concretized for us in a variety of ways, and can be used, similarly, to deepen our sense of relationship, and also occasionally to provide us with the additional leaven of humor. Maybe we can think of ourselves as walking through life toward the setting sun much as in the fade-out of a Chaplin movie. As we head toward that distant horizon, it might be fun, in the mind's eye, to flip a little side kick or a hitch of the belt as Charlie used to do, a gesture that adds just that extra touch of humor and modesty to the journey.

References

Bandura, A. Effecting change through participant modeling. In J. D. Krumboltz and C. E. Thoresen (Eds.), *Counseling methods.* New York: Holt, Rinehart and Winston, 1976.

Bandura, A. *Social learning theory.* Englewood Cliffs, New Jersey: Prentice-Hall, 1977a.

Bandura, A. Self-reinforcement: Theoretical and methodological consideration. *Behaviorism,* 1977b.

Beck, A. T. *Depression.* New York: Harper & Row, 1967.

Bogen, J. E. The other side of the brain. *Bulletin of the Los Angeles Neurological Societies,* 1969, 34, 135–162.

Bourne, L. E., Ekstrand, B. R., and Dominowski, R. L. *The psychology of thinking.* Englewood Cliffs, New Jersey: Prentice-Hall, 1971.

Bruner, J. S. The course of cognitive growth. In P. C. Wason and P. N. Johnson-Laird (Eds.), *Thinking and reasoning.* Baltimore: Penguin, 1968.

Eisenstein, S. *The film sense.* New York: Harcourt Brace, 1942.

Ellis, A. *Humanistic psychotherapy: The rational-emotive approach.* New York: Julian Press, 1973.

Freud, S. Jokes and their relations to the unconsciousness. In *Standard edition of the complete psychological works* Vol. 8. London: Hogarth, 1960.

Gazzaniga, H. S. The split brain in man. *Scientific American,* 1967, 217, 24–29

Gill, M. Topography and systems in psychoanalytic theory. *Psychological Issues, Monograph 10.* New York: International Universities Press, 1963.

Hariton, E. B., and Singer, J. L. Women's fantasies during sexual intercourse: Normative and theoretical implications. *Journal of Consulting and Clinical Psychology*, 1974.
Horowitz, M. J. *Image formation and cognition.* New York: Appleton-Century-Crofts, 1970.
Horowitz, M. J. Intrusive and repetitive thought after experimental stress. *Archives of General Psychiatry*, 1975, 32, 1457-1463.
James, W. *The principles of psychology.* 2 vols. New York: Dover (1890), 1950.
Janis, I. L. Human reactions to stress. In E. Borgotta and W. Lambert (Eds.), *Handbook of personality theory and research*, New York: Rand-McNally, 1968.
Jaynes, J. *The origin of consciousness in the breakdown of the bicameral mind.* Boston: Houghton-Mifflin, 1977.
Johnson, D. M. *The psychology of thought and judgment.* New York: Harper & Row, 1955.
Kaplan, H. S. *The new sex therapy.* New York: Brunner/Mazel, 1974.
Kris, E. On preconscious mental processes. In: D. Rapaport (Ed.), *Organization and pathology of thought.* New York: Columbia University Press, 1951.
Lazarus, A. (Ed.). *Multimodel behavior therapy.* New York: Springer, 1976.
Lewin, K. *A dynamic theory of personality.* New York: McGraw-Hill, 1935.
Meichenbaum, D. *Cognitive behavior modification.* Morristown, New Jersey: General Learning Press, 1974.
Meichenbaum, D., and Turk, D. The cognitive-behavioral management of anxiety, anger, and pain. In P. O. Davidson (Ed.), *The behavioral management of anxiety, depression and pain.* New York: Bruner, Mazel, 1976.
Mischel, W. *Personality.* New York: Wiley, 1971.
Mischel, W. Toward a cognitive social learning reconceptualization of personality. *Psychological Review*, 1973, 80, 252-283.
Paivio, A. *Imagery and verbal processes.* New York: Holt, 1971.
Perls, F. *Gestalt therapy verbatim.* New York: Bantam, 1970.
Pope, K. S. The flow of consciousness. Unpublished doctoral dissertation. Yale University, 1977.
Pope, K. S., and Singer, J. L. Some dimensions of the stream of consciousness: Towards a model of on-going thought. In G. Schwartz and D. Shapiro (Eds.), *Consciousness and self-regulation.* New York: Plenum 1978a.
Pope, K. S., and Singer, J. L. (Eds.). *The stream of consciousness.* New York: Plenum, 1978b.
Pope, K. S., and Singer, J. L. Determinants of the stream of consciousness. In G. Davidson, and R. Davidson (Eds.), *Human consciousness and its transformations.* New York: Plenum, in press.
Rapaport, D. *Organization and pathology of thought.* New York: Columbia University Press, 1951.
Rapaport, D. The psychoanalytic theory of motivation. In M. R. Jones (Ed.), *Nebraska Symposium on Motivation.* Lincoln, Nebraska: University of Nebraska Press, 1960.
Reich, W. *Character analysis.* 2nd ed. New York: Orgone Institute Press, 1945.
Reyher, J. Free imagery: An uncovering procedure. *Journal of Clinical Psychology*, 1963, 19, 454-459.
Richardson, A. *Mental imagery.* New York: Springer, 1969.
Rizley, R. C. The perception of causality in depression: An attributional analysis of two cognitive theories of depression. Unpublished doctoral dissertation. Yale University, 1976.
Rodin, J., and Singer, J. L. Laterality of eye shift, reflective thought and obesity. *Journal of Personality*, 1977.
Schachtel, E. *Metamorphosis.* New York: Basic Books, 1959.
Schwartz, G. Biofeedback as therapy: Some theoretical and practical issues. *American Psychologist*, 1973, 28, 666-673.

Schwartz, G. E., Davidson, R. J., and Maer, F. Right hemisphere lateralization for emotion in the human brain: Interactions with cognition. *Science*, 1975, *190*, 286-288.
Schwartz, G., and Shapiro, D. (Eds.). *Consciousness and self-regulation: Advances in research*. Vols. I and II. New York: Plenum, 1975-1977.
Seidman, J. M. (Ed.). *The adolescent. A book of readings*. Revised. New York: Holt, Rinehart & Winston, 1960.
Seligman, M. E. P. *Helplessness*. San Francisco, California: Freeman, 1975.
Simonton, O. C., and Simonton, S. S. Belief systems and management of the emotional aspects of malignancy. *Journal of Transpersonal Psychology*, 1975, *7*, 29-47.
Simpson, O. J. Newspaper interview, New Haven, Conn. Jan., 1977.
Singer, J. L. *Imagery and daydreaming methods in psychotherapy and behavior modification*. New York: Academic Press, 1974.
Singer, J. L. *The inner world of daydreaming*. New York: Harper & Row, 1975.
Singer, J. L. Imaginative play and pretending in early childhood: Some educational implications. *Journal of Mental Imagery*, 1977, *1*, 127-144.
Singer, J. L., and Sugerman, D. Some thematic apperception test correlatives of Rorschach human movement responses. *Journal of Consulting Psychology*, 1955, *19*, 117-119.
Sperry, R. Hemisphere disconnection and unity in conscious awareness. *American Psychologist*, 1968, *23*, 723-733.
Starker, S., and Singer, J. L. Daydream patterns and self-awareness in psychiatric patients. *The Journal of Nervous and Mental Disease*, 1975, *161*, 313-317.
Strupp, H. H. Specific vs. non-specific factors in psychology and the problem of control. *Archives in General Psychiatry*, 1970, *23*, 393-401.
Suinn, R. M. Body thinking: Psychology for Olympic champs. *Psychology Today*, July, 1976, *10*, 38-43.
Tauber, E. S., and Green, M. G. *Prelogical experience*. New York: Basic Books, 1959.
Tomkins, S. *Affect, imagery, and consciousness*. Vols. I and II. New York: Springer, 1962-1963.
Turk, D. A multimodal skills training approach to the control of experimentally produced pain. Unpublished Doctoral Dissertation. University of Waterloo, 1977.
Ulam, S. M. *Adventures of a mathematician*. New York: Scribner's Sons, 1976.
Wilson, E. Review of *Ulysses. New Republic*, 1922, *3*, 164.
Witkin, H. A., and Goodenough, D. R. Field dependence revisited. *Research Bulletin*, Educational Testing Service, 1976.
Woolf, V. Modern fiction. In *The common reader*. New York: Harcourt, Brace, 1953 (1925).

PART II

Psychoanalytically Oriented Uses of Imagery

Introduction

The chapters grouped in Part II of this volume reflect the work of psychotherapists and theorists with strong commitments to some aspects of the psychoanalytic theory of personality and psychopathology. Dr. Horowitz, a distinguished investigator of imagery and psychopathological processes, has made important contributions toward integrating broader issues of human information processing with the psychodynamic conflict emphases of classical psychoanalysis. His contribution to this volume provides a framework closely related to cognitive psychology that can help toward organizing the diverse uses of imagery and fantasy.

The chapters by Reyher and Shorr describe extensive applications of imagery or fantasy methods within the psychoanalytic framework. Reyher's approach represents a continuation of the classical free association method with, however, an emphasis on image rather than verbal associations. One wonders how psychoanalysis might have developed had Freud clung to his early emphasis on image association rather than shifting around 1900 to the verbal emphasis. Shorr's approach involves a more active form of intervention with much more direction from the therapist. Both contributors work within Freudian and Sullivanian theoretical orientations. Reyher has already made important contributions to the experimental study of imagery processes and Shorr is beginning to experiment with an imagery questionnaire.

2

Controls of Visual Imagery and Therapist Intervention

Mardi J. Horowitz

1. Introduction

Visual imagery has been a part of therapeutic intervention throughout recorded medical history. Dreams, for example, were prominent moments in the treatment afforded supplicants at the Aesculapian temples of ancient Greece. Recently, there has been a surge of widely varied imagery techniques in many brands of psychotherapy (Singer, 1974). The use of any of these imagery techniques usually means a shift in how patients control their visual mode of representation. Their regulatory processes are altered because of interventions by the therapist. Such interventions may be interpretive as in classical psychoanalytic psychotherapy. Interpretations tell the person what they are doing. The focus of attention on the specified process or content leads to altered controls, especially if volitional effort is added. Interventions may also be directive. The person is told how to alter his volitional control over the stream of thought. This chapter offers a theoretical model for understanding the visual mode of representation, the controls that influence depiction of ideas in this form, and the way that interpretations or directions alter visual thinking and subjective experience.

Mardi J. Horowitz • Department of Psychiatry, University of California School of Medicine, San Francisco, California 94143.

2. Image Formation as a Mode of Representation

Modes available for the conscious expression of meanings include enactive, image, and lexical representations (Horowitz, 1978). In ordinary wakeful thought, these modes blend richly; reflective awareness seldom distinguishes one from another. This multimodal thought is symbolized, in Figure 1, as the center of the sphere of attention. As the periphery is approached, there is less blending, and one may be aware that a train of thought is pictorial rather than verbal, is in auditory images rather than subvocal speech, or is a flow of word meanings without sensory qualities. Each mode has its own special utility and organizational properties as elaborated in Table I.

Enactive thought depicts information in trial actions, with minor tensing of muscles. Competing action tendencies can be compared and

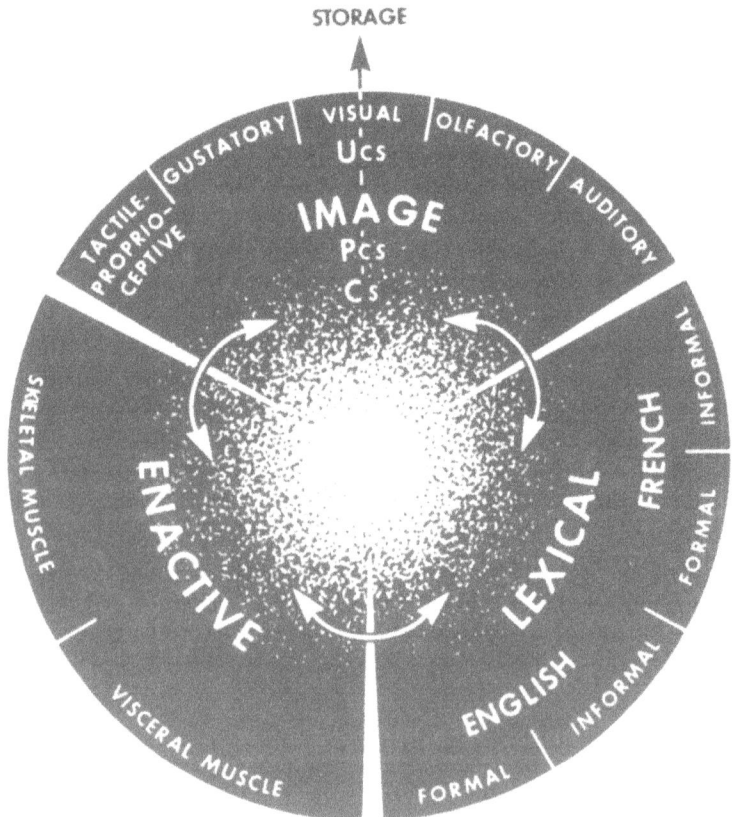

Figure 1. Systems of representation of thought.

Table I. An Outline of Modes of Representation (from Horowitz, 1978, p. 89)

Mode	Subsystems	Sample organizational tendencies	Sample statement	Sample of complex units of represented information
Enactive	Skeletal neuro-musculature Visceral neuro-musculature	By directionality and force, by operational end-products	X does this	Gestures Facial expressions Postures
Image	Visual Auditory Tactile-kinesthetic Olfactory-gustatory	By simultaneous occurrence, spatial relationships, concrete categorization of similarities and differences	X is like this X is like Y X is there and Y is there X and Y happen together X does this to Y	Introjects Body images Relationship between self and object
Lexical	(Different languages?)	By sequentiality and linear structure, by abstract categorization	IF X and Y *then* Z because X + Y → Z	Phrases or sentences Stories and histories

the flow of enactive thoughts may be reflected in micromomentary gestures and facial expressions (Haggard and Isaacs, 1966).

Image thought allows continued information processing after perception and, as in dreams and daydreams, can lend a sensory configuration to emergent ideas and feelings.

In lexical thought the essential ingredients are word meanings and grammatical organization. Conceptualization, reasoning, and abstract generalization are most secure in this mode.

Each mode is composed of subsystems. Enactive systems may be organized by functional activities such as different work sets or sports. Image systems are divided by sensory modes: auditory, visual, olfactory, gustatory, tactile, and proprioceptive. The visual mode is the focus of this paper. The lexical system may be organized by different languages, each with specific vocabulary and rules for grammatical construction.

Emergent ideas enter a system, the information may then be translated from one mode to another (indicated by arrows in Figure 1). Regulatory processes act at the boundaries of systems to inhibit or facilitate these entries and exits.

3. Utility of the Visual Image System

Visual images are private experiences, rarely communicated by pictorialization, more often communicated by translation into words. Perhaps because of the early development of image formation, before conscientiousness or superego formation, or perhaps because of the privacy inherent in this mode, images often carry into awareness ideas censored from lexical representation. Such properties lead to the extremes of image use noted in clinical settings: at times the spontaneous flow of images seems almost like a direct expression of unconscious thought, as suggested by Freud (1900) and later by Jung (1916) in explanation of his active imagination technique; at times reversion to images is a withdrawal from verbal communication, a form of resistance (Kanzer, 1958).

Images of dreams and waking fantasies often carry the first awareness of a newly emergent theme. Other clinical observations have shown that it is in this mode that preverbal memories (Kepecs, 1954) and unresolved traumatic episodes may reenter awareness after a long period of repression (Horowitz, 1970, 1976). Even if a theme has not initially gained entry into awareness in image form, extension of ideas into image form often is associated with intensified emotion. The images can depict the intensity of a wish or fear because they reveal particular actions between persons. Finally, image experiences, even of entirely internal origin, may have a quasi-perceptual quality that allows the person a sense of interaction with them, on an "as if real" basis. The more common examples are the experience of introjective "presences" and the temporarily restorative fantasies of missing objects, from the fantasy of food in a starving person to the fantasy of a separated lover, to the imaginary companion of a lonely child.

If these are the utilities of image representation, what motivates therapists to use interventions that increase image formation rather than those that encourage the continued employment of lexical thought? The most common aim is to short-circuit repression and elicit expression of warded-off ideas. The second most common aim is to short-circuit the partial repression involved in the more complex defenses of isolation and undoing, in order to uncover the emotion arousing properties of thought.

Most frequently, the material then expressed in image form is composed of traumatic memories, conflicted interpersonal fantasies, and disavowed but dynamically powerful self-images. It is the conflict between current conscious attitudes and the wishes and fear inherent in these emergent images that generates emotional responses to the images experienced. This conflict can then, hopefully, be worked through. As one step in working through such conflicts, image experiences are translated into word meanings. This extends awareness of meaning and alters the earlier state of censorship.

4. A Model of the Image System

Having described some of the properties of the image system, we may now consider a model of the system in order to focus on the possible sites for the accomplishment of defensive aims. Figure 2 provides a visual metaphor of such a model.

Stimuli enter the mind as information in the form of images. Eventually the information is transformed into the enactive and lexical forms suitable for usual interpersonal communications.

For a time, the process of image thinking may take place in separable trains of thought, organized by relatively primary process as well as relatively secondary process regulations. The same stimulus situation is contemplated in different ways, with eventual comparison and even competition among these ways before there is conclusive interpretation of a stimulus or decision on action.

Information enters the visual system from at least four and probably five sources, as shown in Figure 3. One source is perceptual input, including entoptic sensations. The second source is internal information that includes both the schemata necessary to construct perceptual images and the storehouse of long-term memory and fantasy. The third input is from codings retained from prior episodes, episodes retained in a kind of short-term or active memory with a property of recurrent representation. The fourth input is translation from thought cycles occurring in other modes. The hypothetical fifth source is from parallel image-forming systems. Entry of information from a primary-process type of image formation into an image system that has been regulated by secondary process is the instance of concern here. Defensive aims can be accomplished through the regulation of each of these forms of input.

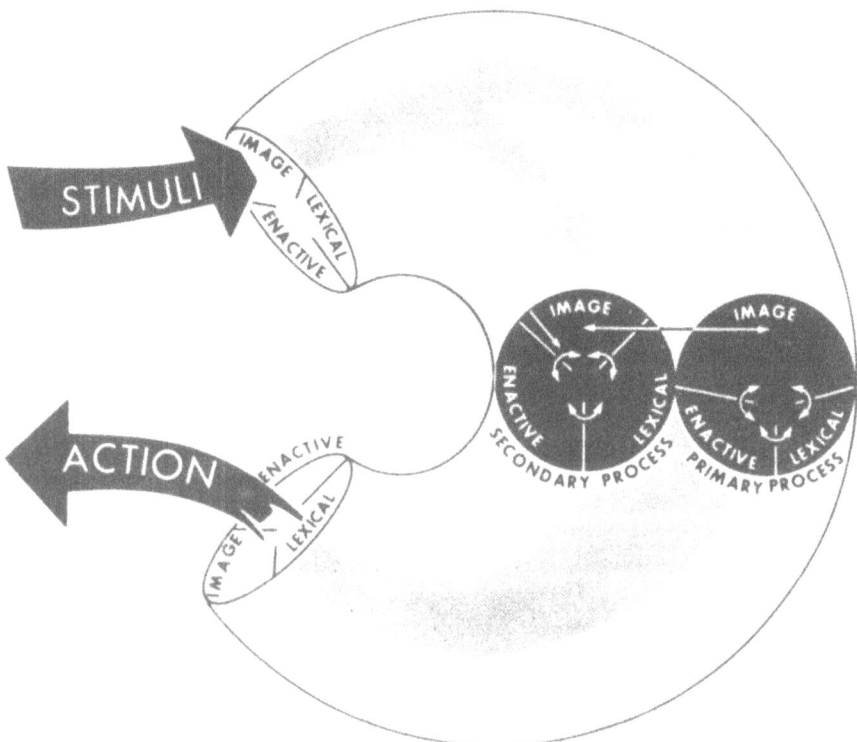

Figure 2. The "Black Tube" metaphor of minimum complexity.

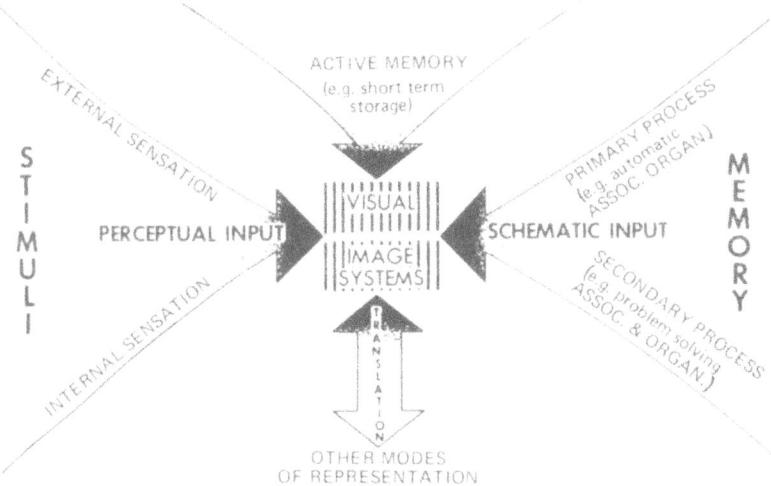

Figure 3. Model of input into the image systems.

5. Defenses and the Process of Working-Through

Working-through involves recognition and reconciliation of discrepancies between reality and fantasy, between current possibilities and inner attitudes or aims. Recognition and confrontation mean that ideas and feelings usually warded off are now expressed within a safe and therapeutic relationship. This process requires change in defensive operations, and most generally, a change in the inhibitory maneuvers that accomplish repression. The model of representational modes presented here illustrates sites where inhibitions prevent the free flow of information in the form of visual images. One may now consider therapeutic interventions aimed at alteration of such inhibitions. The presence of a therapeutic relationship will be assumed.

6. Techniques to Alter Inhibitory Operations

The five most frequent inhibitions of entry of information into the visual image system are illustrated in Figure 4 as follows:
1. The failure to attach word labels to images.
2. The converse, which is avoidance of image associations to contents expressed in words.
3. Inattention to dim or fleeting image episodes.

4. The prevention of primary process or spontaneous flow types of image formation.
5. The nontranslation of enactive representations into imagery.

Overstated examples of interpretive and directive kinds of interventions are provided in Table II (Horowitz, 1978). These are illustrative only. The directive remarks included in Table II are comparatively gentle in that they suggest to the patient changes in the form of thought. In guided fantasy techniques and behavior therapy techniques, direction is more extensive, with suggestion of specific contents to conceputalize. The choice of interpretive or directive intervention for a given type of inhibition as well as the timing, dosage, and nuances of intervention are dependent on the current state of transference and the potential for transference topics not amenable for discussion here.

But, without going too far into the choice of interpretation or direction, what can be said about the difference between these techniques for the same type of inhibition? The directive interventions are similar to those of a teacher. If the assumption of a developmental lag is indicated, that is, if the patient has not yet learned to make full use of various modes of thought, if inhibition has been in fact a long-standing limitation of cognitive style, then a simple directive statement may help the patient learn new ways of using thought processes. Interpretive remarks are, of course, also covert suggestions. The patient hears such remarks as implications that he ought to try doing what he is told he is avoiding. But interpretive remarks give much more information and so require much more inference or knowledge on the part of the therapist. If this information is accurate and well timed, interpretations place the patient

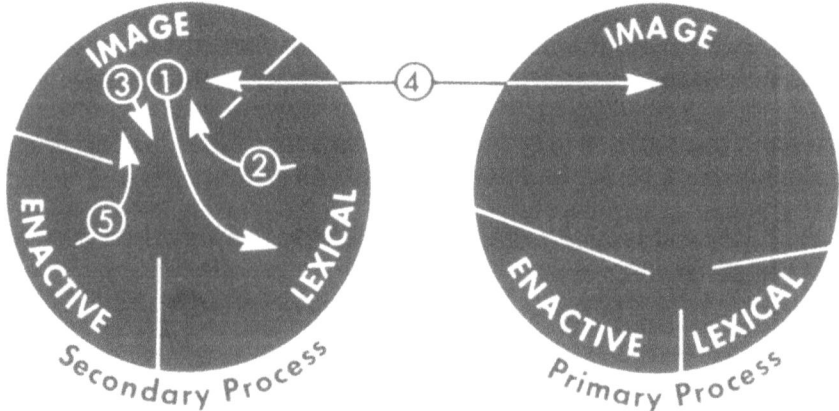

Figure 4. Topology of inhibitory processes influencing visual image formation.

Table II. Defensive Inhibitions and Sample Interventions (from Horowitz, 1978, p. 340)

Site of inhibition	Sample of an interpretive intervention	Sample of a directive intervention
1. Images not associated with word meanings	"You do not let yourself describe those images you are having because you are afraid to think clearly about and tell me about those ideas."	"Describe your images to me in words." "Tell me what that image means."
2. Lexical representations not translated into images	"You do not let yourself think that idea visually because you are afraid of the feelings that might occur if you did."	"Let yourself think in visual images and report whatever you experience to me."
3. Vague images (preconscious) not intensified (conscious)	"You are afraid to let that fleeting image become really clear in your mind because you are afraid you will feel or act badly if you do."	"Try and hold onto those images and 'tune them up.'"
4. No cross translation between secondary process and primary process images	"You are afraid to let yourself have daydream images because you are afraid that bizarre ideas will take over and you will lose control."	"Let yourself kind of dream about this right now."
5. Enactive representations not translated into images	"You are afraid to picture in your mind the implications of your present posture and facial expression; you are afraid the self-image that would result would shame you."	"Try to picture yourself in your mind with that posture and expression on your face."

in a position of greater control. He can consciously choose to continue or to set aside the inhibitory processes set in motion by unconsciously made decisions.

The errors possible in intervention by direction or interpretation also influence the therapist in choice of technical style. Directive intervention, especially the suggestion of particular contents in guided fantasy techniques, may put the patient in a passive position in which the directive acts of the therapist provide a nidus of reality for the elaboration of a transference in which the therapist is like a parent telling the patient what to do, a person he can hold responsible as he complies or stubbornly resists in an overt or covert manner. Interpretative interventions can provide erroneous information that the patient may then believe or else use against the therapist. An example is when the therapist interprets a behavior as defensive when it is in fact due to a lack of regulatory capacity; the interpretation does not help the patient gain control over his thought process.

7. Facilitations and Inhibitory Failures

The avoidance of images can be contrasted with the intrusion of images. These episodes of unbidden images are more complex because they may result from either active facilitation or failure of inhibition. An example of interpretation in an instance of facilitation of imagery follows. Suppose the patient has become flooded with emotion because he has formed vivid images of a painful memory. The therapist might then interpret the transference meanings: "You are upsetting yourself by forming lurid images of that event because you hope I will be compelled to comfort you if I see you cry." While this is an ordinary transference interpretation, albeit without a link to an earlier figure, it also conveys information about how cognitive processes are used. This is contained in the phrase "by forming lurid images." As mentioned before, such information puts the patient in a slightly better position to exert conscious choice over his ensuing thought process.

Such an interpretation would be inappropriate if the main reasons for the lurid images were failures of inhibition. In this context, directive remarks may help the patient gain control. For example, the therapist may say, "Please contemplate that idea in words. You feel sad remembering this event. What did it mean to you?" At times, therapists suggest even more dramatic shifts to other modes as a way of learning control, as when Beck (1970) showed a patient with intrusive images that he could stop these images by clapping his hands.

It would also be possible for the therapist to direct attention to another topic, or to stay on the same topic but suggest specific images, as is done in behavior therapy techniques. For example, in systematic desensitizations, the therapist takes phobic imagery, assembles a hierarchy of images from least to most threatening, and tells the patient when to start an image, what to image, and when to stop. This maneuver teaches the patient control over image formation; if the therapist can tell him to start and stop, he can tell himself the same thing.

8. More Complex Defensive Operations

Defenses such as undoing and isolation are more complex than repression because they involve multiple cognitive operations. A brief clinical vignette provides an illustration of the play of such defenses at the boundaries of representational systems:

> Early in a course of psychoanalytic psychotherapy an obsessional man was describing a situation with his work supervisor. He concealed from himself his hatred of this man.

The supervisor gave him more work than the patient thought he could do. As he tried to describe his response he oscillated between feelings of respect and feelings of dislike for the way his supervisor told him to try to take on more work. In a given sentence, he would add undoing clauses: he admired the firmness of the supervisor but he didn't like being given more work; he ought to do more but it irritated him to be told to; he respected the supervisor, but the supervisor was too authoritarian, he spoke up to the supervisor, but in a wishy-washy way, and so forth.

The lexical system is the principal mode of representation here and lends itself to undoing because of its sequential organization. The therapist attempted to hold the patient to his irritation: Wasn't he saying that he did not like the supervisor when he gave him extra work?

The patient complained of the way the therapist said "did not like." That wording was too strong; sometimes he did admire the supervisor, at other times he felt less respect. The patient fell silent for a while, then reported the image of a door on which a red-hot branding iron had just emblazoned an arrow. He could not think of what the image might mean, but felt vaguely frightened.

Reconsider the two states. In one the patient is thinking in words and communicating these mental contents. In the other he has shifted to images, and for a time does not communicate. In the first state he manifests little emotion, in the second he reports feeling frightened. We know from other evidence that in both states he avoids clear depiction of himself as angry and destructive. In the lexical state he accomplishes this avoidance by using neutral words such as "respect" and "disrespect" and changing his way of ascribing even these mild attitudes to himself. The requirements of grammar fix the subject and object as self or other: he respects or does not respect the supervisor.

In contrast, in the image system, the impulses are rather clear: the door is burned by the forcefully assertive branding iron. The patient avoids thinking of himself as angry by leaving the self and object designation unstated. Symbols are present—the door, the arrow, the iron, burning—but he does not identify himself with any of them. Instead, he is frightened. In his kind of image-thinking his position as the subject or object of action can remain unclear; he is either the injured door, and hence frightened, or the out-of-control injuring iron, and hence frightened that he might hurt someone else.

As he translates the images into words, and thinks of possible meanings related to himself, he can still accomplish undoing by verbal juggling (Salzman, 1968) by changing ideas from self as victim to self as aggressor, with resulting cancellation of anger by fear and fear by anger. The end result is, of course, only a vague sense of guilt and self-doubt.

To recapitulate, a given defensive aim, such as undoing, can be accomplished differently in different systems of representation. Some information leaks through to each system, and use of both systems can increase what is known. In the lexical system, subject and object are designated, but several oppositional interactions are asserted in order to maintain the protective confusion. In the image system, the emotional quality of the contemplated action is made clear, but the self-designation such as victim or aggressor is left unclear. The separation of the modes accomplishes isolation of idea from affect. The therapist, however, does not have to segregate information from either system; it is possible to pick up the emotional clues from the images, and the ideational clues from the words. Information derived from both states can be put together, the defensive codes broken, and the underlying threat recognized.

Intervention to help the patient set aside defenses in order to expose and deal with this threat will be a much longer process. It will involve interpretation of what is warded off, the manner of warding off, and the various cognitive maneuvers used to maintain defense. Change in cognitive style will involve the patient learning to put together information, using both representation systems, just as the therapist has done.

9. Summary

There are several modes for the representation of thought. Thinking usually combines and orchestrates those modes, but each mode has a particular utility and is regulated in different ways. In particular states, especially in conflict when emergent ideas and feelings are avoided by control operations, the modes may be experienced as separable vehicles for expressing meanings. Defenses are accomplished by control operations at the boundaries of each mode. An understanding of the cognitive process may help therapists choose interventions, either interpretive or directive, that are at the level of the patient's method of processing information. Such interventions may place a patient in a position of greater control, at a point where he can decide to experience thought in new ways, more consciously, expressively, and expansively.

References

Beck, A. T. Role of fantasies in psychotherapy and psychopathology. *Journal of Nervous and Mental Disease*, 1970, *150*, 3-17.

Freud, S. (1900) *The interpretation of dreams*. Standard edition, L. Strachey (Ed.), London: Hogarth Press, 1959.

Haggard, E. A., and Isaacs, K. S. Micromomentary facial expressions as indicators of ego mechanisms in psychotherapy. In L. A. Gottschalk and A. H. Auerback (Eds.), *Methods of research psychotherapy*. New York: Appleton-Century-Crofts, 1966.

Horowitz, M. J. *Image formation and cognition*. New York: Appleton-Century-Crofts, 1970, 2nd ed., 1978.

Horowitz, M. J. *Stress response syndromes*. New York: Aronson, 1976.

Jung, C. G. (1916) *The archetypes and the collective unconscious*. New York: Pantheon, 1959.

Kanzer, M. Image formation during free association. *Psychoanalytic Quarterly*, 1958, 27, 465–484.

Kepecs, J. G. Observations on screens and barriers in the mind. *Psychoanalytic Quarterly*, 1954, 23, 62–77.

Salzman, L. *The obsessive personality*. New York: Science House, 1968.

Singer, J. L. *Imagery and daydream methods in psychotherapy and behavior modification*. New York: Academic Press, 1974.

3

Emergent Uncovering Psychotherapy: The Use of Imagoic* and Linguistic Vehicles in Objectifying Psychodynamic Processes

Joseph Reyher

1. Introduction

Spontaneous visual imagery does not characteristically occur in an interpersonal relationship; hypnogogic and hypnopompic images, nocturnal dreams, daydreams, fantasies, and hallucinations are private events. Spontaneous visual imagery is unpredictable and idiosyncratic and, therefore, irrelevant to the purposes of most interpersonal relations. As we shall see, spontaneous visual imagery has aversive properties both in an interpersonal relationship and in one's private ruminations. In the former, it undercuts the self-protective function of security operations whereas in the latter it is a ready vehicle for the gratification of anxiety-producing unfulfilled needs and the depiction of repressed impulses.

Spontaneous visual imagery, like free association, may be acknowledged only under circumstances wherein one individual (a client)

---

* This term is used rather than *imagistic* or *imaginal* because of their multiple meanings. However, it should not be confused with *imago*, which has biological and psychoanalytic definitions. The term *imagoic* is used as an adjective denoting visual images.

Joseph Reyher • Department of Psychology, Michigan State University, East Lansing, Michigan 48823.

has pledged himself to report everything that comes to mind (the Basic Rule) when asked by another individual (a psychotherapist) to describe visual imagery (free imagery). However, the client's success in honoring his pledge is opposed by the anxiety piqued by the initial, incipient act of self-disclosure imposed by the Basic Rule. The resulting anxiety-driven compromise behaviors are face-saving devices that are subsumed under what Sullivan (1953) called *security operations.* These behaviors create the illusion that the client is honoring his pledge while disrupting the procedure, e.g., asking questions. Security operations reduce anxiety by returning the interpersonal relationship to the familiar and relatively safe conversational form.

There are two other points of anxiety in the unfolding course of events that undermine the client's resolve to abide by the Basic Rule. If the onset of visual imagery is characterized by trivial, childish, offensive, or bizarre imagery, the client is likely to feel demeaned by it and, therefore, will engage in redeeming and disruptive security operations. If the visual imagery should continue, a point is eventually reached where the images become anxiety-producing, even when they appear innocent, and the client's eyes pop open. These images turn out to be anxiety-laden vehicles (derivatives) of dissociated conceptions and repressed impulses.

There is little doubt that the foregoing anxiety-driven behaviors contribute to our ignorance of spontaneous visual imagery, which are homeostatic-like mechanisms for preventing the lowering of self-esteem and the peculiar pain associated with it. Other possible contributing factors for our ignorance are the purposes that motivate the observer and/or the imager. These purposes almost always involve directed imagery rather than free imagery, e.g., systematic desensitization, implosive psychotherapy, guided imagery techniques, incidental learning, and problem solving. Psychotherapists and research investigators both tend to dislike asking individuals to do things that produce disruptive reactions including anxiety and anger, and which appear to be meaningless. In other words, their own security operations (looking good in the eyes of the would-be imager) cause them to desist. This reluctance to press for spontaneous imagery becomes the focal point in the training of neophyte psychotherapists who, for the most part, are intimidated by the client's aversive reactions. Finally, one must be an old-fashioned Freudian to believe that spontaneous visual images are meaningful drive derivatives, but it is decidedly unorthodox to use imagery instead of free association, particularly when Freud used imagery (concentration technique) and abandoned it.

If spontaneous visual imagery is to be observed, the interpersonal situation must be structured in such a way as to identify and obviate security operations. These structuring procedures are called "emergent uncovering psychotherapy" because they progressively objectify a wide variety of psychodynamic processes and identify two sources of anxiety—one Sullivanian and the other Freudian. Thus, psychotherapy becomes a reliable procedure that can be learned by a psychotherapist and experienced by a client.

2. Procedures for Objectifying and Differentiating Awareness and Interpersonal Behavior

The physical arrangements are informal—which means the psychotherapist is not sitting behind a desk—preferably with two identical chairs and a recliner or couch nearby. I like Sullivan's term *participant observer* to characterize the involvement of the psychotherapist and the term *collaborator* to characterize the involvement of the client. Although the phenomena that are produced are those described by Sullivan, the management of the interview is much different because of the planned interventions. The psychotherapist intervenes at entrée points (indicators of anxiety, a manifestation of resistance, a symptom, or a security operation). This form of intervention increases pressure for client self-disclosure if certain guidelines (interpretive observations, nondirective prompting, and interpersonal inquiry) are followed and interpretations are not proffered. These constraints on the psychotherapist insure the objectivity of the phenomena observed by both participants. The client experiences what the psychotherapist might otherwise interpret, providing the procedure is affective. If the emergent uncovering techniques work well, the objectivity of the proceedings have important implications from the perspectives of both the individual and science. For the client, it means that he knows the self-discoveries are valid, and the increased differentiation of self-awareness corresponds to an increase in ego-strength, where *ego-strength* is defined as the ability to accept the anxiety generated by self-disclosure. Since the application of the method is unbiasing and invariant, it becomes a useful scientific tool.

2.1. Self-Disclosure

Self-disclosure entails great risk to a client's self-esteem because in his personal histories he has been belittled, demeaned, or ridiculed for ill-advised revelations of his innermost thoughts as well as for the customary put-downs of everyday life. Psychotherapy, therefore, places a client's self-esteem in jeopardy, generating anxiety. It is this anxiety that makes the prospect of consulting a psychotherapist so utterly terrifying. Even psychotherapy clients of long standing continue to experience anxiety upon the act of self-disclosure because they are more highly invested in maintaining and advancing the good will and esteem of their psychotherapist. However, because of their commitment of candor and their increased self-awareness, they are more apt to identify their anxiety, recognize its source, and catch a security operation in midflight. Most importantly, they recognize the projection of their own self-rejection onto the psychotherapist, which causes them to expect rejection. As Sullivan observed, attention, like a searchlight, only illuminates cues relating to matters of self-esteem.

2.2. Entrée Points: The Exploration of Self-Awareness

During the initial interview, the psychotherapist draws the client's attention to dissociated behavior (e.g., a clenched fist) and manifestations of affect and anxiety. These perturbations in the flow of the client's behavior are called *entrée points* and call for an interpretive observation (Wallen, 1956). An interpretive observation merely draws the client's attention to the behavior in question ("Your fist is clenched") and thereby puts pressure on him to account for it. Physiological and behavioral expressions of anxiety are much in evidence during the initial sessions, as are security operations. Common indicators of anxiety are autonomic nervous system effects, such as blushing, blanching, swallowing; somatic nervous system effects, such as tics, tremors, stammering; or behavioral effects, such as erratic gestures, shift in body position, and breaking eye contact. The most reactive indicators of this genre are the feet: they wiggle, rotate, and bend upward.

These perturbations in the ongoing flow of behavior may be contingent with a particular topic or a reaction to the psychotherapist's behavior, which implies a relationship between them. For example, the psychotherapist observes the client's cheeks reddening and says in a nonconfronting manner, "Your cheeks seem to be getting red", and waits for the client to infer the significance of this behavior. In contrast, interpretations and confrontations too often serve as self-enhancing security operations for the psychotherapist. These undermine the client's collaborative role and polarize the relationship in terms of mentor–student, parent–child. Furthermore, since the implications an interpretation are experienced as opprobrious, most clients receive it as a painful, narcissistic injury (lowering of self-esteem due to reflected, negative appraisal). However, some clients cannot admit to their injury and to their anger because the psychotherapist is merely doing his job. They must suppress their feelings and give an illusion of thoughtful consideration because the psychotherapist otherwise might think that they would be bad clients or might become angry and retaliate with superior knowledge. Clients are put under tremendous pressure to dissemble (a security operation), i.e., "Hmm, that's interesting," "You might be right about that," "I never thought about that before," then say, "But. . . " or they change the subject—another security operation.

An exploration of clients' subjective awareness should be initiated following their responses to an interpretive observation. This exploration often reveals a struggle between opposed motives to self-disclose but, at the same time, to suppress the self-demeaning self-conceptualization it inspires. More often than not, this generates anxiety and cues security operations to prevent a narcissistic injury, e.g., denial, rationalization, etc.

An interpretive observation prompts clients to cast an inward eye on their immediate experience. Sometimes clients are able to get in touch with the anxiety and/or with whatever is producing it. Those clients lacking psychological mindedness or low motivation for self-exploration are most apt to deny any significance to indicators of anxiety. Psychotherapists merely accept these denials, but, of course, they use this information to their advantage by recognizing that any proffered observations, interpretations, and recommendations would be discounted by the client. By focusing on the client's reality problems and frustrated aspirations, sufficient motivation for self-exploration may be developed. For those clients who are curious about the significance of their contingent reactions, nondirective techniques used in connection with interpretive observations have potent uncovering properties with respect to suppressed material. A variety of techniques for gently urging the client on can be used. These are: "Huh, huh," restating affect-laden words and any statement that encourages the client to continue in a particular direction, "That's interesting," or "How is that?" or "Can you tell me more about that?" Reflections are to be avoided unless the affect-laden thoughts are very clear, otherwise a reflection really is an interpretation.

Language itself is replete with entrée points, chief of which are vague, nondenotative words that we all use to cover up our true feelings. These include such words as "upset," "bothered," "disturbed," "concerned," "bad" or "out of sorts" and such colloquial expressions as, "freaked-out," "spacey," and "bummed-out." The psychotherapist tests this suppression of affect-tinged thought by saying, "Upset in what way?" or "Can you tell me more about that?" This use of nondenotative words and expressions gives the listener the illusion of self-disclosure while at the same time maintaining suppression. The substitution of one word for another after pronouncing the first syllable is an instance of conscious editing that provides a particularly powerful opportunity for helping clients see how they select words (suppression) to avoid making an unfavorable impression on the psychotherapist. The same is true for cutoff sentences. The psychotherapist makes the needed observations by saying, "Can you complete that thought?" When and if the client is able to retrieve the dropped word or complete the cutoff sentence, the psychotherapist says, "What do you make of that?" or something to that effect. If the client is unable to get in touch with the underlying affect-tinged thoughts, the psychotherapist watches for the intensification of anxiety and the mobilization of fresh self-protective maneuvers. A focus on language presents an opportunity *par excellence* for psychotherapists to help their clients get in touch with their desire to make a good impression and their anxiety about the prospect of making a bad one.

Many clients feel betrayed by an entrée point and become reluctant to look into it. In examining their resistance to pursue the implications of an interpretive observation, they discover features of their personality they would rather disown; a need to deny, rationalize, or justify their behavior at all costs (all security operations). They may discover a desire for others to see them as perfect, or that they must be in control of themselves and others at all times. Anger, hostile thoughts about the psychotherapist, withdrawal, and paranoid ideation are not infrequent. The focus on resistance leads clients to an examination of their character traits which they loathe to do because this is what others see; it is their visible selves. Character traits constitute the interface of interpersonal relationships wherein most of us are avoiding signs of disapproval. In emergent uncovering, the focus on resistance takes precedence over anything else. Of course, this is standard practice in psychoanalytically oriented psychotherapy.

To avoid being regarded as a sadistic inquisitor by anxious clients who generate entrée points at a high rate, the psychotherapist might forego making interpretive observations and make reflections such as, "You appear to be nervous." If this does not prompt the client to self-disclose, then the psychotherapist observes the client's ensuing behavior for the elicitation of impromptu security operations and other fresh contingency reactions. It is important to be careful using the word "why," which we use so naturally, because it connotes an evaluative attitude and thereby prompts rationalizations. Since it puts the user in a position of power, it often functions as a security operation, particularly for psychotherapists. Consequently, it is a difficult interpersonal behavior to modify.

Interpretive observations must be made gently because they are inconsistent with the client's striving to appear to the psychotherapist as an intact and worthy person. Since these observations are intrinsically demeaning, the client may perceive them as an expression of the psychotherapist's hostility. In the initial interviews, the psychotherapist should help the client verbalize his reactions. To initiate this increase in pressure for self-disclosure one might use a comment such as, "Were you wondering about my impression of you when I brought that twitch to your attention?" Such a comment, which is termed an interpersonal inquiry, usually elicits contingency reactions, and the client may at times be nonplussed, an entrée point. The posing of such a question by the psychotherapist may be perceived as a dreaded concretization of the client's inner conviction that the psychotherapist dislikes him or her. The employment of nondirective techniques at this point can help the client verbalize his self-loathing and its projection.

2.3. Eyes Closed Free Association

Sooner or later most clients are able to cope with the psychotherapy interview without generating obvious entrée points and security operations. The psychotherapist then increases uncovering pressure by asking the client to recline (in a reclining chair or a nearby couch) and to free associate without omitting a thing, while both remain face-to-face. Free association increases pressure to self-disclose because the client agrees to cooperate as per instructions before appreciating the implication of the phrase, "without omitting a thing." The client usually complies with the psychotherapist's request to avoid disapproval. However, when the client closes his eyes, another source of anxiety is cued, putting him in a double bind. Asking the client to free associate without omitting a thing is a request for full disclosure of thoughts without the benefit of self-protective monitoring and editing security operations. Upon hearing this request, some clients experience a rush of anxiety, manifest resistance, and generate security operations suited to the exigencies of the moment, e.g., "You've got to be kidding," "This is foolishness," "Is this the psychoanalysis that nobody uses anymore?" or self-effacement, "I'm not good at doing this kind of thing." Disparagement enhances a client's self-esteem by putting down something else, whereas self-effacement enhances a client's self-esteem because of the patent display of courage in admitting to an insufficiency. Not only does this counteract the client's experienced lowering of self-esteem, but it prevents the psychotherapist from saying the same thing, which would be a more severe narcissistic injury. Another facet of self-effacement is that it tends to elicit reassurances. The psychotherapist's task is to restate the client's wording of the security operation and to use other nondirective techniques, as needed, to move in to explore the underlying painful affect and feelings of inadequacy. For those clients who opened their eyes (an entrée point), this means repeating the instructions after the employment of an interpretive observation ("You opened your eyes") and nondirective techniques ("What do you make of that?"). For those clients who do not open their eyes but remain silent (an entrée point), this means an immediate examination of their inability to free associate by employing, of course, interpretive observations and nondirective techniques.

In addition to the added pressure of self-disclosure, free association generates feelings of insufficiency because criteria for assessing adequacy of performance are absent (Stern, 1974). This feeling of insufficiency prompts clients to believe the psychotherapist is evaluating them negatively on the basis of definite criteria that he has not shared. They open their eyes and look at the psychotherapist. An exploration of their immediate awareness usually reveals their need for reassurance, which they suppress or deny. These security operations are secondary to a more primary security operation of dissembling, viz., behavior conveying a prized self-conception such as "I'm alright Jack!" "I'm cool." Thus, an already complex situation for clients frequently is complicated by concurrent and incompatible strivings to impress the psychotherapist with their psychological integration while at the same time accepting the role of client in psychotherapy which implies being dysfunctional in some way(s).

If they keep their eyes closed, many clients assert that only trivial or fragmentary thoughts come to their attention. The psychotherapist then says, "Can you recall what these were?" Since this question applies pressure on clients to disclose suppressed material, the psychotherapist watches closely for entrée points. The client usually agrees to comply but then blocks as he experiences resistance. The psychotherapist responds by making an interpretive observation, "You seem to be having some difficulty," and it often turns out that the suppressed positive or negative conceptions and/or affects concern the psychotherapist. One immediate effect of the client's verbalization of these items is a subsequent weakening of suppression.

In addition to the increased need for security operations because of interpersonal threats to self-esteem (anticipation of a narcissistic injury), the supine position promotes a feeling of passivity—a pathogenic interpersonal situation for some clients—and vulnerability (insufficient self-protective mechanisms). Most clients hesitate to recline upon request, and, when they do, they may experience a reluctance to close their eyes. This objectification of resistance is of momentous importance because it reveals to clients that a part of their mind, which they do not understand, opposes the procedure. Not only does it pique their curiosity, but it defines the immediate goal of psychotherapy, which is the analysis of resistance. When clients finally close their eyes, usually after an exploration of their immediate experience, they often reopen them in a few seconds, sometimes involuntarily, and go on to describe symptomatic reactions, engage in security operations, and look directly at the psychotherapist. These behaviors and reactions initiate more exploration of their immediate experience which, like resistance, can be of momentous significance because clients realize that their symptomatic reactions are being produced by some process outside of awareness. The exploration of their immediate awareness often reveals that feelings of inadequacy (low self-esteem) is the pathogenic (symptom-producing) instigator. These feelings also create a compelling need for reassurance from the psychotherapist; hence, clients open their eyes to scan the psychotherapist's countenance for signs of approval and disapproval. They hope to see the former but dread seeing the latter, which they feel is more probable.

To illustrate the foregoing procedures and phenomena, the following verbatim excerpt was taken from the protocol of a twenty-three-year-old, self-referred male whose presenting problem was premature ejaculation. His coping mechanisms with respect to environmental stress were adequate and he was succeeding in his teaching career.

2.4. The Verbalization of Suppressed and Dissociated Material: A Clinical Illustration

T: Now I would like you to do something that might prove to be helpful. Would you mind leaning back, closing your eyes, and describing everything that crosses your mind?
C: All right. (He keeps them closed for a few seconds and then opens them.)
T: I see that you have opened your eyes.
C: Oh, I didn't know how long you wanted me to keep them closed. (His resistance

is rationalized and is probably *not* experienced. Rather than interpret the resistance, the procedure that produced it is reapplied to promote experiencing the resistance.)

T: Would you mind closing your eyes again and describing everything that crosses your mind?

C: Okay. (About 20 seconds elapse.) I just got a sharp pain, a sharp twinge in my chest.

T: That's interesting. I also notice that your eyes are open.

C: Yes, I just opened them, I guess, when I felt that twinge.

T: Is there pain now?

C: No.

T: I wonder what the pain and your eyes opening are all about?

C: Beats me. (His resistance is not experienced, but neither is it rationalized, a distinct gain in confidence. The procedure is reapplied to promote further mastery.)

T: How do you feel about closing your eyes again?

C: Okay, I guess. (Note the implied resistance.)

T: Would you close them again? (Ten seconds go by and C has not closed his eyes.)

T: I see that your eyes are still open.

C: I'll close them. (His resistance presumably produced fear that I might get angry with him for not closing his eyes; he hesitates.)

T: It might be useful if you could tell me what is going on inside yourself right now.

C: Nothing in particular. (Conscious withholding—suppression.)

C: Well, to be honest, I was just trying to make up my mind to close my eyes.

T: You were trying to make up your mind?

C: It was just hard for me to make up my mind to do it. (The first verbalized experience of resistance is of great moment and is exploited to promote further confidence and understanding.)

T: It's interesting how one part of your mind will oppose what another part wants to do.

C: This *is* interesting. It sure is. (Uncovering pressure is increased by asking C to take note of his feelings.)

T: Can you recall what you were feeling when you said, "I'll close them"? (The client squirms in the chair and avoids eye contact, an entrée point.) Does your moving about right now mean anything about how you are feeling?

C: Well, I, I feel silly. (Lowering of self-esteem.) You asked me to close my eyes and I did, but then I opened them. You asked me to close them again and I didn't do it right away. (The client is on the threshold of verbalizing feelings of insufficiency and the inevitable generation of anger, which is turned inward. The word "silly" is an entrée point.)

T: You said you felt silly.

C: It seems dumb that I can't close my eyes and keep them closed.

T: Are you being hard on yourself right now?

C: I suppose so.

T: You suppose so?

C: Well, I'm letting you down. I can never do anything right. Sometimes I hate myself.

T: Was it difficult to tell me those things?

C: Yes.

T: Any reason in particular?

C: You'll find out what an idiot I am and think I'm hopeless.

T: Does that mean I won't want to work with you?

C: Yes.
T: Are you convinced of that?
C: No.
T: You're of two minds on that?
C: It's obvious from the way you talk and look that you're not going to ask me to leave.
T: How are you feeling now?
C: Better.
T: What about that chest pain.
C: It's gone.
T: Is that surprising to you?
C: Yes, now that I think of it.
T: Would you like to find out more about that? (This is a crucial test of his ego strength.)
C: Yes.
T: Well, then close your eyes again and describe everything that crosses your mind without omitting a thing.
C: OK, I'm getting uptight, my heart is pounding and I want to open my eyes.

The significance of these initial interactions cannot be exaggerated because the client *experiences* symptomatic behavior that he cannot explain. He experiences resistance contingent with anxiety and/or symptoms and accepts the attempt to understand these reactions as the immediate goal of psychotherapy. If the client has sufficient ego strength and motivation to accept this immediate goal, emergent uncovering is off to a good start.

Eyes closed free association proceeds:

C: Say, that pain is back again and I seem to want to catch my breath. (He opens his eyes and looks at T.)
C: What do you think is causing that?
T: How are you feeling right now?
C: Okay.
T: What about the pain in your chest and the catch in your breath?
C: They're gone.
T: Let's see, as soon as you close your eyes you want to open them and you have symptoms. Have you ever noticed these things when you are alone and when your eyes are closed?
C: No. Does that mean it has something to do with closing them in here?
T: What do you think?
C: I don't know. Do you mean that it has something to do with you?
T: I'm not sure. How do you feel?
C: Scared. You know, I've never been to a shrink before. You might think I'm crazy or queer or something. (Previously suppressed thoughts are being verbalized presumably because his confidence in the relationship has increased. He has not been unsympathetically confronted or demeaned.)
T: How do you feel when I ask you to close your eyes?
C: The same—scared.

T: Would you mind closing your eyes?
C: No. (He closes his eyes.) I'm scared all right and I feel like I would like to lift my arms up in front of my face to protect myself. That's funny; I just thought of my father giving me a swat at the dinner table when I was a kid. (This blatant transference reaction, or parataxic distortion, opens up a new direction to the proceedings.)
T: What do you make out of that?
C: You're not my father, but, in a sense, I seem to expect the same treatment from you that I got from my father.
T: You expect the same treatment from me?

The above example illustrates how the client experienced contingencies between objective events: closing his eyes, symptoms, and resistance. After he realized the critical (pathogenic) factor was not being able to see the psychotherapist, he was able to experience that his father and the psychotherapist were equivalent sources of threat. Since it was he who discovered the determinants of his own personal experience, the uncovering proved to be a self-esteem enhancing, confidence-building procedure.

2.5. Relevant Laboratory Investigations

Two investigations by Stern provide the first experimental elucidation of security operations. In his first investigation (1974), Stern compared three conditions to determine the effect of eyes open versus eyes closed on the production of primary-process intrusions in college males. The three conditions were free association with eyes open, free association with eyes closed, and free imagery with eyes closed. These conditions were administered with no attempt to build rapport. Upon meeting the subject, the experimenter perfunctorily asked him to be seated in a reclining chair and then gave him the instructions for one of the conditions, thereafter maintaining absolute silence. Contrary to his expectations, the Holt method for scoring primary process did not differentiate among the three conditions. The two free-association conditions were equally pathogenic (anxiety-producing), and, surprisingly, both were significantly more pathogenic than free imagery. The greater pathogenicity of the two free-association conditions was unexpected because he had anticipated that the visual imagery conditions would be associated with a high degree of drive representation and primary-process intrusions. Signs of anxiety appeared shortly after the beginning of all three conditions, and they were evenly distributed throughout the 10-minute sessions. Thus, it appears that the anxiety was associated with the ambiguity of the task rather than the activation of repressed, drive-related impulses.

Stern's assessment of the experimental conditions, in terms of the challenges they posed for the subjects' feelings of self-esteem, was fruitful. In the two free-association conditions, the subject was faced with an unusual task that lacked criteria for making self-evaluations of their own performance. The enigmatic experimenter allegedly knew these criteria but said nothing, thereby inducing a feeling of insufficiency (lowering of self-esteem) and anxiety in these subjects. This was not as true for the free-imagery condition wherein subjects were asked to perform a specific task on which some self-assessment of performance was possible; that is, one can see images to report. The fact that the subject "sees" images satisfies the task demands, which therefore poses less threat (lowering of self-esteem) than does free association.

In his second investigation (1975), Stern succeeded in manipulating the threat of eyes closed, free association by using two sets of instructions. To maximize threat, subjects in one condition were given feedback to the effect that they were not doing what was expected of them. To minimize threat, subjects in another condition were given feedback that they were doing what was expected of them. A third group was given no feedback. As in the previous investigation, the verbatim protocols were scored for signs of anxiety, but this time there were no differences among the conditions; however, a relationship emerged between expressions of reduced self-esteem, verbalized anxiety, total number of symptoms (anxiety signs), and being female.

When the number of anxiety signs was plotted against the number of words spoken, a curvilinear relationship emerged that suggests that subjects who experienced the most threat suppressed disclosing both their associations and their symptoms of anxiety. In contrast, those subjects who experienced less threat disclosed more, including their symptoms. Even though they might have experienced fewer symptoms of anxiety, they disclosed proportionately more. As threat decreases, the frequency of words spoken and symptomatic reactions also increases until a pivotal or turnover point is reached which is followed by decreasing signs of anxiety as the number of words spoken increases. This curvilinear function was verified recently by LeBaron (1976).

The foregoing investigations show that the frequency of anxiety signs can be manipulated by the nature of the task and type of feedback, and they suggest that the frequency of symptoms is a function of a lowering of self-esteem.

3. Objectifying Repression and Repressed Drive-Related Impulses

There is no question that an exploration of subjective awareness, particularly during eyes closed, free association, considerably increases clients' more differentiated perceptions of themselves and others while enjoined in an interpersonal relationship. They come to appreciate the impoverishment of their interpersonal relationship because of the projection of their own self-demeaning conceptions and the profusion of security operations thereby generated. Nevertheless, some clients continue to be plagued by feelings of inadequacy and remain ill at ease around people. Focal symptoms have proven to be intractable. Something else needs to be done.

Whenever clients are able to free associate with their eyes closed without displaying obvious entrée points and security operations, the psychotherapist can introduce visual imagery by asking them if they have noticed any images or pictures in their mind's eye. With few exceptions, clients will answer in the negative. The psychotherapist can then say, "I would like you to describe whatever pictures come into your mind's eye, making note of any feelings and bodily sensations that come to your attention." Most clients verbalize resistance in some form: they do not see anything, or images flit in and out before they can recognize them. Some clients even open their eyes saying they cannot do it or that they simply do not want to proceed. The psychotherapist draws their attention to their resistance, which is palpable and objective; however, this time their resistance seems to have mysterious origins. In no immediate way does it appear to have anything to do with their relationship with the psychotherapist. Once again, their mysterious origin piques client curiosity which then prompts them to close their eyes and proceed. For those clients who cannot form images, the psychotherapist can often get them started by saying, "Can you picture your car in your mind's eye?" or "Can you see what you had to eat for your last meal?" After this initial success, the psychotherapist says, "Now please describe whatever changes take place or whatever other images come into your mind's eye."

Most clients are able to image after brief resistance and, occasionally, the eruption of symptoms. Typically, the client's initial imagery is a veridical recollection of prosaic everyday experiences. Nothing seems amiss, but sooner or later an innocent image or scene (e.g., a sandal with a long heel; the prow of a boat ploughing through the water; a duck with an outstretched neck; a catfish lying in the gutter flipping over onto a curb and exposing its stomach; a rear-end view of a heifer that turns its head around and looks at the client), will be accompanied by contingency reactions. Common symptomatic reactions, specified by a Symptomatic Reaction Scale (Burns and Reyher, 1976; Stern, 1974), most commonly include: verbalized anxiety, indicators of anxiety (tremors, dry mouth, tachycardia), psychosomatic symptoms (pain behind eyes, headache, dizziness, nausea) and hysterical symptoms (numbness, floating, paralysis). Common manifestations of resistance are, "I don't want to close my eyes," "My eyes popped open against my will," "I can't get images anymore," or "I don't want to do this anymore."

The disparity between an innocent image and the eruption of contingency reactions often piques the curiosity of the client which, hopefully, presents a mystery to be resolved. Sometimes however, it is only the psychotherapist's curiosity that is piqued, and the client is reluctant to proceed. This reluctance is treated like any other entrée point. Subsequent uncovering shows that these disparities are indicators of repressive insufficiency. An insufficiency of repression means that the repugnant, anxiety-producing aims and objects of certain drive-related impulses are finding more direct expression in the client's imagery and behavior. These presumed indicators can be converted to objective indicators when contingency reactions are elicited upon repeated requests to revisualize these images but not to other images. Therefore, the former are called hot images.

Although an insufficiency of repression is objectified by an operational definition, the aims and objects of a repressed, drive-related impulse are not. If the client has the motivation to proceed, repressed impulses become more blatantly depicted, often in highly implausible and bizarre ways. Visual imagery obviously has become a vehicle for the representation of repressed impulses and their dissociated aims, i.e., "An eagle is attacking my father at the dinner table"; "I see my father; now I'm grabbing someone by the cock and throwing him over my shoulder"; "I see myself standing in front of my class nude; I have an erection. I'm shitting and I'm cracking a whip over their heads"; "I'm looking up at a face. I'm crawling up my mother's nose. The sides are smooth and free of boogers and hair." Thematic integration may disappear due to the intensification of repressed impulses, e.g., "I saw a rabbit ears TV antenna, then I saw a fish, and now I see a caterpillar." With further intensification of repressed impulses, the internal cohesiveness of a percept is attenuated and just fragments pass by, e.g., "I see a mouth, now an ear, then an eye." These fragments often are creatively synthesized into new percepts (images), e.g., "My father and I are fishing and he pulls in this large fish that has an elephant trunk," or "I see the Loch Ness monster with the head of Teddy Roosevelt," or "I'm looking down at my dick and see a long, pointed, glass tube. Now I see a woman with her legs spread, but instead of a vagina, I see an electric plug."

To become objective indicators of repressed impulses and their dissociated aims, the foregoing imagoic derivatives must be associated with expressions of anxiety and guilt. The anxiety might be verbalized or expressed in symptomatic behavior. The guilt generally takes the form of repugnance, self-derogation, or the anticipation (projection) of rejection by the psychotherapist. Clients will not understand the significance of blatant, imagoic, drive representations in the absence of the above contingency reactions. Only when they are present does he or she realize the adaptive, self-protective functions served by repression, providing, of course, that the psychotherapist has maintained objectivity by not making interpretations. Uncovering is complete whenever the client is able to experience the drive-related affects and impulses that were subject to repression and is able to verbalize its repugnant aims. Unfortunately, it takes many months for objectification to include experiencing. Some clients will terminate psychotherapy following blatant and painful objectification. For example, an impotent young male said he had been obsessed all week by a TV advertisement of a woman selling rugs. I asked him to recline and visualize the commercial. He described an older, attractive woman who selected a rug and reclined upon it, pulling a lower corner over her pelvic area. Then he saw a disembodied erect penis move toward her and stop about eight feet away. A drop of liquid formed on the tip of the penis and turned into a fish that swam over to her. As the fish drew near, the woman, now nude, pulled back the rug and the fish swam up her vagina partway and got stuck, with just its tail showing. The woman then laughed maniacally as the fish struggled vainly to extricate itself by violently swishing its tail. It finally succeeded, but it was reduced to a skeleton, and the woman was now his mother. The client's anxiety was so acute that he opened his eyes and did not want to resume free imagery for several sessions. Although he realized his Oedipal strivings, the lust and other related affects were not experienced. Out of his extreme anxiety came the verbalization that he did not want to explore any further his feelings about his mother.

The skeptical reader should consult the published documentation of comparable uncovering via visual imagery (Morishige, 1971; Morishige and Reyher, 1975; Reyher, 1968, 1977b). Although individuals vary in the degree of bizarreness of their free imagery, the revisualization of a dream is a particularly powerful method of intensifying repressed impulses (Morishige and Reyher, 1975; Reyher, 1977a) and generating bizarre imagery. The onset of bizarreness seems to be related to the intensification of anxiety and serves as a mechanism of defense. Clients who might be characterized as having hysterical features often describe highly dramatic and bizarre visual imagery. The bizarreness is the handiwork of primary process in standard Freudian psychoanalysis; however, an exploration of an alternate conceptual scheme was found to be both parsimonious and promising.

4. Modes of Information Processing

There appear to be two major modes of information processing in human beings (Reyher, 1977b). One is intrinsic to the nervous system and forges perceptions from the electro-chemical representation of the energy impinging on the receptors (Reyher, 1977b). The principles or functions regulating perception also govern the retrieval of percepts (images) from our encoded perceptual history. It is called the *analogic-synthetic mode of information processing.* The other mode of information processing which enables us to understand and use written and spoken symbols is called the *semantic-syntactic mode of information processing.*

The semantic-syntactic mode has independent expressive and receptive components. Listening is different from speaking. Listening is a digital (words) to analogue (cortical potentials) conversion, whereas speaking is an analogue to digital conversion. Listening is designated as the receptive semantic-syntactic mode and speaking as the expressive semantic-syntactic mode. The expressive mode can be broken down into *conceptual-verbal* representation (abstract referents) and *depictive-verbal* referents (words denoting concrete objects).

The essential and unique features of the expressive, semantic-syntactic mode are the representation and communication of meaning through the use of symbols and syntax. That is, the speaker or writer uses vehicles (*morphemes*) to represent something other than themselves (their referents), which are arranged in a particular order according to consensually validated rules. These are not passive, spontaneous processes. The communication of one's thoughts is active, interpersonal, and the speaker or writer directly apprehends the meaning of what he wants to communicate.

The analogic-synthetic mode of information processing not only synthesizes perception but also synthesizes visual imagery. Normally, our waking images are iconic; that is, they are retrieved from our encoded perceptual history. Iconic images are not semantic vehicles of representation; the imager merely takes note of visual images in the same way that he takes note of visual perceptions. Neither images nor perceptions are cognitive processes. They are synthesized effortlessly by percept-forming Gestalt principles of organization while being modulated by the neural records of past percepts. This modulation of sensory input by past experience proceeds along gradients of physical, functional, and qualitative similarity. With respect to imagery, sensory input is restricted to interoceptive, proprioceptive, and intrapsychic stimuli some of which are drives; that is, they are response-producing. Needs of the self, particularly those involving unfulfilled strivings for recognition, are the referents governing the retrieval of percepts and provide the thematic organization (synthesis) of percepts relevant to fulfillment. We know these as daydreams. The images are iconic and depictive of ego-syntonic strivings.

The identification of referents is not clear in the case of nocturnal dreams and hot images wherein ego-dystonic, drive-related impulses and their dissociated aims are indirectly depicted because of prohibitive anxiety associated with direct imagoic depiction. Indirect and involuntary, imagoic depiction of the aims and objects of a drive-related impulse is not mediated semantically; hence, its lack of meaning. Indirect imagoic depiction is mediated on gradients of similarity (physical, functional, and qualitative), such as the relationship between cow and mother and between snake and penis. They are aptly described as drive derivatives in standard psychoanalytic nomenclature. As such, they function as indicators of a process. An indicator does not stand for something other than itself (a phallic symbol is a misnomer because it does not have representational or symbolic functions). An indicator merely registers the existence of some process. In this case, however, we only can infer the presence of a process because derivatives of a given drive-related impulse can assume infinite guises. Unfortunately, most derivatives do not convey to the observer the relevant dimensions of similarity. Drive derivatives, therefore, are variable and unreliable diagnostic signs, the significance of which is unknown. Objectively assessing the referents of derivatives must await indentification by the imager even though they seem obvious to the observer. Imagoic drive derivatives are more easily identified than are the conceptual-verbal derivatives of free association because they bear some resemblance to their referents. Conceptual-verbal derivatives are obscured by dimensions of semantically mediated comparisons, identities, allusions, and symbolization. Free association is generated by dissociated concepts constituting the aims of repressed impulses whereas free imagery depicts the percepts constituting the aims.

Records show that depictive, imagoic presentation alone is too concrete to represent affects and sentiments such as love, loyalty, reverence, transcendentalism, Zionism, socialism, democracy, and so forth. These meanings are mediated by conceptual-verbal representation, although concrete, imagoic, exemplifications of them can be formed concurrently. Both our laboratory investigations (Reyher, 1977a) and clinical observations show that free imagery intensifies repressed drive-related impulses and that cognition (understanding) involves the conceputal-verbal labeling of dissociated affects and concepts associated with the aims and objects of these drive-related impulses.

5. Relevant Clinical Illustrations

In the two illustrative protocols below, the reader might take particular note of the differences between them with respect to the use of conceptual-verbal representation (abstract referents), depictive-verbal referents (words denoting concrete objects), and imagoic derivatives. Both depictive and conceptual-verbal representation involve the conscious (we choose our words) or cognitive communication of meaning via symbols (words and their referents), but this is not the case for spontaneous imagoic drive presentation in the mind's eye. These visual images are unbidden.

The protocol below was produced by a highly intelligent, self-referred, single female who was sexually inactive, inorgasmic, and whose major emotions were isolated. Her coping mechanisms with respect to environmental stress were exceptionally good and she had amassed a wide variety of competencies:

"I thought of a couple of the pictures that I saw of just my father. ("Can you describe the pictures?") Well, they were just about the same. They were just taken of him standing and looking at the camera. Has a real light suit on, one with a hat on, and one without a hat. He just looked so young and was very slender. . . . The room is changing dimensions. Oh, well, there's a great separation between the two of us. ("How far away do I seem?") The room is extremely long and you're at the other end. . . . ("Tell me what comes into your mind's eye and what sensations and feelings you notice.") I went back to thinking about a little boy and a little girl. ("The little boy that put his hand up the little girl's dress?") Uh-hum. It just seems like there's times that I'm a little more nervous (connection between unconscious drives and physical symptoms established in previous sessions) or tense than at other times; it seems like any little thing can make me jump. ("What do you see?") Nothing. No, it's like the back of the chair is going to tip over. ("Just keep on describing every little thing, no matter what it is.") I feel very cold.—I'm just very cold and it feels like it's getting light.—It's very cold.—I just see this light. ("Just describe whatever you see and feel.") I'm very cold—I, um, just seems as if I'm relaxing and I just have two spoons in my hands, a spoon in each hand.—I thought of, I saw myself like running downstairs or something in these shoes that were much too long for me. I just, I'm very cold. I think, well, of getting my coat to get warm. I seem to be a little frightened. I don't know. ("Keep on describing everything that you notice.") I thought of the little boy and the situation out at school, boys fighting. ("Anything in your mind's eye?") I thought of the fish we have out at school, and I thought one had an extremely large stomach and I thought of them. And I saw myself like pinching these fishes. ("Pinching the fish's stomach, the large stomach?") I get like I'm so relaxed, and then there's something that starts frightening. ("Pinching the fish's large stomach?") I thought of, um, I saw like the backs of two people, I don't know. It has something to do about, um, a navel or something. ("A navel, backs of two people, a navel. Tell me everything that you see and feel.") My eyes, it seems always hard to keep them closed. I thought of some money out at school. I thought of two boys out at school and some money. I saw—I saw a big person like bending over, and he has a sailboat, a small toy sailboat, and I saw the sails go up. I become frightened. ("That frightened you?") I thought about, when you said that, I thought about this man that I used to date that had a sailboat. ("Can you get an image of that long fish with the big stomach?") It seems that by pinching the stomach, I'm forcing the fish to go to the bathroom. ("What do you see?") I see I'm pinching the stomach, and I see the fish going to the bathroom, going to the bathroom. ("Urination or a bowel movement?") A bowel movement. . . . I just thought of when I did see a fish, and one of the students in the class asked me what was that hanging from the fish, and I told him. . . . I thought about pinching my father's stomach with my knee. ("What's happening now? Pinching your father's stomach with your knees.") I also thought how like the trailings of the bowel movement of the fish could be like my father's penis, or something. ("The last time you thought about sitting on your father's stomach, you were aware of his genitals behind you. You thought if you moved backward you would be sitting on them.") I, in saying that, like I want to say that I never said that; or I don't remember saying that. ("What's happening?") I was just thinking about it, and I thought about intercourse. I thought about it because, you know, when I thought about the penis it was an erected penis and I thought about sitting on it. When I thought about it, I was sitting on the erected penis. ("Your father with the erected penis?—You're kind of wincing, frowning.") Well, it's bothering me that I want to say that: I don't think that it's my father's. I just thought about it. ("In what way is it bothering you?") I, um, I just don't—oh, I don't know. I just don't like the ideas there's something. ("One part of you does, and one part of you doesn't. It keeps coming up all the time.")—I, um, I don't know, I just, like I had to stop thinking about him. Like I was just thinking about what I was going to do when I left."

Client A is a good example of the presentation in awareness of imagoic derivatives generated by the genital-sexual impulses associated with her Oedipal strivings and the apparent intensification of these by continuous, spontaneous visual imagery. Client B is a good example of the conceptual-verbal representation of affects and sentiments apparently in response to the intensification of the genital-sexual impulses associated with his Oedipal strivings during the presentation of imagoic derivatives. He was a twenty-one year old, self-referred, sexually impotent male of average intelligence who was failing his college studies. His ego strength and methods of coping with environmentally induced stress were significantly less than that of Client A.

"I feel kind of tight right now. I'm thinking right now about a sensation I had when I was telling you about Susan. I feel right now like I did then. The back of my head is hot, muscles are tight, legs are numb, and just real hot. I see a forest on the right and a wall behind me. I always seem to see walls and barriers of some sort. Like I can visualize that wedge-shaped field, pointing to the farmhouse. What comes to mind is my philosophy toward you, for digging down into my subconscious. I guess I'm sort of patting myself on the back right now for seeing my problems so clearly. I seem to be able to analyze myself. Funny, I'm very conscious of my penis right now. I don't know why. My hand is on my abdomen very close to it, I guess. Think about my mother; the feeling is almost overbearing. Seems like a corridor and she's blocking it. Like it's dark at the other end of the corridor, and I want to get past and see what's there. My throat and mouth are dry. ("What do you see?") Like a broomstick handle. Like an erect penis. I'm really awfully conscious of my penis right now—.("What's happening?") I have a headache starting. It's kind of black with little gold specks—it's like I'm looking off far away. Way far away I see the sky, field, and fence. ("I see you are scratching your neck?") Yeh, I have itches and tickling sensations all over. My nose, and side of my face, and back of my head. Just trying to relax as much as possible. Something like a science-fiction novel with mental telepathy, and the first principle is noneffort. I guess I'm feeling that way—not to try at all. Mother—soft, among other things. ("What are those other things?") Oh, not frightening, but repressing, keeping me back, not letting me have my way. See her almost as wedge-shaped."

Susan appeared to be an imagoic derivative of the client's mother, and the wedge-shaped field appeared to be a derivative of her pubic hair. These inferences were supported (retrospective confirmation) when his attention was drawn to his penis at which point conceptual-verbal representation mediated four affectively toned conceptions of his mother: she was frustrating, overbearing, sensually appealing (soft), and anger-provoking. Continuous visual imagery apparently intensified the genital-sexual impulses associated with his Oedipal strivings. Despite the blatancy of both imagoic and conceptual-verbal vehicles of representation, the client did not recognize their significance (insight-uncovering) in this session. Most psychotherapists would mistakenly make interpretations at this point. Uncovering was far off. The eruption of symptoms and his seeming "*la belle indifférence*" toward them has systematic significance apropos another line of research involving posthypnotic conflict (Silverman, 1976). These investigations have shown that the degree of repression determined, in part, the particular type of symptom manifested; that is, there is a particular order or sequence of symptoms generated by the lifting of repression. The protocol of Client B illustrates this progression of psychopathology.

The immediate effect of a switch from conceptual-verbal representation to imagoic-depictive presentation in awareness is the apparent intensification of drive-related impulses and their repressed aims and objects, and the magnitude of such intensification is indexed by contingency reactions and the blatancy of imagoic presentation of these strivings (aims and objects of drives). Contrary to orthodox psychoanalytic theory, the impression of the two illustrative protocols, and many others, is that spontaneous visual imagery does not involve disguised gratification of a repressed striving, but it merely seems to allow for the presentation of the aim and object of a repressed drive-related impulse via derivatives. The revisualization of hot images and dreams by the client seems to have a strong intensifying effect on drive-related impulses, in contrast to conceptual-verbal representation, because they are spontaneous imagoic presentations that have particularly intimate connections with a salient drive or drive-complex (e.g., an Oedipus complex).

6. Laboratory Investigations of Drive Intensification

An investigation by Reyher and Smeltzer (1968) supports our clinical observations of drive intensification via free imagery. We had our subjects respond with either verbal associations or visual depiction, in a counterbalanced design, to blatant sexual and aggressive words and to words denoting family relationships. As expected, visual depiction was accompanied by an increase in the presence of drives, greater defense demand, and less successful defense than was verbal association. Also, the frequency of GSRs to visual imagery was greater than to verbal associations. Thus, anxiety-producing, drive-related affect and impulses achieve more direct expression via imagoic derivatives than via conceptual-verbal representation.

Morishige and Reyher (1975) were able to show that dream images tend to be hotter than those of free imagery (spontaneous visual imagery) with respect to a variety of electrophysiological measures, and that an emergent uncovering condition (revisualization of hot images) increased the blatancy of drive presentation for client-subjects, but not for student-subjects. Undistorted imagoic depiction of the latent content of dreams was achieved for several of the client-subjects as a result of having them revisualize these as well as other hot images identified by the GSR, subjective report, behavioral signs of anxiety, symptoms, and resistance.

An excerpt from the verbatim protocol of one client-subject (Client A) who was asked to visualize a dream illustrates the intensification of repressed impulses and the direct imagoic depiction of the latent content of her dream. In the manifest content, she dreamed that she had awakened and then became frightened because she could neither move nor awaken. Somehow she found herself in the bathroom standing before the sink trying to splash water on her face, but she could not get her cupped hands to her face. She then looked up into the mirror and saw a photographic negative of herself. She awakened in reality feeling very anxious and reluctant to bring the dream into the laboratory.

("Describe the dream again and make a note of any images that happen to come into your mind's eye.") "I was lying in bed. And I couldn't wake up. I tried to wake up and I tried to move my hands except they wouldn't move at all. I am, I was trying to wake up, and I couldn't move anything, and I laid in bed and thought if I could get some water on my face it would wake me up. I'm having different visions. ("Can you describe them?") I have a vision of a male standing at a toilet going to the bathroom. ("Describe the image.") He's just holding onto his penis and just going to the bathroom. I went to the sink to try and get some water and I could feel it on my hands but couldn't. When I put my hands to my face I couldn't feel anything. So I looked up into the mirror and there wasn't anything there and I was just a negative (opposite sex). ("Describe what you see.") I don't actually see it. I just remember so—I remember that there was nothing there but just black and white. Then I see the toilet, but the toilet is not in the right spot. ("Is the man still there?") No. ("What's happening?") I was trying to figure out the man at the toilet. ("What's he wearing?") Plaid shirt, but I don't necessarily know if it's a man. I think it could have been me. ("Do you see the penis now?") I don't know. ("What's happening?") Nothing. (Resistance.) I was just thinking about, I just became aware of what I wasn't—a machine. ("Are there any feelings and sensations connected with that thought?") I just realized that I didn't switch on the light. (Resistance.) ("Do you see yourself or what seems to be yourself at the toilet?") This was when I saw myself looking down into the sink basin . . . and moving my hands to cup the water. All of a sudden I saw the hands moving toward the penis. I saw the figure. ("What's the faucet like in the sink?") It's a turn handle . . . it's, huh, cold and hot on either side. (Testes.) ("Do you see the faucet itself?") Oh, it comes up the center . . . I don't know . . . I feel as though I'd like to sit up and open my eyes or something. (Resistance.) ("Do you see anything?") No. ("Do you know why you'd like to open your eyes?") I'm supposed to take a break or something."

Dramatic instances of uncovering like the above present cogent clinical evidence for psychic determinism—the point-for-point correspondence between every detail in the manifest and latent contents (repressed strivings) of the dream. Note that the image of the faucet was too hot to revisualize.

7. A Conceptual Integration

The objectifying properties of emergent uncovering psychotherapy have made the verification of many clinical observations by psychoanalytic practitioners a matter of mere empirical documentation rather than inference (Reyher, 1977a). Prominent among these are Freud, Sullivan, and Horney, with the constructs of the first two being the most relevant. Their theoretical constructs, however, are wanting in that they are not susceptible to operational definition. This is particularly true for Freud's metapsychogical explanations. In fact, the only empirically based construct that we did not verify happens to be crucial to his metapsychological explanations, namely, gratification drive discharge (wishfulfillment) of nocturnal dreams. Dreams are supposed to be a type of psychic safety valve. Instead of offering some relief, we find that the revisualization of nocturnal dreams intensifies repressed impulses and their dissociated means of gratification, exacerbating existing symptoms and producing new ones.

Both Freud and Sullivan conceptualized anxiety as an instigator of defense against internal danger and the anticipation of external ones, although they differed markedly in their emphases and on the nature of the mediating mechanisms. Freud emphasized the former (instincts) whereas Sullivan emphasized the latter (interpersonal relationships). My own psycholinguistic construct development does not square entirely with theirs because of the distinctive methods embodied in emergent uncovering psychotherapy. The phenomena produced by these methods do seem to clarify some conceptual issues, particularly the nature of psychic pain, its sources, and its consequences. The constructs of dissociation and repression are both useful and appear to represent different mechanisms and serve different functions. If a drive is operationally defined as any disposition that is response-producing, then drives can be classified as either endopsychic or intrapsychic. Intrapsychic drives are generated by our conceptions of ourselves and of others, particularly while we are engaged in real or imaginary interpersonal relationships, whereas endopsychic drives are those that have a biological substrate.

7.1. Intrapsychic Drives

Many affects with response-producing properties are generated by changes in self-esteem, particularly those that involve anticipated narcissistic injury and the aftermath of an actual injury. Since they originate in public and/or interpersonal circumstances, they are highly susceptible to being defined operationally. When we are threatened (anticipation of a narcissistic injury) or when we experience an actual injury, we engage in efforts either to maintain self-esteem (face saving), to minimize an experienced loss (save our skins), or to make attempts to increase it (face-lifting). These actions constitute distinctive classes of security operations and they often, but not always, are accompanied by distinctive affects. Self-esteem maintenance is identified by security operations designed to prevent a decrease in self-esteem by justifying one's self, e.g., excuses, rationalizations, externalizations, etc. Minimizing is identified by security operations that are dysjunctive. They stop an unfavorable course of interpersonal events wherein one is already in anguish and anticipates that any action will worsen an already bad situation, e.g., "Count me out," "No thanks," "You do it," "I don't want to," etc. Self-esteem enhancement is identified by security operations that are designed to impress (produce a positive conception) another person(s) to head off a threat, e.g., bragging, lying, exaggerating, showing off, being a know-it-all, disparagement, doing favors, being a nice guy, etc.

Primarily, we all strive to impress (form a conception) others positively, particularly those who are significant (family, friends, opposite sex, our heros and mentors), and, coordinately, we all strive to avoid making negative impressions. We are vigilant for behavioral cues relating to approval (positive-reflected appraisals) and disapproval (negative-reflected appraisals), and we hope that our positive strivings will be rewarded (accolade) by public recognition, e.g., loyalty, doing a good job, hard work, being a good person, etc. We dread public disapproval (ignominy). Making others laugh, showing interest, agreeing with us, endorsing our opinions, and doing as we say are all standard signs of approval. Accolades (a hero's welcome, Nobel prize, etc.) are only received in response to special merit.

We cannot give ourselves the aforementioned positive and negative appraisals. What we think of ourselves is secondary. For example, those of us who pick our noses in private without misgivings would experience ignominy if this action were publicly observed. The same is true of masturbation and other personal habits. We dread having petty, vengeful, or spiteful behavior identified by others. Our clients invariably acknowledge, with great difficulty, the disparity between self versus other locus of appraisal. Being inner-directed is a positive value in our culture, and clients expect the psychotherapist to endorse this value. Some of us who appear to be inner-directed more than outer-directed in the locus of our values may really be behaving with respect to an absentee reference group constituted by one or more live or dead persons (a hero or religious figure). A clinical example might be helpful. A client arriving late and breathless for an appointment almost always will apologize immediately upon arrival. This is a standardized security operation (abiding by the amenities) that is given automatically without a second thought. However, when treated as an entrée point, useful insights emerge. The exploration of subjective awareness reveals a desire to make amends for having kept the psychotherapist waiting, assuming possibly that he or she dislikes waiting for clients. This calls for making an interpersonal inquiry, "On your way here, did you wonder what I might be thinking?" Such an inquiry usually reveals that the client was acutely aware of the possibility of disapproval and that he or she hoped to forestall it by a breathless apology and/or to placate (security operation) the psychotherapist by a recitation of the reasons causing the delay. Clients, nevertheless, are reluctant to say that altering the psychotherapist's impressions was the primary determinant for an apology. Of course, one does not question an apology, because the same issues will repeatedly come up in various guises for the same or different reasons, all of which prompt an interpersonal inquiry. Most people simply do not like viewing themselves as chameleons and, accordingly, expect to be rejected. In any event, it usually turns out they have been reluctant to admit, or even to think, that their major concern was that the psychotherapist should think of them as being thoughtless, irresponsible, insincere, shallow, etc. Their eventual identification of the true locus of their concerns often reinforces their motivation to become less dissembling in their intimate relationships; rather, the ones that ought to be intimate.

The strivings elucidated by the exploration of subjective awareness are not those that clients like to own up to and to inculcate in others. Jung's *persona* is an apt term to use in this context. We have a public self and an inner self. Most of our waking lives are spent promoting increases (success-mastery-recognition) and avoiding decreases (failure-insufficiency-rejection) in self-esteem, whether this is done in reality or in compensatory fantasy. Those with low self-esteem tend to anticipate negative appraisals from significant others and, therefore, inhibit themselves while those with high self-esteem tend to anticipate positive appraisals and, therefore, are able to actualize themselves.

7.1.1. **Syntonia and Dystonia.*** Each directional movement in self-esteem leaves a trail of kindred affects and emotions in its wake. To simplify communication, the term *syntonia* is used to designate the pleasant component of the affects generated by an upward movement of self-esteem, and the term *dystonia* to designate the unpleasant and painful components of the affects generated by a downward movement of self-esteem. Syntonia is characterized by the use of such words as satisfaction, high spirits, joy, euphoria, happy, ecstasy, etc., and, therefore, does not constitute the main focus of this communication.

Dystonia is generated whenever we feel that a prized and/or per-

---

* The psychoanalytic definition rather than the neurological or psychiatric definitions of the term *dystonia* is used in this chapter. In terms of the former, dystonia designates an abnormal muscular tonicity; in terms of the latter, it designates a disharmony within the psyche.

sonal conception of ourselves has been controverted by our own behavior or that of another person(s). It is a narcissistic injury because the particular conception is an important aspect of our persona. For most of us, some conceptions are more important than others (Rokeach, Reyher, and Wiseman, 1968), e.g., being honest may be more important than being orderly, and being loyal may be more important than being prompt, and being independent may be better than being dependent. Since we are frustrated in our efforts to impress others favorably, anger is generated along with a guilt-tinged pain attached to the realization that we have been insufficient. We have failed others and ourselves. Dystonia is instantaneous. In competitive sports when a player makes an error or mistake, we often witness all its components in graphic form: we see a searing psychic pain as evidenced by grimacing and moaning; anger is directed inward as evidenced by hitting one's self and verbally castigating one's self, or it is directed outward as evidenced by blaming the equipment (wrapping a golf club around a tree); guilt is evidenced by a dysphoric mood and self-attributions of being no good, lousy, etc.; and security operations are elicited as evidenced by the making of excuses, lying, feigning injury, and other suitable face-saving behaviors.

The components of dystonia often are objectified upon the request for eyes-closed free association. There are indicators of anxiety such as eye opening to detect cues in the psychotherapist's behavior relating to approval and disapproval (guilt), and indirect requests for reassurance—a security operation.

Severe dystonia wrecks lives by prompting avoidance of all risk taking. The alternatives to avoidance are suicide, psychosis, or becoming a recluse. The misery of intense dystonia is exquisite, filling one's awareness with negative self-attributions and anxiety cued by the expectation that one will be abandoned by friends and family. This guilt-tinged, painful, self-awareness is complicated by the intense anger of chronic frustration. Anger originating in frustration must be repressed, turned outward, or turned inward, all of which have distinctive and grave consequences. Horney (1950) graphically described the self-contempt of her clients and the face-saving devices (security operations) they use to offset or avoid injury to their exaggerated pride.

Sleep can be a respite. While awake we search for ways to blunt the pain or to anesthetize ourselves. Eating is one way to blunt it, and it also may have the secondary effect of removing us from the risks of the romantic marketplace, once we become fat and undesirable. Compensatory romantic fantasies then blunt the pain of sexual privation and loneliness. Obesity is a haven.

Others may anesthetize dystonia with alcohol while harboring compensatory or heroic fantasies, viz., striking it rich at the gaming table or by a shrewd business deal. Still others use drugs to alter their perceptions in order to experience the syntonia that otherwise is absent from their lives. Yet others support compensatory fantasies with hard work and dedication to a goal. They become grinds or "workaholics" whose guiding, compensatory fantasies can be actualized only by becoming the first or the best in their line. A few even risk their lives by climbing Mount Everest or by going over Niagara Falls in a barrel.

The most extreme suffering is observed when early childhood conceptions of being unloved, hated, abandoned, or killed by parents emerge via visual imagery, e.g., "I see myself standing between my parents. I'm just a baby. They chop off my head, and then they seem to be picking at things in my neck." Visual imagery such as this probably is generated by conceptions developed in what Sullivan aptly calls the *parataxic mode of experience.*

7.2. Dissociation

Dissociation represents the inability to cognize (understanding via conceptual-verbal vehicles) negative conceptions (personifications) of one's self and others because of prohibitively aversive dystonia. Since these require conceptual-verbal vehicles for their comprehension, exclusive use of free imagery would be ineffective. Conceptual-verbal representation will complement, unless it is prohibited, whatever concrete facets of these personifications are being depicted in the mind's eye of the client. Client B is a good example of the interweaving of the two modes of information processing. He would manifest contingency reactions whenever he started to cognize negative conceptions (personification of the bad mother) of his mother, i.e., the cold, unloving mother and the intrusive, sexually provocative mother. To prevent this, he avoided labeling features of herself and her behavior relevant to either of these personifications. Dissociation dissappears following the objectification of repressed drive-related impulses via direct imagoic depiction. When a dissociated personification or conception is removed by complete labeling of its relevant features, more differentiated veridical perception of the person in question ensues.

Both dissociation and repression are similar because they are motivated by the guilt-tinged psychic pain of dystonia which is a concomitant of a lowering of self-esteem. But this is as far as the similarity extends, because they seem to be subserved by different mechanisms. Dissociation involves the interruption of a microgenesis (Werner and Kaplan, 1953) of cognition which is indexed in variable ways: *para-*

praxes described by Freud; forgetting what one was about to say, not knowing why we said what we did; getting confused in the middle of a sentence; sighing or crying without knowing why; feeling depressed without apparent reason; identifying with criminals, which we do not like to admit to ourselves and about which we feel chagrined; rooting consistently for the underdog or the champion, and so forth.

The most impressive index of an interruption in the microgenesis of cognition is referred to as *precognitive auras* (Reyher, 1977a). In the course of reporting hot imagery, some clients verbalize not wanting to proceed even though they do not know what a particular hot image means. It is as if they have some inkling as to its aversive nature without being able to verbalize it. This is considered to be an indicator of an interruption in the microgenesis of cognition rather than verification of a preconscious system in Freudian psychoanalysis. It always turns out that some developing conception would controvert a conception that is essential to maintaining self-esteem (Rokeach *et al.*, 1968), e.g., "I am not a man (or a woman)"; "I'm a pervert"; "My mother doesn't love me"; "I am a wanton evil person." Psychopathological instances of the acting out of these dissociated self-conceptions are the behaviors of fugue states, drunken episodes, and alternate personalities (multiple personality). The self-protective amnesia in these cases are extreme examples of an interruption in the normal process of concept formation (cognition). The interruption of the microgenesis of cognition probably takes place at a point where concepts are integrated with percepts, and it is cued by the incipient dystonia generated by intensified repressed impulses.

Repression differs from dissociated conceptions insofar as it involves the inhibition of impulses associated with the dystonia-producing aims (concepts) and objects (percepts) of drives. Thus, we see that the repression of impulses is coordinate with the dissociation of concepts and probably involves a neurophysiological negative feedback mechanism that reduces the intensity of the impulses (Reyher, 1963; Reyher and Basch, 1970; Sommerschield and Reyher, 1973). Our data do not warrant the invocation of psychoanalytical metapsychological explanation.

It appears that repression is secondary to dissociation; that is, impulses related to objectionable aims must be inhibited in order to maintain dissociation. Fortunately, not all the possible aims and objects of a drive are unacceptable (controvert an important self-conception); otherwise, we could never resolve by displacement an Oedipus complex which, for most of us, is inevitable.

7.2.1. Anxiety and Induction of Dystonia. Dissociation does not necessarily involve the repression of impulses. This is particularly true for dystonia-inducing public behavior (a performance or an examination). The dystonia is not initiated by a drive-related impulse. Take as an illustration an individual learning to type. When the same error is made repeatedly, there is the familiar, guilt-tinged anguish that includes self-directed anger, but not anxiety. The anxiety, however, would appear when the student anticipated a test while error prone. It is an index of the anticipation of publically recognized (interpersonal) failure and hurt pride (a controverted prized self-conception) which is accompanied by incipient, guilt-tinged pain (feelings of inadequacy) and security operations that brake a lowering of self-esteem and allow the anger to be turned outward, e.g., criticizing the course and/or the instructor. The anxiety is the response of fear to a known potential threat. If the student indeed failed the examination, then the dystonia is subject to dissociation and the generation of security operations (e.g., rationalizations, excuses, sour grapes, etc.). If we should reminisce, our reminiscence is tinged with dystonia. (We favor the recall of pleasant experiences.) Once again, the anxiety is absent, and for the same reasons. However, should our course record be reviewed by some significant person, then the anxiety is reexperienced. Anxiety is a function of the anticipation of interpersonal threat.

For some individuals, particularly macho males, a symptom or indicator of anxiety can possess drive properties and motivate security operations. A visible display of anxiety, such as a stammer, increases the likelihood that it will recur. We also observe that the dystonia (embarrassment) generates security operations (e.g., "I'm thinking faster than I can talk," an excuse) and covert behaviors (e.g., avoiding certain words). The eruption of visible anxiety controverts, particularly in an observer, self-conceptions essential to the maintenance of self-esteem. These self-conceptions are embodied in their persona, e.g., "I'm tough," "I'm brave," "I'm fearless," "I'm the greatest," "I'm cool," "I've got it all together." In this context, it appears that anxiety is merely an index of threat, and it is the threat that has drive properties.

Clients reveal that anxiety may not be the prime motivator of the psyche when it comes to psychopathology and defense, including security operations. Rather, it appears that the guilt-tinged pain of dystonia serves a signal function. The principal evidence is that our clients verbalize pain that is generally experienced in the context of feeling guilty, embarrassed (a form of guilt), repugnant, and self-loathing. Anxiety is often absent during the emergence of these affects, although it was present earlier in the process of uncovering. Thus, it seems to be related to the anticipation of a narcissistic injury by the psychotherapist. This observation verifies the psychoanalytic conception of anxiety as having signal functions, but it is inconsistent with the conception that the signal is to activate mechanisms to avoid even greater anxiety.

Anxiety does not even serve as a signal when it merely indexes fear associated with an imminent narcissistic injury. Evidence in favor of this interpretation is that some individuals verbalize the experience of anxiety (obsessive-compulsives) and others (hysterics) do not. This variability across individuals seems to be a function of the degree to which dystonia is generated by the process of controverting a particular conception. Conceptions vary in importance (Rokeach et al., 1968) to self-esteem with the most important ones having been acquired early in life, particularly before cognitive maturity (Sullivan's parataxic mode of experience). These early autonomous conceptions representing parental values and love (Freud's superego) are inevitably controverted by the aims and objects of pregenital and Oedipal strivings. The severity of the dystonia generated is indexed by the anxiety experienced. That an audience is not a necessary condition for the activation of these early conceptions is evidenced by anxiety-dreams, anxiety attacks while alone, irrational guilt, and depression. It is their autonomous function independent of interpersonal activation that inclines us to personify their evaluative feedback as "the voice of conscience," superego, or incorporated objects.

7.3. Security Operations and Defenses against Impulses

Security operations differ from the standard psychoanalytic mechanisms of defense against repressed impulses because they exist only in real and imagined interpersonal meetings. Any kind of behavior can participate in a security operation, e.g., repetitive head-nodding, automatic laughter, gestures (shrugging shoulders), making faces, pasted on smile, flashlight smile. These behaviors only have meaning because of the individual's interpersonal strivings to form positive conceptions in others and to receive sought after confirming positive appraisals.

More than likely the user of a security operation is unaware of its instigation and import; he may be aware only of its ostensible referent, i.e., a comment on the weather, passing along gossip, the punch line of a joke. Considerations of propriety may even be forsaken, such as joking at a funeral; interpersonal sensitivity may be blunted by bragging; acquaintances may be alienated by officiousness; employers may be dissatisfied by obsequiousness or negativism; romance may be ruined by seductiveness or being on the make, and so forth.

A security operation is a paradox. Although its intent is to offset rejection or disapproval and/or produce approval, the threatened individual expects eventual disapproval—it is this conviction that prevents the making of eye contact. The certainty of rejection merely is attenuated by success in eliciting signs of approval. Reassurance is sought but cannot be realized. Since security operations do not provide respite from the anxiety that elicits them, they are recurrent even when they are counterproductive. We are helpless in the immediacy of dystonia generated by interpersonal situations, some more than others. The individual so afflicted listens closely to the encountered person's utterances for thinly veiled insults and scrutinizes that person's expressive behavior for smirks, mocking smiles, an arched eyebrow, an edged voice, etc. This scrutinizing of others renders the user liable to misinterpretation of cues (imagined slights) and confirmation of the anticipation of rejection. Perceived signs of approval are discounted even though this is the purpose of the security operation. Thus, the underlying feelings of dystonia continually cue fresh security operations.

Even the lighting up of a cigarette symbolizes a disparate way, learned in childhood, of easing dystonia. It activates any one or more of the self-conceptions, "I'm grown up," "I'm tough," "I'm sophisticated," and functions as a security operation in threatening adult interpersonal relationships, particularly at cocktail parties or when walking into a strange bar. Like most security operations, its ameliorating effect is trifling and transient but relentlessly repetitive, because the conditions that produce it remain unchanged. Finally, smoking is sustained by an initially offensive taste having been converted into a pleasant one. To be sure, underlying pregenital strivings and fixations predispose the generation of particular security operations as well as particular psychoanalytic defenses, but matters of self-esteem in the crunch of the interpersonal here and now preempts all other drives, even that of survival, e.g., accepting a death defying dare or a duel.   Security operations escape our notice because their true purpose is inconsistent with the ways in which we want to conceptualize ourselves and, even more important, the impressions that we hope others will form of us. Self-other conceptions may include all or one of the following as well as others: "I'm sincere," "I'm authentic," "I'm open," "I'm self-consistent," "I'm integrated," "I'm rational," "I'm fair," "I'm honest," etc.

We see attenuated expressions of dystonia in *les faux pas* of everyday life, such as forgetting a name of a friend or introducing someone by the wrong name, knocking over a glass of wine at a dinner party, and forgetting protocol or a point of etiquette at an important social event. Students feel it when they cannot answer a question put to them in class by the teacher or when they fail an examination. Most of us know the pain of being proven wrong, insulted, rebuffed, or rebuked, and the ensuing frantic search for an effective face-saving security operation. These might include a physical assault, murder, or paranoid delusions.

Security operations are not all bad. Without the standard clichés about the weather and the automatic "How are you?," we would feel isolated from one another, and our feelings of inadequacy would intensify. Anyone who doubts the motivating force of forming favorable impressions and avoiding unfavorable ones should attempt going to work or school dressed out of fashion and without color coordination. Similarly, anyone who doubts the necessity of amenities and manners (complementary security operations) should attempt to pass by acquaintances and work associates without initiating or acknowledging greetings. Most of us cannot bring ourselves to do this because of the intensity of the incipient dystonia.

The resistance of security operations to jettisoning or change is a measure of the intensity of feelings of inadequacy and self-derogation. All attempts at reassurance and exhortation fail because these feelings are utterly irrational and are rooted in childhood. In our clinical experience with emergent uncovering pschotherapy, they are based upon negative self-appraisals by both ourselves and others before logic and causality are available (Sullivan's parataxic mode) to controvert these. Logical and rational appeals as in rational-emotive psychotherapy are of little or no value. Failure to respond may even exacerbate feelings of inadequacy and guilt. Some of our clients respond favorably because they experience the goodwill and sincerity of the psychotherapist when they self-disclose. Even this is insufficient in many cases when negative self-appraisals are generated outside of awareness (interruption of microgenesis) by repressed pregenital, Oedipal, and murderous strivings. These promote the conscious experience of being unworthy, unlovable, or even despicable. Symptomatic approaches such as behavior modification cannot succeed in these cases.

7.4. Endopsychic Drives

Our clinical experience with emergent uncovering psychotherapy shows that hunger, thirst, and eliminative endopsychic drives do not find expression through spontaneous visual imagery. It is not uncommon for endopsychic drives, with the exception of sex, to intensify during a session without the client's imagery giving any hint whatsoever of their activation. This does not mean that clients cannot volitionally form images depicting gratification of these drives, if they choose. The conspicuous absence of endopsychic drives probably is not a function of their relevance to their lives or problems because to them most of their imagery is irrelevant anyway. Our student-subjects (Morishige and Reyher, 1975) do not describe imagoic depiction of endopsychic drive gratification either. Perhaps it is the imperious insistence of these drives that motivates adaptive responses (motility) to bring relief. Substitutive attempts at gratification (e.g., eating, urination) via visual imagery simply are unfulfilling, although under prolonged deprivation of gratification an individual may conjure up relevant imagery volitionally in a futile effort to obtain relief.

The sex drive is unique in having a neurohumoral substrate complete with diffuse cortical projections. Perhaps this accounts for its ubiquitous presence in dreams and in free imagery in the guise of imagoic derivatives. The eruption of hysterical symptoms during emergent uncovering psychotherapy suggests that the dissociated aims (conceptions) and objects of the sex drive can also easily find derivative presentation in systems (hysterical symptoms) other than visual imagery (Burns and Reyher, 1976) in the same way that hypnotic suggestions influence systems outside of voluntary control (Reyher, 1977b). Both hypnosis and hysterical symptoms have been related to mediation by the right cerebral hemisphere. Stern (1977) reported that hysterical symptoms favor the left side of the body by a ratio of five to two. This, of course, implicates the analogic-synthetic mode of information processing that is intrinsic to the nervous system. Since pregenital and Oedipal strivings must be frustrated, their intensification must generate secondary guilt and anger. These secondary drives are salient in dreams, free imagery, hysterical symptoms, sexual dysfunctions, sexual perversions, and schizophrenic thought. Our protocols show that these are blended by the synthesizing function of the analogic-synthetic mode. It is this blending that underlies the constructs of condensation and overdetermination (Reyher, 1977a) which, with the addition of displacement, are the principal components of primary process. Only sex is an endopsychic drive; anger and guilt are intrapsychic drives.

7.5. Free Imagery: The Mechanisms of Image Retrieval

In order to explain the process of image formation during free imagery, it is assumed that drives are integrated with perception by the analogic-synthetic mode, and that the retrieval of percepts (images) from the encoded perceptual history of the individual involves the same processes that formed the percept in the first place. Instead of the reactivation of encoded percepts similar to current visual input, as in perception, percepts are retrieved from the encoded perceptual history of the individual with respect to their similarity with the percepts constituting the aims and objects of repressed drives, not the concepts associated with them. Distinguishing between percept and concept is not new and is recognized by such terms as *pars pro toto* and *transduction* (Rapaport, 1959). Freud (1959) used this presumed separation to explain schizophrenia, and Werner and Kaplan (1953) referred to it as "physiognomic thinking." The separation of percept and concept is self-evident upon the inspection of protocols that show a progression of increasingly blatant imagoic drive derivatives prior to objectification (Reyher, 1968), and when the true aims and objects are suddenly depicted (Morishige and Reyher, 1975). The protocols included herein are good examples of the former. As noted above, even the cohesion of a percept is attenuated, and the images become a series of disconnected fragments, each of which, however, is related (displacement) to percepts embodying the aims and objects of the repressed drives involved. Bizarreness is increased dramatically when disparate fragments are synthesized to form fantastic percepts (condensation). Thus, we see that primary process (displacement and condensation) is not a principle unique to a dynamic unconscious but is, instead, the combined operation of analogic and synthetic functions of the analogic-synthetic mode of information processing that constructs our visual-spatial world. It is the semantic-syntactic mode that gives it meaning. One may assume that dystonia activates a homeostatic mechanism that prevents the semantic-syntactic mode from infusing percepts with their personal and conventional meanings. If percept retrieval is indeed mediated by the same principles that govern perception, then the feature detectors may play a crucial role. Both Rock (1970) and Ganz (1971) suggest that the feature detectors must be suppressed for perception to occur. This implies that the feature detectors interfere with the semantic-syntactic mode from further identifying and selecting percepts for retrieval once they have been "tuned" by the feature detectors. In other words, they need to be suppressed just as soon as they provide a cue function mediated by gradients of similarity. The disinhibition of feature detectors provides a homeostatic function for the diminution of dystonia which is disorganizing and interferes with adaptation because of the separation between percept and concept (the concretization of thought). An encoded percept that has something in common with the percepts constituting a repressed striving is tuned and likely to be retrieved when the striving becomes active and anxiety-producing. One other assumption may be added to this heuristic model to give it greater explanatory power and to account for the day residue of dreams. The operation of a recency effect can be assumed; that is, the more recent the encoding of a perception (memory), the greater the probability of its being tuned and retrieved. Thus, a given encoded percept is more likely to be retrieved if it is recent and in proportion to the number of features it has in common with the percepts embodied by conceptions subject to dissociation.

This heuristic model of percept retrieval accounts for the implausibility and bizarreness of free imagery, dreams, psychotomimetic drugs and schizophrenia. If there is some threshold of dystonia intensification in which the integration of concept with percept is prevented, then any means of reducing dystonia with drugs, alcohol, transcendental meditation ought to "normalize our thinking."

7.5.1. Imagoic Depiction and Self-Conceptions. During free imagery, there is a conspicuous absence of imagoic derivatives of an individual's enhancing self-conceptions, e.g., "I'm smart," "I'm cool," "I'm tough," but there are occasional imagoic derivatives of critical self-conceptions in the guise of caricatures. The more abstract self-conceptions, such as "I'm a loving person," "I'm law-abiding," "I'm untrustworthy," never seem to generate imagoic derivatives. Perhaps abstract conceptions of any kind require exclusively conceptual-verbal representation because they are mediated by subvocal speech (thinking to one's self), but this is doubtful. More likely, these self-conceptions are acquired late in development and, therefore, are relatively peripheral to self-esteem.

7.5.2. Imagoic Depiction and Security Operations. Security operations seldom, if ever, are imagoically depicted during free imagery. The reason for this lies in the immediacy of the interpersonal situation. An anticipated or real narcissistic injury requires direct and immediate remedial action. If a security operation cannot be created on the spot, the client will open his or her eyes to scan the psychotherapist's countenance for signs of approval and disapproval, providing, of course, that feelings of inadequacy are not sufficiently intense to motivate denial and indifference (security operations). Another putative reason for the absence of security operations in visual imagery is the same as that used to account for the absence of abstract self-conceptions. A security operation is mediated by the expressive, semantic-syntactic mode of information processing in real or imagined interpersonal relationships. Imagoic depiction cannot present the semantic relationship between word and referent.

7.6. Uncovering: Pathogenesis and Therapeutics

Uncovering represents the cognizing of dystonia-inducing opprobrious self-conceptions that formerly were subject to dissociation—an interruption in microgenesis—and the experiencing of the drive-related impulses that initiated the microgenesis and that were formerly subject to inhibition (repressed). Chronic neurotic symptoms and anxiety reactions index the interruption in the microgenesis of cognition by pregenital and Oedipal strivings even when there has been reasonably good parenting and the formation of positive self-conceptions. Schizophrenia may develop in the absence of good parenting because there are no positive self-conceptions to controvert; there are only negative self-conceptions and the anticipation of negative appraisals. Unlike the neurotic individual, there is no attempt to maintain one's positive self-conceptions with security operations. Instead, there is a withdrawal from interpersonal interaction and the cessation of communication. Since the expressive, semantic-syntactic mode is no longer engaged, the analogic-synthetic mode fills awareness with its own products (primary-process thinking).

Thus, we see that emergent uncovering techniques activate pathogenic processes but, fortunately, in a relationship with another person who has nothing to gain but doing a good job. If the client is instrumental in satisfying other needs of the psychotherapist, then there is likely to be uncontrolled countertransference which poses a threat to the client because he or she responds to the psychotherapist's expressive behavior (analogic-synthetic presentations). The psychotherapist's affects pose a threat because they are suppressed, which implies that they are dangerous. To obviate this threat and to promote self-disclosure by the client, the psychotherapist must self-disclose also, whenever he becomes aware of affects (love, lust, anger, guilt, admiration, etc.). This also underscores the relationship between the participants as one of collaborators. Successful uncovering appears to be contingent upon a continuing disconfirmation of the client's expectations that the psychotherapist is making implicit negative appraisals. In the face of "damning" self-disclosures and the scrutinizing of moment-to-moment behavior, the psychotherapist remains accepting and inquiring. This attitude controverts the client's projected self-appraisals and permits the formation of positive ones. This Rogerian demeanor is blended with Freud's understanding of a dynamic unconscious and Sullivan's participant observation.

Objectification and uncovering will not take place unless the individual is experiencing enough dystonia to motivate a commitment to self-disclosure and is given the opportunity to experience both semantic-syntactic and analogic-synthetic modes of processing drive-related impulses and the concepts associated with their aims. Consistent with these clinical observations, Burns and Reyher (1976) failed to uncover a hypnotically implanted paramnesia (a made-up story) that was heavily laden with Oedipal strivings, despite strongly worded posthypnotic suggestions to recall it. Morishige and Reyher (1975) have shown that student subjects do not show progressively more blatant depiction of repressed impulses during the visual-imagery procedures of emergent uncovering psychotherapy. Nevertheless, hot images (those that elicit contingency reactions) were much in evidence. In addition to not having had an opportunity to work through self-protective security operations, the failure of the posthypnotic suggestions and the emergent uncovering is undoubtedly due, in part, to a lack of commitment to self-disclosure which only psychotherapy clients in distress are able to make.

The phenomena generated by our clinical and laboratory investigations do not seem to be a function of demand characteristics. Schofield and Platoni (1976) could not induce their laboratory subjects to produce bizarre imagery despite explicit instructions to "see" crazy images. Neither does it appear to be a matter of suggestibility. A recent investigation (Reyher, Wilson, and Hughes, 1978) showed that a condition of verbalized free imagery was associated with significantly lower suggestibility than a nonverbalized condition and a formal induction of hypnosis. This expected outcome was attributed to the engagement of the expressive, semantic-syntactic mode during which verbalized free imagery, a left-cerebral hemispheric function, putatively is antithetical to suggestibility, a right-cerebral hemispheric function (Gur and Gur, 1974; Reyher, 1977b).

8. Conclusions and Wider Implications

8.1. Domains of Phenomena

It might seem incongruous to some investigators that many of the empirical and operational constructs of both Freud and Sullivan proved to be well founded. There is nothing strange about this because the data are not homogenous; they represent different domains of phenomena. This reflects a general principle that is self-evident in the physical sciences but which is easily overlooked in the behavioral sciences. The circumstances of observation (cloud chamber versus naked eye) determine the phenomena observed and the phenomena observed require different constructs (quantum theory versus Newton's theory). In terms of emergent uncovering psychotherapy, the phenomena generated by the interpersonal techniques are categorically different from the phenomena generated by the imagoic techniques. The two domains of phenomena are generated by two different modes of information processing and require different theoretical constructs. This means that Sullivanian and Freudian theoretical constructs are complementary rather than antithetical. One of the main reasons for the continuing controversy is that the proponents of each theoretical orientation uncritically generalize well beyond their respective data bases. That is, phenomena associated with the expressive, semantic-syntactic mode of information processing cannot be explained by constructs developed from phenomena generated by the analogic-synthetic mode, and vice versa. The two domains of phenomena are incommensurate. For example, nocturnal dreams cannot be explained by the construct of security operation and, conversely, the construct of security operation cannot be explained by the dream work. Theory and psychotherapy alike must include both Freudian and Sullivanian constructs and perhaps others, if procedures are developed to objectify phenomena relevant to them.

8.2. Can Spontaneous Visual Imagery Be Symbolic?

On rare occasions a client might describe imagery reminiscent of Jungian symbolism, but this possibility is indeterminate because of the lack of criteria or means of objectification. In any case, archetypes, a collective unconscious, and a residue from a primordial past are not evident under the conditions of free imagery in the laboratory or under the conditions of emergent uncovering in the consulting room. Neither is there conventional symbolic reference such as a crucifix for Christianity, a hammer and sickle for Communism, or a swastika for Nazi Germany; nor are there ad hoc symbols such as a policeman and policewoman for law and order or a covered wagon for frontier America; nor natural symbols such as the sun for generativity and the bird for flight. The protocols uniformly verify Werner and Kaplan's (1953) assertion that a visual image or a dream image is not a symbol. At best, it is a *protosymbol*. A protosymbol always bears a resemblance to its referent (e.g., cow and mother) even if the image were chosen intentionally to designate a referent which, of course, is not the case in free imagery. To the imager, images mean only themselves in their factuality. Thus, a penis has never symbolized male power and freedom. In fact, a penis almost always is indirectly presented as a hot image (phallic symbol), and when the male genitalia are directly presented, it is always a feature of repugnant, repressed, drive-related impulses and dissociated concepts. The penis only becomes a symbol in conceptual-verbal discourse. By definition, a symbol requires an intentional act of denotative reference and can bear no resemblance to its referent. Women who identify themselves as feminists and who demean Freud for his views on penis envy experience exquisite dystonia when their publicly announced and committed views (self-conceptions that they want to form in others) are controverted by their own spontaneous visual imagery. These findings should not be interpreted to mean that all females who endorse feminism and denounce Freud have dissociated conceptions of possessing a penis of their own. The preceding assertions and arguments apply equally to homosexual males who have dissociated conceptions of possessing female genitalia.

8.2.1. **Imagoic and Conceptual-Verbal Representation of the Aims and Objects of Drive-Related Impulses.** According to the organismic theory of language acquisition (Werner and Kaplan, 1953), the undifferentiated aims and objects of drives (strivings) of the infant are embedded in a perceptual-motor-affective substrate. With increasing perceptual-cognitive development, the strivings become more differentiated in types of satisfiers (kinds of food), modes of satisfaction other than sucking make their appearance, and, finally, the child is able to verbalize those aims and objects of strivings that are socially approved. Semantic-syntactic representation (symbolization) has superceded but has not replaced analogic-synthetic presentation in behavior that includes other, perhaps all, biological systems as well as visual imagery (Reyher, 1977b). The infantile aims and objects of drives, including pregenital sex, become inconsistent with the child's growing self-conceptions, but they are not erased. Socially condoned adult aims and objects only characterize our waking lives, not our nocturnal dreams and free imagery.

8.3. Creativity

The novel and transformed percepts produced by displacement (analogic function) and condensation (synthetic function) have implications for creative problem solving, e.g., Kekule's discovery of the molecular structure of benzine (Gordon, 1961) which was suggested during a dreamlike vision of dancing molecules that formed a snake which seized its tail and whirled around. Although the snake, most likely, was a derivative of a repressed drive-related derivative, Kekule recognized its implications with respect to a problem at hand and roused himself from his reverie. As others (Sheehan, 1972) have observed, a period of fruitless effort or confusion may be followed by a flood of images.

Two investigations in our laboratory conform to the heuristic model, although they were conceptualized in terms of standard psychoanalytic constructs. An investigation by Gur and Reyher (1976) required hypnotized subjects to visualize the tasks of the Torrance test of creativity and to report relevant responses mediated by spontaneous visual imagery. They found that visual imagery plus hypnosis, but not visual imagery without hypnosis, enhanced scores on the figural tasks. There was also the expected increase in drive representation. My interpretation of these findings is that drives activated by free imagery found ready-made derivatives in the encoded elements of the tasks which were readily retrieved because of their recency. In another investigation, Davé (1976) solicited individuals who were at an impasse on some problem. Following the visualization of the elements in their problem, these elements were used as the instigators for three consecutive hypnotically induced dreams. Almost all the subjects in this group resolved their impasse whereas almost all the subjects in a rational-cognitive group did not. None of the subjects in a control group had any success whatsoever. When these subjects were reassigned to both treatment groups, only the dream treatment was successful. As expected, there was an increase in drive activation, and some of the dreams were extremely bizarre and fraught with conflict. The dream protocols were more like those of clients in psychotherapy than they were of student subjects (Morishige and Reyher, 1975; Wiseman and Reyher, 1975). An inspection of some of these protocols strongly supports the psychoanalytic point of view (Freud, 1959; Rapaport, 1967) and the heuristic psycholinguistic model; namely, percepts are retrieved because of features that resemble those of percepts embodied in the aims and objects of repressed, drive-related impulses and their dissociated concepts.

8.4. Implications for Freudian and Sullivanian Theory

Unfortunately, Sullivan did not follow up his empirically based clinical observations with a corresponding zeal for systematic construct development. Like Freud's terms of *Ego* and *libido,* Sullivan's constructs of *self-system* and *dynamism* are not susceptible to operational definition and empirical demonstration. Although Sullivan lacked Freud's systematic zeal, this might prove to be a blessing in disguise since we have the benefit of his astute, clinical observations without the burden of proving and disproving a vast assortment of theoretical constructs.

The conceptual coupling of the four functions represented by the analogic-synthetic and semantic-syntactic modes of information processing serve as a parsimonious alternative to psychoanalytic metapsychology which, according to Freud, could be jettisoned without affecting the clinical foundation of psychoanalysis. The constructs of cathexis, countercathexis, libido, Id, Ego, and Superego are not needed. As noted earlier, the central tenet of drive gratification discharge (wish fulfillment) of visual imagery and nocturnal dreams are inconsistent with increasing disturbance created by the revisualization of hot images and dreams alike (Reyher, 1977a). Whatever the investigator's theoretical predilections, the objectifying procedures of emergent uncovering psychotherapy identifies fundamental processes that are surprisingly susceptible to operational definition, manipulation, and control.

References

Burns, B., and Reyher, J. Activating posthypnotic conflict: Emergent uncovering psychotherapy, repression, and psychopathology. *Journal of Personality Assessment*, 1976, *40*, 492–501.

Davé, R. P. The effects of hypnotically induced dreams on creative problem solving. Unpublished master's thesis. Michigan State University, 1976.

Freud, S. The unconscious. In *Collected papers* (translated under supervision of J. Rivière) (Vol. 4). New York: Basic Books, 1959.

Ganz, L. Sensory deprivation and visual discrimination. In H. L. Teuber, (Ed.), *Handbook of sensory psychology* (Vol. 8). New York: Springer-Verlag, 1971.

Gordon, W. J. *Synectics: The development of creative capacity*, New York: Harper & Row, 1961.

Gur, R. L., and Gur, R. E. Handedness, sex, and eyedness as moderating variables in the relation between hypnotic susceptibility and functional brain asymmetry. *Journal of Abnormal Psychology*, 1974, *83*, 635–643.

Gur, R. E., and Reyher, J. Relationship between style of hypnotic induction and direction of lateral eye movements. *Journal of Abnormal Psychology*, 1973, *82*, 499–505.

Gur, R., and Reyher, J. The enhancement of creativity via free imagery and hypnosis. *American Journal of Clinical Hypnosis*, 1976, *18*, 237–249.

Horney, K. *The collected works of Karen Horney*. New York: W. W. Norton, 1950.

LeBaron, S. Visual imagery and posthypnotic conflict in relation to psychopathology. Unpublished master's thesis. Michigan State University, 1976.

Morishige, H. H. A psychophysiological investigation of anxiety and repression during free imagery recall, dream recall, and emergent uncovering. Unpublished doctoral dissertation. Michigan State University, 1971.

Morishige, H., and Reyher, J. Alpha rhythm during three conditions of visual imagery and emergent uncovering psychotherapy: The critical role of anxiety. *Journal of Abnormal Psychology*, 1975, *84*, 531–538.

Rapaport, D. *Organization and pathology of thought*. New York: Columbia University Press, 1959.

Reyher, J. *Hypnosis*. Dubuque, Iowa: William C. Brown, 1968.

Reyher, J. Spontaneous visual imagery: Implications for psychoanalysis, psychopathology and psychotherapy. *Journal of Mental Imagery*, 1977a, *2*, 253–274.

Reyher, J. Clinical and experimental hypnosis: Implications for theory and methodology. In W. E. Edmonston (Ed.), *Conceptual and investigative approaches to hypnosis and hypnotic phenomena*. Annals of the New York Academy of Sciences. New York: New York Academy of Sciences, 1977b.

Reyher, J., and Basch, J. A. Degree of repression and frequency of psychosomatic symptoms. *Perceptual and Motor Skills*, 1970, *30*, 559-562.

Reyher, J., and Smeltzer, W. The uncovering properties of visual imagery and verbal association: A comparative study. *Journal of Abnormal Psychology*, 1968, *73*, 218-222.

Reyher, J., Wilson, J. G., and Hughes, R. Suggestibility and type of interpersonal relationship: Special implications for the patient-practitioner relationship. *Journal of Research in Personality*, 1978, in press.

Rock, I. Perception from the standpoint of psychology. In *Perception and its disorders*, Research Publication A.R.N.M.D. (Vol. 47), 1970, pp. 1-11.

Rokeach, M., Reyher, J., and Wiseman, R. An experimental analysis of the organization of belief systems. In M. Rokeach (Ed.), *Beliefs, attitudes, and values*. San Francisco: Jossey-Bass, 1968.

Schofield, L. J., and Platoni, K. Manipulation of visual imagery under various hypnosis conditions. *American Journal of Clinical Hypnosis*, 1976, *18*, 191-199.

Sheehan, P. W. A functional analysis of the role of visual imagery in unexpected recall. In Sheehan (Ed.), *The function and nature of imagery*, New York: Academic Press, 1972.

Silverman, L. H. Psychoanalytic theory, "The reports of my death are greatly exaggerated." *American Psychologist*, 1976, *31*, 621-637.

Sommerschield, H., and Reyher, J. Posthypnotic conflict, repression, and psychopathology. *Journal of Abnormal Psychology*, 1973, *82*, 278-290.

Stern, D. B. The uncovering properties of visual imagery, verbal association with eyes closed and verbal association with eyes open: A comparative study. Unpublished master's thesis. Michigan State University, 1974.

Stern, D. B. Signs of anxiety during three verbal association conditions. Unpublished doctoral dissertation. Michigan State University, 1975.

Stern, D. B. Handedness and lateral distribution of conversion reactions. *Journal of Nervous and Mental Diseases*, 1977, *164*, 122-128.

Sullivan, H. S. *The interpersonal theory of psychiatry*. New York: W. W. Norton, 1953.

Wallen, R. W. *Clinical psychology: The study of persons*. New York: McGraw-Hill, 1956.

Werner, H., and Kaplan, B. *Symbol formation: An organismic-developmental approach to language and the expression of thought*. New York: John Wiley & Sons, 1953.

Wiseman, R. J. The Rorschach as a stimulus for hypnotic dreams: A study of unconscious processes. Unpublished doctoral dissertation. Michigan State University, 1962.

Wiseman, R. J., and Reyher, J. Hypnotically induced dreams using inkblots as stimuli: A test of Freud's theory of dreams. *Journal of Personality and Social Psychology*, 1975, *27*, 329-336.

4

Clinical Use of Categories of Therapeutic Imagery

Joseph E. Shorr

1. Introduction: The Function of Imagery

Psycho-imagination therapy is a phenomenological and dialogical process with major emphasis on subjective meaning through the modality of waking imagery.

The phenomenological aspects are based on the proposition that the individual needs to become aware of how he defines himself in relation to others and how he feels others define him. Such as:

How I see myself   How I see you seeing me
How I see you   How you see me seeing you

The phenomenological "in-viewing" is in the context of the self-other theories of Harry Stack Sullivan (1953) and R. D. Laing (1962). In brief, the developmental personality factors are related to confirmation and disconfirmation from others. That is, each child as he develops, must fulfill two basic needs in relation to the significant others in his life. The first is the need to make a difference to the other. The second is the need to seek confirmation of acknowledgement from the other. These occur contemporaneously. When these needs are not fulfilled, the child develops false positions.

If a person is not confirmed for his real self, then he develops strategies to secure confirmation for a false self. The security operations

---

Joseph E. Shorr • Institute for Psycho-Imagination Therapy, Los Angeles, California 90048.

he involves himself in serve to maintain his identity even in the absence of true acknowledgment.

Major emphasis in the therapeutic interaction itself has to do with separating one's own view of oneself from the attributed self as defined by the significant others in one's childhood. In short, the "true" identity is helped to emerge and the "alien" identity hopefully is eliminated.

This "in-viewing" of interpersonal and intrapersonal interactions and the individual's strategies within the self and other relationships are best seen through the systematic use of waking imagery. A person's imagery can show how he organizes his world, his style, and can reveal the marked individual differences to which we, as therapists, should be attuned.

Imagery provides a primary avenue to the self and others through which thoughts, wishes, expectations, and feelings can be most effectively reactivated and re-experienced. Essentially, the employment of visual imagery predominates. Recently, strong evidence has been advanced that demonstrates that the phenomenological report shows vision predominating at the level of conscious mechanisms (Posner, Nissen, and Klein, 1976).

Imagery, unlike other modes of communication, usually has not been punished in the individual's past and is therefore less susceptible to personal censorship in the present. Because of this, imagery provides a powerful projective technique resulting in a most rapid, highly accurate profile of the individual's personality and conflicts.

The method involves asking the patient to relax and close his eyes and to trust his images. The therapist then suggests the appropriate imaginary situation to elicit the desired material.

I will attempt to show in this chapter the systematic categorization of imageries that can be woven in the fabric of the therapeutic interaction.

Fromm (1955) stated that more active methods than conventional free association are needed to stimulate the patient for greater affect:

> There are other active methods to stimulate free association. Let us assume you have analyzed the patient's relationship to his father, but want more unconscious material than he has offered in his associations; you tell the patient: "Now, concentrate on the picture of your father, and tell me what is the first thing that comes to your mind." I might draw your attention to the fact that there is a certain difference between asking the patient, "What comes to your mind about your father?" and the second way of telling him: "Now, concentrate, focus on your father." Or, "Visualize your father now, and tell me what is on your mind." There seems to be only a slight difference in wording. However, there is a very great difference in the effect. Another way of stimulating free association lies in giving the patient the picture of a certain situation, then asking what comes to his mind. For instance, you

tell the patient: "Assume tomorrow morning your telephone rings and the person calling tells you I have died. What comes to mind?" Well, you will find that there are very interesting free associations which come up.

Imagination is viewed as the central kernel of consciousness and an important means of access to the uniqueness of the individual's world. The active introduction and conscious use of imaginary situations is used as a stimulating investigative tool, a way open to action possibilities. It allows the patient to explore more safely and openly, to differentiate, to experiment with, and to integrate fantasy and reality, all within the context of a cooperative therapeutic alliance and encounter.

The combination of imaginary situations and their possible sequence is a consequence of the direction the patient's responses lead. What is he opening for examination? What is he willing to face? Where is he going? What is he ready for? What does he appear to deny?

It is not wise to push the patient to image if none are forthcoming after a long interval: one may want to go either to other imaginary situations or perhaps just to current concerns. The patient must be brought to believe that material is always on hand for awareness and meaning regardless of whether or not he is involved in imagery.

2. The Technique of Psycho-Imagination Therapy

Psycho-imagination therapy uses four techniques, namely: (1) finish-the-sentence; (2) most and least question; (3) the self and other question; and (4) the imaginary situation (IS). However, it is the quality of ubiquitous waking imagery elicited through the imaginary situation that is the essence of the phenomenological method.

The theoretical purpose of using imaginary situations is based not only on seeing how the patient views his world, but also being able, in time, to "open up" the "closed system of internal reality." Fairbairn (cited in Guntrip, 1964) describes this internal world as a "static internal situation" that is precluded from change by its very nature so long as it remains self-contained. It is my contention that the better able the patient and the therapist are to see this "tight little inner world," the easier it will be to deal with the whole of the patient and his world.

When the patient is asked to imagine himself in certain structured situations, responses may be elicited that accurately bring into the "here and now" states of feeling that have their roots in the past. By stressing the situation with patients and encouraging them in their choice of action within the situation, they are ultimately helped to greater choice of action in their external reality.

Thus, although I had some interesting results from guiding a person in going into a house and telling me what he or she saw therein, far more was revealed when either I suggested introducing a significant "other" into the situation, or the patients did this for themselves. I could then urge the patient not only to tell me how he felt in the various parts of the house, but how he felt in relating to the other person in the situation.

Sometimes it is so urgent to develop a high degree of specificity that the imaginary situation will relate so specifically to one particular patient that it would never again be used with anyone else.

As the patient becomes accustomed to this kind of therapy it is less and less necessary to make interpretations for him. With specific cross-checking, including the most-or-least method, the finish-the-sentence technique, and the self-and-other technique, it would be possible to help focus the patient to greater awareness, where he would be forced to face the truth for himself.

Certain types of image categories were delineated from the imagery productions of hundreds of patients, imagery workshop participants, and university students in classes in the use of imagery. These specific imagery categories are separated for instructional purposes so that the trained therapist using imagery can have a systematic understanding of what certain kinds of imageries purport to do and what general expectancies of reactions appear to occur most consistently. The broad array of imagery instructions are intended to be a comprehensive and systematic guide for clinical use. I also encourage the therapist and the patient to use their own imagination in therapy to come up with imagery scenes that will lead to increased awareness.

Psycho-imagination therapy attempts to put the individual, through his own imagery, into a particular situation that would evoke a set of interactions that would be useful not only in revealing major problems in the areas of significance in the patient's life, but that would also permit him to relive experiences. Singer (1974) wrote, "Shorr uses an almost infinite variety of images geared very much to the specific characteristics of the patient and the specific developments in therapy."

The dialogical processes that result from the patient's imagery productions in interaction with the therapist to gain greater awareness and to focus for change are minimally included, since to include complete dialogue would be of a magnitude beyond the scope of this chapter.*

---

* For verbatim therapist-patient interaction printed tapes, the reader would do well to read the author's *Psycho-Imagination Therapy* (1972) and *Psychotherapy through Imagery* (1974).

Another emphasis in psycho-imagination therapy is subjective meaning. Escalona suggests that it is mental imagery that may offer a unique opportunity to study the integration of perception, motivation, subjective meaning, and realistic abstract thought (1973). In the course of describing his image, the imager begins to relate it to something of meaning in his personal life. Events, attitudes, feelings, motivations are attached to the image and can be used to explore further its interpersonal implications.

It is possible to achieve images that bypass the censorship of the individual in any type of imagery, daydream, or dream. What I am trying to show is that by asking the person to respond to specific types of imagery, certain kinds of reactions seem to emerge in their productions. Obviously, this is not an absolute since a person may reveal his areas of conflict, his style of defenses, and even focus certain images for change in any of the types of imageries I am categorizing. Yet, certain kinds of things are better revealed by offering one kind of imagery systematically than by offering another kind. For example, in self-image imagery I ask the person to imagine (IS): "There are two of you. One of you is looking through a keyhole at the other you." From the response of the person it is possible to get at not only self-image but areas of conflict, styles of defenses, and unconscious attitudes. Yet, I introduce self-image imagery as a separate category because it invariably adds a dimension of awareness that may be overlooked if it is not included, thus adding comprehensiveness.

The principle of categorization involves rules for grouping entities on the basis of some common or shared attributes. Here are the categories of imagery with common attributes.

3. Spontaneous Imagery

The use of spontaneous imagery is generated in two ways. One method is to ask the patient to allow any images that he "sees" to emerge and then to report them. As the sequence of images flows, certain ones can and often do become affect laden. These images can then serve as a vehicle for further dialogue or possible release of feeling.

A second method is to ask the patient to offer the next five consecutive images that occur to him. He is then asked which of the five gives him the most reaction. From the one selected, a dialogue or release of feeling may occur. On occasion, the therapist can ask the patient to "become" in his imagination the image that he had the strongest reaction to, and to complete certain sentences as if he is the image. It is possible to have the patient finish the same sentences for each of the five images.

Here is the actual example of a male, thirty-three years old, with a history of violent behavior.

The five consecutive images are (1) a lake; (2) a tree; (3) a motorcycle; (4) a woman; and (5) death in a hood similar to the one that danced in the Woody Allen movie.

I then asked him to imagine he was Death, since he immediately responded that it was the fifth image that caused a very strong reaction in him and to finish these sentences as if he were the image.

I feel *lonely*.

Adjective that best describes me: *power*.

I wish I *had something to do besides collecting bodies*.

I must *collect bodies*.

I need *a vacation*.

I secretly *don't like this job, but God gave it to me*.

I will *do my job*.

Never refer to me as *irresponsible*.

From those responses we were able to get into a meaningful dialogue. I will not attempt interpretation but as you can see, a lot can be revealed in a short time.

Another possibility with five consecutive images is to ask the patient if he can find some sense out of the pattern of the five images. It is also fruitful at times to ask for an additional five consecutive images either at the same session or at later sessions.

In addition, spontaneous imagery can be stimulated by suggesting that the patient imagine walking down a road and reporting everything he sees.

The most common form of imagery in man is spontaneous and arises before our "inner eyes" without any apparent stimulus from any specific source. Augusta Jellinek (1949), originator of the term "spontaneous imagery," put it most aptly when she stated, "These images are experiences as they would originate independently as though we were only spectators, and not the source of these productions." Anyone who has asked a person to "just imagine anything that comes to you," with no regard for directions or specific content, will know that surprises never cease for the person imagining, who may express discovery, amusement, or shock, and for the therapist himself, who may be quite astonished by the unexpected nature of the imagery. Most frequently the imagery seems to flow into a continuous stream of scenes and actions.

As a person grows to trust his spontaneous imagery during the therapeutic dialogue and begins to see meaning and direction from it, he can begin to trust his spontaneous imagery when he is outside the therapy situation and can begin to derive his own meanings and directions.

4. Directed Imagery

Directed imagery is the primary method used, except where spontaneous imagery is used or where patients volunteer images that are "now" occurring to them or images they have had in the course of time that they wish to examine for meaning. Certainly intrusive images the patient presents should be examined for meaning and release of feelings, as it would preclude the need for directed imagery.

Directed imagery can capture the flow of imageries that are constantly going on in our minds. There are certain times when the spontaneous flow of images may seem to be without theme or apparent coherency, going in an endless fashion of shots and sequences. The intervention of directed imagery can be used then to capture the flow and bring coherency and integration to the production. My experience validates those of Horowitz and Becker (1971), who say that the specificity of instructions for reporting visual images increases the tendency to form as well as to report images.

The therapist is urged to allow the flow of imagery to go as far as it seems it can go before offering new imaginary situations. Dialogue should be engaged in when the flow appears to stop.

The incidental remarks the patient makes while imaging are not to be ignored. I will offer one of many possibilities. For example, there are persons who are competitively motivated to offer only seemingly creative-sounding imagery. Such persons might say they are offering boring imagery, and they must be reassured to report all and be told, too, that no imagery is insignificant and all have potential meaning.

5. Self-Image Imagery

All of us have a theory of ourselves, about what kind of person we are. Our self-concept of competent or incompetent, attractive or repulsive, honest or dishonest, etc., has enormous effect on our behavior. Personality theorists have suggested concepts such as self-esteem, self-confidence, self-negation, self-doubt, self-respect, etc. There is considerable evidence to support the belief that each of us has a self-system, a set of attitudes we have about ourselves. This self-system is how we define ourselves. Yet, inextricably bound to our self-definition is our perception of how others see us. Sullivan (1953) has stated that even when we are alone, our thinking, images, and behavior always relate to other people, real or imaginary.

The individual's self-image or self-definition may be revealed in any type of imagery, daydream, or dream. Yet, an even more clear picture with accompanying feelings may emerge if the effort is made to concentrate on the person seeing images of himself alone, in a situation.

Self-image imagery can be categorized in the following manner:

1. Those imaginary situations in which the patients are asked to imagine there are two of them. Then they are asked to imagine such things as "kissing yourself," "hugging yourself," "sitting on your own lap," "holding yourself up," etc. Attitudes of self-acceptance or non-acceptance, shame, or self-revulsion may emerge. This self-observation may reveal conflicts and style of defenses heretofore concealed to the imager.

2. Those imaginary situations again in which the persons are to imagine there are two of them. Then they are to imagine "looking through a keyhole and see yourself," or "two of you sitting in easy chairs facing each other in a dialogue." This helps us see ourselves and talk to ourselves.

3. Those in which there are two of you but with one of you in need of help, i.e., "You are in a boat—another you is in the water in the middle of the ocean. What do you do?" Often this imaginary situation and other variations of the same phenomenon indicate a person's attitude toward self-help or accepting help.

4. Still another group of imaginary situations that tends to elicit self-images combined with reminiscent images are, i.e., "image of yourself in a classroom," "image of yourself in a child's playground."

6. Dual Imagery

Psycho-imagination therapy is predicated on the premise that a person's inner conflicts are brought about by the opposition of two strong and incompatible forces, neither of which can be satisfied without exacting pain, fear, guilt, or some other emotional penalty. Of course, to become aware of these antithetical forces within oneself, these ambivalences, is to begin to recognize the complementary opposites within experience. Once this can be accomplished the patient can attempt to change his reactions to reality situations; can, in effect, negate conflict; can indeed actualize his own personality.

A rather remarkable phenomenon appears to occur when a person is asked to imagine two different forces, dolls, trees, animals, impulses, etc., and then to contrast each of them with each other. In the great majority of the reported imageries (but not all), there appears to be some form of bipolarization between them. This can be better demonstrated when one asks the imager to assign an adjective to each of the two images. The adjectives may reflect opposite forces of some kind. To enhance the opposing or contrasting forces, one can ask the person to imagine one of the images speaking to the other image, then to imagine the answer back to the first image from the second image. Again, this can be reversed, with the second image speaking to the first image and the first image's remarks back.

Dual imagery is so fertile that from here it is possible to develop it in many directions. I will demonstrate a few directions:

First Image		Second Image
	the person	
Statement to person from image		Statement to person from image

Another direction:

First image		Second image
	the person	
Statement from image to person		Statement from image to person

Another direction:

Suggest that the first and second image walk down a road together (or appear together in some way) and become aware of what their interaction appears to be.

Another direction:

First image		Second image
	the person	
(M/L) The most unlikely (or difficult) statement from the image to the person		(M/L) The most unlikely (or difficult) statement from the image to the person

Another direction

First image		Second image
	the person	
Statement from the image to a significant person in the person's life		Statement from the image to a significant person in the person's life
or		or
Statement from the significant person in the person's life to the image		Statement from the significant person in the person's life to the image
or		or
Statement from the therapist to the image		Statement from the therapist to the image
or		or
Statement from the image to the therapist		Statement from the image to the therapist

There is no absolute formula for using dual imagery. When I suggest that patients image two trees, or two animals, or two women

I usually find that some items are neutral and others are affect laden. It is difficult to tell in advance what the patient will respond to with strong emotion. Thus, I suggest that you engage the patient first with what seem to be neutral images and work into the affect-laden imagery according to the patient's readiness to deal with sensitive material.

The major emphasis is on awareness of conflict; the particular way in which the patient views his world; the dialogue that may ensue; the release of feelings; and the readiness to enter into the focusing approaches such as cathartic or task imagery.

Experience with dual imagery as a means of discovering areas of conflict and expanded awareness seems to fall into the following general groupings:

1. Those that compare two images of things: two rocking chairs, two tables, two rooms, two bathtubs, two houses, etc.

2. Those that compare two images that are alive but not human: two flowers, two trees, two animals, etc.

3. Those that compare two images that are human: two women, two men, two children, etc.

4. Those that compare the person in relation to forces or impulses. Those include: (IS) Above you is a force. What do you feel and do, etc.? (IS) You awake from sleeping in a field at night and there are footsteps over your body. Over what part of your body are the footsteps, and whose are they? Or: (IS) You walk down a road and somebody taps you on the shoulder, etc.

5. Those that compare two of you: (IS) You are in a cave. You are also outside the cave. Call to yourself. Or: (IS) You are in a boat in the ocean and you are also in the water. Throw a rope from that you in the boat to the you in the water, etc.

6. Those that compare two body parts of one person: (IS) Imagine what your heart says to your head. (IS) What does the left side of your brain say to the right side of your brain, etc.?

7. Those that compare body parts of one person to another person: (IS) What does your heart say to the heart of another person, etc? (IS) What does the heart of the other person say to your heart, etc.?

8. Those that compare differences in physical space directions: (IS) You walk down a shallow river and you see something on each side. Or: (IS) You look ahead and see something; then turning, what do you see, etc.? Image in front and image behind.

9. Combined cateogires of dual imagery: (IS) Imagine two different animals in human situations, or any other possible combination of dual imagery conceptions that may occur creatively in the operational use of imagery that seems to help delineate conflict areas.

The dual images frequently represent the two parts of self in conflict, that is, self versus self. Then, at other times it is the self versus the other person. In any case, dual imagery can serve to make a person aware of his internal conflicts and those conflicts with other persons. A dialogue is a natural outgrowth of the reporting of the dual images leading to further meaning of the conflicts.

When a person is asked to image two bipolarized images together and then to imagine them as one image, he may experience great difficulty as he attempts this. Some persons protest and say it is impossible. One person brought the two images together and then exploded them in his imagery so that they would disappear. Apparently, the more bipolarized the dual images, the more difficult it is to imagine them in a unitary manner.

In the use of dual imagery with detached or schizoid persons, I have observed changes in their imagery when the detachment lifts. What appeared in detachment as dull and limited seems to enlarge and expand and become more vivid. At other times, with some detached people, one of the dual images has upon examination revealed itself as the "secret self" of that person.

7. Body Imagery

All of us tend to look at our body image through the eyes of others so, for example, what we see in a mirror is interpreted through a set of social values. We invariably evaluate our body image against an ideal or preferred standard reflecting a cultural bias.

The idealized body image also relates to those body images we may have of ourselves with our eyes closed. Such self-observation may reveal internal satisfaction or its opposite, self-hatred.

Empirical evidence indicates that persons tend to be able to sense a body-part core of their identity when asked to identify such a body correlate.

Furthermore, introjection of parental figures can be evidenced when persons are asked to imagine in what part of their body their parents reside. They can see their parents in their heart, guts, arms, etc. Most patients are not overly surprised by the body reference to particular organs and respond quite naturally to such a question.

In the developmental process, if a person has been falsely defined by the significant other, false definition may take on bodily form. The mother or father who "resides" in the patient's chest appearing hostile is in reality the false identity or the neurotic conflict internalized.

The patient is asked to "exorcise" the bad parental figure out of his body and to remove the influence of the other; and when accomplished, it can lead to a healthier, more independent identity.

The following are 13 examples of different types of body imageries:

1. In what part of your body does your body-part core reside? Statement from core to other.
2. In what part of your body does your anger, love, joy, guilt, shame reside?
3. In what part of your body does your mother or father reside? (Introjection-body exorcism)
4. Enter your own body. Describe the journey.
5. Have mother or father, etc., enter your body. Describe their journey.
6. Enter your mother's or father's body. Describe your journey.
7. Dual body imagery: (IS) image of chest; image of back. (IS) A force that goes into your head; a force that comes out of your head.
8. Statement from your own: head to heart; head to guts; head to genitals—statements back.
9. Statement from you to other person: (IS) head to head; head to heart; head to guts; head to genitals, etc.—and all can be reversed in direction of other to you and their statements.
10. Imagery that relates to "buffer-zone" areas and self-touching: (IS) What is the closest you will allow a stranger to come near you? (IS) Imagine what parts of your body you find easiest to touch and what parts do you find most difficult?
11. Imaging one's own body in relationship to attractiveness, size and shape, masculinity or femininity, and strength: (IS) Sensing your body, which part seems most attractive or least attractive? (IS) Sensing your body, which part of your body are you most aware of? (IS) Sensing your body, what is the most secret part of your body, etc.?
12. Body-holding imagery involving others: (IS) Imagine holding your mother's or father's face in your hands. (IS) Reverse and imagine them individually holding your face in their hands.
13. Composite imagery: (IS) your parent and your body as merging and then separate out your own.

8. Sexual Imagery

Individuals can fantasize or imagine sexual happening from memory images nearly congruous in feelings to their past actual occurrence. Empirical evidence indicates that sexual imagery can be so vivid that the physiological response can cause increased heartbeat rate, a rise in temperature, rapid breathing, vasocongestion, and even orgasm. Of course, other imageries besides sexual ones can be near-re-creations, but sexual images are certainly the example par excellence.

In fact, my experience indicates that when persons say they cannot have images, they will respond when I ask them if they can imagine sexual scenes or recall sexual memories. So far this has resulted in no failures.

Sexual themes are a fertile area for the imagination to play upon. They have power because of their importance in our lives. Images of sexuality we have during intercourse or in place of it, as in masturbation, are as common as rain. Then there are other images related to the strategies of interaction between men and women that anticipate sexual outcomes, acceptance, or rejection.

Sadistic or masochistic images may emerge, as well as images of dominance, rejection, jealousy, unfavorable comparisons, feelings of heartbreak, joy, sin, being dirty, etc.

Since sexual conflicts deal with the most vulnerable, the most tender, the most shame-inducing, and the most guilty feelings, they are the most difficult to disclose to oneself and others. In order to get at these conflicts, I start with general imaginary situations that have no obvious sexual overtones, but that have, through clinical use, proved to be sexually revealing.

The range of sexual imageries is so vast that one would have to be encyclopedic to categorize them. I offer the following categories as the most productive from my clinical experience.

The imageries can be systematically categorized in the following manner:

1. In about 98% of the persons who are offered the following imaginary situation, sexual feelings and attitudes are expressed. The 2% of individuals are those who relate this imagery to death or burial and those, like prisoners, who regard it as an escape hatch. Since 98% do respond to it and reveal themselves sexually, it can be a powerfully important sexual imagery: (IS) Walk into the middle of a room. There is a hole in the floor. Look through the hole and tell me what you see. Then imagine going down into the hole and tell me what you feel and do.

Here is an actual response from a thirty-year-old woman. I will not attempt interpretation or patient-therapist dialogue: "The room is dark—it's very hard to find the hole. When I look through I see a crocodile. Wow! I just can't go down—but I'll try. Whoo, my dress flies up—I'm an easy target (laughs). Roger the crocodile will do me in—I don't belong there."

2. There is a special imaginary situation in which the person is asked to imagine three doors—a left, middle, and right door—and then to imagine entering. Experience indicates that nearly always the response to the middle door relates to either sexuality or love relationships or the lack of them even if the manifest content is not explicitly sexual. The left and right doors do not follow a predictable fashion, but can be used for further information and awareness in any case.

3. There are those imageries that ask the person to image sexual parts. Examples are: (IS) Imagine an animal that comes out of a penis and an animal that comes out of a vagina. (IS) Remove lint from the navel of ———(someone the person is intimately involved with).

4. Certain sexual imageries that are useful to attitudes between the sexes are as follows: (IS) Escort a group of women (or men) prisoners one mile away to another station. What happens? What do you do and feel, etc.? (IS) Imagine a woman (or man) on a six-foot mound of earth, etc.

5. Imageries that involve parents such as: (IS) Take a shower with your father or mother. (IS) Stare at the naked back of your father or mother. (IS) Have each of them stare at your naked back, etc.

6. Imageries that relate to sexual fantasies such as: (IS) Imagine the fantasy a person of the opposite sex would have about you. (IS) What is your sexual fantasy about an ideal sexual partner, etc.?

9. Predicting Imagery

To predict the reported imagery production in another person one has encountered for the first time would be virtually impossible. Yet, when two persons, intimately involved, are asked to predict each other's imagery in separate and private reports, surprising results may occur. For example, I have asked married couples privately and silently to report five consecutive images and then to write them down on paper. I then asked each partner to predict the imagery of the other. A bimodal distribution of predictions seems to occur. That is, some couples were able to predict a good many of the other partner's imagery while others seemed to have little awareness of the other's imagery. The results of the dialogue that follows when one partner reveals his or her own imagery to the other partner can be of great therapeutic value. It can heighten the degree of awareness for the person and the partner. Increased communication invariably results because the partner is seeing the other through his or her way of viewing the world. Even those who are poor at predicting the other's imagery now have a chance for awareness of the other that has been heretofore overlooked.

10. Task Imagery

Other investigators have indicated that highly therapeutic results can be achieved when a patient is asked to face difficult symbolic forces and "transform" them into images that are more readily handled. The various forms of confrontation, whether it be staring, killing, exhaustion, magic fluids, etc., are designed to "transform" the symbolic demons, thus reducing anxiety and sometimes terror.

My own experience indicates it is possible to offer certain imagery that I refer to as task imagery, that can offer the possibilities of "working-through" a conflict. These imaginary situations involve him in mastering a piece of work or action. Invariably, this is followed by asking the patient to redo or reexperience the imaginary situation (IS). This very often results in a changed self-concept in the person.

While Leuner (1969; and see also Chapter 5) and Hammer (1967) use a standard set of confrontation imagery, I use a great variety of imagery. For the most part, the task imagery involves nonsymbolic or concrete imagery, though it may take on symbolic forms at certain times.

My own use of task imagery stresses the use of dialogue between myself and the patient.

As the therapist utilizes and gains experience with task imagery, he may develop his own creativity and flexibility in the choice of imaginary situations.

Task imagery may reveal the patient's internal conflicts, his style and manner of approach, his defenses and fears; and also it can serve as a vehicle for focusing for a changed self concept in the "working-through" of the imaginary task. Task imagery affords the possibility of a patient's facing himself and then attempting to change his self-concept. The important ingredient following the initial flow of imagery is to reexperience or redo the imagery in a manner that leads to a possible healthy conflict resolution.

In repeating the same imaginary situation with a person, one can attempt to increase the intensity of the desired response, focusing for greater feeling response each time. This is especially true when the feeling response seems devoid of affect. In repeating the same imaginary situation, one may offer the instruction to "say something with more feeling." An example of this was asking a man a dual imagery, "to imagine two different rocking chairs and then to imagine somebody different in each." He imagined an old man in one rocking chair and a young man in the other. I then instructed him to make a statement to each of the men. He started with an abstract statement in his initial response. His second response was a factual statement about the furniture. I repeated the imaginary situation, urging him to make an emotional statement about each man. This time, he was more feeling in his statement and expressed some concern about "the other man's son who was lost in Vietnam." From this initial feeling spark, more profound expression of feelings emerged.

All of these and many more are helpful and offer the patient the possibility of working for change. But it must be remembered that the patient must be ready to focus for change. The elements determining this readiness are the patient's awareness of his internal conflicts; the release of feeling connected with contributory traumatic incidents; cognizance of the undermining strategies of behavior of the significant others; and recognition of his own counter-reaction strategies.

Gardner Murphy (1947) anticipated the concept of the transformation of imagery when he stated, "But Images . . . are manipulable just as muscular acts, to give new and better satisfaction."

Here are some of the main types of task imageries that can be used with reference to what it purports to do and to the "working-through" of some form of conflict resolution and enhanced self-image.

1. Those task imageries that are related to the achievement and power motive: (IS) Imagine climbing a thousand steps to the top; (IS) imagine building a bridge across a gorge.

2. Those task imageries that allow the person to fight powerful forces: (IS) You are caught in a blizzard and you must find your way to safety. (IS) Herd a group of horses into a corral one mile away.

3. There are those task imageries that allow the person to fight for a new start against guilt and shame: (IS) You are an embryo about to birth. (IS) Imagine taking your first steps as a baby.

4. To fight against loss of control and return to your own mastery are these task imageries: (IS) Imagine backing through a paper wall. (IS) You are stuck on top of a ferris wheel and you are to get down safely.

5. One of the most powerful task imageries relates to fighting rotten feelings about oneself. Here are two such imageries: (IS) You are in a tank of the foulest liquid. How does it feel? You must get out. (IS) You are in a sewer full of rats. Get out.

6. Creating order out of disorder through imagery exercises such as: (IS) Imagine cleaning an oily, scaly piece of metal until it is clean; (IS) Imagine a very knotty rope and unravel it.

7. Imagery related to rescuing oneself and others: You are asked to fight and overcome danger. (IS) Lead people out of a swamp. (IS) Imagine successfully removing the fuse from a bomb.

8. To feel greater control over overpowering forces: (IS) Ride a Sherman tank over bumpy fields. (IS) Control a steel ball swinging into and felling buildings.

9. Transforming weak or negative images into strong or positive images. For example, if there is a rabbit or snake in your guts, one can concentrate on transforming it into a more positive or stronger image.

11. Cathartic Imagery

There are certain kinds of imaginary situations in which the patient is asked to imagine the "bad" parent in front of him and openly, in psychodrama fashion, to define himself in a positive manner. Imagination can substitute in many persons for actual face-to-face confrontations. Obviously, this kind of focusing procedure requires a supportive therapist aligned on the side of the patient, and equally important, a readiness on the part of the patient to liberate himself from a false identity. Of necessity I will not discuss patient readiness but will limit my remarks to the imagery approaches. The following are types of imageries that lend themselves to cathartic expression on the part of the patient:

1. Those imageries relating to being wrongfully accused of a *non sequitur* accusation: (IS) Imagine the parental figure accusing you and then reverse the process by accusing the accuser to the point of rightfully asserting your true position.

2. Certain finish-the-sentence items may be used as:
I am not ——— : I am ——— :
Never refer to me as ——— , etc.

3. Certain traumatic incidents recalled in reminiscent imagery may also be used in this fashion.

4. Parental imageries: (IS) You and your parent in a dry well a hundred feet down with a ladder to the top. Describe the reactions, etc.

12. Depth Imagery

Depth imagery is not an accurate descriptive term since any imaginary situation can cause a person to react from the very depths of his feelings, which appear to come from the unconscious forces within.

Yet, there are certain imageries that seem to get at depth or unconscious forces, nearly always eliciting a profoundly deep set of reactions, no matter who the patient may be.

These highly emotionally charged imaginary situations should be employed with caution and with awareness of what the patient is ready to face.

Here are a few examples: (IS) Imagine that you are a child and you are crying. Now imagine your mother or father "licking" away your tears. (IS) Your mother or father walks into a room and finds you dead on the bed.

In addition to these are those imageries that seem to plumb the unconscious forces within but do not involve parental figures: (IS) Imagine a sealed can underwater. Open it. What do you see, feel, and do? (IS) Imagine putting your hand into a cave three times, each time going a little deeper. What do you do, see, and feel?

13. General Imagery

For purposes of categorizing therapeutic imagery, there are those imaginary situations that are not specifically dual imagery, task imagery, body imagery, sexual imagery, self-imagery, etc., and yet exist as a vast area of the function of the imagination. These imaginary situations I refer to as general imagery. Again, as with any other type of imagery, meaning and dialogue leading to awareness and change are most important. Here are a few examples.

1. Try to imagine an image of a "molecule of you"; "your conscience"; or "Paradise." What do you do and see and feel?

2. Imagine you are a walnut, or an amoeba, or a sandwich on a plate, etc. Speaking as that image, what do you do and see and feel?

3. Allow yourself to have a fantasy or daydream.

4. Image of a pair of scissors cutting something; image of a fire end of a stick; image of a knife, etc. What do you do and see and feel?

5. (IS) Imagine a light beam and follow it up into the sky. What do you do and see and feel? (IS) Stare into a fire. What do you do and see and feel?

The creative possibilities are so vast and the directions that general imagery can go in are so various as to defy ordinary classification. As a therapist, you may find unchartered imagery areas so fertile and new that it carries with it wonderment and excitement. New possibilities can and do occur.

14. Detection of Resistance in Imagery Production

Clinicians using imagery generally agree that patient responses can bypass the censorship of that person to reveal hidden aspects of personality. It is this special ability of reported imagery that provides us with therapeutic awareness that verbalizations alone may not reveal. Despite this, imagery used in therapeutic interactions is not free of resistance.

Resistance is the patient's mechanism in the service of keeping buried repressed material because he wishes to avoid the anxiety that would ensue were this material revealed. The concept of resistance is so complex that I am restricting my remarks to the detection of resistance in imagery production.

First we need to distinguish between those who consciously resist, and those who, despite honest attempts, seem not to have any images—those who will not and those that cannot. Both are resisting. Those who will not will do so in a more conscious style. Those who cannot will resist for more hidden or unconscious reasons.

Individuals who will not image are aware of their fight against revealing themselves. Among the enormous variety of reasons for actively refusing to respond we find: fear of exposure, fear of not being able to compete with the assumed high level of other persons, hostility to the therapist and the idea of therapy, fear of loss of control, or the belief that imagery is just another trick to entrap him, etc.

To the refusal to image must be added the dimension of *defiant imagery*. There is a defiant imagination that, in open opposition, may defy the therapist by showing him that none of his efforts can bypass the patient's resistance.

Certain patients will report fake imagery; they fabricate or manufacture imagery. I find this occurring only rarely. However, the falsely reported imageries are still subjective productions and must be examined for possible meaningfulness. The detection of such false imagery is difficult and requires that vaguely defined skill called clinical experience.

Moreover, one must not overlook voice cues since much is revealed in the telling of imagery. Raised and lowered tones, sudden silence, hesitancies, changes in volume must be individually examined to reveal defiance and resistance.

In my own work, perhaps because of selective factors, those who will not image comprise a very small percentage of the therapeutic population. The following, obviously incomplete list of resistance patterns should aid in detecting resistance among the overwhelming majority of patients who readily involve themselves in imagery. I must reemphasize that these kinds of resistances appear in the imagery productions of persons who ordinarily have good imagery flow.

1. *Unreported imagery:* If certain imagery sequences seem to bring up feelings of great anxiety or shame and guilt, the person may say he has images but is having great difficulty revealing them at this time. Encouragement by the therapist or a temporary shift into dialogue may break this barrier and eventually allow the patient to report the imagery.

2. *Foggy, clouded, or vague imagery:* This is especially revealing when it occurs only sporadically as a general phenomenon. Feelings states such as anger or joy may be resisted by the individual when this occurs.

3. *Stick figure or cartoon imagery:* If this occurs only on occasion, it probably indicates resistances are in operation at those periods. Sometimes the patient may recognize his own resistance. One, for example, told me, "I'm getting those cartoon images again. I'm probably resisting."

4. *Distancing themselves from the therapist:* The patient may say that during his imagery responses he imagined the therapist at a great distance. One patient, whenever her imagery had a sexual content, told me, "You are a mile away." Yet, in her other imagery productions, I appeared a few feet from her.

5. *Diversionary imagery:* Specific kinds of imagery recur as a diversion when the patient is resistant. One patient said that whenever he was involved in difficult imagery he saw food. A typical statement from this man was "I know I'm resisting, because I'm getting those food images again."

6. *Reduced images:* This is manifested in imagery productions where the patient suddenly sees tiny images, almost microcosmic in size. When this is contrary to their ordinary imagery flow, it may represent aspects of themselves they do not wish to see.

7. *Inability to image the self:* The inability of persons to see themselves in imagery is sometimes evidence of resistance. For example, some patients have difficulty seeing their faces in imagery. Some can see only their backs. Often this is a resistance to feelings of shame and guilt. When these feelings are eliminated, they are usually able to see their faces and the front of their bodies.

8. *Lack of affect:* When persons offer imagery without the concomitant matching feelings, they are probably expressing resistance. When, in time, their imagery productions and feelings merge and feelings are expressed, resistances are usually overcome.

9. *No imagery:* If no imagery occurs after repeated attempts in a relaxed state, the patient may be feeling depression, or emptiness of existence, or feelings of nothingness. This is an example of cannot rather than of will not.

15. Group Therapy Imagery

It would be neither appropriate nor practical to attempt here a comprehensive analysis of group therapy and its myriad forms. I shall restrict my remarks to psycho-imagination group therapy as it relates to the use of imagery.

Psycho-imagination group therapy emphasizes the patient's self-definition and the degree to which his self-concept permits or constricts his behavior vis-à-vis the other group members. His awareness of how others in the group define him becomes crystallized. Furthermore, the group can become the arena for re-enactment of old family interactions that molded the patient's false positions and negative self-image.

The overall purpose of interaction within the group is to help each and every patient become aware of his or her conflicts and then take the risks inherent in focusing for change. While, broadly speaking, nearly all of the imagery approaches suggested for individual therapy can be utilized in group therapy, there are several factors that must be taken into account. First, groups involve interaction between men and women together; some patients find it considerably easier to express feelings and imagery to members of the same sex and sometimes find it difficult to express feelings to members of the opposite sex. This is especially true of those persons with problems relating to exposure of sexual inadequacy. Overcoming this kind of reluctance, permitting oneself the free flow of imagery and emotional expression without the feeling that one is weird, is a barometer of the patient's growth.

Second, the factors of peer competition and belonging, while not always evident in one-to-one therapy, may surface in group contact. The disclosure of such feelings and the coping with them are part of the group process. Also, basic trust of authority figures and basic trust of one's peers are areas that may be subjected to considerable emotion and conflict within the group setting. By example, by identification, by stimulating one another, by giving increasingly free play to their fantasies, dreams, imagination, and unconscious production, co-patients often afford the conflicted group member a chance to develop and nurture the courage for new alternatives.

The use of imagery in group therapy may take the following directions:
1. Imagery within the person subjectively experienced.
2. All the persons in the group engaging in imagery about a single member.
3. That member's reactions and imagery in response to the others' imagery.
4. One person engaging in imagery about every other person in rotation.
5. All of the other people, then, engaging in imagery about that one person in return-reaction imagery.
6. All of the persons engaging in imagery about the therapist at various points in his past or present life (or the future).
7. The therapist engaging in imagery about each of the group members at various points in their past or present lives (or the future).
8. All of the persons interacting in imagery without any directed consecutiveness, but yet having its own internal consistency in the sequences of reactions, depending on the particular group.

While the main thrust of this discussion involves imagery, it would be unwise to assume that imagery is the sole method used in group therapy. I have found that the "finish-the-sentence" questions can also be of invaluable help as "group starters." Among these "FTS's" are:

1. The more I know you the more I ——— .
2. I cannot give you ——— .
3. The most difficult thing to tell you is ——— .
4. If only you would ——— .
5. I like you best for your ——— .
6. The adjective that describes you best is ——— .
7. Sooner or later you will find me ——— .
8. Never refer to me as ——— .
9. I will not allow you to define me as ——— .
10. My best defense against you is ——— .
11. I have to prove to every woman or man ——— .
12. Your strongest point is ——— .

There are countless other "finish-the-sentence" approaches that can be used. Not only are they useful group starters, but they can also be used at any time in the group interaction for the purpose of clarifying reactions and feelings. They may also very well serve as leads into imagery if they result in particularly strong reactions. There are times, especially in the focusing approaches, that certain imagery may lead back to an appropriate "finish-the-sentence" question, as in cathartic imagery. The possibilities are extremely varied and can be created effectively at almost any moment of feeling and interaction.

Group imagery in which the entire group is simultaneously presented an imaginary situation permits participation of each person's imagination for a time and then the imagery is shared by all. Following this, interaction usually occurs on many levels depending on the particular group. Examples are: (IS) Imagine the entire group is in prison and then imagine that we all find a way out. (IS) We are all in a stagecoach and we are going on a journey. What do you imagine will happen to us as we go?

A use of dual imagery might be for each person in the group to react to a single patient, as in: (IS) Imagine standing on Steve's shoulders. How would it feel and what do you imagine will happen? Bipolarization of feelings and conflicts may be indicated between the central person of the situation and each of the other members in the group. For example, John's response was "I can't get on Steve's shoulders because my heels would dig into his shoulders and hurt him. I will be too much of a burden on him." I then asked Steve (IS) what he would feel if John were standing on his shoulders. "I'd be in competition with him," Steve said. "I'd have to show him I can carry him with ease and never flinch even for a second. I can never show another man I'm weak. That's unmasculine."

As the group members take turns giving their imagery in standing on Steve's shoulders, and as he responds to them, it will be quickly revealed with whom, among them, he is in greatest conflict. At any point in time a sequence of intense interaction may occur between two persons, or among several. The emphasis, to reiterate, is on helping the individual become aware of his internal conflicts, his negative self-image, his own self-definition, and the difference between how he defines himself and how others define him. This awareness may serve to engender in him the strength to attempt behaving differently, more in line with his "true" identity. If, as a result of the reactions to an imaginary situation, anyone in the group is being defined falsely, he or she must of course be encouraged (by me as well as the other group members) to assert himself or herself and insist, "You cannot define me that way."

In group therapy it is also possible to combine imagery with some form of psychodrama to help increase patient awareness of internal conflicts. I asked one man to (IS) imagine two different animals, and he visualized a koala bear and a panther. I then asked him to imagine that he *was* the koala bear and then to make a statement as the koala bear to each group member. When he had finished I asked him to imagine he *was* the panther and then to make a statement to each group member as the panther. Without going into the details of his responses, I can say that his experience was highly therapeutic and effective both for him as well as the other group members.

Needless to say, such combined use of imagery and psychodrama can be utilized with effectiveness in other imaginary situations. The group therapy setting helps focus and crystallize the reactions for greater awareness and therapeutic change. For example, (IS) one person in the group is to imagine himself as a child and acts out how he attempts to get adopted by two other group members who act as a couple who may want to adopt him.

Body imagery can be introduced into the group interaction by the following imaginary situations. This is directed to one person in the group: (IS) Imagine handing your heart to each group member in turn. Say what you feel, see, and do.

Of course, each group member will likely react to accepting or rejecting, etc., the heart of that one person. Following the same procedure, one can have each person in turn (IS) imagine holding the face of each group member in your hands and tell the group what you see, feel, and do. Then each group member can share his reactions to that person, etc.

Self-image imagery can be introduced by asking the group as a whole in turn (IS) to look through a keyhole and imagine seeing —— — (a group member) in the room. Each person then reports his or her imagery and that person then reacts to the individuals in the group. Another form of self-image imagery is to ask each group member to (IS) imagine you are in a child's playground alone. Then each group member is to report his or her imagery, which subsequently leads to interaction, possible reminiscent imagery, or other imagery productions.

Sexual imagery can be introduced by asking each person to (IS) imagine picking lint from the navel of ——— (a group member). The interaction of that person and the other group members tends to follow naturally. This can continue in turn with all the group members and their interactions. Another sexual imagery that can be introduced in group therapy is to ask each person to (IS) imagine escorting a group of women or men prisoners to another area one mile away. After each group member reports his imagery, interaction at many levels is possible, leading to awareness and changed self-concepts.

General imagery of an infinite variety is possible in group therapy. I shall only mention a few: (IS) One group member imagines a bird on the head of each other group member. Their reactions in turn to that person's imagery again serve as a point of reference for interaction. (IS)

One group member imagines an image on the chest of each person in turn, etc.

Depth imagery can occur in any of the previous dimensions of imaginary situations. Those that seem nearly always to elicit reactions of a profound nature invariably leading to the focusing approaches, including cathartic imagery, are as follows: (IS) Imagine you are a baby and you are being passed from one group member to another in turn around the group. What do you feel and see and do? (IS) One group member is to imagine being chained to the leg of each group member in turn. The reactions of the other group members to him are important as well as the feelings and actions, etc.

Task imagery can be utilized in group therapy by asking each person to (IS) imagine being seated on a gold throne and then to cope with the group in any way the imagery directs. The reactions in return from the other group members may result in either a certain kind of interaction or into that person redoing the imagery within the framework of a healthier self-concept.

(IS) Each person in the group is to imagine himself as an embryo about to birth itself. The imagery can be shared and interactions at various levels usually occur.

I must emphasize that the group sessions are not so structured that imagery is the only function involved. Anything may be brought up at any time: a particularly traumatic situation or decision a person is involved with; carry-over reactions from previous sessions; thoughts and feelings people have had about some of the others in the days between group meetings. Also included may be such awareness and feelings as patients have gleaned from individual sessions and wish to bring up spontaneously in the group situations. Nothing, certainly, should deter spontaneous behavior unless the spontaneous behavior is used as a cover-up for some difficult internal conflict. To keep the structure and the spontaneity of the group unfettered is a fine goal for any group therapist.

16. Current Research

A projective test of visual imagery was developed in 1974 by the author that is comprised of fourteen imaginary situations and four sentence completions. A scoring system was developed so that a quantitative score can be made as to the conflict level of that person. Qualitative analysis of the testee of a psychodynamic nature can also be made. It is individually administered. Norms are based on 118 college freshmen and sophomores. The group (SIT) can also be used.

At present, studies are under way with the use of the Shorr Imagery Test (SIT) with drug-abuse people and men prisoners. The results of the studies are not yet ready and will be offered for publication in the near future.

ACKNOWLEDGMENT

The author wishes to thank Dr. Peter Wolson for reading portions of this chapter and for his valuable suggestions.

References

Desoille, R. *The directed daydream*. Monograph No. 8, The Psychosynthesis Research Foundation, 1965.
Escalona, S. K. Book review of *Mental imagery in children* by Jean Piaget and Barbel Inhelder (New York: Basic Books, 1969). *Journal of Nervous and Mental Disease*, January, 1973, *156* 70-71.
Fisher, S. *Body consciousness*. Englewood Cliffs, New Jersey: Prentice-Hall, 1973.
Freud, S. *Theory and technique*. New York: Collier Books, 1963.
Fromm, E. Remarks on the problem of free association. *Psychiatric Research Reports* 2, American Psychiatric Association, 1955.
Guntrip, H. *Personality structure and human interaction*. New York: International Universities Press, 1964.
Hammer, M. The directed daydream technique. *Psychotherapy*, November, 1967, *4*(4), 173-181.
Horowitz, M., and Becker, S. S. The compulsion to repeat trauma: Experimental study of intrusive thinking after stress. *Journal of Nervous and Mental Disease*, July, 1971, *153*(1), 32-40.
Jellinek, A. Spontaneous imagery: A new psychotherapeutic approach. *American Journal of Psychotherapy*, July, 1949, *3*(3), 372-391.
Laing, R. D. *The self and others*. Chicago: Quadrangle Books, 1962.
Leuner, H. Guided affective imagery (GAI): A method of intensive psychotherapy. *American Journal of Psychotherapy*, January, 1969, *23*(1), 4-22.
Murphy, G. *Personality. A biosocial approach to origins and structure*. New York: Harper, 1947.
Posner, M. I., Nissen, M. J., and Klein, R. M. Visual dominance: An information processing account of its origins and significance. *Psychological Review*, March, 1976, *83*(2).
Sheehan, P. W. *The function and nature of imagery*. New York: Academic Press, 1972.
Shorr, J. E. The existential question and the imaginary situation as therapy. *Existential Psychiatry*, Winter, 1967, *6*(24), 443-462.
Shorr, J. E. Psycho-imagination therapy: The integration *of phenomenology and imagination*. New York: Intercontinental Medical Book Corp., 1972.

Shorr, J. E. In what part of your body does your mother reside? *Psychotherapy: Theory, Research and Practice*, Summer, 1973, *10*(2), 31-34.

Shorr, J. E. *Psychotherapy through imagery*. New York: Intercontinental Medical Book Corporation, 1974a.

Shorr, J. E. *Shorr imagery test*. Institute for Psycho-Imagination Therapy, Los Angeles, California, 1974b.

Shorr, J. E. The use of task imagery as therapy. *Psychotherapy: Theory, Research and Practice*, Summer, 1975, *12*(2).

Shorr, J. E. Dual imagery. *Psychotherapy: Theory, Research and Practice*, Fall 1976, *13*(2).

Shorr, J. E. *Group Shorr imagery test*. Institute for Psycho-Imagination Therapy, Los Angeles, California, 1977.

Singer, J. L. *Daydreaming: An introduction to the experimental study of inner experience*. New York: Random House, 1966.

Singer, J. L. Imagery and daydream techniques employed in psychotherapy: Some practical and theoretical implications. In Spielberger, C. (Ed.), *Current topics in clinical and community psychology*. Vol. 3. New York: Academic Press, 1971.

Singer, J. L. *Imagery and daydream methods in psychotherapy and behavior modification*. New York: Academic Press, 1974.

Singer, J. L. *The child's world of make-believe*. New York: Academic Press, 1975.

Sullivan, H. S. *The interpersonal theory of psychiatry*. New York: Norton, W. W. Col., 1953.

Part III

Mental Imagery Therapies

Introduction

The papers grouped in Part III reflect a development toward an even more extensive utilization of imagery in psychotherapy, approaches that begin to move away from more traditional psychotherapies. Leuner's guided affective imagery (GAI) represents the most systematic of the European mental imagery or waking-dream approaches that reflect the influences among others of Jung's active imagination method, Schultz's autogenic training, and Desoille's *Rêve Eveillé* method. Leuner's theoretical orientation remains close to psychoanalysis despite the fact that his therapeutic method is more structured and emphasizes chiefly the symbolic working-through of conflicts without active therapeutic interpretation.

Greenleaf's active imagination method reflects an extension of Jung's contribution to dream analysis into a total psychotherapeutic orientation. The speculative and far-ranging chapter points to links of imagery to Oriental practices and even to current theories of mathematical applications to the behavioral sciences.

Ahsen's eidetic psychotherapy as represented in Sheikh's chapter reflects a transition from the broader emphases and Freudian or neo-Freudian orientations of the earlier chapters and the more specific, symptom-focused behavior modification uses of imagery. Sheikh's account of eidetic theory represents a new personality theory, one still to be elaborated or tested but certainly novel and stimulating. The emphasis on the internalized parent figure; the separation from parents through imagery does have lines to modern psychoanalytic views of object relations and ego-boundaries but the therapeutic approach is a far more direct one. In many ways because of its focus on repeating the image and avoiding narration or imagery trips, the technique described is closer to the behavior therapies than to the free associative or active imagination approaches described in chapters 2-6.

5

Basic Principles and Therapeutic Efficacy of Guided Affective Imagery (GAI)

Hanscarl Leuner

Translated by Augusta Arthur

1. Introduction

The individual words in the term guided affective imagery (GAI) characterize in themselves the procedure of the psychotherapeutic daydreaming technique described here (Leuner, 1969). The procedure was first described by the author in 1954, and subsequently systematically developed into a psychoanalytically oriented psychotherapy (Leuner, 1955; 1970). At present more than 80 articles and books exist on the procedure and its effects. In Europe there is an International Society for Guided Affective Imagery with chapters in West Germany, Switzerland, Austria, and Sweden. In German-speaking territory the procedure was introduced by the author as *katathymes Bilderleben* (catathymic imagery). The term "catathym" was first coined for fantasy by H. Maier, senior physician to the late Eugen Bleuler, to characterize its dependence on affects and emotions (Greek, *kata* = dependent; Greek, *thymos* = soul, i.e., emotionality). For use in practice, the term "symbol drama" has been adopted (Krojanker, 1966).

Guided affective imagery is more than a therapeutic procedure. It represents a system of graduated methods and management models for

---

Hanscarl Leuner • Department of Psychiatry, University of Göttingen, Göttingen, West Germany.

manipulation of the daydream in psychotherapy. In contrast to other forms of therapeutically applied daydreaming, it stands out as being highly systematized and, in terms of bringing the unconscious portion of psychological problems into focus, is capable of being highly structured (Singer, 1974). On the other hand, it permits completely free individual and creative unfolding of the patient's fantasy. Because of this polarity, GAI allows a high degree of adaptation to the personality structures of both the patient and the therapist, as well as to the therapeutic task at hand.

One domain of the procedure includes short-term psychotherapy of from 15 to 30 sessions, and crisis intervention. Another is treatment of longer duration, changing the patient's personality structure with GAI in a comparatively short period of time. The procedure can also be applied successfully to patients with a low level of education. Even in child and adolescent therapy it is superior as short-term therapy in comparison with many other methods, as is pointed out in a recently published book (Leuner, Horn, and Klessman, 1977) about its application for this age group.

Guided affective imagery has historical precursors that focused in an unsystematic manner on the potential of fantasy and the analogy of daydreaming to nightdreaming (Silberer, 1909; Frank, 1914; Kretschmer, 1922), as well as formulations for image meditation (Happich, 1932). The author was not yet familiar with the "other" daydreaming technique of Desoille (1955) when he developed his procedure. The latter adheres to a different basic principle from GAI and is founded on another, less systematic, more pragmatically oriented technique.

2. Theoretical Foundations

Like all daydreaming techniques, the concept of GAI and its formulation were an outgrowth of experience with the state of deep psychophysical relaxation that occurs spontaneously at the point of falling asleep or waking up (Silberer, 1912), and that can also be systematically produced by means of relaxation techniques such as those of Jacobson (1928) and the autogenic training of J. H. Schultz (1970), or through simple verbal suggestions of relaxation by the therapist. In this manner a regressive level of experience is attained that can give spontaneous rise to optical phenomena of an imaginative nature.

Thorough studies of fantasies thus produced, e.g., in the "filmstrip thinking" of Kretschmer (1922), have shown that they give expression to the subject's unconscious problems in the form of images, and that the manner in which they appear follows Freud's dream theories

(Freud, 1900). Fantasies of this kind therefore provide direct information about deeply rooted psychopathology. From a technical point of view, unsystematically created fantasies are not adequate when the goal is to develop a procedure for a systematic daydreaming technique.

As an additional constituent impulse to relaxation, substantive models that free psychological material in the hypnagogical field of experience—at first free of consciousness—had to be introduced. This is easily accomplished by asking the subject to imagine something specific in his hypnagogic state. If, for example, it is suggested to him that he imagine a house, he can usually achieve this without difficulty. Phenomenologically speaking, an object in fantasy generally remains characteristically colorless and must be held in place by a certain willful assertion of mental energy. However, in a state of relaxation a new impulse appears. The object of fantasy becomes considerably more vivid; it increases in color and plasticity, develops into a three-dimensional object, and is located in surroundings through which the subject can walk in his optical fantasy. For example, he can walk around the imaginary house and observe the rear of it. In other words, at the full realization of the fantasy stimulated into being by therapists (catathymic fantasy), a quasi-realistic and perceivable world develops in the consciousness of the subject or patient. He is able to move freely in this world of optical fantasy, although he is always aware that he is in a state artificially fostered by the therapist, and that the things he perceives in his daydream therefore do not represent reality.

At fullest immersion in the catathymic fantasy, the person in question is strongly emotionally involved, and his feelings correspond to the content of the daydream. Precise observation has shown that there is a close functional correlation between the state of relaxation and the stimulated motif in the fantasy. As the fantasy becomes more active, the state of relaxation deepens; this, in turn, renders the fantasy increasingly more lively and colorful, which brings about a further deepening of the relaxation state. Thus, a cyclical process is developed that places the subject in a deep hypnoid state, despite a minimal initial level of relaxation, without resorting to or attempting hypnosis.

3. Mobile Projection

Suggesting the idea of a fantasy to a patient provides a structured field of experience (at first empty of content) in a mild state of relaxation, even when the request to imagine something is deliberately given quite vaguely by the therapist. Initially, the subject is to imagine any house or other building, and not, for example, a specific home or a house that he likes. From a psychological point of view, what we have here is a projective test. Analogous to the TAT, in which a picture is given to the subject with a request to make up a story about it, or to the World Test for Children, in which the child is to create a scene from the plethora of available play material, the material produced by suggestion in GAI corresponds to the structure of the unconscious psychodynamics. The vague suggested motif serves as a crystallization point, with the purpose of stimulating a projective process in the realm of visual fantasy. The image emerges by means of a projection into darkness and is experienced one meter before the patient's closed eyes. Because of the lack of specified material, in contrast to the above-mentioned projective test procedures, every emotional reaction, no matter how small, is immediately projected onto this screen. Thus, every change in the subject's emotional state also stands out, abruptly and without hindrance. We call this "mobile projection."

The possible uses of mobile projection are many. Two examples should suffice to make that clear:

3.1. Diagnostic Aspect

This is an example of the diagnostic aspect, with simultaneous management of the therapeutic process (Swartley, 1963). On top of a mountain (a standard suggested theme or motif) climbed in her daydream by one of the first patients I treated with GAI, my patient imagined an old castle ruin that blocked her view into the valley. This image repeated itself often in testing, in which I asked her to imagine the same situation on the mountain top over and over. She could "see" every detail, every individual stone of the unchanging ruin standing there. I took the patient into treatment after she had been on the waiting list for eight weeks. After I knew her case history well, I decided on a direct interpretation of the image of the ruin, which was a fixed stereotype ("fixed image" type) and therefore necessarily had special significance for her. The patient had lost her father at the age of seven through her parents' divorce. She had loved him very much, but had never seen him again. I myself associated with the image of the ruin a sort of chivalrous romanticism, little girl's dreams, and an Oedipal situation.

I had formed the hypothesis that if a correct interpretation was made, that is, one that corresponded correctly to the symbolic content of the image, a transformation or complete change in the image would occur, in the sense of mobile projection (transformation phenomenon) (Leuner, 1954). And that is what happened: I cautiously offered my patient an interpretation of the image of the ruin. Shortly afterward, the ruin, which until then had been repeatedly imagined in a stereotypical fashion, changed. Stones fell from the walls, which became thinner and lower. The next day I asked her to imagine the same situation again. Now the ruin had completely collapsed. Only a few stones lay on the meadow, and the patient had a beautiful view of a sunny summer landscape spread out at her feet.

3.2. Spontaneous Projection

This is an example of the mobile projection, during a *spontaneous emotional change* which is the result of life events. The same patient, in the same stereotypical manner, when asked to imagine a house, had imagined various different houses, which nonetheless all served business purposes—for example, an office building, an inn, a bakery; the dwelling rooms were all for single occupancy only and were located in a tiny space up under the roof. During the patient's stay at the clinic, she fell in love with an attractive older man, and could often be seen walking with him. My hypothesis was that, insofar as a house is an expression of one's own personality, the patient's acute love feelings would present themselves there directly. Once more I asked her, without specification, to imagine any house. She spontaneously imagined a forester's house in the middle of the woods, surrounded by a large garden. In the garden she found large ripe pumpkins and long cucumbers. In the house she found a library on whose walls hunting rifles and deer antlers had been hung. One can hardly imagine a clearer representation of Freudian symbolism in the garden and house. I now wondered to what extent my twenty-year-old patient, still behind in the development of her feminine identity, was ready to realize more intimate relationships. I therefore inquired about the bedroom of the house. She entered a room under the roof. Two beds stood far apart on opposite walls, and between them was a window. As I expected from my knowledge of her case, she was apparently unable to imagine a marital type of situation with a double bed.

The simple, informal experiments recounted here confirm a number of hypotheses:

1. The structuring of the imaginative field through inner conflicts
2. The presence of mobile projection with transformation phenomena onto fixed (stereotypical) images
3. Relatedly, manipulation of the effect of the imagery as a result of either therapeutic intervention or spontaneous penetration of experience

3.3. Synchronic Transformation

In addition to transformation caused by direct intervention in the imagery, and to interpretively significant spontaneous transformation caused by life events, we found a phenomenon that we called "synchronic transformation." It is based on the following observation.

In the course of therapy, changes can also occur in those images in the fantasy that are not brought about either by therapeutic intervention or by life experiences, but that seem instead to turn up involuntarily more or less in passing. An example is the view from the mountain to be climbed. As therapy progresses, the landscape observed by the patient from the mountaintop changes little by little, without ever being therapeutically addressed. The landscape at the beginning of therapy is often desolate, as it looks in Germany perhaps in March or late winter. Vast woodlands often stretch out into the distance, and signs of human activity are scarcely to be found—no towns or cities, no streets, no railroad tracks, no traffic, no people in the fields. In the course of a therapeutic effort of 20 to 30 sessions, the landscape, intermittently recalled, gradually changes into a summer landscape, right through to the ripening of the grain. The woods are broken up by streets and railroads. Towns appear, men work in the fields, and in the distance a larger city can be seen. This synchronic transformation occurs in the most varied realms of the imaginative panorama of the landscape as therapy progresses, during which time specific lines of development can be identified. This phenomenon, observed regularly in successfully progressing treatment, confirms two further hypotheses:

1. Apparently independent variables, expressed by contents of imagery, can be applied to analysis of the therapeutic process.
2. All motifs of the fantasy are dynamically associated with one another and mutually influence each other. Theoretical propositions of holistic psychology and Gestalt psychology find support here (Salber, 1960).

4. Bringing Core Conflicts into Focus

I will now return to the structuring of the field of experience by use of an imaginary motif offered by the therapist. In this connection we put forth the hypothesis that, as a consequence of the reality of the meaning underlying a symbolic motif in neurotic patients, typical cycles of conflict can quite often be brought to projective representation

(Leuner, 1955a; Zepf, 1973). We follow the model of a computer by trying to recall the relevant data on the individual conflict from the memory bank. We cautiously request the patient to imagine certain standardized stiuations. Such themes can center directly on particular realms of conflict or, by their broad structure, stimulate the projection of problems as yet unidentified but perhaps pressing and acute. An example of such directed focus could be inhibited aggression in the broadest sense, often a relevant realm of conflict in neurotic persons. Here is an example:

A patient had been sick for a year with severe cardiac neurosis, could no longer work, became depressed over it, and suffered from vegetative disturbances. He had the external appearance of a strong, healthy man. When I tried to reconstruct the event that had triggered the appearance of the symptoms, I discovered that the cardiac fear symptoms had appeared after an accident. The patient worked in a VW repair shop. When he was about to make an adjustment on the motor of a car and the customer turned on the engine, the car moved backward toward the patient (the customer had forgotten to take the car out of reverse gear). The patient was pinned against the wall of the shop. In medical terms this was a trivial trauma. The next day the cardiac complaints began, from which the marked syndrome soon developed. The patient characterized the customer as an arrogant man who had annoyed him for years, but said he had not been able to retaliate because with him the "customer is king." There was no doubt that the patient suffered from expressly inhibited aggressive urges and that the minimal aggression of the customer, against which he had not been able to defend himself, had triggered his symptoms.

It was my intention to confront the patient with the extent of his aggressive inhibition and to get for myself some diagnostic hints for the therapy to be taken—for example, the extent of the aggressive inhibition in the patient's self-perception. For the purpose of directly addressing the realm of conflict between aggressive feelings and the ability to carry them out, I chose, on the basis of certain considerations, the motif of a lion. I requested the patient to imagine a lion. A masculine lion appeared, well formed and without peculiarities. Now I tried for an encounter between the lion and the patient's adversary. I asked him whether he could imagine the customer he disliked in an encounter of that sort. He could, and the customer appeared on the scene. I expected the lion to demonstrate a reaction appropriate to the patient's aggressive disturbance. This expectation was confirmed. When the adversary appeared on the scene, the lion pulled in his tail like a timid dog, moved toward the patient, and lay down at his feet. In so doing he shrank to the size of a lap dog. This mobile projection in the form of the behavior of the lion (as symbol and core of the realm of conflict of "aggressive readiness") when confronted with an aggressor demonstrates what is evident without further scientific proof—the inability of my patient to take aggressive action against an opponent.

I then treated the patient with GAI. After 25 sessions the symptoms had improved considerably. Four weeks after an attempt at returning to work I saw him again and carried out a test. I had the lion appear again, and thereafter the unloved customer. The scene had now changed. When the adversary appeared, the lion ran toward him. The man ran, with the lion behind him and appearing to catch up. At this moment, however, a wall appeared. The man jumped over the wall, and the lion followed. In other words, the inner stage-manager of the daydream blocked the patient's view of the expected aggressive act. The patient, so to speak, spared himself the confrontation with the obvious battle. In his actual behavior, however, the patient had taken a different attitude and developed his career with the help of improved ability to cope effectively with competitors.

This example clarifies the principle of bringing important areas of conflict into focus in GAI by means of an imaginary motif or theme suggested by the therapist.

The motif of the lion and some of the themes yet to be described are structured to focus closely on a particular problem. We also have thematic suggestions (a meadow, for example) that permit a wide range of projections; these motifs are suitable for the projection of existing problems without addressing them directly.

5. Standard Themes

The following overview surveys the 10 standard motifs of GAI and their most commonly occurring symbolic content (Table I). It must not be forgotten that the motifs can address many different problems of the patient, since the projections produced are always of an individual nature and any given theme may be interpreted differently depending on the individual patient's history. Collective interpretations can only be adopted as generalizations, and only for a certain percentage of the patients in question. Precise analysis of the antitheses of collective and individual meanings of the prescribed imagery brings us to the old dialectic of collective and individual symbolic interpretation that dates back to Freud and Jung.

The interpretations of the standard motifs presented in the following section therefore have significance only as guidelines.

5.1. Standard Motifs of GAI

5.1.1. Elementary Level. The elementary level is intended for the therapeutic trainee and can be considered the general foundations of the therapy.

5.1.1a. Meadow. Frequent starting point for stimulation of the daydream. From here the GAI can develop on an individual basis. The meadow is fitting as an entrance motif because of its overwhelming pleasant qualities. It calls up fantasies of the Garden of Eden, of summer sunshine, of fertility, of the chance of rest and encountering people, and of common experience. Persons with neurotic disturbances, however, project their problems here already. In depressives, for example, the meadow can be infertile, brown, and burned; in people who feel caged by a compulsive personality structure, there is often

Guided Affective Imagery

Table I. Overview of the Therapeutic Instruments and Strategies of GAI

Level	Standard motifs	Structure	Therapeutic techniques	Management models (symbolic operation)
Elementary	1. Meadow	broad	I. Training procedure	a. Reconciliation
	2. Brook	medium broad	II. Unfolding of creative fantasies	b. Feeding and enriching
	3. Mountain	broad		
	4. House	medium broad		
	5. Edge of the woods	broad		
Intermediate	6. Encounter with relatives	narrow	III. Associative procedure	c. Inner pacemaker
	7. Sexual attitudes (rosebush, take a lift)	narrow	IV. Night dream	d. Confrontation
	8. Aggressive orientation	narrow	V. Bringing acute conflicts into focus	
	9. Ego ideal	narrow	VI. Introspection of bodily organs	
			VII. Satisfaction of wishes and archaic needs	
			VIII. Working-through	
			IX. Transference analysis	
Advanced	10a. Cave	broad	X. Combination with conventional psychoanalysis	e. Tiring and weakening
	10b. Swamp	narrow	XI. Graphic representation of imagery	f. Magical fluids
	11. Volcano	narrow		
	12. Folio	broad		
Musical GAI (1–8 Focusing possible)			III. Associative procedure	
GAI in groups (1–8 Focusing possible)			A. Individual fantasies	Feedback techniques
Didactic possibilities			B. Group fantasies	

a small meadow bordered by a barbed-wire fence. A sixteen-year-old adolescent boy saw a bunker on the meadow, such as those found in World War II, but without a door or other opening. It appeared as a symbol of his own contact disturbance and communication problems. The correlation between the frequency of certain imaginary situations in the meadow motif and other standard motifs with certain types of experience and behavior patterns can be statistically investigated. That has been done, for example, for the depressive affect (Prindull, 1964).

5.1.1b. Brook. After many trials, we adopted and developed further other motifs in nature that originally appeared spontaneously in the meadow motif. The patient is asked, for instance, whether he can imagine a brook in the meadow. As a rule he is able to do this. We presume that the brook, as a flowing body of water, can be followed from its source to the sea, to some extent as a conduit of the emotional development and unfolding of the person. The patient is directed to think of following the brook as a goal to be achieved in his fantasy, and, as he chooses, to follow the brook either upstream to its source or downstream to its mouth. Return to the source often symbolizes a "return to the breast," whereby we think of oral relationships to the maternal world. The clinical impression predominates that in patients who have difficulty drinking the spring water (e.g., because no water comes from the spring, the water tastes bad, they fear it could be poisonous or contaminated), an early disturbance in the area of oral drives is suggested.

While pursuing the brook downstream, neurotics often come upon what we call obstructive motifs, that is, situations that hinder the free flow of the brook. They find blockades, the water falls into a deep hole and disappears underground, or it pours into a large reservoir or small pond from which it cannot flow out again. In the course of treatment these obstructive motifs are pushed further and further back, until finally the considerably improved patient can follow the course of the water to the sea without difficulty. This motif can also serve as an indicator of therapeutic progress.

5.1.1c. Mountain. The task is to view a mountain from the meadow and, after exact description of the mountain, to try to climb it. From the peak the patient should have a panoramic view. The mountain motif suggests the masculine-paternal world in general and thereby also the authority and rivalry question. A study by Kornadt (1958) yielded evidence of a statistically significant correlation between the height of the mountain and the subject's level of aspiration. Depressive patients either have very low mountains or the opposite, extremely high ones that they refuse to climb. Admiration of masculine authority or fear of male predominance is depicted in attributes that indicate how viewing the mountain is experienced emotionally. Inability to climb the mountain suggests neurosis of considerable degree. Minimal willingness to climb it suggests a low level of motivation to achieve. The ability to have a panoramic view in all directions from the mountain represents the behavior of a healthy person. The disturbed person has a limited view, whereby characteristics of the perceived landscape once more offer clues to the nature of the disturbance.

5.1.1d. House. In connection with the house motif in dreams, Freud himself referred to the slogan designating a friend as an "old house." He recommended regarding the house motif as an image of the individual's personality. Entering a house can also be conceived of, however, as a sexual motif, though this is relatively rare. Imagining the house is usually no problem for the patient. Depending on the type of disturbance from which he suffers, it can be a small hut, an uninhabited barn, a feudal mansion manifesting the unconscious wishes of the person in question, or a purely functional building without living quarters. Viewing the interior is revealing: the kitchen, symbolizing the oral sphere; the common rooms, the floor, and the basement, in which memorabilia such as family albums may be found; the bedroom; and the contents of closets with clues about partner relationships and the Oedipal situation (proximity of the patient's clothes with those of other people). Dependence on parents, grandparents, and other people can also be expressed in the house motif. As a rule it leads directly to the patient's problems and signifies for him a powerful confrontation with deeply repressed conflicts, which should therefore be offered to him with the greatest caution.

5.1.1e. Edge of the Woods. In the beginning we avoid having the patient enter the woods, which not infrequently can be found in the vicinity of the meadow. The woods are generally seen as a symbol of the unconscious. By some, especially children, they are experienced as a sanctuary of security, and by others as a place of threatening dangers. Fairy tales such as *Hansel and Gretel* provide important clues. A mildly depressed twenty-year-old female patient with marked conversion symptoms encountered in the woods a group of former friends who had all died an unnatural death. Among them was a former fellow patient who had committed suicide and who, in the patient's fantasy, offered her poisonous berries with the request to follow her into death. Depressed patients often get lost in the woods, which creates difficulties for the therapist.

In order to avoid that sort of undesirable incident, in this motif the patient is led to a sheltered spot in the meadow from which he can look into the darkness of the woods. He is told in advance that figures, either humans or animals, will sooner or later step out of the woods.

Both types of figures, experience has shown, can be identified as dynamic structures that C. G. Jung characterized as "shadows." They are unconscious behavioral tendencies and wishes that are tabooed by the patient's superego—for example, when a gunman emerges from the woods in the imagery of an impotent man, or a young girl sees a lone tramp, a shy deer, sometimes a cunning fox or other animals from a mouse to a snake, all these take on meaning. The mere fact that these figures, slumbering in the dark until now, see the light of day, has diagnostic and therapeutic effect.

5.1.2. Intermediate Level. The intermediate level is intended for the therapist in advanced training.

5.1.2a. Encounter with Relatives. Father, mother, or their derivatives, siblings, the patient's own children, and bosses can be summoned either in symbolically disguised form (an elephant as father, a cow as representation of the maternal world) or also as the actual person. The behavior of these figures toward the patient (behavioral observation) is informative, as soon as the attempt is made to have the patient approach them, talk to them, and touch them, in order to ascertain his unconscious attitudes toward them.

5.1.2b. Motif for Testing Sexual Attitudes. For men we make use of the poem by Goethe entitled "Das Heidenröslein" ("The Hedge-rose"), in Schubert's famous song. We ask the male patient to imagine a rosebush at the edge of the meadow. Then we ask him to pluck a rose and put it on the table at home. [Singer (1974) assumes that transcultural values would prevent the American man from having anything at all to do with flowers.] An eighteen-year-old saw delicate white roses that were "too delicate" to be plucked; a man with long-standing marital problems found only a withered rose, but in the background he saw two "wild shoots" with which he associated his extramarital relationships.

5.1.2c. Motif for Clarifying Aggressive Orientation. The motif of the lion mentioned above has stood the test. The lion can exist in free hunting ground, it can lie on the ground lazily and idly, it can appear harmless due to its soft, beautiful coat and felinity and like to be petted, it can jump through a burning hoop at the circus, it can pace back and forth in a cage, and much more.

5.1.2d. Motif for Manifestation of the Ego Ideal. The patient is instructed to give without forethought the first name of a person of the same sex, and subsequently to visualize the person to whom this name belongs. Relatives and friends usually appear, often people possessing particular characteristics the patient would like to have had, that is, people who have played an important role as competitors in the patient's life. In women this is often another woman, of opposite hair color and with qualities the patient feels lacking in herself. Working through this motif can lead to clarification of identity problems.

5.1.3. Advanced Level. The advanced level is intended for the fully trained therapist.

The following symbolic figures are motifs that call forth deeply repressed archaic material above all.

5.1.3a. Cave Motif. As in the woods motif, the subject is first asked to imagine himself in a place at a safe distance from a cave, and to wait to see what emerges from it. As an "opening of the earth" this theme taps deeper material than the woods motif, and releases a stronger dynamic. Often giants, ghosts, and animal figures appear that clearly suggest behavior patterns of which the patient is not aware, even if he also demonstrates them in real life. The patient with cardiac neurosis mentioned above, for example, observed a bear that came out of the cave, lay down on the meadow, and fell asleep. The bear seemed to symbolize not only the patient's physical strength, but also the underlying tendency of this man, who had always been hardworking and industrious, to live lazily and idly as he did during the time of his illness. Entering the cave can also have the meaning of introitus in the sexual sense. Finally, entering the cave can lead to an encounter with the make-believe world of the earth's interior, with fairy-tale-like content, and can also give expression to deeply repressed wishes and unconsciously initiated actions.

5.1.3b. Swamp Motif. This was introduced on the hypothesis that boggy soil has aspects of anal "partialism" (Freud), a snake can be related to creation, and in our civilization it simultaneously represents the frequently abhorent world of filth (anal defense). A related aspect is that of "anal-eroticism" found in some sexually immature persons.

The patient is told ahead of time that a swamp will appear at the edge of the meadow. He is to stray at a safe distance and observe the swamp, from which some figure will emerge. As a rule heterosexual figures appear—at first archaically a frog, a snake, a giant fish that snaps, but also a naked man in the case of a female patient, etc. The patient attempts to coax the figure onto solid ground, and in some circumstances to feed it (compare above). The material set forth here generally releases a strong anxiety-ridden dynamic. For this reason this motif is reserved for the advanced level, since its application remains the province of only very experienced and highly trained therapists. Therapists should be warned against using it in patients with a weak ego structure.

5.1.3c. The Volcano. The introduction of a volcano is based on the idea that eruptive processes from the depths of the earth can be represented here; synonymously eruptive, e.g., undirected and strong, pressing aggressive impulses of the patient. The motif is well suited for crisis intervention in patients with accumulated aggression. Not infrequently eruption does not take place in the fantasy. The volcano can then be viewed from above by flying over it in a helicopter. One then often finds that the volcano has cooled down, or that there is a steel lid on it preventing the eruption, as an indication of existing repressive tendencies. If the volcano erupts, an instant unloading of the patient's pressing aggressive impulses can be attained. Objects can sometimes be pulled from the volcano that offer a direct clue to the patient's problems, such as the shoes of a patient's husband that she feels she always has to polish, or pots and other domestic items if the patient hates her role as a housewife, etc. Occasionally the eruption is so powerful that it destroys surrounding villages and towns as a singular indication of self-destructive impulses.

5.1.3d. Folio Motif. In patients who come up with little material, or with whom the therapist has the feeling that he should rummage around more deeply, this motif is a possibility. The patient is told ahead of time that there is a picture book buried somewhere, usually in the basement of the house, and that he is to search for it. Usually a volume of pictures, sometimes an old Bible, is found. The patient is requested to look at the pictures closely and to describe them. The material is partly in archaically coded form, but it does give clues to underlying behavior patterns that otherwise would not be apparent until much later. This motif is also to be used with the greatest caution, since the basic technology of GAI adheres to the notion that the only material to be used is that which allows the patient's psyche to express itself spontaneously and without resistance (analogous to Freud's contention that only surface material should be worked with).

The very brief presentation of the basic motifs provided here may give the impression that they serve largely diagnostic purposes. In the form of ISP, Swartley (1963) has already described this aspect of the themes. It is true, as has already been shown, that the procedure can be viewed as a highly sensitive projective test. The proper approach toward the patient's fantasies in therapy, however, is decidedly different from a purely diagnostic orientation. I will expand on this later. In any case, the standard motifs described here serve the following purposes: (1) they give the patient a starting point for the daydream; and (2) they identify various conflict areas in loose sequence and allow the patient to develop his own projections freely, with the primary aim of bringing him face to face with them at first preverbally and later also verbally, that is, confronting him with them carefully and with restraint. Insight is thereby gradually transmitted that has been designated by Kosbab (1972) as "self-interpretation of the imagery in GAI."

6. Therapeutic Techniques

In the therapeutic techniques of GAI we find a polar structure just as we do in the system as a whole. On the other hand, the therapy can be highly structured at the beginning of each session by the use of standard motifs.

6.1. Specific Techniques and Strategies

6.1.1. Training Procedure (I). In this technique, the patient practices starting each session with one of the standard motifs, in order to be led spontaneously further from there (Leuner, 1970).

However, the therapist can loosen this structure by allowing the fantasy to unfold from the introductory motif in an individual and creative fashion (II). Newer studies, such as Landau (1976), have given extraordinarily positive insight into the creative potential, which so far has not been fully utilized. Whether and to what extent the creative scope of the imagery increases from session to session can indeed serve as a measure of therapeutic progress in GAI. Prestructuring a therapeutic session by suggesting a standard motif to the patient at its onset can further this process. In patients who have a great deal of difficulty in setting their creative imagination free, the next session can be more strictly and specifically structured by the use of more detail. The therapist can guide the course of the fantasy and elicit more precise observation of its imaginary content with questions and hints. This detailed structuring has disadvantages in addition to the advantages. It evokes certain transference reactions of the patient toward the therapist, such as a feeling of dependence similar to that between pupil and teacher or child and parent—situations in which accomplishments are expected and demanded. These transference reactions can stimulate an emotional response of pliancy, subordination, and dependence.

6.1.2. Associative Procedure. In polar contrast to such an experimental orientation of the standard motif at the elementary and intermediate levels, we have developed the associative procedure (Leuner, 1964). In analogy to the free associations of classical psychoanalysis, the free associative river of the fantasy of the patient for whom the procedure is appropriate is stimulated by loosely structuring its initiation with a broad motif such as a meadow, brook, or mountain. Associations in GAI are made in "pictures" rather than in words. In a fashion similar to the verbal chain of association in psychoanalysis, the associatively connected pictures here repeatedly circle the relevant core conflict, and impulses and resistances act on each other until finally the core conflict or infantile trauma is resolved. The associative technique is undertaken with a minimum of direction and an extremely reserved therapeutic approach. Beyond that the therapist can, by the use of technical measures, expand the associations either into the past, in order to identify the genetic roots of the conflict, or into the present in order to work out real situations in everyday life and characteristic maladjustments. The goal is to work through this material in order to make the interrelationship between the images and the current maladjustments and their respective origins clear to the patient.

The deliberate directing of the daydream in the experimental procedure described earlier (elementary level), accomplished through its emphasis on guiding the daydream (in contrast to the associative procedure), guarantees the patient explicit protection from unexpected negative images and impulses that cause, for example, anxiety or depression in severely disturbed patients. The associative technique of the intermediate level is, by contrast, based on the assumption that the patient has a strong enough ego structure that the images and impulses, powerful at times, can be taken, so to speak, in self-prescribed doses. They can then be tolerated by the patient without strong attack on the ego and worked through in the sense of "suffering and bearing it" and therefore also as catharsis of traumatic neurotic impulses. This technique demands of the patient as well as of the therapist that he be able to confront and tolerate his anxiety; at times it can be very trying, especially when archaic, that is, regressive, strongly emotion-packed material forces its way into consciousness. The experienced therapist choosing to apply the associative procedure knows how to integrate elements of the experimental procedure into it in order to give the patient some degree of protection in appropriate situations on the one hand, and on the other hand to bring the negative impulses and affects to light in a therapeutically fruitful way. The associative procedure has the great advantage that age regressions often occur spontaneously, in which a psychic trauma of early childhood can be dealt with, relived, and brought to abreaction (Barolin, 1961). This plastic reenaction of early childhood is known to us otherwise only through the use of hallucinogens (Leuner, 1962) or in hypnosis (Leuner, 1971). Therapeutically it is especially effective (Schneck, 1955). In GAI, flashes of the past stand in organic connection to spontaneous confrontations with current conflict-ridden problems that are a part of a determining dynamic network that includes behavioral patterns in the patient's present life.

6.1.3. Reinstatement of Night Dreams (IV). Night dreams, especially uncompleted ones, can be recalled in the fantasy of GAI and continued as a daydream in order to determine their expected endings under the therapist's protection. It is also possible, by guiding the dream, to offer solutions that the night dream never found.

6.1.4. Bringing Acute Conflicts into Focus (V). Instead of structuring the daydream by means of a thematically defined standard motif, the attempt can be made to leave the structuring to a dormant acute conflict. The potency of its imaginary symbolic representation often leads to a convincing confrontation for the patient. Spontaneous or carefully directed trial actions and imaginatively realized solutions can thus be strived for. The technical procedure is that in an introductory conversation the conflict is addressed emotionally. In the subsequent initiation of GAI an especially broad motif is chosen that is of emotional significance for the conflict-ridden person, either symbolically or realistically—for example, a problematical person appears from the woods.

6.1.5. Introspection of Bodily Organs (VI). Either the patient is asked to imagine that he is looking from the outside into bodily organs that ail him, or he undertakes a journey through his own body as in *Gulliver's Travels*. To this end he makes himself small, enters through the mouth, and inspects the affected organ. A study by Roth (1976) examined psychodynamic representation in tension headache, and another by Freiwald, Liedtke, and Zepf (1975) in *Colitis ulcerosa* and cardiac neurosis with special attention to the manifested object relationships. However, the therapeutic significance of this technique should not be overestimated.

6.1.6. Satisfaction of Wishes and Archaic Needs (VII). We have only recently discovered that an unexpected therapeutic effect can occur if the therapist always takes on an especially permissive attitude when the patient seeks to satisfy wishes and archaic needs. The latter includes above all the need for devotion and shelter with oral overtones ("anaclitic therapy"). From a psychoanalytic point of view, conflicts related to resistance strategies can be avoided, and frustrated needs can be met through regressive completion of emotional phases of development. We must also consider the idea that only in GAI is a conflict-centered and confrontation procedure therapeutically effective. Even in cases where overwhelming patterns of resistance become apparent, clinical success, especially in psychosomatic cases, can be attained by uninterrupted use of the associative procedure (Leuner, 1964). Resistance structures are evidently transformed, and lead to a strengthening of the ego (Leuner and Wächter, in press).

6.1.7. Working-through in GAI (VIII). As in the recommendation for psychoanalytic short-term therapy, working-through resistances and repetition compulsion in the personality in GAI does not play a decisive role, since GAI is generally carried out as short-term therapy (up to 30 sessions). However, working-through can be initiated wherever long-term behavior modification therapy directed at the neurotic personality structure and repetition compulsion becomes necessary, as long as the patient is able and willing and the therapist is suitably trained.

The experienced, psychodynamically oriented therapist will have no difficulty working-through the material, often spontaneously evident, in the form of confrontation with the use of meaningfully introduced imagery. In this way, self-analytic impulses will be stimulated, and certain firmly entrenched behavior patterns will resolve themselves through abreactions and recourse to early genetic roots. In our opinion, there is therefore less need for classical working-through in GAI than there is in psychoanalysis. We have developed certain techniques for working-through in GAI, such as goal-directed confrontation with pathological behavior patterns. We tend to prefer them to verbal working-through, which can also replace them in part.

6.1.8. Transference Analysis in GAI (IX). For reasons to be explained later, analysis of transference does not play a central role in GAI. However, the psychodynamically trained therapist should be able to interpret imagery in GAI at the transference level. In cases where transference resistances hinder the progress of therapy, they must be attended to verbally with psychoanalytic techniques so that they can be brought to light by means of fantasies, in which acute conflicts are brought into focus.

6.1.9. Combination with Conventional Psychoanalysis (X). This combination can ensue in three forms (Leuner, 1970): (a) The material already treated in GAI can be worked on further by expanding the field of associations. This can be especially important for sophisticated personalities. The patient brings to the next session a detailed record of a previous GAI session (taken from the tape recording), which then becomes the basis for further treatment. (b) GAI is introduced as a tool in conventional psychoanalysis, in order to resolve stubborn resistance patterns. (c) GAI may serve as a substitute for dreams in patients who don't dream.

6.1.10. Graphic Representation of Imagery (XI). GAI therapy can be effectively supplemented by having the patient draw self-selected sequences from his fantasies (or having him set them to music). This material can be treated further in a therapeutic session such as that described in (III) above, or, if necessary, in a group session with other patients.

6.1.11. Music and Related Group Techniques. Because of limited space, the use of music for stimulation of fantasies in GAI (Leuner, 1974b; Leuner and Nerenz, 1964; Nerenz, 1965, 1969) and related group techniques (Kreische, 1977; Plaum, 1968; Sachsse, 1974, in prep.) will not be discussed here.

7. Management Models in Symbolic Drama (Symbolic Operation)

Our experiments led to another method of structuring the imaginative field: involving the patient in directed activity at the symbolic level. Its makeup grew out of observations of spontaneous courses of action. From these observations we drew the following hypothesis: Certain dramatic activity or reactions during the fantasy that are characteristic of the primary process in dreams (Freud, 1900) can be used for direct intervention in the unconscious dynamics and thereby also for rapid changes in behavior, without having to address them verbally or even interpret them. We call this technique, described below, "symbolic operation" (Leuner, 1957). All of these operations require of the therapist carefully thought-out goal definition and a precisely described therapeutic demeanor.

7.1. Two Examples

Two simple examples will demonstrate the mechanics of symbolic operation. Another will point out the dangers of faulty operation, as well as theoretical implications.

Example 1

A 20-year-old chemistry student, whom I knew well from long-standing counseling of his family, came to see me during my office hours. He had an exam to take at his institute, and had done well on the test with a lower-ranking faculty member. However, when the department chairman tested him routinely, the student experienced affective disturbance and was not able to mobilize his knowledge. He was then given the opportunity to repeat the test the next day. From my knowledge of the family I had no doubt that the patient had transferred his considerable fears of his father, a high-ranking military man, onto the professor. Psychoanalytic treatment of the problems in the father-son relationship would have necessitated lengthy therapy. In the matter at hand, crisis intervention was indicated. On the basis of my previous experiences, in this patient's case I applied a management model of symbolic drama that I have designated as "feeding and enriching" and "reconciliation." I asked the patient to imagine that the chemistry professor was stepping out of the darkness of the woods. After lengthy resistance this was accomplished. I now suggested to the patient that he overcome his timidity, greet the professor, and begin a conversation with him. Once again this was possible after considerable hesitation. Finally, I suggested to the patient that he ask the professor to join him for a picnic on the meadow, and indicated to him that he had in his bag all the things necessary for a picnic, chicken, bread, and a bottle of good red wine. With some resistance the professor accepted the invitation. After some time both men sat on the meadow, eating eagerly and drinking wine. The mood improved considerably, and when the picnic was over, each gave the other a friendly slap on the shoulder. A reconciliation had taken place. I asked the patient to imagine once more before going to bed, that he was giving the professor a great deal to eat, and pointed out that an attitude of great generosity (in contrast to the retentive attitude of many neurotics) was especially important. The next day the patient reported to me with some satisfaction that he had passed his exam with the professor without affective disturbance.

We deal with many examples of this sort. The father-son problem of the patient was certainly not resolved by this procedure. But at least it was temporarily successful in better assimilating the hostile and overpowering introjected father image. A great deal of significance should be attributed to the reconciliatory aspect (Stierlin, 1969).

Example 2
In this case, I would like to give an example of premature and faulty (overpowerful) application of symbolic operation. A thirty-two-year-old war widow with three children was in treatment with me for severe character neurosis, maladjustment, and psychogenic disorders. Over a long period of time she repeatedly found her grandmother in the imaginary house, lying sick in a farmhouse bed. This grandmother, from whom the patient stood to inherit a large farm, had in fact played an extremely significant role in her illness. When therapy had apparently failed to resolve this dependence on the dominating grandmother image, I believed I should proceed more vehemently and with a higher level of intervention. I asked the patient to throw her grandmother out of bed and to drive her from the house. The grandmother reacted with rage, but finally disappeared into the nearby woods. On the following day the patient called me. She seemed very upset, and said she had not slept all night and felt "split in two." She could find no peace and was tortured with guilt feelings about her grandmother. I had the patient come to the clinic and asked her to reimagine the scene. The grandmother came out of the woods and appeared tired and hurt. I recommended to the patient that she take the grandmother back into the house. She succeeded without effort. At the end of the 30-minute session the patient stood up from the couch, felt considerably relieved, no longer "split in two," and was completely appeased.

From a number of similar observations we developed the hypothesis that a functional unity exists between the imagery and the patient's unconscious dynamic structures. "Operative" intervention in the symbol can directly affect the intrapsychic dynamic conflict structure.

7.2. Theoretical Excursus

These empirical findings receive theoretical support in the concepts of symbolic psychodynamics as found ontogenetically in psychological development (e.g., of an infant) (Buhler, 1931) and in the psychology of so-called primitives (Werner, 1953), as well as in regressive processes, for example, of schizophrenics (Beneditti, 1965). Such cases follow the mechanics of the primary process (Freud, 1900): the imagery is not a reflection of the inner psychic state, but rather is experienced as the state itself. For example, when the subject-object barriers are removed by controlled regression of GAI (hypnoid state), the grandmother image above encompasses the sum of all the patient's experiences with her grandmother. The grandmother has now become *introjected*, a part of the patient's self. The grandmother's departure from the house in the patient's fantasy is for the patient *psychic reality;* a portion of her identity is thereby taken from her. The image of the grandmother is more than just an image; it is with full inner obligation a piece of the patient herself. That is why the patient suffers during enactment of the symbolic operation and afterward feels disturbed and "split in two." The psychoanalytic hypothesis about introjection that becomes part of the ego finds empirical confirmation here (Leuner, 1960). This example can serve as a model for the dynamic interaction noted here and can also give an important clue as to why systematically and thus conceptually correct intervention on the part of a therapist directing the daydream, especially in the form of management models, can have direct therapeutic effect and is suitable for crisis intervention. As the example shows, however, the therapist must be warned against explicitly rational intervention (oriented to the secondary process). In therapeutic training for GAI, the trainee must learn a demeanor that is oriented to the primary process. The management models described below are an alternative between highly structured manipulation of the experimental procedure on the one hand and the completely unstructured nature of the associative method on the other. Above all, they offer a means to handle actively the rising symbolic figures. We proceed from the observation that in GAI a progressive, therapeutically supportive principle and a conversely directed neurotic principle are represented (Leuner, 1955b), and that both can appear in opposition to each other in symbolic-dramatic form. The management models were developed in order to lend support to the therapeutic principle in situations with that sort of conflict, that is, in order to weaken the functioning neurotic principle (Leuner, 1957). The latter occurs through assimilation of neurotically separated imaginary material, as described in the example of the exam anxiety of the chemistry student, or through liberation of accumulated feelings of hate with the tendency to act out aggressive impulses. In addition, positive imaginary material or authority figures can temporarily take on a leadership function in the daydream ("pacemaker") (Leuner, 1969).

The following management models have proven themselves worthy of being included in the standard instructions for GAI:

7.3. Elementary Level

7.3.1. Reconciliation. In this model attempts are made at reconciliation with strange or mildly hostile figures by approaching them with gestures, touching, and demonstrations of tenderness, that is, behavior indicating well-intentioned acceptance of these figures. One example of such reconciliation is the last act of the chemistry student's encounter with his professor: After the picnic he touched him, slapped him on the shoulder, and both engaged in friendly laughter.

7.3.2. Feeding and Enriching. This model is based on the idea that in the case of hostile symbolic figures, an oral gift, in the form of food offered in generous quantities, leads to pacification of the figure and subsequent assimilation, e.g., reconciliation. Not only symbolic figures such as animals or humans can be "enriched" by this method, but also such symbols as holes in the ground or other very abstract images; in the latter instance, analogous and interpretatively appropriate symbolic material (for example, in the case of the hole as a feminine symbol, a large ball to be thrown into the hole) can be added. In all probability a transformation phenomenon will be stimulated, in a therapeutically positive direction. An actual transformation of the symbolic figure may occur: For example, a figure may lose its hostile nature because it is satiated and therefore tired and comfortable, and fall asleep.

7.4. Intermediate Level

7.4.1. The Pacemaker (Leuner, 1969). Positive figures in symbolic drama, such as friendly animals, a maternal figure, a friendly, helpful giant, or the magic carpet in the fairy tale *A Thousand and One Nights*, can serve as leadership figures for the patient, who is requested to confide in them. He often reveals to them important symbolic material that can lead to resolution of a conflict or to new material.

7.4.2. Confrontation (Leuner, 1955c, 1975). Confrontation is an explicitly active and directive method in dealing with hostile figures. It leads to rapid abreaction of anxiety and other affects. Similarly, it can lead to quick transformation of symbolic figures in a therapeutically positive direction. The technique works as follows. The therapist stops the patient face-to-face with a hostile figure and asks him to describe it precisely, to describe the expression of the eyes, to stare down its hostile look, and to banish the figure with his own look. With the support of such suggestions from the therapist, the patient's anxiety is liberated and the figure changes its outward appearance. Occasionally a few sessions with this confrontation technique are enough to successfully treat the phobias of children and adolescents, at times even of adults, in the sense of problem-oriented therapy. Connections to behavior therapy are clear; however, our basic therapeutic assumptions are of another sort.

7.5. Advanced Level

7.5.1. Tiring and Weakening. Experience with and understanding of this management model is associated with the often spontaneous tendency of patients to attack symbolic figures they recognize as hostile. Dynamically, an anal-sadistic or reactive hate impulse is present in such cases as a rule. It is not infrequent that the aggressive feelings that surface are directed at part of the person himself (self-destruction). A cautious management technique has therefore proven valuable, which can be applied in a therapeutically successful way without danger of traumatization. Instead of directly attacking the symbolic figure, as the patient would often prefer, he is generally advised to harm the figure little by little. The patient is asked to chase the figure (a hostile animal, a witch, death in the form of a skeleton) through the countryside, in order to exhaust it gradually until, as a rule, it finally collapses and dies. Sooner or later, a transformation phenomenon usually takes place, and brings about a rapid change of behavior. This occurrence documents the powerful effect of this management model.

7.5.2. Magical Fluids. On the basis of our hypotheses, there is no imagery in GAI that does not possess great symbolic significance for the patient. That is also true, of course, for any fluids that appear spontaneously in the landscape or in association with symbolic figures. Therapeutic effects can manifest themselves even in the water of the brook or a lake, or in the fresh water of a spring from which the patient can drink. Water can be experienced as refreshing or revitalizing. Physical symptoms can disappear when the affected body regions are massaged with water. Transformation phenomena can occur. These can only be explained by the existence of functional unity between the imagery and the dynamic structure of the patient.

For example, a female patient in a constant state of nervous excitement requested permission to swim 20 minutes a day in GAI, an experience that gave her great joy and soothed her. After six days her condition had improved considerably. She was allowed to leave the hospital, and the planned thyroid operation was cancelled. Even more unusual effects are caused by the application of bodily fluids such as cow's milk, human breast milk, saliva, or even urine. Application of these can sometimes have highly explosive effects, so that only the trained and very experienced therapist knows how to handle it. We do recommend the use of water, however, for the elementary and intermediate levels as well.

In review, the management models of symbolic drama outlined here are arranged in order of the respective levels of the therapist's training. They are to be applied with greatest caution, under supervision, and only when a genuine need for their use is indicated. Theoretically, they are founded on the concept of symbolic operation mentioned above and on the notion of functional unity between symbol and dynamic innerpsychic structure.

8. Investigative Findings

The introduction of a new psychotherapeutic procedure is justified only when it makes possible the attainment of therapeutic goals that exceed those of other procedures in some way, even if only because of its simplicity or easy teachability. We are aware, of course, of the problems inherent in comparing the efficacy of psychotherapeutic procedures.

8.1. Literature

In the literature, a number of advantages of the procedure are pointed out, which will be repeated here, at first only briefly.

Even at the elementary level, GAI accomplishes a substantial amount of therapeutic work. The elementary level can be learned by therapists who are trained in general psychotherapy in a discernible period of time (about two hundred hours) by regular participation in seminars and courses, as well as in supervised clinical cases.

The duration of treatment in GAI, compared with other procedures, is surprisingly short. *Short-term therapy* from 15 to 25 sessions has had significant results in controlled statistical studies (Wächter and Pudel, in press; Kulessa and Jung, 1977).* Follow-up observations up to eight years later have shown that the number of relapses is limited.

GAI therapy does not treat individual symptoms, but rather *exerts influence over a broad psychodynamic base* in the affected person by working with sometimes pressing preconscious and unconscious ma-

---

* *Bibliography for the KB-Therapist*, AIGKB, Göttingen, 1967 (through the Secretar D-34 Göttingen, von Sieboldstrasse 5).

terial: frequently it spontaneously aims at the core conflict. This explains why various simultaneously occurring symptoms can be considerably improved with GAI even in short-term therapy. This point is illustrated in the study by Roth (1976) reported in detail below. Women with psychosomatic abdominal problems have not only lost these symptoms through short-term therapy, but have lost existing frigidity and dyspareunia at the same time without the couples therapy that is recommended today for such cases.

Moreover, GAI is well suited for *crisis intervention* with the help of goal-directed techniques centering on the problem in question.

With technical modification the procedure can be used with especially good results in the treatment of children and adolescents, as well as drug addicts (Leuner *et al.*, 1977).

8.2. Statistical Studies

Three controlled statistical studies of the efficacy of GAI in clinical treatment will be reviewed here in abridged form. In all three cases, the subjects were patients who had been referred to the outpatient department of a psychiatric university clinic and who had been randomly placed into the treatment program. One can assume that these cases represent a negative selection compared to the average patient clientele, since psychiatric university clinics represent on the whole the "last resort" after other therapeutic attempts by practicing physicians, practicing psychiatrists, and psychotherapists have failed.

8.2.1. Program 1. Fifteen women between the ages of eighteen and thirty-five who suffered from psychosomatic gynecological symptoms were treated by Roth (1976) at the psychiatric clinic of the University of Bern (Switzerland). The therapy was designed so that each patient was treated as long as was necessary, until the expected success came about. Therapy took anywhere from 6 to 50 sessions. Table II lists the symptoms and reports the improvement reached by therapy; symptoms, duration of treatment, and improvement ($N = 15$).

Four patients interrupted therapy prematurely, some because of transference problems and others because of insufficient motivation. Follow-up was made on the average after 10 months. Roth emphasizes that in contrast to the couples therapy of Masters and Johnson (1970) or to any other cases where there is an inclination to treat both partners, in GAI this is no longer required for the treatment of women's sexual dysfunctions. A further advantage was found in the fact that bleeding and other functional disturbances were addressed simultaneously through GAI. Preselection of patients according to their symptomatology or selection according to the severity of the symptoms was not

Table II. Roth Study. Results of GAI Therapy Administered to 15 Women (Aged 19–35) with Psychosomatic-Gynecological Problems by Number and Type of Problem (Length of Treatment 6 to 50 Sessions)

Symptom	Number of patients	Cured/ improved	Unaffected
Secondary amenorrhea	1	1	—
Premenstrual dystonia	8	6	2
Dysmenorrhea	6	4	2
Dyspareunia	6	4	2
Organic problems	12	8	4
Absent or lowered sexual desire	3	2	1
	35	22	11

necessary, since the procedure is not symptom-centered therapy. Correction of disturbances in marital relationships was apparently effected spontaneously through behavior change in the women treated.

8.2.2. **Program 2.** Wächter and Pudel (in press) presented a controlled study with 14 randomly selected neurotic patients referred to the psychiatric clinic of the University of Göttingen (Germany) and treated with GAI.

This group was contrasted with a control group of 15 patients on the waiting list. The duration of treatment and period of waiting were about the same. This was also true for the grouping of patients by age, duration of symptomatology, and diagnoses (Tables III, IV, and V).

Table V and Figure 1 show the result of the change in condition before and after treatment with GAI in comparison to the control group. The result was a significant improvement in measures for psychosomatic difficulties and psychopathological symptoms in contrast with the control group, which demonstrated only random changes.

Table III. Wächter Study. Short-Term Psychotherapy with GAI of 15 Sessions, with Grouping of Patients by Age and Duration of Symptomatology

		GAI-group	Control-group
N		14	15
Male/female		4/10	10/5
Average age (years)		27.3	28.3
from/to (years)		18–39	18–40
Duration of	0–2	1	1
symptoms (years)	2–5	5	5
	5–10	6	7
		8	9
	more than 10	2	2
		14	15

Guided Affective Imagery

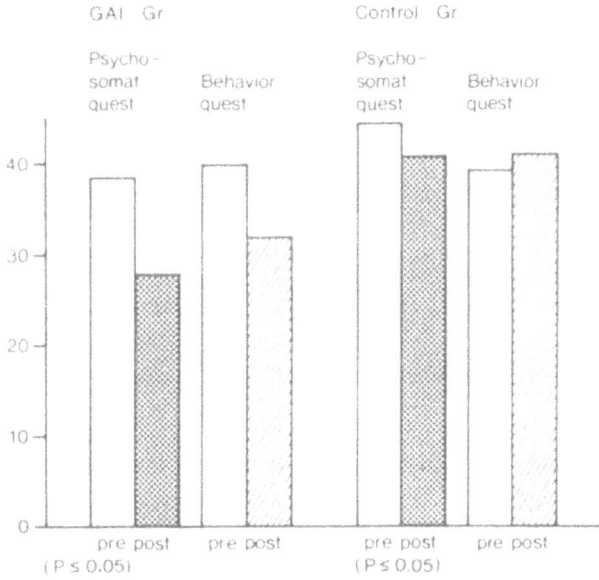

Figure 1. Study of Wächter. N = 14, GAI group; N = 15 control group. Short-term psychotherapy pre/post values of the Giessen list (psychosomatic questionaire) and the Göttingen list (psychopathologic questionaire).

Table IV. Wächter Study. Short-Term Psychotherapy with GAI of 15 Sessions with Grouping of Patients by Diagnoses

Diagnoses	GAI-group	Control-group
Depressive neuroses	3	5
Anxiety states, phobias	6	5
Abuse	2	2
Borderline	1	—
Psychosomatic diseases	2	3
	14	15

Table V. Wächter Study. Pre/Post Values, Giessen and Göttingen Lists

Questionnaire	GAI-group pre/post			Control-group pre/post	
Psychosomatic list (Giessen)	38.67	27.6*	(D 10.05)	44.6	40.6
Manifest behavior (Göttingen)	39.8	33.25*	(D 10.05)	39.4	40.6

* $P > 0.05$ t-test.

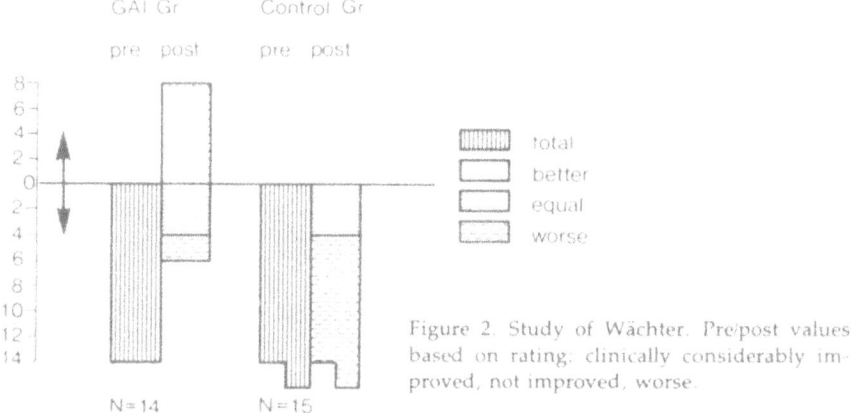

Figure 2. Study of Wächter. Pre/post values based on rating: clinically considerably improved, not improved, worse.

Clinical judgment of a rating team can be seen from Figure 2. Of the 14 patients treated, nine from the GAI group improved by one or two levels, two remained unchanged, and three got worse ($p > 0.01$). Psychological tests that measure influence on neurosis, extraversion, intraversion and rigidity (N-NR-E) according to Brengelmann (1960), as well as manifest anxiety (Taylor, 1953), show that a comparison of data from the GAI group with that from the control group demonstrates a significant improvement for anxiety and a nearly significant improvement for neurosis through GAI (Fig. 3). The other data, which according to Eysenck (1959) measure stability of personality, remained unaffected by the therapy.

8.2.3. Program 3. A newer study by Kulessa and Jung (1978) gives results of GAI therapy of 20 sessions administered to 26 similarly randomly chosen outpatients with psychoneuroses and character disorders, as well as vegetative disturbances (Table VI, VII, VIII and Fig. 4).

Table VI. Short Term Psychotherapy with GAI of 20 Sessions with Grouping of Patients by Diagnoses[a]

Clinical-diagnostic grouping	Number of patients
Phobias and anxiety neuroses	9
Depressive symptomatology	6
Cardiac arrest phobia	2
Psychosomatic disturbance	2
Sexual dysfunction	3
Character neuroses	3
Acute adjustment reactions	1
	26

[a] Kulessa and Jung, 1978.

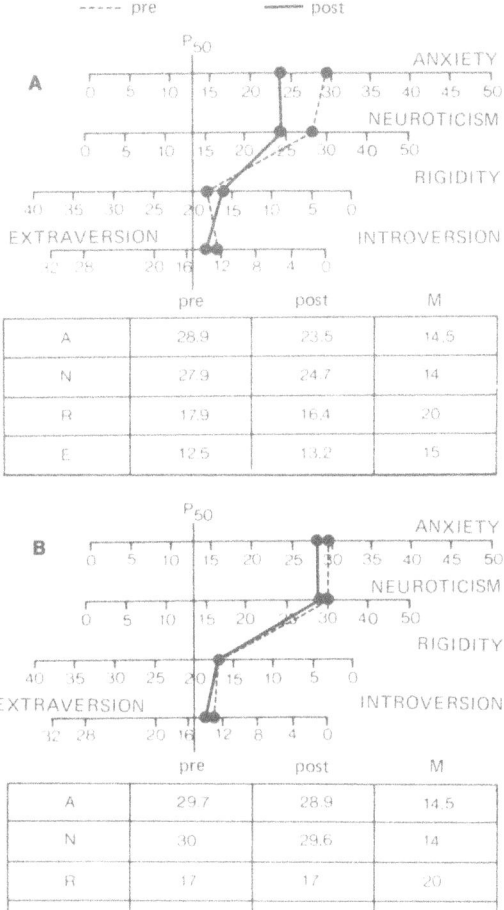

Figure 3. Study of Wächter. Pre/post values in anxiety (Taylor); neuroticism, rigidity, and extra-introversion (Brengelmann). (A) GAI group (15 sessions, 54 days treatment period); (B) control group (46 days waiting list).

Table VII. Short-Term Psychotherapy with GAI of 20 Sessions with Grouping of Patients by Duration of Symptomatology[a]

Duration of symptoms	Number of patients
Less than two years	1
2 to 4 years	7
5 to 9 years	9
10 years or more	9
	26

[a] Kulessa and Jung, 1978.

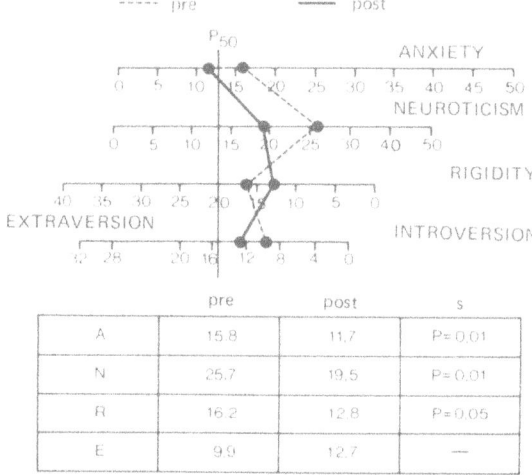

Figure 4. Study of Kulessa. $N = 26$, 20 sessions GAI; pre/post values in anxiety (Taylor); neuroticism, rigidity, extra- introversion (Brengelmann).

Table VIII. Kulessa Study. Changes in Psychosomatic Problems Effected by 20 GAI Sessions, Giessen List ($N = 26$).

Zenz syndromes[a]	Mean score		T	DF	p
	Pre	Post			
Chronic fatigue	7.08	2.50	2.8	25	0.009
Cardiac/circulatory problems	5.73	2.65	0.46	25	0.640
Stomach/intestinal problems	4.00	21.5	2.0	25	0.052
Shoulder and neck pain	4.08	2.04	4.0	25	0.010
Vegetative symptoms	6.81	3.27	2.5	25	0.023
Sexual and sleep disturbances	2.58	0.96	3.7	25	0.013

[a] The syndromes found by Zenz to be statistically significant are presented. The significance of syndromes I and IV is on the 1% level, and of syndromes V and VI just within the 2% realm.

8.3. Case Histories

This statistical material will be supplemented by clinical illustration of the achievements of GAI through five briefly presented patient histories.

Case 1 (Dr. A. B., 1976).
A thirty-two-year-old doctor had suffered for eight months from a disturbance related to work that finally came to a dramatic climax. During his most recent faculty

appointment, he had failed to complete a large quantity of written work such as patient records and forms, "work that weighed me down like a heavy boulder." Finally, a depressive state of complete helplessness developed, in which he cried and capitulated in the face of the increasingly urgent and numerous sharply worded letters of admonition from the head office of the clinic. In this condition the doctor called up a clinical psychologist whom he knew well, and presented his problem to her. In a GAI session of about 50 minutes over the telephone from a distance of 200 kilometers, the following crisis intervention took place. After a few verbal suggestions of relaxation, the therapist introduced into the patient's fantasy a vacation landscape in southern France known to him. There, she said, was a rocky mountain that the doctor was to climb. Finally, he made his way to the top with effort, and expressed a desire to climb the old tower standing there. The door to the stairway was locked, so, gathering all his strength, he scaled the steep outer wall of the tower. There he found the key to the door, and could now also let his lady companion in. The session ended with both sitting very relieved and relaxed up in the tower, enjoying the "overwhelming panorama" and watching a sunset. With one session the severely depressive state had improved considerably. In the next few weeks the doctor had finished what he was working on constructively, and in two or three months had completed the "gigantic mountain of forms" in a "surge of energy." (He later took training in the therapeutic techniques of GAI.)

The apparently severely depressed patient owed this success to a crisis intervention of 50 minutes of GAI over the telephone, in which the motif of mountain-climbing was used with the help of a therapist 200 kilometers away. The appropriately applied motif brought the young man's problems symbolically into focus. By accomplishing the task posed in the one-hour session, a behavior change of short latency set in, through which the patient was able to solve his problem himself. (Of special interest is the fact that a transference situation is indicated in the fantasy: at the point of reaching the set goal the therapist is present in the fantasy.)

Case 2 (Dahlgren, 1973).

This is a history of short-term treatment of chronic depression in 10 sessions with GAI. A thirty-five-year-old married female patient had suffered since 1965 from chronic depressive affect. When she began therapy with GAI on April 5, 1971, she had already carried out two suicide attempts, had been treated as a psychiatric inpatient five times, and was treated regularly as an outpatient with psychoactive drugs. The first interview, undertaken as preparation for treatment with GAI, uncovered a 10-year-long frigidity. Her marital relationship with her husband, who suffered from multiple sclerosis (no impotentia coeundi) and was bound to a wheelchair, was not hopeless despite the patient's aversion to the man. It seemed that the relationship between the partners, which had always been strained, contributed considerably to the depressive mood of the patient who was in any case contact-inhibited. In the patient's record we find the following entry after the fifth session: "The patient came beaming but somewhat nonplussed to treatment. She said that the last time she had gone home, she had fallen on her husband with kisses and caresses. He wondered whether she was "enchanted." Her husband wanted to meet his wife's therapist to express his thanks. The reason no intercourse had taken place between the married couple was that the patient wanted to spare her husband, who had recently undergone an operation.

After the tenth and last session the patient wrote in a letter to the therapist: "For me this was a fantastic form of treatment. After having believed that I was nothing but an ice-cold woman, I have now become a warm and loving human being. It changed our married life unbelievably. I must confess that I was skeptical at first, but as therapy progressed I noticed a change. I was spurred on when my husband, too, noticed a change. I hope that many patients can be helped in this way." Follow-up over three and a half years gave no hint of relapse into the depressive state. The patient felt even-tempered and balanced, and could also cope with other crises such as the now appearing impotence of her ailing husband.

Case 3 (Wächter and Pudel, in press).

A twenty-two-year-old student of education suffered from depressive moods, fatigue, somatic disturbances, and a primary symptom of diffuse anxiety and inner unrest that occurred daily in spells, as well as labile self-esteem, lack of concentration, and fear of academic pressure that severely affected his studies. These symptoms had existed ever since he had begun the study of German literature four years before; he had given up this study early on because he suffered from crying fits. Two further attempts at studying at another institution likewise ran aground. The diagnosis was designated as "anxiety neurosis with hypochondriacal traits." Verbal therapy (Rogers) enabled him—with effort—to work in a library to earn some money. Treatment in a psychiatric university clinic had been unsuccessful. GAI treatment followed in the framework of a controlled therapeutic program of 15 sessions. The therapist was Dr. H. M. Wächter from the psychiatric clinic of the University of Göttingen.

After completion of treatment the patient had become clearly more self-assured and active. His anxiety had disappeared completely. His ability to concentrate had improved. He took up his studies again and had his first successful experience with them. Six months after completion of treatment he wrote to the therapist: "The semester will soon be over, and I can say that for the first time in a long, glorious student career I have attained all the goals I set for myself. Realistically and with almost no trace of neurosis, I have faced all obstacles that threatened me with failure." He reported that he had resumed his artistic endeavors and was preparing his first exhibit of his pictures and posters.

Case 4 (Wätzig).

A thirty-six-year-old merchant suffered from the development of anxiety neurosis with cardiac symptomatology and depressive mood. The symptoms had existed for 23 years. The patient was referred from the Neurology Department of the University of Kiel, where he had been thoroughly examined for a brain tumor because of violent headaches on one side. For three months he had been unable to work in his store or to drive a car, and had avoided contact with other people because of his attacks of anxiety. For years he had been taking tranquilizers and sleeping pills regularly in dosages from medium to high. Because of many physical problems he had been thoroughly examined on many occasions, both as an inpatient and as an outpatient, always without any sort of pathological finding. The situation at home was disharmonious. The patient had always been an anxious child and even in childhood had neurotic symptoms such as bedwetting and thumb sucking, which in part lasted into adulthood. He felt rejected by his father, who favored the older brother. When the patient was seven his father had been killed in a bomb attack. The patient himself sustained head and leg injuries and was only able to walk again after several operations. Later he was often sickly, and blamed difficulties in school on his "war injuries." He had an overprotective upbringing, and his mother allowed him no association with the opposite sex. The main symptom of his anxiety attacks, "fear of heart stoppage," first appeared when the patient was confronted by a lady boss whom the patient experienced as threatening. GAI therapy was introduced in a six-week inpatient treatment, then continued on an outpatient basis with weekly sessions. At the end of the inpatient treatment (about 25 sessions), the massive attacks had already ceased. The patient was able to control other anxious reactions. He had it out with his overprotective mother, increasingly asserted himself socially, became completely competent again in his business, and at the completion of treatment after eight months was able to take a vacation for the first time without his mother and free of anxiety attacks. Follow-up analysis one year later showed that the patient had maintained a relatively stable condition since the completion of treatment.

The example shows the potential of GAI to treat even an extreme chronic neurosis with a necessarily poor prognosis in a relatively short period of time.

Case 5 (Wächter and Pudel, in press).

This last case is an example of failure in short-term therapy with GAI due to poor motivation of the patient and inability to change. A twenty-four-year-old economist suffered from contact problems, shyness and inhibition (especially with women), nervous unrest in encounters with other people, as well as depressive moods. The symptoms had begun five years earlier when he allowed his parent to choose his area of study and, dissatisfied with his own lack of decision-making ability and dependence on his parents, began to drink. In his history it is interesting to note that he had neurotic symptoms in childhood up to the age of eight, and treatment attempt at a student counseling service and with a neurologist has been unsuccessful. His behavior during treatment with GAI was conspicuous for his strong tendency to overanalyze and intellectualize. The patient soon developed an ambivalent, even negative, attitude toward treatment, which he approached passively. He was not capable of expressing his feelings of transference.

The results of treatment were unsatisfactory. Subjectively the patient did experience the treatment as pleasant and soothing, but stated that it could not fully contribute to the solution of his problems. He said merely, "Of the last six years of my frustration about one and a half have been made good again"; his passive expectation of failure is clearly expressed in this statement. His problems remained untouched; however, the patient had at least come to realize that he needed more of his own initiative to solve them. He gave the impression of being somewhat more calm, and did reach the point of taking a bank job (which was below his capabilities).

Unfortunately, because of limited available space, it will not be possible to relate long passages from individual histories of patients treated with GAI and to discuss their relationship to the case history. Detailed casuistic reports of this kind have been published elsewhere (Adelsson, Ahlborn, and Ask, 1976; Henle, 1977; Holfeld and Leuner, 1969; Koch, 1962, 1969; Rechenberger, 1963).

8.4. Didactic Possibilities

In the training of psychiatric residents and psychotherapists of all kinds didactic possibilities can also contribute to the positive findings in studies on GAI. Kosbab (1972, 1974) has investigated and published ways in which it can be applied in the training of psychiatric residents. Additional wide-ranging possibilities were collected from experience in seminars of ISGAI* and its sections (Leuner, 1977). Beyond training

---

* International Society for Guided Affective Imagery and Imagery techniques in Psychotherapy and Psychology, Secretar: Friedländer Weg 30, D-34 Göttingen (F.R.G.)

therapy specifically for GAI, they helped to increase general sensitivity to the dynamics of unconscious processes, associations in psychoanalytic symbolism, and transference and countertransference relationships, including their nonverbal aspects.

9. Some Theoretical Reflections on GAI

At various points in the text I have already referred to hypotheses we made where no other hypotheses were available, and which formed the basis for the dynamic phenomena of the fantasies as presented above.

A few additional psychoanalytical viewpoints, of interest in the context of GAI, will be discussed below.

9.1. The General Psychodynamic Concept

Guided affective imagery represents a broad psychodynamic concept. The procedure is rooted in every theorem of personal psychodynamics. Its scope covers unconscious motivation, the interpretation of symbolism, resistance mechanisms, and the role of transference and countertransference, as well as the therapeutic significance of liberating affective impulses. The author is of the opinion that psychoanalysis, as based on Freud and developed further, including the most recent theory of "primitive internalized object relations" (Volkan, 1976), offers the most suitable dynamic concept for GAI. But the ideas of C. G. Jung, to whom the author owes much of his intellectual stimulation for GAI, also form a theoretical foundation for the method. The so-called archetypical symbols, however, also go back to primitive object relations, as shown in experimental investigations of the technique of symbol confrontation (Leuner, 1955c). Fear of the "manipulation of archetypes" in the daydream technique, expressed by representatives of the Jungian school, can be regarded as irrelevant from theoretical and practical aspects (Leuner, 1955c).

9.2. What Is Therapeutically Effective in GAI?

The question of efficacy presents major problems in every psychotherapeutic method. One must rely on clinical observations and judgments, as well as on the drawing of comparisons. The simple statement that GAI is effective because it brings unconscious and preconscious psychodynamics into consciousness (Freud's thesis: from *id*, *ego* must be made) is not sufficient; in part it is even wrong, because a large portion of the metaphorical content of the fantasy is only partially or not at all conscious in the cognitive sense. The following overview will sketch our conception to date of the effective aspects of GAI, without elaboration.

1. During the daydream, the patient is *protected from anxiety* by the therapist and engages in dialogue with him, whereby a considerable portion of both rational-intellectual and character defense mechanisms are run under.

2. Problematical unconscious material is uncovered step by step at the patient's own rate, with the help of refined introspection through the hypnoidally changed state of consciousness.

3. The conflict (represented by a perceivable object in fantasy) has a countereffect on the defense structure, as a result of the easy displacement of libidinous cathexis through liberation of feelings and affects ("microcatharsis").

4. The testing of actions on the fantasy level [as opposed to Freud (1915), who designated thinking as the way in which actions are tested] is made possible.

5. Relatedly, special effectiveness is attained by giving impulse to the patient's creative potential, which allows him to anticipate solutions to problems on a metaphorical level.

6. The patient can act out defenses and basic urges in fantasy, as well as *"catch up"* on atrophied oral, libidinous, and expansive-aggressive basic needs, ultimately on a regressive-archaic level.

7. Infantile traumatic scenes are reawakened (age regression), whose abreactions ultimately lead back to the basic conflict and subsequently to an attempt at a corrective emotional experience [new beginning in the sense of Balint (1970)].

8. Goal-directed working-through is demanded by confrontation with the substantive content of the repetition-compulsion.

9.3. The Nature of Transference Relationships in GAI

Precise examination reveals that transference relationships exist on many levels in GAI. On the one hand, transference is characterized by the controlled regression of the patient during the hypnagogic daydream. Following R. Spitz (1956), we can speak of an anaclitic transference (submissive type, Freud), that is, submitting to the therapist who calls forth the daydream, is responsible for it and guides it, and submitting to the world of the developing fantasy. On the other hand, there is the "infantile patient" (Spitz) in GAI, in a relatively independent position in the "other world" of his fantasies. He has to deal with their content intellectually, encounter dangers, and accomplish assigned tasks. He can even be stopped and asked to ponder over any problems that arise. In this way, the role of the patient in GAI as we see it is considerably different from that in psychoanalysis (e.g., Spitz). Depending on the therapeutic approach, the protective role of the therapist or the self-reliance of the patient is increased. This cooperative situation is consciously enhanced by the setting in the daydream session. Instead of sitting behind the head end of the couch as in conventional psychoanalysis, the GAI therapist sits next to the patient at head height. If desired, each can look at the other. Emotionally, a peer situation is consciously intended by this arrangement; the therapist accompanies the patient on his excursions into the strange inner world of emotion-laden fantasies. This concept can best be illustrated by the following model: as in the old technique of diving excursions, the patient steps from the surface (a ship) and goes underwater. All ties to the outside world are regulated by the leader of the expedition from on board the ship. Oxygen is provided through a hose, instruments are supplied for completion of the mission, and suggestions and comments are made by telephone. The diver's activities and experiments on the ocean floor and the unexpected dangers and problems that arise must be dealt with by the diver alone, but he can always seek advice from the leader of the expedition on board ship.

This model (Leuner, 1970) covers a portion of the specific transference relations found in GAI, with respect to the polarity between the patient's self-dependent activity and his dependence on the therapist. This joint probing of the psychological depths creates a unique working alliance, in which the patient is both performer and recipient of analysis. All his ties to reality and the outside, i.e., the parts of his mature ego, are thus delegated to the therapist.

In training for GAI therapy, a nondirective approach is learned. It is based on the therapeutic variables of the Rogerian method (Rogers, 1973; Kretzer and Breuer, 1974), supplemented by the congruence of the substantive context. It is then possible in practical GAI therapy, especially under the conditions of short-term therapy, to guide the course of treatment for long passages in the framework of a "positive transference." This stable transference, very beneficial to therapy, is given decisive support by an additional factor. Instead of projecting infantile feelings onto the therapist, as occurs in psychoanalytic techniques in which the therapist is the only projective screen, in GAI it is the fantasies that receive the overwhelming proportion of the projective dynamics of the acute conflict in question. Relatedly, all transferences can be perceived together on the fantasy level. This situation makes treatment with the daydream technique much less trying than verbal psychoanalytic therapy, and explains why in many cases it can be completed without the disturbing transference resistances of psychoanalysis. If these resistances do occur, however, it is often (a) because of the narcissistic dominance of a therapist who may seem endowed with magical qualities (a situation that is avoided by emphasis on the peer-setting), or (b) because of the expectation of increased demands on the patient to "produce" imaginary material. The experienced therapist learns in his training how to detect the transference reactions of the patient and his own countertransferences as well as how to analyze transference resistance in complex therapeutic situations.

9.4. Symbolic Concepts

First of all, GAI makes use of psychoanalytic symbolism as found in the dream theories of Freud (Leuner, 1974a). The images in the subject's optical fantasies are understood as phenomena of regressive psychic functions produced by the hypnoidally altered state of consciousness. They thus follow the functional laws of the primary process (Freud, 1923; Redlich and Freedman, 1966): condensation, displacement, repeal of the thesis of contradiction, increased emotional excitement, easy displacement of libidinous cathexis, minimizing of the thought process and control of reality, etc. It is therefore immaterial whether or not the imagery represents reality. Every image has metaphorical significance for the subject. The nature of the image is always determined by a variety of factors. It is a form of abstraction from a large collection of emotionally consequential life events (including the renunciation of instinctual drive), which appear under a common qualitative denominator. The symbol is the result of a psychic compromise between instinctual drive and resistance. It can be a symbol for extrapsychic relations [objective level of Freud (1900)] or express innerpsychic problem areas [subjective level of Jung (1960)]; the two frequently interact. Therapeutic intervention in the imagery grasps "with one blow" at the various dimensions of the network of emotional relationships between aggregated portions of experience of the self. The result is the high level of effectiveness attained in daydream therapy, as opposed to purely verbal psychotherapeutic techniques. The hypotheses underlying this concept are empirically and in part experimentally verified, including the differentiated relationships (not discussed here) between regression, level of repression, and the influence of affects or instinctual drive and their symbolic representation. Object relations, as reflected in the imagery, can also be represented quasiexperimentally.

10. Indications

The indications for GAI are relatively broad in scope. They can be outlined briefly as follows:

General Indications
1. So-called vegetative disorders and psychosomatic illnesses
2. Abating of functional or psychic components in internal or other diseases
3. Anxiety and phobias
4. Neuroses with primarily psychic manifestation, with the exception of compulsion neurosis
5. Adjustment reactions due to personality disorders
6. Psychoneuroses and personality disorders of childhood
7. Adjustment reactions in puberty and adolescence

Contraindications
1. Low intelligence with an IQ below 85
2. Acute or chronic psychoses, or prepsychotic conditions
3. Organic brain syndrome
4. Expressly depressive affect (also neurotic type)
5. Poor motivation, even for simple noninsight therapy
6. Expressly hysterical neuroses
7. Symptomatology older than twelve years

11. Summary

1. The psychotherapeutic procedure of guided affective imagery may be distinguished from other daydream techniques by the following basic principle: clearly defined and systematic structuring of the projective field of imagery by means of motifs that serve as crystallization points. Relevant cycles of conflict are thereby stimulated to imaginary-projective representation.

2. Moreover, diagnostic experiments and systematically controlled studies of the psychotherapeutic process are thus made possible.

3. The polar nature of specific therapeutic techniques and strategies

permits their adaptation to the individual therapeutic situation and the therapist's level of training.

4. Goal-directed techniques based on the primary process were developed for therapeutic action with symbolic figures as representatives of object relations.

5. The effectiveness of guided affective imagery is demonstrated in literature and statistical studies, and illustrated with case histories.

6. Theoretical reflections center on psychoanalytic concepts, including recent findings about primitive object relations, which form a valid basis for the GAI procedure. The specific nature of transference in GAI is illustrated with a metaphorical model.

7. The most important indications in neurotic, psychosomatic, and related disturbances are formulated, followed by contraindications.

TRANSLATOR'S ACKNOWLEDGMENTS

I would like to express special thanks to my husband, Kevyn Arthur, for his invaluable editorial counsel, and to my friend, Dr. Jeffrey Blum, for his kind technical assistance.

References

Abralsam, G. La figidité. *Psychosomatic Medicine*, 1972/73, 3/4, 168.
Adelsson, U., Ahlborn, S.-E., and Ask, G. Symboldrama enligt Leuner-en korttidsterapeutisk metod vid behandling av neuroser; 3 fall studier. CDI-arbete Vt-76, Göteborgs Universitet, Psykologiska Instituten.
Balint, M. Therapeutische Aspekte der Regression: Die Theorie der Grundstörung. Stuttgart: Klett, 1970.
Barolin, G. Spontane Altersregression im Symboldrama und ihre klinische Bedeutung. *Zeitschrift fuer Psychotherapie und Medizinische Psychologie*, 1961, 18, 77–91.
Benedetti, G. Die Handhabung der Regression in der individuellen Psychotherapie schizophrener Psychosen. Verh. VI, Internat. Kongr. Psychother. Part I. Basel: Karger, 1965.
Brengelmann, J. C., and Brengelmann, L. Deutsche Validierung von Fragebogen der Extraversion, neurotischen Tendenz und Rigidität. *Zeitschrift fuer Experimentelle und Angewandte Psychologie*, 1960, 7, 291–331.
Bühler, Ch. Kindheit und Jugend. Leipzig: Barth, 1931.
Dahlgren, H. Symboldrama, En pykoterapeutisk metod, Lukasstiftelsens Utbildningsinstitut, Stockholm, 1973.
Desoille, R. Introduction a une psychothérapie rationelle. Paris: L'Arche, 1955.
Eysenck, H. J. Der Maudsley Personality Inventory als Bestimmer der neurotischen Tendenz und Extraversion. *Zeitschrift fuer Experimentelle und Angewandte Psychologie*, 1959, 6, 2.

Frank, L. Affektstörungen. Berlin: Springer, 1914.
Freiwald, M., Liedtke, R., and Zepf, S. Die Imagination des erkrankten Organs von Patienten mit Colitis ulcerosa und funktionellen Herzbeschwerden im experimentellen katathymen Bilderleben. *Zeitschrift fuer Psychotherapie und Medizinische Psychologie*, 1975, *25*, 15-32.
Freud, S. (1900) Interpretation of dreams. In J. Strachey (Ed.), *The standard edition of the complete works of Sigmund Freud*. Chicago: The Hogarth Press, 1953.
Freud, S. (2., 1915) The unconscious. In J. Strachey (Ed.), *The standard edition of the complete works of Sigmund Freud*. Chicago: The Hogarth Press, 1953, Vol. 14, pp. 186-188.
Freud, S. (1923) The ego and the id. In J. Strachey (Ed.), *The standard edition of the complete works of Sigmund Freud*. Chicago: The Hogarth Press, 1953.
Happich, C. Das Bildbewusstsein als Ansatzstelle psychischer Behandlung. *Zentralblatt Psychotherapie*, 1932, *5*, 633-643.
Haronian, F. The ethical relevance of a psychotherapeutic technique. *Journal of Religion and Health*, 1967, *6*, 148-154.
Henle, I. Anwendung des katathymen Bilderlebens bei der Therapie der ehelichen Virginität. In P. Hahn and H. Herdickerhoff (Eds.), *Materialien zur Psychoanalyse*. Göttingen: Vandenhoeck A. Ruprecht, 1977.
Holfeld, H., and Leuner, H. Der Vatermord als zentraler Konflikt einer psychogenen Psychose. *Nervenarzt.*, 1969, *40*, 203-221.
Jacobson, E. *Progressive relaxation*. Chicago: University of Chicago Press, 1928.
Jung, C. G. *Psychologische Typen, Gesammelte. Werke, 9*. 6th edition, Zurich: Rascher, 1960.
Koch, W. Psychotherapeutische Kurzbehandlung somnambuler Fluchtzustände mit dem Symboldrama nach Leuner. *Praxis der Psychotherapie*, 1962, *7*, 1.
Koch, W. Kurztherapie einer zwangsstruktuierten Neurose mit dem katathymen Bilderleben. *Zeitschrift fuer Psychotherapie und Medizinische Psychologie*, 1969, *19*, 187-191.
Kornadt, H.-J. Experimentally excited images as function of dynamic systems. Proceedings of the XIII. Congress Int. Ass. Applied Psychol., Rome, 1958.
Kosbab, F. P. Symbolismus, Selbsterfahrung und die didaktische Anwendung des katathymen Bilderlebens in der psychiatrischen Ausbildung. *Zeitschrift fuer Psychotherapie und Medizinische Psychologie*, 1972, *22*, 210-231.
Kosbab, F. P. Self-analysis in guided affective imagery. *Archives of General Psychiatry*, 1974, *31*, 283-298.
Kreische, R. Technik von 2 Formen der Gruppentherapie mit dem katathymen Bilderleben und ihre Ergebnisse. *Med. Diss.*, Göttingen, 1977.
Kretschmer, E. Medizinische Psychologie. 1st edition, Leipzig: Thieme, 1922. 13th edition, Stuttgart: Thieme, 1971.
Kretzer, G., and Breuer, K. Beziehungen zwischen Gesprächstherapie und Katathymem Bilderleben. In *Ausgewählte Vorträge der Zentralen Weiterbildungsseminare der AGKB*, Göttingen, 1974.
Krojanker, R. J. Leuner's Symboldrama. *American Journal of Hypnosis*, 1966, *9*, 56-67.
Kulessa, C., and Jung, F. Ergebnisse einer 20stündigen Kurzpsychotherapie mit dem katathymen Bilderleben, eine testpsychologische Untersuchung. *Zeitschrift fuer Psychosomatische Medizin und Psychoanalyse*, 1978.
Landau, E., and Leuner, H. Experiences with GAI in the creative process. Göttingen Seminary, 1976 (unpublished).
Leuner, H. Kontrolle der Symbolinterpretation im experimentellen Verfahren. *Zeitschrift fuer Psychotherapie und Medizinische Psychologie*, 1954, *4*, 201-204.

Leuner, H. Experimentelles katathymes Bilderleben als ein klinisches Verfahren der Psychotherapie: Grundlegungen und Methode. *Zeitschrift fuer Psychotherapie und Medizinische Psychologie*, 1955a, 5, 185-203.

Leuner, H. Experimentelles katathymes Bilderleben als ein klinisches Verfahren der Psychotherapie, Ergebnisse. *Zeitschrift fuer Psychotherapie und Medizinische Psychologie*, 1955b, 5, 233-260.

Leuner, H. Symbolkonfrontation, ein nicht-interpretierendes Vorgehen in der Psychotherapie. *Schweizer Archiv fuer Neurologie und Psychiatrie*, 1955c, 76, 23-49.

Leuner, H. Symboldrama, ein aktives nicht-analysierendes Vorgehen in der Psychotherapie. *Zeitschrift fuer Psychotherapie und Medizinische Psychologie*, 1957, 6, 221-238.

Leuner, H. Das Landschaftsbild als Metapher dynamischer Strukturen. In *Festschrift zum 70. Geburtstag von E. Speer*. Munich: Lehmanns Verlag. 1959.

Leuner, H. Die Verifizierung der existentiellen Bedeutung des Symbols durch Symbolprovokation. In B. Stokvis (Ed.), *Aktuelle Fragen der Psychotherapie*. Basel, New York: S. Karger, 1960, Vol. 3, p. 45.

Leuner, H. Die experimentelle Psychose. Springer Serien Heft 95. Heidelberg: Springer, 1962.

Leuner, H. Das assoziative Vorgehen im Symboldrama. *Zeitschrift fuer Psychotherapie und Medizinische Psychologie*, 1964, 14, 196-211.

Leuner, H. Guided affective imagery (GAI): A method of intensive psychotherapy. *American Journal of Psychotherapy*, 1969, 23, 4-23.

Leuner, H. Katathymes Bilderleben. Unterstufe—ein Seminarkurs. Stuttgart: Thieme Verlag, 1970.

Leuner, H. Halluzinogene in der Psychotherapie. *Pharmakopsychiatrie, Neuro-Psychopharmakologie*, 1971, 4, 333-351.

Leuner, H. Grundzüge der tiefenpsychologischen Symbolik (unter Berücksichtigung des Symbolismus im katathymen Bilderleben). In *Ausgewählte Vorträge der Zentralen Weiterbildungsseminare der AGKB*, Göttingen, 1974a.

Leuner, H. Die Bedeutung der Musik in imaginativen Techniken der Psychotherapie. Lecture at the Easter Symposion of the Herbert von Karajan Foundation, Salzburg, 1972. In W. J. Revers, G. Harrer, and W. C. M. Simon (Eds.), *Neue Wege der Musiktherapie*. Düsseldorf and Vienna: Econ, 1974b.

Leuner, H. The role of imagery in psychotherapy. In S. Arieti and G. Chrzanowski (Eds.), *New dimensions in psychiatry: A world view*. New York: John Wiley and Sons, 1977.

Leuner, H. Erinnern, Wiederholen, Durcharbeiten im katathymen Bilderleben. Paper presented at the 5th Central Seminar on GAI, March 27-30, 1976, Bad Lauterberg.

Leuner, H. Guided affective imagery: An account of its developmental history. *Journal of Mental Imagery*, 1977, 1, 73-92.

Leuner, H., and Nerenz, K. Das musikalische Symboldrama und seine psychotherapeutische Wirkung. *Heilkunst*, 1964, 77, 330-341.

Leuner, H., Horn, G., and Klessmann, E. *Katathymes Bilderleben bei Kindern und Jugendlichen*. Munich: Reinhardts-Verlag, 1977.

Leuner, H., and Wächter, H.-M. Kurzpsychotherapie einer chronischen Neurose und Acné excoriée mit dem katathymen Bilderleben (KB), ein Beitrag zur Theorie und Praxis der anaklitischen Therapie, in press.

Maier, H. W. Über katathyme Wahnbildung und Paranoia. *Zeitschrift fuer die Gesamte Neurologie und Psychiatrie*, 1912.

Masters, W. H., and Johnson, V. E. *Impotenz und Anorgasmie—Zur Therapie funktioneller Sexualstörungen*. Stahlberg: Goverts-Krüger, 1970.

Nerenz, K. Die musikalische Beeinflussung des experimentellen katathymen Bilderlebens und ihre psychotherapeutische Wirkung. *Med. Diss.*, Göttingen, 1965.
Nerenz, K. Das musikalische Symboldrama als Hilfsmethode in der Psychotherapie. *Zeitschrift fuer Psychotherapie und Medizinische Psychologie*, 1969, *19*, 28-33.
Plaum, G. Erste Ergebnisse des musikalischen katathymen Bilderlebens in seiner Anwendung als Gruppentherapie. *Med. Diss.*, Göttingen, 1968.
Prindull, E. Die Manifestation der depressiven Verstimmung im katathymen Bilderleben. *Med. Diss.*, Göttingen, 1964.
Rechenberger, H. G. Das Symboldrama in der psychotherapeutischen Praxis: ein Fallbericht. *Zeitschrift fuer Psychotherapie und Medizinische Psychologie*, 1963, *13*, 239.
Redlich, F. C., and Freedman, D. X. *The theory and practice of psychiatry.* New York: Basic Books, 1966, p. 469ff.
Rogers, C. R. *Die Klient-bezogene Gesprächstherapie.* Munich: Kindler, 1973.
Roth, J. W. Katathymes Bilderleben als Kurzpsychotherapie in der psychosomatischen Gynäkologie. *Schweizer Rundschau, Medizinische Praxis*, 1976, *65*, 252-260.
Roth, J. W. Diagnostik und Therapie von Patienten mit Spannungskopfschmerz mit dem katathymen Bilderleben, 1978, in preparation.
Sachsse, U. Über die Psychodynamik in der Gruppentherapie mit dem KB. In *Ausgewählte Vorträge der Zentralen Weiterbildungsseminare der AGKB*, Göttingen, 1974.
Sachsse, H. Gruppentherapie und Gruppendynamik mit dem katathymen Bilderleben im Versuch mit führerlosen Gruppen. *Med. Diss.*, Göttingen, in prep.
Salber, W. Qualitative Methoden der Persönlichkeitsforschung. In P. Lersch and H. Thomae, (Eds.) *Handbuch der Psychologie. Vol. 4. Persönlichkeitsforschung und Persönlichkeitstheorie.* Göttingen: Hogrefe, 1960.
Schneck, J. M. G. Spontaneous regression to an infant level during self-hypnosis. *Journal of Genetic Psychology*, 1955, *86*, 183-185.
Schultz, J. H., and Luthe, W. *Autogenic methods.* New York: Grune and Stratton, 1970.
Silberer, H. Bericht über die Methode gewisse symbolische Halluzinationserscheinungen hervorzurufen und zu beobachten. *Jahrbuch der Psychoanalytischen und Psychopathologischen Forschung*, 1909, *1*, 302-342.
Silberer, H. Symbolik des Erwachens und Schwellensymbolik überhaupt. *Jahrbuch der Psychoanalytischen und Psychopathologischen Forschung*, 1912, *3*, 621-660.
Singer, J. L. *Imagery and daydream—Methods in psychotherapy and behavior modification: The guided affective imagery of Hanscarl Leuner.* New York: Academic Press, 1974, p. 82.
Spitz, R. A. Übertragung und Gegenübertragung. *Psyche*, 1956/57, *10*, 63-81.
Stierlin, A. *Conflict and reconciliation.* New York: Anchor Books, Doubleday, 1969.
Swartley, W. Initiated symbol projection (ISP). In R. Assagioli (Ed.), *Psychosynthesis.* New York: Hobbe, Dorman, 1963.
Taylor, J. A. Personality scale of manifest anxiety. *Journal of Abnormal and Social Psychology*, 1953, *48*, 285-290.
Volkan, V. D. *Primitive internalized object relations.* New York: International Universities Press, 1976.
Wächter, H.-M., and Pudel, V. Kontrollierte Untersuchung einer Kurzpsychotherapie (15 Stunden) mit dem katathymen Bilderleben. *Zeitschrift fuer Psychotherapie und Medizinische Psychologie*, in press.
Werner, H. *Einführung in die Entwicklungspsychologie.* 3rd edition. Munich: 1953.
Zepf, S. Die Beziehung zwischen Motivvorstellungen und imaginierten Inhalten im experimentellen katathymen Bilderleben. *Zeitschrift fuer Psychosomatische Medizin und Psychoanalyse*, 1973, *19*, 157-170.

6

Active Imagining

Eric Greenleaf

1. Introduction

> The analyst may well learn from ordinary life and be guided by it. It is astonishing to see how difficult this can be for analysts. (Guggenbuhl-Craig, 1970)

In the course of this essay I'll describe some guiding principles of the work of active imagining. What I will say about therapy is heuristic; it ought to be tried on for size. If you viewed situations in this way, what would you do? How would you act? What would you say? And are these ways an aid, or at least some comfort, in rough weather? And, did the patient achieve what he came to you for? Can everyone agree, no matter his or her therapeutic language, on the value of the therapy?

Most of these considerations are gauged by appeals to one's own experience of life. Yet, the work has several important antecedents in alchemy, yogic practices, and shamanism and has affinities with several modern investigations into the relationships obtaining among brain functions, perception, language, imagery, and mathematics.

Throughout this writing, I refer to *dreams*, which I take to mean all imaginations—what Singer (1974) calls "oneiric" events—ranging "from those of sleep through daydreaming and waking imaginative thought under conditions of reduced arousal or relaxation," and *active imagining*, meaning dreaming guided by oneself or another person while relaxed and alert.

Eric Greenleaf • Private practice, Berkeley, California.

2. Dream Action and Dream Meanings

> The most valuable part of the dream philosophy presented that I can use and assimilate in my own life is the idea of noninterpretation. All that is needed to resolve a situation is at hand. This makes for action instead of intellectualization. The meanings aren't hidden. The dream action is generally simple and straightforward—often deceptively so.
>
> I had an elaborate dream with four or five people chasing me, and I was very uncomfortable. When I awakened, I could project all sorts of sexual and social implications in being chased. But the next morning I had a sequel dream, or rather a summation dream, and the "meaning" this time was "Don't get ahead of yourself." The idea of not getting ahead of myself because it makes me uncomfortable is not only a more useful idea in my life, but also carries no confusion or guilt or other such baggage with it.
> —Student in a "dream group"

Consider psychotherapy: Two or more persons sit in chairs in a room. Often, one lies down on a couch or pillows. Gesture is generally confined, as is posture; rarely are there integrated, complex actions involving the skeletal muscles, such as occur in sports, sex, war, adventure. There is talk, and the most generous range of emotion and thought and dramatic circumstance. The terror and joy are experienced intensely, but as in the theater or cinema, or in dreams or reverie. All therapies use the night dream and daydream and the odd spontaneous fantasy to promote their efforts. While stressing the likeness the entire therapeutic encounter bears to the situation of dreaming, we also insist on the important aspects in which dreams are to be treated as situations in life.

Now dreams provide a picture of our circumstances in life, and the dreams of therapy are often unresolved situations, most often interrupted by fear or anxiety. The "unfinished business," "fixation," "impasse," or "bind" of a given life is brought before the therapist's attention. He or she must guide the patient through the ambiguity and uncertainty that has brought that life's development to a halt. It is certain that the patient exposition of meaning or pattern in a person's life is salutary, but, as the student's dream of "being chased" makes plain, a type of exposition that promotes action or change is what is called for, not simply one of the several available psychological "interpretations." The dream and active imagining of a patient in analytical psychotherapy elucidates this:

> A year or two ago I dreamed of a gigantic, sheer granite mountain, an overpowering mass, its ruggedness towering above the valley beneath, thrusting its tremendous spires into the sky. I was on a wide ledge of this mountain, so far up that the trees of the orchard below flowed together. I desperately wanted to get off that ledge, away from that threatening, cold grayness, but could find no way though I searched and searched.

Active Imagining

Finally, I saw an old, white-bearded Chinese man sitting at a table near the edge of the ledge. I went to him and told him I wanted to get down the mountain but could find no way. I asked if he would help me. He took me by the hand and led me to a path.

(She comments: Again the dream wasn't saying anything. Where was the hint from the unconscious? The archetype of the "old, wise man" was a familiar one in my dreams, but this time he was too inscrutable. The dream was so vivid, so real that I felt it had an importance for me that I had better not ignore. So I decided to converse with him in active imagination.)

I asked him what he had to say to me. He went and sat at a table on the cliff. So, I went to him and told him, as in the dream, that I needed help to get down. He went to the back of the ledge and wrote on the face of the mountain and stepped back. He had written in Chinese characters and I can't read Chinese. I didn't know what to do. He knew I didn't read Chinese! Being desperate, I went to him again and told him I couldn't read his message, and he told me I could learn. Feeling both a little scared and a little angry—what kind of old wise man is this?—I said to him: "I don't have time to learn Chinese now. I need to get down off this mountain. Will you help me?" He stood, and looking very directly at me, said, "Sometimes we have to ask more than once," took my hand, and led me to the path.

The first therapeutic task is to attend to the patient's wants and concerns, especially to statements of agency ("I desperately wanted to get off that ledge") as one may hold, with many modern therapists (Haley, 1963, 1967; Greenleaf, 1971), that pathology is agency denied. The next task is to utilize a person's own competence to allow change to occur. Taking the simple instance of the dream, Hazel was asked to use her own feet to walk down the path: first one foot, then the other. She was told to "Let me know if anything difficult or interesting happens." This statement allows both the intensity of self-involvement and the possibility of rapport with a guide or therapist that move the work along. It also sets a rule for interchange between the dreamer and her guide somewhat like that rule followed in close friendship or adequate parenting: relationship is mandatory for the novel, compelling, and delightful event; also, for events that call forth dilemmas or problems. At other times, we explore on our own.

Following the suggestion to begin walking on the path, Hazel was able to come to the valley, then to a city, and was no longer on the threatening, cold ledge. Still, such is the seductiveness of ideas, she might have stayed there indefinitely, badgering the old man for his "wisdom" and neglecting to set her own feet in motion, had she not been requested to do this. This "resistance" or "rationalizing" was overcome with a nudge, not by explanation. Milton Erickson's lifelong work is a testament to the utilization of small actions that breed small but expanding changes in large systems of human interaction.

Even in the use of intriguing or complex dreams, it is usually possible to translate the dream material into a coherent situation and to suggest action appropriate to that situation. These dreams are often nonobvious in meaning, and the translation process is difficult to describe. In the dream that follows, for example, I had gotten the sense of something hidden that must be found, and this intuition informed the suggested action. Cory's dream follows:

> I had gone to visit a friend, Jean, who was to be married. I was to be her only attendant. I entered Jean's home, a very large, stately home. She was very excited about her marriage and explained, too, that in the spring she would be twenty-one and receive her inheritance. Jean then gave me a ring identical to the one she wore. We climbed a narrow spiral staircase, one complete revolution, to the chapel. Over the altar hung three heads of animals. End of dream.

Cory was asked to complete the dream as a waking imagining, and she saw Jean, but was distressed to find no groom. "The bride and I at times seemed to be one and the same." Suggestions to read a book set on the altar led to "many rapidly changing and very overwhelming emotions":

> I then turned around, and saw Jean standing next to her boyfriend. I, being the only attendant, married them. I then went to the left side of the altar and looked in my new handbag (this having been suggested) and took out a crystal necklace—a rosary. I put it on. When putting on the necklace it momentarily became a crown of thorns. Wearing the necklace, I experienced joy.

Cory later revealed that this dreamwork had freed her from a painful and anxious identification with a martyred saint, which had held her since childhood.

The inference used to form suggestions for continuing the dream was "Something is missing, incomplete. Where can it be found?" Then, "When given a present, put it on; see how you feel wearing it." Thus, though I knew no Catholic theology and little religious symbolism, it was possible to give adequate suggestions based on simple action potentials in the dream situations that could be pursued according to shared values for action (try on a necklace received as a gift), even though shared symbolic meanings were unavailable.

The first principle in this sort of work, then, is to complete the dramatic action of the dream, using the person's own images. This may be done in some organized fashion, as with Senoi dreamwork, (Greenleaf, 1973; Stewart, 1951), or it may use the structure of the dream itself as the imagined situation. The injunction to "complete the dramatic action" applies as well to life situations, dreams, imagined activities, and hallucinated or delusional understandings. But the second principle must be to use the common sense to identify what must be done. Attempting to fly from the cold ledge must not be done. In like wise, murder and death are subject to severe constraint in active imagining, as they are hoped to be in the realms of action in life. Discussion with the interior guide or the therapist is a catalyst allowing useful decisions about action to replace catastrophe in carrying forth the dream.

3. Human Competence

> The (therapist) is. . .a serious student of practical aspects of human personality and living. (H. S. Sullivan, 1954)

Although psychotherapies have originated from the attempt to deal with human suffering and ineptitude and the literature of therapy is a record of these sufferings, there are many examples at hand of the way people function at the heights of human achievement. These ought to guide us.

The briefest glance at the most brilliant of athletes, musicians, or scientists shows their persistence, ability to act though in pain or discomfort, steadfastness when fearful and, most important for our own work, a thorough reliance on methods of mental rehearsal using images. As the boxer, Ken Norton, reminds us, "What the mind can conceive, the body can achieve" (*San Francisco Chronicle*, August 13, 1976). Many professional golfers won't putt until they can see the ball enter the cup in a mental rehearsal of the next stroke. Or, consider Einstein's "thought experiments," which picture relativity theory as a set of everyday events, such as watching a train pass by (Capra, 1975). Or, Rostropovich, speaking of Prokofiev:

> Very often he treated musical instruments as if they were living beings. For example, slow, low notes on the tuba made him think a beetle was sitting in the note. With great pleasure he would listen to the beetle climbing from one note to another. (*San Francisco Chronicle*, July 22, 1976)

The famous instances of discovery in dreams, like Kekule's grasp of the structure of the benzine ring, can be multiplied by countless instances from the waking thought of competent persons. Since we hope to encourage patients to use their own power and competence in living, we might show them the availability of the methods of competent thought and action in the commonplace activities of their lives, the most ordinary of which may be said to be dreams and daydreams. Too, what one can do at work, say, by way of interacting with others and persisting against difficulty to solve problems, is applicable to "problems at home" in nonobvious ways. Again, Erickson is the best guide to ways of aiding people to bring existing competencies to bear from one segment of experience to resolve dilemmas in another part of life (Haley, 1967).

In the situations that patients bring to therapy, then, it is not important that we try to determine what the situation "means" so long as we are capable of acting to resolve it. To accept the reality of the person's portrayal is crucial, in whatever form it is offered, and though the situation is easiest to describe when dealing with dreams, it applies to *all* disclosure: dream, play, play therapy, psychodrama, anecdote, even film or tape. So, we treat the dream as a real circumstance requiring action, just as we recognize the dramatic imagination at work when we speak of "real life." In deciding, along with another person, what to do, it's simplest to identify a resolved situation both would value; a goal to work toward: getting off the mountain, bargaining with an adversary, binding a wound, sinking a putt, singing on key, reading a letter. The problem of comparative values is reduced in size by this approach to the dream as a life problem to solve by action, as "Fewer meanings arise from direct experience as compared with the number available through cogitation (Zucker, 1967)." Too, the nasty harpies of interpretation can be silenced here, as they are for most of us while watching a play or, when playing. Again, the examples of grace and intense concentration afforded us by athletes and performers are excellent guides to the pursuit of ordinary human competence.

To really "see" and "do" the necessary action in continuing the dream allows access to spontaneity and to the "unconscious mind." Stanislavski (1926) writes in *An Actor Prepares:*

> Let me remind you of our cardinal principle: "Through conscious means we reach the subconscious.". . . Whenever you have truth and belief, you have feeling and experience. You can test this by executing even the smallest act in which you really believe and you will find that instantly, intuitively and naturally, an emotion will arise. . . . If you just feel the truthfulness of this (imaginary) act, your intention and subconsciousness will come to your aid. Then superfluous tension will disappear. The necessary muscles will come into action and all this will happen without the interference of any conscious technique.

So, using dreams and emphasizing acting in the dreams, continuing the dreams, the therapist propels a patient through the impasse that occurs with fear or anxiety. Then "superfluous tension" disappears and natural emotions arise, and this occurs without a great deal of conscious understanding of "meanings," but with agreements to act (in imagination) in certain ways. The parallels with other techniques, such as hypnosis, are obvious if, with T. X. Barber (Barber and Spanos, 1974), we note that hypnotic subjects

> . . .respond overtly and experientially to suggestions when they become involved in imaginings. . .actively imagining those things that are suggested. . .precludes the possibility of simultaneously focusing on information that is inconsistent with the suggestions.

Or, as Erickson has put it (Haley, 1967):

> ...the technique (of hypnosis) in itself serves no other purpose than that of securing and fixating the patient's attention. . . . There is then the opportunity to proffer suggestions and instructions serving to aid and to direct the person in achieving the desired goal or goals.

Singer's use of "oneiric" also includes the relaxation characteristic of states of attention and ease that the therapist, collaborating with the patient to meet his or her needs and goals, promotes by dealing with images. Desensitization techniques, T.A. rescripting, Gestalt dialogue, hypnotherapy, and bedtime storytelling all partake of this therapeutic control over anxiety and the safety provided by a guide to utilize imaginings or dreams by way of helping persons in fearful situations.

4. Realism in Dreamwork

The involvement of the patient in his work and experience is everywhere held to be crucial to change, both of emotion and behavior. The involvement of the therapist is equally crucial, and disjunctions in involvement between the two are evident in the patronizing, "educative" tone assumed by some therapists. This tone may be starkly in evidence when the "real meanings" of events are discussed. By comparison, complete sympathy with the reality of emotions, thoughts, and dreams—of life brought into the consulting room—often translates into some concept and experience in the patient of respect for his own life.

The heuristic value of such a stance is perhaps most evident in our dealings with the more obtuse twists of experience, like hallucination, inchoate emotion, and uncanny dissociations of consciousness. A work of psychotherapy on which L. R. McCartney and I collaborated (Greenleaf and McCartney, unpublished) will bring this issue to better focus. In 1972, McCartney and I met once monthly for two to four hours each session. She entered therapy in order to gain some clarity in her feelings about a complex interpersonal relationship. During the eighth hour of this work, she reported a dream:

> I am with Bill, my ex-husband, outdoors somewhere. I ask him, "How are you?" and he says, "I'm fine, but I'm worried about Laura. She's driving me crazy. She's been sick, and she gets on the microphone and says, "ffffff," and she never does her work. Last night I was up 'til four trying to get her work and mine done."
> We have a huge argument over the name of what's wrong with Laura. I try to tell him it's "reflective repression" 'cause someone told me that and I half-believe it. Then, all of a sudden, on the loudspeaker near me I hear Laura's voice, "ffffff," and then this horrible, horrible scream that I couldn't understand. I look at Bill and say, "Go to her, help her!" 'cause I realize she's insane and letting everybody know it. And he doesn't

understand anything. He just looks puzzled. Then, there's another horrible scream that I *can* understand. It says, "Come quick! Cat's sick," in a terribly frightened, panicked, sick voice.

McCartney said that she felt the dream came from deep inside her and that it was related to fear of witchcraft and of cats and of being possessed, and also to feelings of "devastation" when she's unknowingly hurt people. Her journal for that day continues:

> And I told him all these things bang-bang-bang and said that somehow they're all related. I know they are, but I don't know how. And Eric said, well, he didn't know either, but he knew a place we could start working, and it would be to work with the dream, and did I want to do it? So I said, "Yes," and he asked me about Laura. I told him how mostly for me she's been a person who just reminds me of me. And then he asked me to go to Laura, since Bill couldn't go to her; to go to Laura and help her.
>
> I closed me eyes and relaxed. I went to Laura—she was bent over a kitten, crying. I asked her how I could help her. I had a couple of false starts, like, "Well. I think she says. . ." and Eric said, "Wait a minute. Don't tell me what you *think* she says. Just relax and let it come to you." He had me lean back against the wall. So I relaxed for a really long time and then I started to talk to Laura. And she refused to answer me. At last, I realized I was the one who needed help.
>
> Then I said to her, "Laura, I need your help. I really need you to tell me what's wrong." Suddenly, *she* said, "I never thought of myself as a helpful person. Not at all." And she has a New Zealand accent and talks in a very cynical way. Eric asked me about the cat, and she started to scream. *She* screamed, laughed loudly and wildly, lashed about. Finally she collapsed back into the chair exhausted, her arms hanging over the sides, her head back, breathing hard. Eric talked with her for two hours and sometimes I knew what she was going to say and sometimes I didn't. Later Eric said he was surprised at first—when she first appeared. She laughed at him, teased, insulted, but he was good to her.

"Surprise" is a bit mild, of course. When I recovered my soul from its hiding place under my chair, I began to notice that this difficult woman who had suddenly appeared in place of my shy, earnest, humorous "patient," complete with stiff mannerisms, different voice quality, posture, opinions, ethics, style, motives, and "personality"—this new, dreadful person sprung into the office—was herself frightened, proud, stubborn, and very lonely. I acted toward her with wary sympathy. As McCartney said:

> Anyway, it was a very weird afternoon, finding out there's another person inside me I didn't know about, who's all the things I never can be. And I don't know how long she's been there or anything like that. And Eric said he can't help me find out about where she came from or how long she's been there, but he can help me get the two—or more—parts of me together.

So the work was set as a work of reconciliation—bargaining, getting to know someone. Further personalities weren't encouraged to appear, and the historical and ontological questions most apt to bog down our efforts were set aside. The relationship of the two was continued in a sort of couple's therapy, with Lorraine also talking to Laura in daydreams and writing in a diary where each could put her thoughts. About a year later, Lorraine was able to remember the death of a much-loved grandmother and to grieve her loss nearly 25 years after the death:

> I remembered Grandma. I remembered a day at Grandma's house, in a dark bedroom at the foot of the stairs. I was laying on the bed and Grandma was sitting on it beside me. She's telling me things. I feel a little frightened. "You go to sleep now and when you wake up your Daddy will be here and we will ask him about the kitten." My sense is that I didn't see Grandma after that. She got sick, went to the hospital, and died. And this Sunday I finally cried for her.
>
> Laura both held that great big emotion I was afraid of for so long and held off the loneliness. I still hurt. I really do want my Grandma. So often I write in my journal, "Lonesome. I'm lonely." I feel less lonely with Laura here, but it's Grandma I'm lonesome for. The difference between "knowing" about Grandma dying and "experiencing" Grandma's death is indescribable.

Then, a year later still, she writes:

> Good dreams of seeing myself in a beautiful plain white dress. And later finding my Grandma's treasure chest of lace and trims and buttons. I asked whom it belonged to and my aunt said, "To you." I was so delighted—such a beautiful treasure to own and use.

So, the therapy itself, which totaled 18 hours during 1972, was continued by Lorraine herself for several years afterward, using the interpersonal techniques developed in dealings with her "other side." Strategies for this sort of interaction have been discussed by me more fully in a somewhat different context in "The 'Unconscious-Mind Mirror' in Active Imagination" (Greenleaf, 1975). There, an exercise that elicits the unconscious image of the self—"constellates the shadow," Jungians might say—is detailed. But there, too, the use of active imagination in which personified segments of the self are treated like real-life others eventuates in more straightforward treatment of the emotional and historical and interpersonal information that becomes available to the patient. And, the therapy continues in that sense far beyond the point of therapeutic "termination."

Within the active imagining, asking the question, as Weaver (1973) does, "What would you do in life in this case?" proves effective for dealing with "multiple personalities," imagined parents or children, dream monsters, and "archetypes of the collective unconscious." And, in these dealings, therapists may be guided by the interpersonal approaches of such as Ginott (1965) and Sullivan (1954) in their relationship with difficult others. Then, in dealing with the relationships, one tries to progress the action onward to some dramatic conclusion like those found in life, rescue and relief, separation and reconciliation, exploration and discovery, or even death, grief, and renewal. The person's own sense of the completion of an act is usually reliable, though the therapist must watch for instances in which fear, rather than resolution, signals the end of the work. With several hours of time available to the patient and therapist, many works of active imagination seem to take about one and a half hours to complete, after which people often volunteer, "I feel I worked a lot today—not physical work. I'm finished for today." Or, "I felt sick and I felt exhausted. It was just a fantastic amount of hard work to do it." The sense of effort is an important correlate of the use of one's own power and competence to attack difficult objectives, and the sense of personal strength or activity is a commonplace of vibrant lives.

When dealing with individual figures in dream situations, the ordinary and extraordinary difficulty of relating holds sway. Here one speaks of love, hate, sadness, forgiveness, lust, rage, grief, joy, suspicion, trust, and the several other named emotions that occur in two-person relating. Following a line of emotion or emotional exchange is important for clarity of relating, and in special circumstances, such as relating with dream figures, give the true sense to both therapist and patient that, as Lorraine expressed it: "I trust him not to think I'm crazy. In fact, I even asked him that. I trust him 'cause he doesn't treat me like I'm crazy."

5. Modalities of Experience

In some way, the use of active imagining has one do purposively what otherwise occurs to one passively, as do dreams, daydreams, passing thought, and quickly stirred emotion. Haley and his colleagues often note (Haley, 1963; Watzlawich *et al.*, 1974) that the suggestion or demand that one do actively what one must do anyway is by itself highly effective in catalyzing change. Similarly, treating "fantasy" figures as "real" relationships, in the ways I've described, allows patients to deal with those "projections" and what not that they must anyway suffer, all of us having been brought up by "significant others." In addition, dealing directly with dream figures provides a change of framework for the patient, from one in which she is "crazy" or irrelevant or plagued or possessed, to one in which she is pursuing relatedness. Watzlawick, Weakland, and Fisch cite this reframing as a powerful therapeutic tool.

That reframing, or even simple change of venue, is a useful stratagem is confirmed by works both ancient and modern. A recent instance is the pioneering efforts of the Simonton group (Simonton, 1975) to treat cancer with a variety of active imagining. So far we've discussed several such transforms of experience: the continuation of dreaming, which reframes the alien as relationship: the active stance, which reframes a cognitive dilemma as a task or practical problem. It is equally useful to reframe the modalities of somatic experience and vague or confused experience as clear images that may be manipulated.

These difficulties in living, the "psychosomatic" discomfort, the "vague complaint," and even and especially the "sophisticated" patient's total, helpless understanding of antecedents and meanings in his suffering, can be aided when made tangible in dreams. But the dreams may also be created in the therapy itself, as when a person complaining of pain is asked, "Where is it? What does it look like there?" or, of emotion, "What color is it? Where do you experience this in your body?" For example, a man complaining of "depression" may be told, "You remember when you were a school kid; we all did drawings with colored crayons and covered them with black. Then we scraped them with our nails to reveal the colors. Suppose you scrape all the black off and tell me what you see." As in all this work, a matter-of-fact tone in the present tense—"You scrape off all the black"—is pretty good proof against objections to carrying forth simple imaginings. In fact, it's difficult not to picture what another is speaking of. When the colors emerge, compound colors may be separated into primaries and the several colors given shapes by asking, "What shape is the red now?" or, "If the color were a thing, what would it be? Look and tell me." Then, balls may be rolled or thrown, curtains parted, and a general sense of purposeful motion given to a static circumstance or emotion.

Physical distress, such as headache pain, "tightness" of muscles, or plain "nerves" can be translated into images in much the same way. A woman suffering back pain and tension was asked to tell me, "What's going on there? What do you see?" She saw two men, one at the neck, another at the base of the spine, pulling skeins of nerves so tautly between them that some had frayed and were broken. Through dialogue with the figures, one was encouraged to repair the frayed nerves, while the other agreed to leave his tugging and open an office from which to manage the woman's rather disorganized personal habits. In four days, half the back was free of pain; in two weeks, two-thirds.

Another important guideline indicated here is the conservation of the images or system of images through reorientation or transformations. In the "mind-mirror" exercise figures are asked to change or evolve, not to disappear. In the example cited above, the man is given other work to do, not cast out. In the instance of McCartney's two personalities, a later dream showed her frightened, but "doing something to get the two of us together." The metaphorical use of all of the self and all of its materials, or, one might say, the reintegration of projections, equilibration of the system of psychical fields, or the conservation of libidinal energy, however expressed, is a key element in all therapeutic work, the achievement of which provides natural closure to personal difficulty or dilemma.

Consider another instance of both translation of the modalities of experience and their integration: A forty-year-old man entered therapy with me in a state he described as "down in the dumps." He was asked to take on the "depressing" task of sorting through the garbage there and recycling it, to which he replied: "I've thought of this disgusting garbage as attachments to past events, like adhesions. I want to get rid of it." Well, how to do this? We agreed to compost the (mostly organic) garbage in order to provide energy by means of a methane converter. He could then use the "power" generated in this way for whatever use seemed important to him. His choice was to use the gas to power a burner that could cut holes through metal plates that blocked him from the outside world of other persons. As he did this, his feeling of disgust was replaced by one of calm satisfaction and smooth breathing, "like normal, everyday breaths, but easier." He began "down in the dumps," but, after much hard work, he can "breathe easier."

Vague complaints often have about them the irresistible quality of pathos, but they are not often something we can easily come to grips with in therapy. A young man was tormented both by repeated, sudden feelings of humiliation and worthlessness and by severe leg pains whose cause couldn't be determined. After many weeks of therapy he was asked to notice where the feeling of absolute or unconditional worth (not tied to performance) lies. After a moment's thought he said that it was "in the heart" and resembled a spiky oval that grows darker and smoother with increased worth and brighter and painfully burning with decreased feelings of worthiness. He was told to let the feeling grow and was surprised to find it sending a spur into the afflicted leg, with a small, spiky ball on the end. I asked him to draw up and spit out the ball, all the while remembering instances of anger and humiliation suffered in his lonely years of childhood. As he did this, he discovered "hundreds" of the spiky balls stored in his knee joint. He decided to get them all out.

It's long been the fashion in psychotherapy to think of the organism as an integrated system of "psychosomatic" events. The transforms of experience and the "symptoms" that compel our attention are ascribed to some interplay between anxiety and the self or stress and the organism. If we think of anxiety as a formless situation, one in which information is muted, lost, or distorted, and emotion likewise uncertain, like a sort of "white noise," we will make ready to replace this painful meaninglessness with form, and image.

A patient who suffered dream deprivation and *pavor nocturnus* under the influence of "antipsychotic" medication said bitterly to me, "If I only had an image to hold on to." The role of providing these images falls to the dreamer herself, or to the dreamer and her guide. Together, they develop the means that allow safe passage through the straits of uncertainty and fear. This role, and that collaboration, have an ancient lineage, to which we now turn.

6. The Structure of Healing

> They should have apprehended the method of visualization and applied the illimitable virtue thereof for exhalting one's own condition. (*Tibetan Book of the Dead*, Evans-Wentz, 1927)

The *Book of the Dead*, or *Bardo Thodol*, contains texts read to the dying man to guide him through the terrors of death and rebirth, "the fearful ambush of the *bardo*." But the situations for which it prescribes forms of guided meditation are more general still than that of dying. *Bardo* is a term denoting an "intermediate" state, a state of consciousness and of uncertainty, of which six are named: the state of waking consciousness, the state of dream consciousness, the state of trance consciousness in meditation, the state of the experiencing of death, the state of consciousness of rebirth, and the state of the experiencing of reality. In these periods of transition, uncertainty, and, as we would say, anxiety, the person is counseled to be steadfast in face of the attraction and fear exercised on him by the images that "embody (his) own intellect." As with anxiety, this task becomes more difficult the longer uncertainty obtains, and the images confronting the person become more horrific the longer he fails to grasp his "present intellect, in real nature void, not formed into anything. . .the very Reality," or, as we would say, the self.

The Buddhist view makes reality, self, and mind synonymous and, as in the *Bardo Thodol*, provides exercises and guidance in countering fear and anxiety that bar one from the experience of seeing things truly. In her recent biography of Jung, M.-L. Von Franz (1975) claims that his rediscovery of active imagination is a "return to the oldest known forms of meditation, as they existed before the subsequent development into Yoga, Buddhist meditation, and Taoist alchemy." She thus ties Yoga, alchemy, Zen practice, and the devices of Shamanism to their common use of visualization to allow liberation. She cites a Chinese Taoist text:

> The wise man centers himself, concentrates and thus is able to rise to higher spheres and descend into the lower, and distinguish there the things which it would be proper to do.

Again, this guidance about "what to do" in changing situations of life is provided by the *bonze* to the dying Tibetan, or by the shaman to his client. Followers of Jung's work emphasize the function of the analyst in guiding a person's active imagination so that he is able to express the "inferior function" of experiencing through the medium of fantasying. R. F. C. Hull's (1971) bibliography of Jung's references to active imagination is a useful reference for those interested in the correspondences, as is Von Franz's (Von Franz and Hillman, 1971) chapter in *Lectures on Jung's Typology*. Attaining to the "middle sphere" through active imagination is said to create the "transcendant function." Ego awareness is detached from identification with certain functions of experiencing and the person comes to resemble a Zen master:

> At this moment one transmits, as it were, his feeling of life into an inner center, and the four functions remain only as instruments which can be used at will, taking them up and putting them down again. (Von Franz and Hillman, 1971)

I'll return to consider the sources of archetypal psychology in the next section, examining the concept of "archetype" and some of the associated therapeutic methods. Still, *all* psychotherapeutic method has been in the public domain for thousands of years. The Buddha himself proclaimed that he had seen the ancient way, and followed it. There are as many ways of doing therapy as there are of experiencing life, and modern therapies use dance, art, imagination, relationship, attentional processes, and learning, as in: bioenergetics, art therapy, guided fantasy, gestalt therapy, hypnotherapy, and behavior therapy. In just this way, the Yogic disciplines set out from the basic life experiences of vision, posture, sound, and pattern to develop their methods of visualization, *mudra, mantra,* and *mandala.*

Suffering and change are the "problems" to which Yoga addresses its methods (the problems of "stress" and "growth," if we prefer a modern usage). These methods are experimental and use both homology—the similarity of structure between patterns of events, and paradox—"an assertion seemingly contradictory. . .that yet may be true in fact," to liberate persons from that suffering. "Homology" is the basic process of representation itself, as when our words in the therapist's office are taken to represent patterns of our behavior toward our parents years ago. All ritual partakes of this sense that one set of things may represent another, or that thought may represent deeds. Mircea Eliade (1963), the historian of religions, cites homology as the principle of thought binding origin myths, healing practices of the shamans, and current forms of life in a society:

> This fact that the cosmogonic myth can be applied on various planes of reference seems to us especially significant. The man of the traditional societies feels the basic unity of all kinds of "deeds", "works" or "forms" whether they are biological, psychological or historical. An unsuccessful war can be homologized with a sickness, with a dark, discouraged heart, with a sterile woman, with a poet's lack of inspiration, as with any other critical existential situation in which man is driven to despair.

Still, there are methods more appropriate to one sort of situation than to another, or, more accurately, ways of working that utilize common principles in varying ways, according to the attributes of the patient and the customs of the times. Jung (1961) says, "In one analysis I can be heard talking the Adlerian dialect, in another, the Freudian." Von Franz (1971) notes that intuitive types may do active imagination in clay, thinking types by dance, sensation types by writing weird fiction. In the fourth century B.C., Tantric Yoga was developed (Eliade, 1958), parallel to the unfolding of Gnosticism, hermetism, and alchemy, and specifically addressing itself to the men and women of *kali yuga*, the age of greatest darkness and degeneration according to Indian cosmologies. Eliade (1969) says:

> The syndrome of *kali yuga* is marked by the fact that it is the only age in which property alone confers social rank; wealth becomes the only motive of the virtues, passion and lust the only bonds between the married, falsehood and deception the first condition of success in life, sexuality the sole means of enjoyment, while external, merely ritualistic religion is confused with spirituality. For several thousand years, be it understood, we have been living in *kali yuga*.

The appropriate methodology for persons suffering in these ways begins directly with their bodily experience of life, utilizing the passions of sexuality in a Yogic discipline, as with the *Kundalini* (Zimmer, 1960). Further, the "materialism" of the age, that "degeneration of symbolism" (Eliade, 1962) once expressed to me in the maxim, "If you can't eat it, screw it, or sell it, what is it?" is met by special forms of the Tantric Yoga. Zimmer (1960) describes a process of meditation that begins with the observance of cult rituals—"offerings, whispered formulas, a swinging of lamps"—and concrete images of the deities, which are adorned with gifts. Little by little, "the whole outward ceremonial is repeated in a process of progressive visualization," and the rituals are replaced by inner processes:

> Each day the rites become more intense; the inner process they are intended to provoke runs through the seven stages of the Yoga exercise, which is associated with the image of a god: from the contemplation of the material image to the substitution of its inner likeness, . . .then from an inner contemplation of this image in which contemplator and image exist separately to a union of the two *(samadhi)*. . . .

Paradoxically, this concentration on experience can lead one to liberation from the constraints of that experience, just as it is hoped that the Glide Foundation films of every manner of sexual passion will free the viewer from his "hangups" about sexual feeling and expression. The homology of mental and experiential structure is what chiefly interests us in this discussion, and specifically the place of imagery in representation of the world and in the adaptation of organisms to changing circumstances. But paradox is always at work also, in the "reframing" of experience we mentioned earlier, and in the use of ritual to homologize current experience to the "sacred time" of myth, so that the "rupture of the plane" of ordinary space, time, and paired, opposing concepts can occur (Eliade, 1958). Within the structure of ritual healing, initiation, or meditation, paradoxical formulations of speech and relatedness, such as appear in the Zen traditions (Chang, 1969) or, more recently, in the therapeutic work of Erickson (Haley, 1973) and Haley (1963) lead to transcendence of the paired constructs that constrain understanding and living: "Crazy" and "sane" may be transmuted to "crazy like a fox."

The authority of these traditions—ascetic, mystical, or therapeutic—derives, says Eliade, from "the direct, experimental knowledge of all that constitutes the bases and processes of the human body and the psychomental life" (Eliade, 1962). A parallel tradition with that of the Yogic disciplines has been that of alchemy, elegantly researched and described in his *Forge and the Crucible*. There he shows close connections between shamanism, the arts of song, dance, and poetry and the art of the smith and the magician. The overlapping techniques of these disciplines were handed down in initiation mysteries, the structure of which consists in the experience of suffering, death, and rebirth, leading to a transmutation of the person (Eliade, 1962). The alchemical transmutation, the great work of the alchemists, can be seen as an initiation mystery in which they "projected onto Matter the initiatory function of suffering." As the texts cited by Eliade, and by Jung in his *Psychology and Alchemy* (Eliade, 1962) make clear, alchemists sought through relationship to matter to cause it to pass through four phases (black, white, yellow, and red) in order to transform it *and* themselves into the "philosopher's stone," that treasure that is common as water but to which only the adept can find access. The vessel of transformation is best seen as the self and, as the alchemist Zosimos said, "One the procedure, one the vessel, one the stone," (Von Franz, 1975).

To relate with matter, the alchemists sought to use dreams, meditation, and a fantasying, *phantasia vera et non phantastica* that various authors cite as the same activity Jung rediscovered as active imagination. In alchemy the practitioner guides his matter into spirit, as the shaman—the guide, healer, psychopomp (but not priest) of traditional societies—guides souls. That the shaman is "the great specialist in the human soul"—he alone "sees" it, for he knows its "form" and its destiny" (Eliade, 1962)—becomes important to this developing complex of Yoga, alchemy, and shamanism in their relation to active imagination. The shaman suffers initiation, death, and rebirth in his own experience, not "symbolically," and he "sees" the "forms" of life (Eliade, 1962) and thus can "demolish the barriers between dream and present reality" and re-establish the lost soul in the ritual space of the Great Time or the Dream Time.

The method used for these transcending maneuvers is, we have argued, homologous with that of visualization or active imagination. If it is so that a concentration on imagined experience can constrain, change, and transcend physical behavior patterns—and who has ever held otherwise?—then the question of the relationship of these thought-forms to the active, lived experience of life and to the understanding of that life must be asked. Before considering current views of this relationship. we'll examine the Jungian view of "archetype" as it's displayed through active imagination.

7. Archetype and Image

>We approach the id with analogies. (S. Freud)*
>Image is psyche. (C. G. Jung)†

Replication is a cardinal principle of the physical sciences much referred to by psychologists yet difficult to adhere to in experimental situations with persons. In the canons of social science, criteria of replication are usually coupled with attempts at prediction, though it's been suggested that in research where "demand characteristics" (Orne, 1962) are operative, *un*-predictable or spontaneous subject responses can best fit a "scientific" model of psychological research. Spontaneous

---

* See Freud, S. *New Introductory Lectures on Psychoanalysis*, No. 31, J. Strachy (Ed. and Tr.). New York: Norton, 1965.

† See Jung, C. G. *Alchemical Studies, Collected Works*, Vol. 13, Princeton University Press, 1968, p. 75.

subject reactions are especially telling, of course, when the data being considered is "states of consciousness," rather than "behaviors," since human experience is related—told—and verbal report is subject to suggestion and "demand" from the experimenter or observer. The many reports of spontaneously revealed experiences during therapy, in which subjects were unaware of a vast body of literature dealing with identical experience and the therapist had no expectation of such outcomes, can be presented as unpredicted replications of important constancies of mind and emotion. The discovery of archetypal images in the course of his therapeutic work gave rise to Jung's view of the relation of images to what has since been called "the problem of mind."

An instance of the occurrence of an "archetypal image" in the course of psychotherapy will clarify what I mean: Ellen, the patient, came to her session lonely and distraught after the collapse of an intimate relationship. Asked to speak of her emotion, she said she was fearful, and when asked, "What emotion would you feel if you were no longer fearful?" she said, "Sad." "And if no longer sad?" "Angry. But if I wasn't angry, I'd be empty." When she pictured the lonely emptiness, Ellen imagined a long, dark tunnel. But, suddenly, at the depth of despair, she was confronted by the figure of a vibrant, wild, lovely woman. This figure, who appeared when "no one was there," guided her forth, gave her cheer and courage, fought for her, and gave her gifts of great value. One of the gifts was most remarkable. Ellen was given a "golden bough," whose fruit enabled her to enter "an inner world" a vast desert with alien, masculine features and huge rocks among which it was difficult to find a passage.

Now, *The Golden Bough*, Frazer's (1922) classic study, had sat unopened on my shelf for years. Ellen had never heard of the book; I had never read it. When I did, I found that the "golden bough," which Frazer identifies as a type of mistletoe, was held to be able to "open all locks," and that Virgil had the hero Aeneas carry such a bough with him on his descent to the underworld as a living being. The fearful, narrow passageway and the labyrinthine or chthonic journeys are all patterns of initiation (Eliade, 1962), which, we have seen, includes the sequential suffering, death, and rebirth of the initiate.

As a process in living, such initiation may be guided by inner voices or visions, as often with the vocation of shaman, or by outer guides as when one is initiated into the various clubs, societies, professions, and crafts of our time. In therapy, the therapist is guide, but, as with all structures of healing, the guide may be carried as an internal image (Swedenborg, unpublished), either concurrent with the therapist's physical presence or at times when the patient is out of sight of the consulting room. Surely every practitioner has had people tell her with some relief that they "thought of you when I got scared; of what you would say to me if you were here, and that helped pull me through." The archetype of healing, or initiation, exists through this relatedness of patient and therapist or novice and master. It does not reside in either one of them. As Jung said: "The fact is that the single archetypes are not isolated, but are in a state of contamination, of the most complete, mutual interpenetration and interfusion (Casey, 1974). Put another way, the image, or the single word that stands for it, like "therapist," obscures the relatedness that *is* the structure of the image. Eliade (1969) comments:

> It is therefore the image as such, as a whole bundle of meanings, that is *true* and not any *one* of its meanings, nor one alone of its many frames of reference. To translate an image into a concrete terminology by restricting it to any one of its frames of reference is. . .to annul it as an instrument of cognition.

Images are instruments of cognition, and adequate both for dealing with problems of living and for understanding meanings, for "the concepts of complex psychology are, in essence, not intellectual formulations, but names for certain areas of experience" (Jung, 1959). These areas, the phenomena of human psychology, are best represented as events or interactions, not as entities. To discuss these phenomena, one needs a language tied to relatedness and matrix, not to causal sequence. I'm arguing here that "dream language," or the archetypal structures developed through active imagining, provide proper understandings of human events, especially those we cannot speak about in the common language. Imagine describing any *three*-person interaction in English. While dyads have some terms to speak of—"friendship," for example—how can one speak of the relatedness of members-of-a-family-taken-all-at-once? Unless one prefers expostulation, like the ubiquitous "Oh, wow!" there is a real dilemma here. Believing the strictures of the family therapists, systems theorists, or even psychoanalysts, who all remind us that individual life is interdependent, we are left without terms that express this reality when we speak with each other. Even the freak "therapeutic" tongues like T.A. and E.S.T. are poor in nondyadic terminology.

Usually, the dilemma is resolved adequately by the use of anecdote, metaphor, or moral fable. This is apt, I think, for the picturing of relationships through imagery and the consistent vocabulary provided by these images (the archetypal figures and the dramas of life) are perfect representations or homologues of complex human experience. Dreams are what the Tibetans call *rang-snang*, (Evans-Wentz, 1927), one's own thought-forms or visions. This is true whether the dreams are spontaneous or brought forth spontaneously as imaginations in the therapist's office. Dreams provide understandings of what Wittgenstein (1958) calls "what has to be accepted, the given, the forms of life." That is, hearing and visualizing and experiencing an active imagination, one can understand forms of life and relationship. Speaking about the forms of life may be adequately accomplished by telling the dream (Greenleaf, 1973; Zucker, 1967).

Active imagination is seen, in the Jungian notation (Casey, 1974) as a kind of spontaneous amplification of archetypes into images. These images are conceived to be visual forms of the patterns of the organization of thought, "the typical modes of apprehension which. . .form an inner self-image, so to speak, of human instincts or of their structure" (Von Franz, 1975). Weaver (1973) states, "Active imagination leads to the structure of the psyche. . .it is here one finds the basic struggles of mankind, the psychic growth and the forms upon which consciousness rests." Along with an understanding of the dynamic psyche through the interrelated forms of the archetypes, there comes change, and growth, for "we enter into the drama of the psyche itself by participating in what is psychically real: in what is capable of changing us in some basic way" (Casey, 1974).

Whether we emphasize the limitations of English or the ubiquity of visual thinking, dream language, couched in spatial terms like the common language and dramatically structured in visualized forms, provides proper and available understandings of human events, conceived as sets of functional relationships. Jung's concept of archetype is an attempt to represent this state of affairs, but there are, as well, several more recent formulations regarding the explanation of thought, action, and "mind," which converge to support the ancient intuitions described earlier as well as the modern uses of imagery in the psychotherapies. The dovetailing of modern understandings of "hypnosis" with those of "imagery" has been noted. To this we can add writings from the fields of epistemology, paleoneurology, the psychology of vision, comparative linguistics, and mathematics.

8. Images and the Structure of Thought

> We acted as though we had tried to find the real artichoke by stripping it of its leaves. (Wittgenstein, 1958)

I've emphasized that the basis of active imagining lies in action, not in explanation. If the terms are separated, "action" from "meaning," then one would say that understanding "follows" action or that insight is preceded by change. On another view there is no such separation. Gardner's reading of the "structuralists" has it that "one's own knowledge of states of reality comes about through transforming them; thus, the very actions which constitute thought lead ultimately to knowledge of thought." We are accustomed to think that the "actions which constitute thought" are primarily manipulations of "verbal concepts," the more so the more "secondary process," "rational," or "abstract" the thought required. But this assumption is increasingly difficult to maintain.

The question, "How do you know?" was raised recently by Attneave's (1974) Western Psychological Association presidential address. He argues, first, that it is a truism that knowing involves representation, and that representation of one system by another rests on some homologue between system parts and/or relations of parts. He asks in what way representing the world, or "knowing," is important for survival, and concludes that knowing how (rather than knowing why) is the biologically crucial component of "knowing." Knowing how to do things, or where or what they are—how to eat, how to find water, how to mate—is most useful knowledge, and the knower associates objects and processes in the world according to their relations with each other and the integrative functions they serve in living.

Given this situation, what sort of representation is feasible? In what form is the information about relations processed? Attneave considers the representational system of language to be one in which relations are represented by things—words. It is a "digital" system of information processing. Contrasted with this is an analogue system, such as a map, for which relations among categories (rivers, roads, towns) are represented by relations on the surface of the map. Now, Attneave argues that many (though not all) psychological functions entail analogue representation. He cites the representation of number as one such function, certain psychophysiological operations as others. Then, he concentrates his attention on the most important instances of analogue representation: the system for representing physical space, *imagined* space as well as perceived space, since, as he notes, "The animal *knows where* the water hole is." He cites studies by Shepard* that show that when a mental image is rotated, "the representation of the object is in fact going through all of the intermediate aspects in a continuous manner." These imaginary scenes and their active transforms enable a person to experiment with given courses of action before committing himself to act. In this "work space" the associated strong emotions that accompany action may also be evoked and transformed, though Attneave does not make this explicit in his discussion.

Continuing from the analogue nature of representation and its

---

* See Shepard, L., and Metzler, R. *Science,* 1971, *171,* 701-703.

close ties with spatial perception and location, Attneave asks how the representational structures "get their meaning." He notes that descriptions coded in words generate imagery, but goes on to say:

> There is another aspect of meaning that I think is even more essential. I can imagine going for a walk and encountering a dog, or a bird or a wildcat in the woods, but how the scenario progresses beyond that point is highly dependent on which one of the three I imagine meeting. The rules of the game are by no means the same for dogs, birds and wildcats.

So, he argues, the utility of identifying situations and categories of objects lies in our "access" to their rules of interaction with us and with each other, their relationships. The connection of meanings with imagery and with rules of action is shown also by such phenomena as the reports of chess masters (Attneave, 1974) who can reconstruct complete positions after cursory glances at the board. They do this by remembering functional relationships among the pieces—which piece guards which others, for instance—not by memorizing the place of each piece (or of its absence) on each of 64 squares. "In other words, the rules of the game turn out to be quite essential to the way the position is remembered and reconstructed."

The philosophical activity initiated by Wittgenstein makes this relationship among "meaning," "rule," and the "forms of life" a touchstone of the nature of human thought on one hand and of actions between persons in the world on the other. In an earlier paper, "The Schreber Case: Remarks on Psychoanalytic Explanation " (Greenleaf, 1969), I explicated this position and showed its consequences for the understanding of meanings in psychotherapy and for some of the standards of proof obtaining for inferences about "causes" and "motives."

For further confirmation of this epistemological position, those without a taste for philosophy may look to the natural sciences. H. J. Jerison, writing on "Paleoneurology and the Evolution of Mind," in a 1976 *Scientific American*, deals with fossil evidence of the evolution of vertebrate nervous systems. He concentrates on the relationship between sensory-motor systems and the adaptive function of increasing encephalization. For the early hominids, wide-ranging nonarboreal primates, olfactory systems had been much reduced relative to such animals as wolves, who use scent to mark their territories. To develop adequate range-markers then required the use of auditory, visual, and vocal information; so they could develop language as a viable evolutionary direction. The "conscious experience" of the organism would result from a systematic neural integration of sensory information from the different modalities.

This analysis seems to point to language as an integrative modality for understanding and communication among the early ancestors of men and women, but here, as with the other authors I'll mention, Jerison scrutinizes the nature of language for its utility in providing a representation or model of essentially *sensory* events occurring during an animal's life. Language is seen to be a "sensory-perceptual development" whose basic use is in the construction of models of reality *expressed as mental imagery*. The communicative functions of language are seen as clearly secondary; indeed, Jerison claims that if selection pressures had led to the development of language primarily for communication, "we would expect the evolutionary response to be the development of "prewired" language systems with conventional sounds and symbols." These inflexible systems of fixed-action patterns are quite characteristic of bird intelligence, but quite *un*characteristic of mammalian intelligence. In fact, birds and mammals evolved quite separately from two different subclasses of reptiles. Of the birds, Jerison says:

> Their behavior is tightly bound to specific stimuli by fixed action patterns of response, in contrast to an "intelligence" system in which varied patterns of stimuli are transformed into invariant objects.

Dr. Skinner's pigeons are intelligent, true, but of such a different mind (and neural organization) from those humans to whom their acts have been so facilely compared! The flexible patterns and modifiability of our language and sensory integrative systems are organized and represented as mental images, not as stimulus-response patterns without thought. Jerison's conclusions from the fossil record echo other of our major themes:

> We need language more to tell stories than to direct actions. In the telling, we create mental images in our listeners that might normally be produced only by the memory of events. . . . Mental images should be as real as the immediately experienced real world.

How the world is experienced visually and reconstructed in imagery is the subject of Rudolph Arnheim's (1969) elegant book, *Visual Thinking*. He begins with the observation that vision is an active, selective, and purposive process that evolved as a biological aid for survival. To see is never to see aimlessly, in the "blooming, buzzing confusion" attributed to infants. Rather, it is, from the beginning, to see simple shapes, hence, to perform an abstraction. "Releaser mechanisms," which integrate mother-child behavior through the response of the organism to simple shapes and colors (the red spot that gulls peck to induce maternal feeding, for example), are an early form of seeing, a spontaneous grasp of pattern and structure. The perception of shape is itself the grasping of "generic, structural features" of the world. In this sense concepts are percepts, perceptual images, and thought is the handling of these images.

For thinking to be valid, images must be structurally similar (isomorphic to) the features of the situation. But these features—"the primary physical facts from which the sense of sight takes off—are not a bewildering spread of random samples, but highly consistent processes of change." So concepts are, for Arnheim, like the Gestalt term *pragnanzstufen:* phases of clear-cut structure "within a sweep of continuous transformation." Concept formation is then like the perception of structural simplicity and this perception is one of relationships rather than of absolute values and of genera rather than the experience of particulars. Arnheim's biting description of the ways in which digital computers and human beings solve analogy problems—a common test of intelligence—elucidates this notion of concept. Problem-solving is the final function of visual thinking:

> Often a problem presents itself perceptually in the form of something "looking incomplete" and the solution may be found when the situation points to a completion.

Will Attneave meet a dog or a wildcat in the woods? What sort of tail is that near the oak tree? Or, is it just a shadow? Distortion in perception calls forth abstraction and the need to do something to rectify the situation. Again, the "situation" represents a pattern of forces seen as shape, form, concept, and tied to some goal-image, under pressure of which the problem situation restructures itself perceptually: "Whew. Just a shadow of that limb of the tree. No need to run."

Now think again of dreams: Dreams give a picture of our own situation in life. The picture is related to symbols, taking "symbol" to mean "the representation in real magnitudes of something that is essentially an abstract function, an aspect of a relationship," (Watzlawick *et al.*, 1967). Dreams picture functional relationships. As Bateson (1972) quips:

> —A dream is a metaphor or tangle of metaphors. Do you know what a metaphor is?—Yes. If I say you are *like* a pig, that is simile. But if I say you *are* a pig, that is metaphor.—That's right. A metaphor compares things without spelling out the comparison. . . . The dream elaborates on the relationship, but does not identify the (original) things that are related.

For most of these relationships there are no useful near-forms in English, which is a language that treats primarily of entities and objects, not of relationships, at least in the common speech. In fact, Capra (1975), in *The Tao of Physics*, laments the ability of even a technical, scientific form of English to reflect the dynamic condition of relativity and uncertainty and "particle" formation that are currently understood as the nature of the physical universe.

Jerison, Attneave, and especially Arnheim, all place language in some relationship with the imagery that represents our reality to us. From the side of linguistics, Whorf (1956) presents a compelling position that ties language forms to the sort of actions people take and to the concepts (in the form of visual metaphors) that inform these actions. Though I've elsewhere discussed this at length, it's important to note that in his view English and the other "Standard Average European" languages "objectify" basic experience, "so that we can hardly refer to the simplest non-spatial situation without consistent resort to physical metaphors." To cite my earlier discussion of this (Greenleaf, 1975):

> In other words, the language itself, as we ordinarily use it, is so constructed that, if we speak of our "inner experience," feelings and thoughts at all, we must do so in terms taken from the rich description English affords of the world of physical objects apprehended through sight, kinesthesis, touch. Persons seeking help with their lives will naturally and persistently use such metaphors to describe their "feelings." Active imagination techniques provide an excellent way, within the English language, to speak of human experience.

Whorf (1956) contrasts the situation in English and other Standard Average European languages with that in Hopi, where "tensors" convey distinctions of degree, rate, constancy, repetition, increase of intensity, sequence, etc. Gardner's (1973) reading of Piaget emphasizes that infants perceive the "modal" and "vectoral" aspects of behavior (open-closed, force and direction, balance, and so forth) and reproduce these "simple structures" "even while eliminating aspects closer to the physical properties of the stimulus, but differing in dynamic quality." This squares quite well with Arnheim's position regarding perception itself. Here it is tied to action sequences as well, and, through them, to the development of knowledge. But this knowledge, following Whorf, is limited in linguistic expression by the peculiar structure of English and its ties to spatial metaphor. To speak of ourselves in words requires using English, and so, expressing ourselves to one another in spatial metaphor, the language mode of our dreams.

9. Structure Abstracted

> The 'manifest' dream-picture is the dream itself, and contains the whole meaning of the dream. (C. G. Jung)*

---

* See Jung, C. G. *Practical Use of Dream Analysis, Collected Works*, Vol. 16, Princeton University Press, 1966.

> The system is then its own best explanation and the study of its present organization the appropriate methodology. (Watzlawick, Beavin, and Jackson, 1967)

Given the complex, structural nature of human situations and their representation as images, the question now occurs whether there is a suitably abstract formalism that can enable us to represent to ourselves the representations. The attempt to evolve these formalisms resides in the several branches of mathematics. Typically, for psychologists, some sort of elementary mathematical statistics, highly useful for the description of populations of entities having equal valence and arranged in continuous distributions of certain types, is used.

Piaget (1968) has suggested that the concept of the mathematical group is more useful for the sort of developmental structures and operations that compel his interest. Piaget claims that the group concept is useful because, unlike usual forms of abstraction, which draw out properties from things—the more general the property, the more information lost through abstraction (cf. Chaitin, 1974)—the group property conserves information about systems. It is obtained through "reflective abstraction," a method that "does not derive properties from things, but from our ways of acting on things, the operations we perform on them; from the various fundamental ways of coordinating such acts or operations—'uniting,' 'ordering,' 'placing in one-to-one correspondance.'" The external structures of action are tied with the structure of mental operations. In fact, Piaget has claimed an isomorphism between the child's most primitive notions of time, causality, and number and those most sophisticated notions of time, causality, and number held by modern scientists.[*]

The notion of the mathematical group is also utilized by Watzlawick *et al.* (1974) in their analysis of frames of reference and of the types of change that transcend a given frame or system. The analysis of Watzlawick, Weakland, and Fisch in *Change* adds to the group concept Russell's "theory of logical types," so that the framework of group theory, which allows the representation of change in invariant systems, is complemented by the theory of types, which discusses the relationships of member to class and the "peculiar metamorphosis which is in the nature of shifts from one logical level to the next higher."

Their inquiry into the effects of paradoxical communication on change is long-standing, and Russell's writings deal directly with paradox and the reordering of categories of the understanding. The theory of logical types is also applied to instances of what the Jungians term

---

[*] Public lecture delivered at New York University, April 16, 1967.

"enantiadromia," the conversion of something into its opposite. This intertwining of opposites has interesting consequences for psychotherapy and suitably ancient roots, as we've noted, homologue (structure) and paradox having principal place as the instruments of change. We may take structure to mean, with Piaget (1968), "the set of *possible* states and transformations of which the system that actually obtains is a special case." Interestingly, Capra (1975) has made an identical definition for the theoretical description of modern particle physics by "S-matrix theory":

> The structure of a hadron, therefore, is not understood as a definite arrangement of constituent parts, but is given by all sets of particles which may interact with one another to form the hadron under consideration. Thus a proton exists potentially as a neutron-pion pair, a kaon-lambda pair and so on.

We wish to deal both with the question of how to represent structures of thought or action and with the sudden transforms characteristic of human change in action and understanding. Psychotherapy deals with the conditions for change in persons, most usually indexed by emotional changes. It's a commonplace of our understandings that emotions are paired: joy and sorrow, terror and rage, romantic love and disgust, etc. It's also well known that emotions are subject to sudden change, as when a joke overturns anger (cf. Douglas, 1970). Moreover, the sudden changes of action—going on a binge or a fast, religious conversion, fighting or fleeing—are both evident in the fabric of our lives and endlessly puzzling. A recently developed mathematical formalism, catastrophe theory, invented by René Thom and extensively applied by E. C. Zeeman (1976), depicts and maps exactly "those things that change suddenly, by fits and starts."

Catastrophe theory is derived from topology, a mathematics dealing with the properties of surfaces in various dimensions. Topology itself is cited by Piaget (1968) as one of the three "parent structures" of mathematics, and psychogenetically the earliest of the three to appear (the others are algebraic and lattice or network structures). Topology appeals to us intuitively as a formalism for describing human events because (following our argument thus far) those events are best described with imagery, and intuitions about complex events, as Arnheim (1969) notes in his brilliant discussion of "imageless thought," "more often than not require highly abstract configurations, represented by topological and often geometrical figures in mental space." In addition, as Zeeman (1976) emphasizes, the differential calculus, which expresses Newtonian and Einsteinian theories of motion, gravitation, electromagnetism, and relativity, is limited to phenomena for which change is smooth and continuous. Catastrophe theory describes phenomena that are discontinuous and divergent; the actions of disequilibrium modeled by the breakdown of smooth surfaces of equilibrium. Thom has proven that for processes controlled by no more than four factors, there are just seven elementary catastrophes. Zeeman (1976) uses catastrophe theory to map such phenomena as: aggression in dogs, cathartic release from self-pity, the buckling of an elastic beam, the propagation of nerve impulses, and the behavior and treatment of *anorexia nervosa*. In this latter, the theory has in addition the serendipitous effect of explaining the patient's own description of her experiences:

> The seemingly incomprehensible terms in which some anorexics describe their illness turn out to be quite logical when viewed in the framework of the catastrophe surfaces.

This sort of result would be hoped for if our association of image and experience has merit. In addition, catastrophe theory has other now-familiar correlates: First, the "attractor" of a system, the factor that accounts for states of static equilibrium, when it is in dynamic equilibrium "consists of the entire stable cycle of states through which the system passes." So we have a term equivalent to Piaget's "structure" and Capra's "S-matrix." The neural mechanisms of the brain form a dynamic system, the equilibrium states of which can be represented by attractors, and Thom claims that all sudden jumps possible between the simplest attractors are described by elementary catastrophes. Zeeman holds that the model is most accurate in describing the limbic system (concerned with emotion and mood) rather than the more complex activities of the cortex. So the sort of emotional events that concern psychologists can be modeled in their sudden changes, and related to corresponding functions of the brain. Finally, "the model implies the possibility of divergence, so that a small perturbation in the initial state of the system can result in a large difference in the final state" (cf. Haley and Hoffman, 1967). The theory may thus require conditions that will map such equivalent therapies as the family therapies, which aim for just these "small perturbations" in complex systems of human interaction.

Other correspondences also come to mind: For example, the discontinuity that plagues dream sequences might be seen in the light of catastrophe theory as a visual model of the "inaccessible" region of a catastrophe, "through which" the sudden change occurs. The sudden appearance of (or access to) archetypal figures in consciousness is often seen to occur when situations of great conflict or paradox obtain, and the subsequent change from despair to hope is very dramatic. Metacommunications, (cf. Haley, 1963) statements in relationship that communicate about the relationship, provide a reframing, or sudden shift in logical type that sets forth strong, sudden emotion and the associated images that we have come to call "archetypal." The associated notions of rule, image, neural representation, archetype, percept, thought, action, and their structural transforms through homologue and paradox, may find adequate abstract expression in the power and generality of Thom's mathematical language and his maps.

References

Arnheim, R. *Visual thinking*. Berkeley: University of California, 1969.
Attneave, F. How do you know? *American Psychologist,* 1974, 7, 493-499.
Barber, T. X., and Spanos, N. P. Toward a convergence in hypnosis research. *American Pscyhologist,* 1974, 7, 500-511.
Bateson, G. *Steps to an ecology of mind*. New York, Ballantine, 1972.
Capra, F. *The tao of physics*. Berkeley: Shambala, 1975.
Casey, E. S. Toward an archetypal imagination. *Spring,* 1974, 1-33.
Chaitin, G. J. Randomness and mathematical proof. *Scientific American,* March, 1974, 47-52.
Chang, C.-Y. *Original teaching of ch'an buddhism*. New York: Random House, 1969.
Douglas, M. *Natural symbols*. New York: Random House, 1970.
Eliade, M. *Yoga*. New York: Harper and Row, 1958.
Eliade, M. *The forge and the crucible*. New York: Harper and Row, 1962a.
Eliade, M. *Shamanism*. Princeton: Princeton University, 1962b.
Eliade, M. *Myth and reality*. New York: Harper and Row, 1963.
Eliade, M. *Images and symbols*. New York: Sheed and Ward, 1969.
Evans-Wentz, W. Y. *The Tibetan book of the dead*. London: Oxford University, 1927.
Frazer, J. G. *The golden bough*. New York, Macmillan, 1922.
Gardner, H. *The quest for mind*. New York: Knopf, 1973.
Ginott, H. *Between parent and child*. New York: Avon, 1965.
Greenleaf, E. The Schreber case: Remarks on psychoanalytic explanation. *Psychotherapy: Theory, Research, Practice,* 1969, 6, No. 1, 16-20.
Greenleaf, E. The red house: Hypnotherapy of hysterical blindness. *American Journal of Clinical Hypnosis,* 1971, 13, No. 3, 155-161.
Greenleaf, E. Senoi dream groups. *Psychotherapy: Theory, Research, Practice,* 1973, 10, No. 3, 218-222.
Greenleaf, E. Defining hypnosis during hypnotherapy. *International Journal of Clinical and Experimental Hypnosis,* 1974, 22, No. 2, 120-130.
Greenleaf, E. The "unconscious-mind mirror" in active imagination. *Psychotherapy: Theory, Research, Practice,* 1975, 12, No. 2, 202-206.
Greenleaf, E., and McCartney, L. R. Discussions with Irene: An unsuspected dual personality encountered while working with dream images. (Unpublished manuscript)
Guggenbuhl-Craig, A. Must analysis fail through its destructive aspect? *Spring,* 1970, 133-145.
Haley, J. *Strategies of psychotherapy*. New York: Grune and Stratton, 1963.
Haley, J. (Ed.) *Advanced techniques of hypnosis and therapy: Selected papers of Milton Erickson, M.D*. New York: Grune and Stratton, 1967.

Haley, J. *Uncommon therapy: The psychiatric techniques of Milton Erickson, M.D.* New York: Ballantine, 1973.
Haley, J., and Hoffman, L. *Techniques of family therapy.* New York: Basic Books, 1967.
Hillman, J. Anima. *Spring*, 1973 and 1974.
Hull, R. F. C. Bibliographical notes on active imagination in the works of C. G. Jung. *Spring*, 1971, 115–120.
Jerison, H. J. Paleoneurology and the evolution of mind. *Scientific American*, January, 1976, 90–101.
Jung, C. G. *Four archetypes.* Princeton: Princeton University, 1959. (Collected Works 9, part I.)
Jung, C. G. *Memories, dreams, reflections.* New York: Random House, 1961.
Jung, C. G. *The practice of psychotherapy.* Princeton: Princeton University, 1966.
Odier, C. *Anxiety and magic thinking.* New York: International Universities, 1956.
Orne, M. On the social psychology of the psychological experiment: With particular reference to demand characteristics and their implications. *American Psychologist*, 1962, 17, 776–783.
Perls, F. *Gestalt therapy verbatim.* New York: Bantam, 1969.
Piaget, J. *Structuralism.* New York: Harper and Row, 1968.
Sechehaye, M. *Autobiography of a schizophrenic girl.* New York: Grune and Stratton, 1951.
Simonton, C. Belief systems and management of the emotional aspects of malignancy. *Transpersonal Psychology*, 1975, VII, 29–41.
Singer, J. L. *Imagery and daydream methods in psychotherapy and behavior modification.* New York: Academic, 1974.
Stein, R. *Incest and human love.* New York: Third Press, 1973.
Stanislavski, C. *An actor prepares.* Harmondsworth, Middlesex, England: Penguin, 1967 (1926).
Stewart, K. Dream theory in Malaya. *Complex*, 1951, 6, 21–34.
Sullivan, H. S. *The psychiatric interview.* New York: Norton, 1954.
Sullivan, H. S. *Clinical studies in psychiatry.* New York: Norton, 1956.
Swedenborg, S. W. The inner guide to the archetypes. (Unpublished manuscript)
Von Franz, M.-L., and Hillman, J. *Lectures on Jung's typology.* Zurich: Spring, 1971.
Von Franz, M.-L. *C. G. Jung: His myth in our time.* New York: Putnam's, 1975.
Watkins, M. The waking dream in European psychotherapy. *Spring*, 1974, 33–58.
Watzlawick, P., Beavin, J. H., and Jackson, D. D. *Pragmatics of human communication.* New York: Norton, 1967.
Watzlawick, P., Weakland, J. H., and Fisch, R. *Change: Principles of problem formation and problem resolution.* New York: Norton, 1974.
Weaver, R. *The old wise woman: A study of active imagination.* New York: Putnam's Sons, 1973.
Whorf, R. L. *Language, thought and reality: Selected writings.* Cambridge, MIT, 1956.
Winch, P. *The idea of a social science.* London: Paul, 1958.
Wittgenstein, L. *The "blue" and "brown" books.* New York: Harper and Row, 1958.
Zeeman, E. C. Catastrophe theory. *Scientific American*, March, 1976, 65–83.
Zimmer, H. On the significance of the Indian Tantric Yoga. *Papers from the Eranos Yearbooks*, 4, 1960, 3–58.
Zucker, H. *Problems of psychotherapy.* New York: Free Press, 1967.

7

Eidetic Psychotherapy

Anees A. Sheikh

1. Introduction

As Pavlov (1936) remarked, there are "two categories of people—artists and thinkers. Between them there is a marked difference. The artists. . .comprehend reality as a whole, as a continuity, a complete living reality, without any divisions, without any separations. The other group, the thinkers, pull it apart, kill it. . . . This difference is especially prominent in the so-called eidetic imagery of children. . . . Such a whole creation of reality cannot be completely attained by a thinker" (p. 113). It is evident that Pavlov recognized the integrating nature of the eidetic, its power to heal the schism generated by verbal thought processes.

Pavlov's view of individuals may also be applicable to society. Perhaps "a whole era of man can think itself into a trap, and spin without resolving anything, instead creating new problems. When an age decays and uses words as a manipulative weapon to perpetuate what has already lost relevance, the eidetic becomes the symbol of much needed fresh experience" (Ahsen, 1974, p. 282). It appears that after having been severed from visions, warped by words, and stifled by semantics for a long time, Western man is ready to restore his wholeness by returning to the nonverbal springs of his existence. "We witness the return of the dream; we experience the image which precedes the word. If the word splits subject from object, the image restores us to the primal oneness of our deepest self" (Luce, 1968, p. 1).

Anees A. Sheikh • Department of Psychology, Marquette University, Milwaukee, Wisconsin 53233.

In the realm of psychotherapy, the last decade has brought a rapidly increasing interest in the uses of image techniques (Sheikh, 1977). A number of distinct advantages of utilizing mental images during therapeutic interaction have emerged (Singer, 1974). For example, it has been pointed out that details concerning affect and fantasy may be contained in the image but not be available in verbal thought (Sheikh and Panagiotou, 1975). Imagery may provide access to significant preverbal memories or memories encoded at developmental stages when language is not yet predominant (Kepecs, 1957). It appears that especially vivid or traumatic experiences tend to be encoded in imagery. Imagery procedures seem to be particularly suited to dealing with psychosomatic problems (Ahsen, 1968, 1972, 1973). Images are less prone to be filtered through the conscious critical apparatus than is linguistic thought. Since images, unlike verbal logic, are spatial and simultaneous rather than sequential and linear representations, they have greater isomorphism with the qualities of perception and, therefore, a greater capacity for experiential accuracy (Lipkin, 1970).

Eidetic psychotherapy, originated by Akhter Ahsen (1965, 1968, 1972, 1977a, 1977b), relies solely upon the elicitation and manipulation of a type of mental imagery that he has termed "eidetic." Out of the discovery of the functional attributes pertaining to these images, he has evolved a highly complex and innovative system. It fully deserves Lazarus's tribute: "Compared to Akhter Ahsen's penetrating analysis of imagery formation and eidetic processes, all other clinical uses of imagery appear singularly embryonic" (Lazarus, 1972, p. v). But before Ahsen's contributions can be accurately understood and evaluated, it seems necessary to have some ground for comparison with what has gone before and to specify a current consensual definition and classification of mental imagery.

2. Mental Images and Their Classification

Richardson (1969) has compiled the research on imagery and organized the criteria for its classification. However, he does not fail to emphasize the imprecision inherent in the classification along the criterion dimensions in use. He begins with a simple definition of the mental image: it is a quasi-sensory or quasi-perceptual experience that occurs in the absence of the stimulus conditions that would elicit the corresponding true perception. Images may occur in any sense modality, including synesthetic combinations and internal somatic signals, e.g., hunger and pain, or they may reproduce an affective experience.

Some types of images are elicited by or related to recently or presently perceived external stimuli. For example, in the visual mode, illusions, after-images, eidetics, and mescaline images are in some manner based upon present or recent perceptions. Eidetics and after-images occur when the stimulus has been removed. To a limited degree in eidetics, and more markedly in illusion and mescaline imagery, the image may be superimposed upon, but not be isomorphic with perceptual elements.

The unreal nature of images with respect to the stimulus conditions does not necessarily render the quality or intensity of the image different from the genuine sensation, perception, or affect. The hallucination is a case in point; usually a difference does exist in one or both of these aspects of the experience that distinguishes it from reality. Nevertheless, as early as 1910, Perky showed that under certain conditions normal subjects were unable to distinguish a perceptual phenomenon projected upon a screen from their own image. The study was replicated by Segal and Nathan in 1964. An image is likely to be distinguishable from a percept, on the basis of intensity and stability. But the distinctions are not always present: an intense image may have stronger responses associated with it and command more attention than a barely noticed percept. Affective imagery may become sufficiently intense to fully reproduce a genuine affective response. Hallucinations, hypnagogic images, eidetics, and images charged with much emotional response may be as vivid as the perceptual counterparts.

Nineteenth-century investigators Titchener and Wundt attempted to specify distinctions of quality between percepts and images; in particular, they investigated stability (see Richardson, 1969). The stability criterion holds best for the visual mode. A visual percept seems to become more distinct when fixated, but a visual image is likely to elude an attempt to fixate it. However, some visual images, particularly eidetics, may last for a few minutes, and are susceptible to focusing and scanning. In other than the visual modality, even the percepts are unstable.

It is apparent that the dimensions that distinguish imagery from perception and affect are continuous rather than dichotomous. Richardson has shown that the dimensions for imagery classifications have the same trait. On the basis of twentieth-century investigations, Richardson has identified four classes of mental images, which may be compared in respect to clarity, vividness, localization, fixedness or stability, completeness of detail, susceptibility to scanning, and degree of likeness to the sensory percept. The identified classes are as follows: (1) after-images, (2) eidetic images, (3) memory images, (4) imagination images.

2.1. After-Images

This class of images closely resembles a percept, since they have a strong sensory quality. Usually after-images result from actual perception of a stimulus object: they are representation of the object's form and, positively or negatively, of its hue. After-images are usually less vivid than their percepts, but have the sensory quality of literally being seen just as the percepts. After-images are not susceptible to scanning since they move with the movement of the eye. Of all the images, these are least dependent upon central nervous system stimulation; retinal stimulation alone appears to be sufficient to produce them. But several reports suggest that after-images may also result from purely central stimulation: from dream figures or highly colored mental images.

2.2. Eidetic Images

In the traditional sense, eidetic images, are another form of perceptlike images. Two types of eidetic images are reported: those resembling prolonged after-images occasioned by percepts, and those originating in memory or the general process of imagination.* The former may be hue-positive or hue-negative, but may not be entirely accurate representations. Both types are characterized by clarity and detail. Eidetics are relatively fixed and one can scan them for detail as one can examine a photograph. However, a degree of movement of parts of the image may occur with suggestion. Existing studies accept the prevalence of eidetics among children, but among adults they are usually thought to be rare. The identification of an image as eidetic is not altogether reliable since investigators apply different criteria as well as methods.

2.3. Memory Images

Memory images apparently, at times, may approach eidetics in clarity and vividness, but typically do not. They tend to be pallid, fragmented, indefinitely localized, and of brief duration. However, they have the potential for the extreme vividness and clarity, and conceivably could be cultivated for these qualities, and perhaps also for stability and external projection. Attention and affect appear to influence these qualities of memory images.

---

* Ahsen (1977b) has termed these two types "typographic" and "structural" eidetics, respectively. It is the former type that traditionally has been studied more extensively by experimenters.

2.4. Imagination Images

This class of images is significantly influenced by motivational states, and, according to Richardson, generally involve concentrated quasi-hypnotic attention along with inhibition of associations. Imagination images include the following relatively distinct forms: hypnagogic images, perceptual isolation images, hallucinogenic drug images, and sleep-deprivation images. Some of these forms are very perceptlike and assume apparent independence. Imagination images are marked by substantiality and vividness that can equal or surpass that of eidetic imagery. The imaginal forms are given to novelty, symbolism, and condensation.

3. Ahsen's Eidetic Image: The ISM

Previous reviewers have generally described and evaluated only the body of literature pertaining to the study of eidetics carried out through presentation of external stimuli such as a picture (Gray and Gummerman, 1975; Richardson, 1969). It is not very well known that the study of eidetics through external presentation had never been in the minds of the first researchers in the field (Ahsen, 1977b). The initial interest in eidetics arose from reports on internal observations of images that had quasi-hallucinatory qualities and generated tension in the eyeball, yet could not be characterized as hallucinations because the subjects evidently knew them to be internal experiences (Urbantschitsch, 1907).

The study of the eidetic through presentation of an external stimulus was contrived to provide an experimental design for the approach to the internal eidetic (Jaensch, 1930). Unfortunately, soon the eidetic was completely dissociated from its original position as an internal phenomenon, and experimentalists became embroiled in seeking the proof or disproof of a phenomenon that was, in their experiments, at best arbitrarily connected with the internal eidetic image. Even up to the present time, experimentalists have not relinquished the projection of externally presented stimuli. As a result of these "external experiments," the eidetic image has frequently been confused with recent memory. In fact, some of the writers regard the eidetic to be nothing but a recent memory displaying all the attributes of a recent experience (Norman, 1968).

Akhter Ahsen has brought the question of internal eidetics, which he terms as structural eidetics, back into the focus of investigation. Eidetics, as he views them, traverse Richardson's classification, bearing almost equal likeness to the last three of the four classes. They are developmentally determined, affect-laden, vivid, repeatable, and almost universally present images that pertain to key memories and fantasies associated with basic growth and conflict situations, and are arranged in a predetermined sequence. Once elicited, they exhibit incipient tendencies to progress in particular ways, which are not voluntarily controlled. It is often necessary to bring out the incipient movement through repeated projection. The progression of imagery is used to lead to the crux of the problem (Ahsen, 1973, 1974, 1975).

Ahsen views the eidetic to be a semipermanent representation that has been figuratively impressed upon the memory in response to the formative events of life. The visual component, the image, is always accompanied by a somatic pattern—a set of bodily feelings and tensions, including somatic correlates of emotion—and a cognitive or experiential meaning. The eidetic, therefore, is an integral psychosomatic event with a tripartite structure. The three components, the *i*mage, the *s*omatic pattern, and the *m*eaning, led Ahsen to name the complete eidetic complex the ISM.

The eidetic is formed and retained because it represents a highly emotional and significant event or relationship, or a recurrent fantasy in the development of the individual. Therefore, it is to be expected that every important experience, every area of conflict has a corresponding eidetic. The visual component of the eidetic is formed from the experience's salient visual elements, which, however, may be distorted by fantasy responses to the occasion. The eidetic is primarily a memory. Although external events may be overshadowed by fantasy determinants in creating the eidetic, it, nevertheless, is a representation of the individual's perceptions, feelings, and interpretations of these feelings at a particular time. In other words, the eidetic is a representation of a memory, inclusive of the event and the individual's full-scale reaction to that event.

Ahsen demonstrates that at the origin of the ISM, the visual component assumes representational precedence. It spearheads the experience of the total event and, therefore, becomes the psychic cue for the event in its entirety. Ahsen (1968, 1972) reports that through the recall of the visual component, the entire composite event can be fully recalled into the awareness, and the ISM can be experienced in exactly the same way as at the time of the original perception; in fact, it may even release latent affect that may have been arrested or repressed originally.

The image component when first experienced may be relatively vague and elude focusing. Continued concentration, however, renders it more precise, vivid, detailed, and stable. It is fixed and cannot be altered at will by the patient. Even if the patient should succeed in temporarily altering an image, it will not fail to revert to its original form as soon as he loses conscious control or relaxes. The image can be manipulated and mutated only under concentrated attention and only in accordance with the laws under which these images function. Furthermore, when a series of changes are made, they have a corresponding impact on the psyche.

3.1. Visiosomatic Fixation and Dessociation

The tripartite unity of the ISM, and the leading position of the visual component is considered to be a psychic law by Ahsen. He calls it the *Law of Visiosomatic Fixation*. Subsequent to the inception of an ISM, there is a tendency toward a weakening of the link between the three components. This tendency has been termed the *Law of Visiosomatic Dessociation*. Ahsen points out that the separation of the visual cue from the other components is more apparent than real and, therefore, it should not be called *dissociation*. While the visual element is overemphasized in the consciousness, the somatic and meaning aspects are relegated to the fringes of consciousness. They may express themselves in vague response patterns but are not intimately connected with the awareness of the event. The visual component is reduced to a mere picture and remains the only link with the original experience (Panagiotou and Sheikh, 1974). In Ahsen's opinion, this "chromatic overemphasis" accounts for the remarkable efficiency of human memory as well as for man's predisposition to ill-health. He states that "divorced from these space-time references, the visual cues, the experiential states are figuratively blind and appear as vague and haunting affects which cannot be understood or ascribed to any frame of reference" (Ahsen, 1968, p. 85). Fortunately, the visual nucleus always retains at least a vague link with somatic pattern and meaning; and through it, the original experience can be completely revived. It should be noted that sometimes the visual component of one ISM may be confounded with or relegated behind a similar visual pattern of another; consequently, the constituents of two or more ISMs may merge around a single visual nucleus or arrange themselves as a seriality of states. When that happens, it is said that an ISM has been confused with another ISM or pushed "behind a seriality of states," and a retrogressive activation of a seriality of images is necessary to elicit the primary image (Panagiotou and Sheikh, 1977).

3.2. Bipolar Configurations

Ahsen reports another important characteristic of the ISM complex: all experiences are viewed by the ego as either ego-positive or ego-negative:

> If an event happened in a particular way it could as well have happened in an opposite manner. Keeping in view the final issues, the ego confirms one of the poles and leaves the other free to take care of itself. With passage of time, the confirmed pole becomes further magnified and elucidated because of repeated attention paid to it by the ego. The other pole atrophies through lack of attention and visual revival. The final outcome as years pass, is an imbalanced state containing a single strong visual image in the center, suggestive of a monopolar configuration. The opposite pole practically ceases to exist, as its visual representation slips out of attention. (Ahsen, 1968, p. 121-122)

It appears to be Ahsen's position that the ego must choose to identify itself with one of the two poles of an event. However, why such a dichotomy should be regarded a natural law of the psyche is not altogether apparent; for Ahsen also points to a synthesizing function of the ego that is activated in therapy. This division of elements and exaggerated emphasis upon one pole should perhaps be viewed as a pathological response pattern and not as a universal tendency.

The neglected pole of the ISM atrophies but does not completely lose its relationship to the ego: concentration upon the pole selected by the ego always involves a paravisual relationship with the discarded end. "Visual cues pertaining to the suspended pole glimmer in an undeveloped form on the fringes of consciousness" (Ahsen, 1968, p. 122). It is a function of eidetic psychotherapy to attain a balanced visio-fixation upon a newly formed central nucleus. In order to achieve this end, the imagery of the neglected pole must first be developed; only then can the elements of both poles be synthesized around a new nucleus.

3.3. The Magical Laws of the Psyche

Ahsen explains that the behavior of eidetics lawfully corresponds with the functioning of the psyche. Consequently, manipulation of eidetics leads to changes in the personality structures. The therapeutic effect of these images comes about according to four principles that Ahsen discovered as a result of his anthropological study of magic as well as his clinical observations. These "magical laws" of the psyche, as Ahsen terms them, are (1) part is whole, (2) contact is unification, (3) imitation is reality, and (4) wish is action.

Ahsen maintains that these four principles underlie psychic functioning at all levels. The child's mind is profoundly and frankly magical, indulging freely in the play of these four principles. The adult, on the other hand, tends to develop a sense of shame in regard to magic, yet, below this shame, he too continues to be magical, and, in his more spontaneous and honest moods, he resembles the child. It is not uncommon to see a child who wishes to be like his father, put on his father's shoes or clothes and pretend, and then actually *feel* that he is his father. The case histories provided by Ahsen (1968) reveal that adults, not infrequently, have similar experiences. For example, he speaks of a man who experienced "positive psychological streamings" running through his body while holding an eidetic pistol that had come to symbolize security in his mind. He mentions a person who felt jubilant and triumphant after he had in his imagination acquired a simple garment that symbolized a whole drama of sibling rivalry. Still another individual who was very attached to the memory of his mother endowed a quilt that she had made for him with magical powers. When he was asked to creep into this image-quilt, he experienced "a rush of strange psychophysiological feelings, which made him perspire" (Ahsen, 1965). As it is perhaps evident, the magical laws and the objects formed under their influence constitute an important instrument of fast-moving therpeutic maneuvers in Ahsen's approach.

4. Eidetics and Electrically Evoked Recollections

It is of interest to note that the characteristics that Ahsen ascribes to eidetics receive considerable support from Penfield's research (1952, 1958, 1959, 1963, 1975) with the recollections of epileptics, elicited through electrical stimulation of certain points in the cerebral cortex. A few quotations from Penfield's writings will help clarify these similarities:

> There is an area of the surface of the human brain where local electrical stimulation can call back a sequence of past experiences. . . . It is as though a wire recorder, or a strip of cinematographic film with sound track, had been set in motion within the brain. The sights and sounds, and the thoughts, of a former day pass through the man's mind again. (Penfield, 1959, p. 1719)
>
> The subject feels again the emotions which the situation originally produced in him, and he is aware of the same interpretations, true or false, which he himself gave the experience in the first place. Thus evoked recollection is not the exact photographic reproduction of the past scenes and events. It is the reproduction of what the patient saw and heard and felt and understood. (Penfield, 1952, p. 183)

> A song goes through his mind, probably as he heard it on a certain occasion; he finds himself a part of the specific situation, which progresses and evolves just as in the original situation. It is to him the act of a familiar play, and he is himself both an actor and the audience. (Penfield, 1952, p. 108)
>
> Sometimes it would seem that even fancies reappear, as in the case of R. W., a little boy who saw at the beginning of each attack "robbers with guns" such as he had seen pictured in his comic book. (Penfield, 1958, p. 156)
>
> In these examples it seems to make little difference whether the original experience was fact, dream, or fancy. (Penfield, 1952, p. 180)

Whereas Penfield was unconcerned with the psychotherapeutic implications of his investigation, Ahsen's major findings emerged out of his psychotherapeutic investigations. In Penfield's research the instrument of exploration is the stimulating electrode applied to the cortex, while in Ahsen's work it is concentration on an eidetic in a selected area involving emotional conflict. However, it appears that both Penfield and Ahsen are describing the same phenomenon. Both are concerned not with externally but internally evoked experiential pictures; both stress the vividness of the image; both observe that the image has affective or somatic accompaniments and attached meaning or interpretation; both emphasize the repeatability of the image and employ repeated evocation for elucidation and progressive evolvement of the experience. They agree that experience or interpretation that may appear problematic or be unavailable at the beginning becomes accessible as the experiential picture progresses. This observation is particularly relevant to therapeutic practice with schizophrenics who are noted for their inability to regenerate experience. Concentration upon a continuous series of developmental eidetics, over a fairly long period of time, appears to reconstruct a schizophrenic's emotional life and stop and reverse the general splitting process (Ahsen, 1974; Sheikh and Panagiotou, 1975).

It has already been hinted that, according to Ahsen, an event may never have occurred as it is depicted by the eidetic. An eidetic usually represents an experience of hybrid reality: it consists of a combination of the real and the psychic. It need not portray a specific realistic perception but it always represents a meaningful psychic construction. The distinction between fact and fantasy in the mind cannot be made by separating fact from fiction on the basis of rationality or irrationality but rather on the basis of functions. It is remarkable that Penfield's findings give support to Ahsen's contentions in this area also (Sheikh and Panagiotou, 1975).

It is interesting that Ahsen consistently stresses the visual aspect of the pictures, but in Penfield's reports auditory evocation emerges as a predominant occurrence. However, Penfield also reveals that when the electrode is applied repeatedly to evolve the auditory experience further, a complete panoramic reenactment of the original experience takes place and a detailed visual picture emerges in the mind (Dolan and Sheikh, 1977a). It is possible that the initial auditory rather than visual recall is peculiar to epileptics (Kubie, 1952). Ahsen (1973) has found that epileptics, as a rule, are capable of experiencing visual images. But in specific areas their visual imagery gives the impression of congestion or condensation, as if overly tightly packed, and in these areas they manifest an inability to sustain a visual image clearly. These areas, Ahsen reports, pertain to certain problem aspects of the father. This finding raises intriguing questions that invite further systematic scrutiny.

5. The ISM Theory of Personality

According to Ahsen, countless ISMs accrue to the individual during his development and form the repertoire from which he can draw responses for future appropriate or inappropriate adaptations. Among the elements potentially available are the neglected poles of the bipolar ISMs. The conditioned fixation of ISM states may be changed, but only by events of marked impact, such as therapeutic intervention that involves the reliving of the origin of these states. However, in the absence of significant intervention, the conditioned states are inert.

It is left unclear by Ahsen how an individual ceases to form new ISMs in response to novel stimulus situations. Presumably, new ISMs are formed when the stimulus situation lacks elements of similarity that would bring old ISMs into play. However, as time progresses, so many ISMs are in the repertoire that there are few stimulus situations to which these do not generalize. In other words, it appears that the patterns already formed will take over whenever they can. There is evidence for this trend in other theories as well (Martin, 1976). However, at present, the ISM theory seems incomplete in accounting for the learning of new responses that can occur, for instance, through modeling or other interpersonal communications, or through a chance experience in which the individual reacts contrary to prior conditionings and alters an ISM fixation. The theory also does not account for the effects of the self-image of a new ISM that diffuses into and changes existing ISM fixations. For instance, a special success for a person lacking in self-esteem may change his response patterns in areas not related to success. It should be noted that the ISM theory does not specifically exclude other kinds of change, but simply seems incomplete in clearly delineating possible ways out of its determinism:

> If past patterns always control responses, how can changes occur in any way other than directed therapeutic manipulation? Even new impactful events will bring old responses into play. Again, it appears that the inflexible stereotype generalization of response patterns may itself be symptomatic of a developmental course gone awry, just as fixation upon an extreme pole to the exclusion of the elements of its opposite may be a special maladaptive rather than a general pattern of response. (Panagiotou and Sheikh, 1974, p. 234)

Evidently Ahsen (1968) sees in the human mind a vast multiplicity of ISM states rather than a logical oneness: "Under the magical principles every significant state turns out to be active in its own right, seeking its own direction and destiny" (p. 32). Therefore, every significant ISM is given the status of a mini-personality, which he calls a "personality multiple." It should be noted that in respect to this the emphasis shifts from the visual and somatic components to the self-perceptions inherent in the ISM event. About the personality multiple, Ahsen (1968) says:

> It is Mr. X's one image at a particular time when he was feeling or doing something bearing relevance to his problems of existence. As he was vitally involved tens of thousands of times, he has generated an equal number of personality multiples along this line of action. All these personality multiples are now living, feeling, and breathing in him, contending toward the same old aims they completed or left unfinished. They variously live the life they once incarnated while something in the individual tries to force an illusory unity among them.
> They live in him in the form of clearly observable images. At some particular time he wore a striking suit and experienced some significant situation; the memory image pertaining to that situation continues to wear that suit and to emit an influence peculiar to that situation. (p. 141)

How are these "mini-individuals" born? Ahsen states that they come into existence as a result of the association between specific psychological themes and visual configurations from reality or fantasy images. Then, these associations pass through a process of simplification pertaining to the magical plane: part is whole, contact is unification, imitation is reality, wish is action. For instance, an article of clothing may represent an entire psychological drama of conflict with the parents or siblings.

The personality multiples continue to live almost indefinitely, unless they are accidentally or therapeutically resolved. Important multiples are usually formed in respect to the self, parents, siblings, and other animate and inanimate objects that are, at the time, emotionally relevant to the individual's life. Some of the earliest multiples, according to Ahsen (1968), pertain to the mother:

> Her various significant aspects are welded with relevant cues. The personality multiples formed in brothers and sisters usually represent themes of

jealousy and death. Significant dresses worn by brothers and sisters under typical situations come to represent these themes. . . . Personality multiples projected in the father usually deal with themes of protection and discipline or his relationship with the mother, and problems of weaning and transition to his liberating image in the psyche. (pp. 142-143)

It is interesting to note that the feeling of self is projected not only in self-images but also in images of others.

Although personality multiples themselves are not given to unity, the ego exists among them as a force toward rational integration. For the sake of logical integrity, it attempts to centralize experiences around a sense of indentity: it selectively identifies with portions of the past that suit it.

Ahsen admits that a movement in the direction of integration is a natural tendency, and a basic need, but feels that it, nevertheless, involves an "original error." Such a selective personality, he says, is an illusion experiencing itself. He believes that the rejection of certain material and the assimilation of the rest results spontaneously in an overly conceptual approach to the environment. This approach demands that the ego explain the personality in ways that are acceptable to it in view of the self-concept. When the ego has difficulty in accomplishing this, it tends to retreat increasingly behind its own narrow sense of identity and to exclude or distort elements it cannot handle.

In de-emphasizing the function of logic or realism in the unification of personality elements, Ahsen's view diverges not only from classical analysis, but also from most of the popular contemporary theories (Martin, 1976). Contemporary personality theories tend to emphasize the conceptually integrated personality, one that supposedly makes cognitive sense to the individual. Little emphasis is given to the possibility that paradoxical elements co-exist. These theories foster the assumption that existence is lost if one cannot integrate it into a plausible whole and maintain a consistent and logically understandable answer to the question, "Who am I?"

Ahsen does not mean to say that organization and the tendency toward individuality is entirely mistaken, but merely that it is highly overemphasized, in a rational or concept-oriented individual. In order to achieve logically exquisite integrity, the ego exacts a certain price of the individual. He must sacrifice the illogical magical basis of problem-solving that in Ahsen's view is the natural foundation for operation of the psyche at all levels and that has great healing power at its disposal. Also, the individual must exclude or limit psychic materials for adaptation, materials that are potentially valuable but abrasive to the ego's chosen self-image. In extreme cases, it is at the expense of a great deal of energy that the unacceptable material from past states is shut out of awareness (Ahsen, 1968; Panagiotou and Sheikh, 1974).

A truly healthy sense of selfhood is built upon an acceptance of underlying multiplicity. This form of identity fears no enemies in the repressed and needs no rationalizations to defend itself constantly. "It is powerful and dynamic, fearless and all-embracing; it honors categories of living above categories of reasoning" (Ahsen, 1968, p. 34). Ahsen builds his therapy upon the theory of personality as multiplicity. He finds personality multiples an excellent vehicle for analysis, understanding, and catharsis: they can be easily and spontaneously invoked and they circumvent ego defenses.

6. Diagnostic and Therapeutic Procedures

In Ahsen's system, the diagnostic and the therapeutic procedures are inseparably intertwined. The eidetic procedures that he has developed help not only in understanding the underlying dynamics but also in drawing up the therapeutic plan.

Eidetic analysis by Ahsen and by others who have followed his system has indicated that the symptoms are largely caused either by dessociation of the eidetic components, by fixation on the negative pole, or by a partial or complete repression of significant experience. Consequently, the aim of eidetic therapy is achieved mainly by the revival of the tripartite unity, by a shift of the ego's attention to the neglected positive pole, which brings about a more balanced and realistic appraisal of the experience, or by the uncovering of the repressed experience through progression of eidetic imagery. Since Ahsen considers an eidetic event in its full intensity to be the psychic equivalent of the corresponding actual event, the re-experience of personality multiples in the form of eidetics is the re-experience of the individual's history, which thus becomes available for change.

There are three main levels in the eidetic psychotherapeutic process. The first level deals with the symptoms of a psychosomatic or hysterical or phobic nature. Next is the developmental level, which pertains primarily to the widespread problems developed in early life with reference to the parents. Ahsen has developed two major eidetic tests, the *Age Projection Test* (Ahsen, 1968) and the *Eidetic Parents Test* (Ahsen, 1972), that form the basis for diagnosis and therapy at each of the first two states respectively. Ahsen also reports a third universal symbolic level of analysis that may help individuals to attain a deeper understanding and integration of meanings of psychic contents. However, as yet he has not presented this third level of analysis in detail in his published works. Consequently, the discussion of this level will not be included in this paper.

Eidetic Psychotherapy

Eidetic psychotherapy begins with *symptom composition*, which is accomplished through a structured interview during which the therapist tries to specify the exact nature of the physical (i.e., I ache all over) as well as the psychological (i.e., I can't think straight) elements of the symptom complex. The patient is also questioned about the worries or concerns that he may entertain about the symptom (i.e., I am afraid of going crazy). Worries and concerns about various parts of the body are also recorded. The symptom is composed completely in the language of the patient. Subsequent to the symptom composition, the therapist is ready to administer the Age Projection Test.

6.1. The Age Projection Test

The therapist asks the patient to give his first, middle, and last names, nicknames, and any other names by which he/she has been called since childhood, for these names are assumed to refer to an individual's various identities. Next, the patient is asked to pay relaxed attention to what the therapist says. He is informed that when the therapist repeats certain words over and over again, he will see an image of himself somewhere in the past:

> The salient features of the symptom discovered during symptom composition are now reiterated to the patient in his own words in a repetitious manner. In the course of this repetition, the patient is addressed by his various names alternately. This repetition artificially activates the symptom to an almost unbearable acuteness. At this point five seconds of total silence are allowed to elapse. Suddenly the therapist starts talking about the time when the patient was healthy and happy. As the therapist talks about health in those areas where the symptom now exists, the patient spontaneously forms a self-image subliminally. The patient is now suddenly asked to project a self-image and describe the following: (a) the self-image itself; (b) the clothing on the self-image; (c) the place where it appears; (d) the events occurring during the age projected in the self-image; (e) the events occurring during the year prior to the age projected in the image. (Dolan and Sheikh, 1977b)

This procedure usually uncovers an event that precipitated the symptom or that began a series of events that eventually led to symptom formation. Once the self-image related to this event is formed, the patient is asked to project it repeatedly until it becomes clear, and then he is interrogated further about the critical period.

If no relevant event is discovered, the last portion of the test, called "Theme Projection," is administered. The patient is told to see the self-image standing before the parental images, crying to provoke pity and love. Then the self-image takes off one article of clothing and throws it down before the parents, saying, "Take it away, I don't want to wear it." The image proceeds: One of the parents picks it up and deposits it somewhere. The patient sees where it has been placed, what surrounds it, and what objects stand out. He is then asked to report any impressions or memories concerning the objects that stand out in his image.

Alternatively, an important image may evolve spontaneously during the dialogue on imagery between therapist and patient. Ahsen reports, however, that when the Age Projection Test is administered, the meaning and origin of a somatic or quasi-somatic symptom usually become evident. Based on the information revealed by the test, a therapeutic image is then constructed, and the patient is asked to project it repeatedly. This therapeutic image may work in a variety of ways. It derives its therapeutic effectiveness from the four principles of "magical" functioning. Through these symbolic mechanisms, the image may prompt the release of repressed responses, lead to catharsis of accumulated affect, symbolically satisfy unfulfilled wishes, or correct an imbalanced ego interpretation of events by focusing on hitherto neglected aspects of the response (Panagiotou and Sheikh, 1974).

The Age Projection Test is a fascinating procedure with an intriguing rationale (Ahsen, 1968, 1977a). In the area of psychosomatic and hysterical symptoms, stunning successes in an astoundingly brief period have been reported. Numerous case histories are now available (Ahsen, 1968; Dolan and Sheikh, 1977b; Sheikh and Dolan, 1977). As these case studies demonstrate, frequently the symptom is dispelled during the first session. Even when this occurs, further analysis of basic developmental trends may be undertaken through another imagery test. Ahsen has developed a major instrument, the *Eidetic Parents Test* (1972), for analysis at the developmental level.

6.2. Eidetic Parents Test

Ahsen attaches special significance to the patterns of interaction between the patient's parents and the patient's perception of polarities that existed in their relationship. The Eidetic Parents Test (EPT) is designed specifically to uncover eidetics in these areas. They have been shown to reveal to a significant extent the quality of the familial relationships and their predominant pathological themes. This test is central to Ahsen's procedure and provides not only the means for identifying areas of conflict, but also the format for therapeutic procedure. The test involves a systematic scrutiny of features of the parental images to determine the exact nature of the interparental and parent-child patterns of interaction. The first item on the test proceeds in the following manner:

> Picture your parents in the house where you lived most of the time, the house that gives you feeling of home.
> Where do you see them?
> What are they doing?
> How do you feel when you see the images?
> Any reactions or memories connected with the picture?
> (Ahsen, 1972, p. 52)

The entire EPT consists of 30 situation images in which various aspects of the parents and the parental relationships are visualized. In summary, the participant is asked to visualize the following items:

> (1) How and where the parents appear in the house in which the patient was raised; (2) the left-right position of the parental figures in front of the patient; (3) whether the parents look separated or united as a couple in the picture; (4) the feeling of an active-passive relationship between the two figures; (5) which parent seems to run faster in the image; (6) the pattern and purpose of the parents' running in the picture; (7) the freedom of the parental limbs, while running; (8) the comparative brilliance of the parental eyes; (9) the object orientation of the parental eyes; (10) parental eyes—feelings they give, story they tell; (11) the comparative loudness of the parental voices in the picture; (12) the degree of meaningfulness in the parental voices; (13) the parental voices—the feelings they give, story they tell; (14) the degree of hearing by the parental ears in the picture; (15) the degree of understanding by the parental ears when they hear the patient speaking to them; (16) the parents sniffing the house's atmosphere, suggestive of whether they like or dislike the house; (17) the feeling of personal warmth imparted by the parental bodies in the picture; (18) the feeling of acceptance or rejection felt in respect of the parental skin; (19) how healthy the parental skin appears in the picture; (20) the extent to which the parents extend their arms to the patient; (21) the extent to which the patient extends his arms to receive from the parents; (22) the comparative strength of the parental hand grasp in the picture; (23) the parents' manner of swallowing food; (24) the parents' manner of drinking; (25) the pressure in the parental jaws while biting something; (26) the temperature of the parental brains; (27) the efficiency or inefficiency of the parental brains when visualized as thinking machines; (28) the beating of the parental hearts, seen through a window visualized in the chest; (29) the appearance of the parental intestines, visualized in their abdomen; (30) the temperature and appearance of the parental genitals and their reaction to the patient's touching them.
> (Dolan, 1972, pp. 27-28)

Certain of these images perhaps require explanation. In particular, the use of various parts of the anatomy as image stimuli may seem to be a perplexing choice for focal inquiry. Generally speaking, they are utilized to elicit feelings about the soundness versus the infirmity of the parents, which may be apparent in characteristics of the skin, brain, heart, and viscera. The infirmity mentioned need not, of course, be an actual physical condition; these images are presented on account of their mundane symbolism; e.g., the brain represents the thought processes, the heart the emotional processes, and so on. The pathology that shows up in the anatomical images usually ultimately refers to a psychological or emotional inadequacy.

The test includes standard verbatim instructions for presenting the stimuli. Ahsen, to his credit, has left nothing unspecified about the administration of the EPT, nor about the constitution of acceptable responses. After the participant has been introduced to eidetics with a brief practice image, the test is administered in a "piecemeal, phrase by phrase enunciation of each item." If the participant fails to form an image in response to any test item, the instructions are repeated until he responds with an image. If he is totally unable to provide an image response, the clinician is expected to record the overt behavior of the subject.

Every image is repeatedly projected until its essential elements are sharpened and separated from its vague or changing aspects. The participant is allowed to acquaint himself thoroughly with his eidetic image before he is asked to describe it. It is essential to the effectiveness of the EPT that the participant be helped to see the image over and over again, and to describe his experience thoroughly. The examiner may need to do a good deal of rather directive and insistent questioning in order to pin down the core of the eidetic response. The participant is instructed not to force any aspects of the image, but to allow it to grow without any interference. He is encouraged to describe the image in "positive declarative statements."

It should be noted that eidetic responses, unlike oneiric reveries (Desoille, 1965, Fretigny and Virel, 1968; Leuner, 1969), are not narrative. The repetitious, piecemeal projection of segments of the response is considered an important methodological feature in handling eidetics. It helps to construct the rigid sequence of what defines an eidetic area. Any attempt to project in a smooth, narrative fashion leads to a fictional response; the true eidetic, however, is not fictional.

It is apparent that the EPT stimuli are highly structured. The initial presentation of each stimulus permits only a brief response. Repeated projections allow no more latitude in responding; the image unfolds only under the guiding questions of the therapist. This limiting nature of the stimuli and the directiveness of their presentation have afforded Ahsen a rigid basis for comparison between individuals and the possibility of using comparative data for establishing interpretive guidelines.

The faithful reporting of eidetic responses is aided by the fact that they are repeatable to the last detail. The reporting, however, is complicated by other matters, and the first response is rarely a pure eidetic. Ahsen has given the name "eidetic matrix" to the group of phenomena elicited during EPT administration. These include (1) the *first response,* (2) the *primary response,* (3) the *secondary response,* (4) the *interjected response,* (5) the *underlying primary response,* and (6) the *overt behavior.*

The first response reflects the participant's initial reaction to the instruction: this may take a variety of forms, including a manisfestation of resistance, and, of course, will not always be an eidetic. The primary response is the true eidetic. It never fails to be repeatable and tends to recur in an almost mechanical manner. It is usually bright and clear, rich in emotional accompaniment, and has a meaning or set of meanings that the individual can usually recognize with some certainty. Any portion of the primary response may be repeated for elaboration or detailed examination. When repeated, it elicits feelings and memories, and after many repetitions, which may be punctuated by resistances and other types of behavior, it may spontaneously be replaced by a new primary that, in turn, through repetition, may give rise to still another primary. The primaries arising out of repetition of the first primary are termed "underlying primaries." The secondary response, interjected response, and overt behavior are types of reaction that frequently occur between primaries. After a few repetitions, the primary response may suddenly be replaced by material only superficially related to it, such as elements of the individual's ordinary fancy. Such responses are termed "secondary" and are usually used as a defense. Sometimes the individual punctuates the primary response with significant verbal or fantasy material. Ahsen calls this behavior an interjected response and points out that it occasionally contains important depth material that is of use in structuring therapy. Overt behavior refers primarily to the individual's facial expressions, postures, and other acts that express his attitude toward the imagery experience: for example, he may appear interested, indifferent, or irritated.

The repeated projection of the primary response along with the resultant affective elaboration and eventual replacement of one primary eidetic by another and another, is the crux of the full-length diagnostic-cum-therapeutic technique: it is actually through this process that therapeutic progress is made. The reader will recall that the primary eidetic is accompanied by somatic patterns and affective significations. It follows that the repetition of the primary results in a fuller experience of these, along with the visual component; this process implies the acquisition of a degree of conscious recognition of the connections involved, as well as a rather thorough working-over of the affective reactions. It has been observed that only when this process has been carried to completion for one eidetic, does it begin with another. Thus, each progression or change represents a step forward, a deepening and broadening of understanding and assimilation, an illumination of another aspect of the complex problem that the individual is now prepared to examine.

It has been noted above that image figures that are projected repeatedly tend to interact progressively. But at times, strong ego controls cause the images to become frozen at certain points of interaction, often when important trends are about to emerge. In order to break this immobility, Ahsen has developed the *emanation technique*. If the patient is projecting a visual image that holds a self-image (p^1) and an image of another (F^1), the therapist will request the patient to visualize "another self" (p^2) and "another figure" (F^2) emerge from the original images. The patient is then asked to describe the actions of p^2 and F^2 to the therapist. Any number of emanations may be elicited, but Ahsen has found that more than two or three are rarely required in order to restore movement of the images (Ahsen, 1968; Panagiotou and Sheikh, 1974).

An individual's ability to produce a sufficiently rich eidetic response is interpreted as a sign of openness to his internal life. When the imagery reveals what Ahsen calls a "structural defect," it indicates a particularly problematic area. Ahsen has identified two major forms of imagery defects: meager responses and mutilated responses. *Meager responses* may occur in limited areas of eidetic imagery, and reflect the individual's particular problems in relating to those areas. However, insufficient responses may also be a general pattern and point to habitual suppression of emotional experiences. But, both the individual who gives meager responses in a restricted area and he who does so generally often learn to respond adequately, if they are repeatedly encouraged. Yet, Ahsen identifies three sources likely to be the root of extremely persistent imagery repression: (1) a perseverative fantasy theme, such as a phobia, which competes with the imagery, (2) religious or moral aversion to eidetic images, and (3) strong tendencies to acting out. To deal with the first source Ahsen suggests the use of the Age Projection Test: it will bring the dynamics of the perseverative theme to the surface. He interprets the second as a resistance of a disturbed patient to the experience, and suggests that the patient be instilled with an informed conviction that knowledge about his parents is absolutely essential to his well-being. Ahsen believes that the third source, the acting-out tendencies, is likely to be based upon an identification with the negative aspects of one or the other parent. It follows that in order for the individual to realize an internalized image of the parent, he must be able to differentiate himself from that parental image. The aforementioned three sources quite possibly do not exhaust all the causes of the inability to produce adequate imagery responses, and this inadequacy continues to be a nightmare for clinicians interested in using imagery as the main tool for diagnosis and treatment.

In contrast to meager responses, preponderant *mutilated figures* indicate, according to Ahsen, "widespread trauma" in the history of the individual. Common mutilations are undersized, oversized, or entirely absent parent figures. Each of these is regarded to refer to a specific theme: undersized parents generally signify the individual's need to maintain a distance between himself and his parents; oversized parents commonly reveal that the parents are perceived as incorporative; and absent parents, in most cases, mean that the parents made themselves unavailable and the child wished them away or dead. Partially mutilated images with, for example, vague eyes or limbs, faint voices, etc., usually represent related defects in parental behavior. However, grossly mutilated parental images, such as disembodied heads, limbs, or eyes, ghostly bodies, and the like, may indicate "terrorizing themes."

Ahsen specifies that a number of inadequate and mutilated responses to the EPT should be expected. When these are elicited by only some EPT items and do not seem to be a pervasive tendency, they point to the areas of experience to which the participant relates with most difficulty, and which, therefore, are most in need of attention.

The therapists should perhaps be forewarned that it is not uncommon for participants to initially offer some resistance to the EPT. Several rather frequent manifestations of resistance are discussed by Ahsen. The first is "reality resistance": it refers to the participant's tendency to respond in a purely verbal-logical manner that is in accordance with facts rather than with his subjective experience. For example, he might say, "My father runs faster because he is a man"; whereas, if he attended directly to his image response, he would see that his mother was running faster. The individual who has the tendency to ignore the actual image will have to be continually reminded of it by the therapist. Another common form of resistance arises from apprehensiveness about relating to traumatic emotional experiences. The fear may be limited to only a few areas and their corresponding images or it may be pervasive. When the individual is confronted with the task of trying to understand his feelings, he may react by inhibiting his ability to experience his feelings. In such cases, Ahsen attempts to facilitate the individual's re-engagement with his emotional life by instructing him to consider and relate to the possible presence of emotion, even though he is not "feeling" any at the moment. A third form of resistance commonly encountered is a propensity for exaggerated verbalization. The individual tends to respond in a totally verbal manner and avoids seeing an image, or he may describe his image in such profuse detail that its reliability suffers markedly. Under these circumstances, the therapist must insist that the participant curtail his tangential or circumlocutory speech and limit himself to a concise description of what he sees and no more. In other cases, resistance manifests itself in argumentativeness; the patient does not comply with the instructions to visualize and report but instead challenges the therapist in various ways. The therapist obviously must avoid any arguments and again must find a relevant strategy to keep the individual on the track. Resistance can also be expressed by deliberately providing misinformation. However, Ahsen reports this form to be relatively rare and to occur chiefly in individuals who have not sought therapy voluntarily. In still other cases, resistance takes the form of self-condemnation that stands in the way of cooperation in the assigned task. The therapist may be able to direct the individual away from this response pattern through repeated indications that his manner of response is inappropriate to the task and hence unacceptable. Furthermore, in some individuals, according to Ahsen, resistance stems from deep-seated inferiority feelings; they deprive the individual of the confidence to relate to his imagery in the necessary and decisive manner. If it is apparent, then the inferiority feelings must be treated before the images pertaining to the parents can become available for use. In general, Ahsen suggests that any sign of apathy on the part of the participant should be countered by an active imagery approach by the therapist.

It needs to be highlighted that the experience that emerges in the eidetics often is at variance with the patient's conscious views of it. For instance, his experience of a parent in the imagery may differ radically from his conscious opinion of this parent. Generally, the Consciousness-Imagery-Gap (C-I-G) is caused by the need to repress a painful experience. Or, it may be the result of the parents' brain-washing of the patient.

Once the C-I-G has been uncovered, the next step is to challenge the patient's conscious beliefs and attitudes by confronting him with his contrary perceptions revealed in the eidetics. It is vital to take note of the patient's reactions to this procedure. Does he deny the existence of a gap and, thus, reject change? If he resists, what is the form of his resistance? Does he make an effort to bridge the gap? Or, is he eager to learn more about the unknown within himself? Evidently the nature of the patient's reactions to the C-I-G clarifies the problems under investigation (Ahsen, 1972).

Ahsen's method is clearly a directive one. The directiveness is facilitated by the specificity of the instructions concerning the administrational procedures. Ahsen also recognizes the complexity of information that can be drawn from eidetic responses and is very explicit in orienting test users in the analysis of these responses. The repeatability of the images, as seen in the clinic (Ahsen, 1972; Dolan and Sheikh, 1976) as well as in the laboratory (Sheikh, 1976a), leads to a high intra-individual reliability for the EPT. Among imagery techniques the test clearly has the distinction of being the best controlled and, therefore, the most feasible tool for research.

The interpretation Ahsen suggests for the EPT items may strike as surprising to some. A number of items are assigned meanings to which many investigators would readily agree, independent of theory-specific symbolism; these items include, for example, the image of the parents in the home, whether they appear separate or united, whether they look happy or otherwise, and so forth. Other items, however, such as anatomical details, have less logical appeal and may seem to be strange choices unless one follows unflinchingly Ahsen's conception of the importance of psychosomatic symbolism. Need for further research is obviously indicated.

It is important to recognize that Ahsen's EPT and, in fact, his whole eidetic method is a parent-centered approach. Not all clinicians would agree to the central importance of examining the familial interactions in such great detail. It is perhaps also worthy of mention that, in contrast to most other approaches, Ahsen ascribes an important and specific meaning to the function of the father in the development of both male and female children. For a discussion of this topic the interested reader is referred to Ahsen's books (1972, 1977a). It is interesting to note that his views receive considerable support from recent research in this area (Biller, 1971; Lynn, 1974; Popplewell and Sheikh, in press). The therapeutic application of Ahsen's idea of parents as the central nucleus in the psyche is important in the modern technological society, where the parents' role, and particularly the father's role, is being progressively eclipsed.

7. A Case History

Numerous case histories of patients with a wide variety of symptoms are now available in the works of Ahsen and others. The following example is selected because it involves most of the major concepts and techniques of eidetic psychotherapy. It is summarized from a paper by Ahsen and Lazarus (1972).

Mrs. Jay, who was 41 years of age, was suffering from pain in the upper left abdomen, chest, and left breast, from excessive irrational anxieties, including a fear of death, as well as from strong uncertainties and feelings of personal unworthiness. She had undergone behavior therapy with no gain.

After an initial composition of the symptoms, Ahsen administered the Age Projection Test. She reported a self-image around the age of 26 wearing a red blouse and a black skirt. She recollected that her father had died during the preceding year. He had suffered a fatal heart attack but was brought back to life temporarily through cardiac massage. She remembered begging the doctors not to massage the heart and let him die. She also mentioned that at the time she had felt extremely traumatized and had experienced choked hysteria inside.

From the patient's description, Ahsen selected two images dealing with the two opposed ends of the event: (1) massage of the heart (MH) and (2) death of the father immediately after cardiac massage (DF). In response to MH, Mrs. Jay developed the acute symptoms, and in reaction to DF, she became relaxed, though not entirely relieved of all symptoms. The hypothesis presented itself, that just as the doctors wanted to actively revive the father, Mrs. Jay wanted to actively let the father die. During further inquiry about this topic, the patient, on her own, saw images in which she suffocated her father with a pillow on the hospital bed. As she saw these images, she bitterly cried and then became completely peaceful and her somatic symptoms disappeared.

After the disappearance of her main debilitating symptoms, her past as well as her fantasy life started to unfold more freely. She remembered her father's two previous heart attacks. The experience of the images dealing with these events appeared to be laden with powerful affect which brought back the somatic symptoms. In the final analysis, these images, however, proved to be cathartic and strengthened the patient. Mrs. Jay showed keen understanding of the symbolism involved and clearly realized why she wanted her father to die during the cardiac massage.

The eidetics revealed not only her negative view of her father but also a positive one: she saw a jolly man, singing with her as he took her to school or for walks. She immensely enjoyed these images and they restored a feeling of worth in her.

The eidetics uncovered a number of other areas of conflict. An important one among these was her dread of school, where children persecuted her for being fat. Another was the anxiety caused by her first menstruation, her fear of conception and miscarriages, topics which had also emerged during Theme Projection. The EPT elicited many images which led her to the realization that many of her problems were related to her rejecting mother. She consequently felt very angry at her. In short, all these images, with the guidance of the therapist, enabled her to resolve her conflicts. Gradually she was relieved of all her symptoms. A follow-up after one year and another after two years revealed that her progress not only had been maintained but had advanced.

8. Concluding Remarks

In the framework of eidetic psychotherapy, an eidetic image is regarded as a tridimensional organic entity that has extraordinary therapeutic value because of its retrospective as well as prospective relations to psychic processes. It has proven itself as an effective experiential tool for the development of fast-moving psychotherapeutic procedures: they bypass defenses and steer directly toward the experience itself. The rapidity of the process is the crux of the contribution.

The method has been found to be extremely effective with a wide variety of problems (Ahsen, 1968, 1972, 1977a; Dolan and Sheikh, 1976, 1977b; Gerrity, 1975; Jordan, 1977; Sarmousakis, 1976; Sheikh, 1976b; Sheikh and Dolan, 1977). However, it has yielded extraordinarily good results with psychosomatic problems, a category of illness where traditional verbal and behavioral therapies tend to fail miserably. An eidetic is probably the only event in the psyche "which is fundamentally psychosomatic and unites mind and body in a single undifferentiated whole" (Ahsen, 1968, p. 45). It is an economic and comprehensive expression of mind–body unity, and thus contains possibilities that are not available if either of the two is considered separately. Consequently, it is hardly surprising that psychosomatic problems respond particularly well to eidetic procedures (Sheikh and Richardson, in press).

The eidetic procedures have been successfully employed not only in individual psychotherapy, but also in group therapy situations. It is commonly known that subjects with a traumatic past do not readily reproduce their painful experiences. However, they do appear to be very receptive to another person's experience; it seems that the empathic relationship at the imagery level with another's problems is an original ability that is left uncontaminated. This ability has tremendous therapeutic value: when a person experiences another's eidetic image, he interacts at a perceptual level and indirectly brings about a catharsis and subsequent progress in his own mental life. The eidetic images of parents act as an especially intimate medium for empathy. Ahsen has discussed his group therapy procedures in detail in his recent works (1976, 1977a).

Another extremely significant recent extension of eidetic therapy is to the realm of self-analysis and self-education. In his fascinating book, *Psycheye: Self-Analytic Consciousness* (1977a), Ahsen emphatically deplores the persistence of a covert "priesthood" in the mental health field that continues to "corrode the individual's faith in his own sensibilities and his natural capacity to attend his own mind with self-educational benefits" (p. v). He emphasizes that "the center of creative and renewal activity in the individual is always his own self, and no high priest of any sort should be allowed to stand between him and that light" (p. vi). The book provides a comprehensive network of imagery levels that can be very effectively used as the primary vehicle for self-analysis. Individuals interested in this venture simply cannot afford to ignore this highly original work.

Several laudatory reviews of Ahsen's work have appeared during the last few years (e.g., Haronian, 1968; Katzenstein, 1975; Luce, 1967; Piers, 1974; Sarmousakis, 1975; Scobie, 1974; Zaidi, 1974). It has been heralded as a "breakthrough," (Luce, 1967, p. 386), as "one of the most significant developments yet to emerge in psychotherapy since Freud's psychoanalysis" (Scobie, 1974, p. 16), and as "a milestone in the evolution of a truly integrative and comprehensive system of effective psychotherapy" (Lazarus, 1972, p. vii). Ahsen's work certainly deserves a closer look from many more experts in the fields of psychology and psychiatry on account of its contribution to the understanding, amelioration, and elimination of psychopathology.

ACKNOWLEDGMENTS

The author expresses his sincere appreciation to Nancy C. Panagiotou for her valuable assistance in the preparation of this paper.

References

Ahsen, A. *Eidetic psychotherapy: A short introduction.* Lahore: Nai Matbooat, 1965.
Ahsen, A. *Basic concepts in eidetic psychotherapy.* New York: Brandon House, 1968.
Ahsen, A. *Eidetic parents test and analysis.* New York: Brandon House, 1972.
Ahsen, A. Eidetics: A visual psychology. Invited address, American Psychological Association, 81st Annual Convention, Montreal, Canada, 1973.
Ahsen, A. Anna O.—patient or therapist? An eidetic view. In V. Franks and V. Burtle (Eds.), *Women in therapy.* New York: Bruner/Mazel, 1974, pp. 263-283.
Ahsen, A. Eidetic psychotherapy: Theory and technique. Invited address, Department of Psychology, Marquette University, 1975.
Ahsen, A. A. Empathy process. A group therapy technique against mass imagery. Unpublished manuscript, Eidetic Analysis Institute, Yonkers, New York, 1976.
Ahsen, A. *Psycheye: Self-analytic consciousness.* New York: Brandon House, 1977a.
Ahsen, A. Eidetics: An overview. *Journal of Mental Imagery,* 1977b, *1,* 5-38.
Ahsen, A., and Lazarus, A. A. Eidetics: An internal behavior approach. In A. A. Lazarus (Ed.), *Clinical behavior therapy.* New York; Bruner/Mazel, 1972, p. 87-99.
Biller, H. B. *Father, child, and sex role: Paternal determinants of personality development.* Lexington, Mass.: Heath Lexington Books, 1971.
Desoille, R. *The directed daydream.* New York: Psychosynthesis Research Found., 1965.
Dolan, A. T. Introduction. In Ahsen, A., *Eidetic parents test and analysis.* New York: Brandon House, 1972.
Dolan, A. T., and Sheikh, A. A. Eidetics: A visual approach to psychotherapy. *Psychologia,* 1976, *19,* 210-219.
Dolan, A. T., and Sheikh, A. A. Eidetic therapy: Ahsen-Penfield psychotherapy process model. Unpublished manuscript, Marquette University, 1977a.

Dolan, A. T., and Sheikh, A. A. Short-term treatment of phobias through eidetic imagery. *American Journal of Psychotherapy*, 1977b, *31*, 595-604.
Fretigny, R., and Virel, A. *L'imagerie mentale*. Geneva: Mont-Blanc, 1968.
Gerrity, B. Use of Eidetic parents test with adolescents. Paper presented at The 1975 Eidetic Seminar, White Plains, New York, 1975.
Gray, C. R., and Gummerman, K. The enigmatic eidetic image: A critical examination of methods, data, and theory. *Psychological Bulletin*, 1975, *82*, 383-407.
Haronian, F. Book review. *Journal of Projective Techniques and Personality Assessment*, 1968, *32*, 96.
Jaensch, E. R. *Eidetic imagery*. New York: Harcourt Brace, 1930.
Jordan, S. The assertive person: Assertive training through group eidetics. Paper presented at the American Group Psychotherapy Association Meeting, San Francisco, 1977.
Kepecs, J. G. Observations on screens and barriers in the mind. *Psychoanalytic Quarterly*, 1954, *23*, 62-77.
Katzenstein, A. Book review. *Zeitschrift fuer Psychologie*, 1975, *183*, 128.
Kubie, L. Discussion. In W. Penfield (Ed.), Memory mechanisms. *A.M.A. Archives of Neurology and Psychiatry*, 1952, *67*, 178-191.
Lazarus, A. A. Preface. In A. A. Ahsen, *Eidetic parents test and analysis*. New York: Brandon House, 1972, pp. v-vii.
Leuner, H. Guided affective imagery: A method of intensive psychotherapy. *American Journal of Psychotherapy*, 1969, *23*, 4-22.
Lipkin, S. The imaginary collage and its use in psychotherapy. *Psychotherapy: Theory, Research and Practice*, 1970, *7*, 238-242.
Luce, R. A. Book review. *Existential Psychiatry*, 1967, *6*, 386-387.
Luce, R. A. The new eidetic psychotherapy. Paper presented at the Ethical Society, Philadelphia, Pennsylvania, 1968.
Lynn, D. B. *The father: His role in child development*. Monterey, California: Brooks/Cole, 1974.
Martin, D. G. *Personality: Effective and ineffective*. Monterey, California: Brooks/Cole, 1976.
Norman, D. A. Toward a theory of memory and attention. *Psychological Review*, 1968, *75*, 522-536.
Panagiotou, N., and Sheikh, A. A. Eidetic psychotherapy: Introduction and evaluation. *International Journal of Social Psychiatry*, 1974, *20*, 231-241.
Panagiotou, N., and Sheikh, A. A. The image and the unconscious. *International Journal of Social Psychiatry*, 1977, *23*, 169-186.
Pavlov, I. P. *Conditioned reflexes and psychiatry*. New York: International Publishers Co., 1936.
Penfield, W. Memory mechanisms. *American Medical Association Archives of Neurology and Psychiatry*, 1952, *67*, 178-191.
Penfield, W. The role of the temporal cortex in recall of past experience and interpretation of the present. In G. E. W. Wolstenholme and C. M. O'Connor (Eds.), *Neurological basis of behavior*. Boston: Little Brown, 1958.
Penfield, W. The interpretive cortex. *Science*, 1959, *129*, 1719-1725.
Penfield, W. The brain's record of auditory and visual experience-A final summary and discussion. *Brain*, 1963, *86*, 595-696.
Penfield, W. *The mystery of the mind*. Princeton University Press, 1975.
Perky, C. W. An experimental study of imagination. *American Journal of Psychology*, 1910, *21*, 422-452.
Piers, E. How do you see your parents? *Contemporary Psychology*, 1974, *19*, 655-657.

Popplewell, J. F., and Sheikh, A. A. The role of the father in child development. *International Journal of Social Psychiatry*, in press.

Richardson, A. *Mental imagery*. New York: Springer, 1969.

Sarmousakis, G. Review of Ahsen, A. *Eidetic parents test and analysis* 1972. *The American Journal of Psychiatry*, 1975, *132*, 314.

Sarmousakis, G. Eidetic analysis: A comparison with other imagery techniques. Paper presented at Eidetic Analysis Institute, Yonkers, New York, 1976.

Scobie, G. E. W. Book review. Ahsen, A. *Eidetic parents test and analysis,* 1972. *The Glasgow Journal of Psychology*, 1974, *12*, 16.

Segal, S. J., and Nathan, S. The Perky effect: Incorporation of an external stimulus into an imagery experience under placebo and control conditions. *Perceptual and Motor Skills*, 1964, *18*, 385–395.

Sheikh, A. A. Left-right in the brain: Hemispheric projection of eidetic parents among college students. Unpublished data, Marquette University, 1976a.

Sheikh, A. A. Treatment of insomnia through eidetic imagery: A new technique. *Perceptual and Motor Skills*, 1976b, *43*, 994.

Sheikh, A. A. Mental images: Ghosts of sensations? *Journal of Mental Imagery*, 1977, *1*, 1–4.

Sheikh, A. A., and Dolan, A. T. The Age Projection Test: Two case histories. Unpublished manuscript, Marquette University, 1977.

Sheikh, A. A., and Panagiotou, N. C. Use of mental imagery in psychotherapy: A critical review. *Perceptual and Motor Skills*, 1975, *41*, 555–585.

Sheikh, A. A., and Richardson, P. Mental imagery and psychosomatic illness: A critical review. *Journal of Mental Imagery*, in press.

Singer, J. L. *Imagery and daydream methods in psychotherapy and behavior modification*. New York: Academic Press, 1974.

Urbantschitsch, V. *Ueber subjektive optische Anschauungsbilder*. Leipzig: Deuticke, 1907.

Zaidi, S. M. H. Book review. *Pakistan Journal of Psychology*, 1974, *7*, 61–62.

PART IV

Behavior-Therapy Uses of Imagery

Introduction

The behavior modification "movement" that developed chiefly in South Africa, England, and the United States in the mid-1950s has revolutionized the practice of psychotherapy. The seemingly naive directness of the early approaches with their direct attacks on symptoms has given way to somewhat broader views and more sensitivity to the complex expectations and diversity of skills and histories that clients bring to the therapist. The rather mechanical learning theory applied initially has been extensively questioned and newer models that allow great scope for cognitive processes are now incorporated both in theory and practice. Two major contributions of the development may be cited especially. They include a sharpening of the attention of therapists and their clients to behavioral contingencies, a far more systematic and careful attention to the details of one's overt behavior and (more recently) sequences of thought than had characterized the somewhat looser earlier psychotherapies. A second major contribution has been the vast increase in evaluative and analytic research into the psychotherapeutic process. The more dynamic psychotherapies seeking to affect a life-course were harder to study both in terms of what went on in a given session and what the effects of different treatment approaches might be. Behavior therapy, by defining its goals more specifically and by outlining a precise series of therapeutic interventions, opened the way for a huge body of reasonably careful research that has permitted scientific scrutiny of treatment. While there has, of course, been an extensive literature on tests of the assumptions or implications of psychoanalytic theory, relatively little research has examined the psychodynamic treatment processes and their effectiveness (Fisher and Greenberg, 1977; Wachtel, 1977). The chapter by Kazdin in this section provides a small sample of the kind of thoughtful research examination that has emerged in relation to behavior therapies.

No attempt has been made to review all of the behavior-therapy uses of imagery in the chapters that follow. The chapter by Cautela points to a surprising number of possibilities, however, and the chapter by Kazdin elaborates on one method, symbolic modeling, that has been increasingly employed recently. Notice that these approaches minimize elaborate theories of personality development or intrapsychic conflict. They move directly toward modifying behavior through our imagery resources without much concern about introjected parental images or transference affects. Is such a position truly tenable? Meichenbaum's chapter in Part VI amplifies this position but expands it to emphasize the greater role of broad cognitive processes. The earlier chapters by Horowitz and Singer and Pope have also traced some overlapping regions between the various therapeutic uses of imagery, and discussions of common principles may also be found in Singer (1974) and Wachtel (1977). To some extent the outcome should rest ultimately on more careful systematic results evaluating these procedures. For our purposes here it is apparent, however, that even the more structured, symptom-focused and "objective" behavior therapies are relying heavily on the extensive resources for awareness and behavior change that inhere in our imaginative capacities.

8

Covert Conditioning: A Learning-Theory Perspective on Imagery

Joseph R. Cautela and Leigh McCullough

1. Introduction

In recent years there has been a trend in behavioral psychology toward the speculation and development of procedures that manipulate imagery to modify behavior. This is a dramatic departure from the tenets of conventional behaviorism, which held that mentalistic concepts had no place in the scientific study of psychology (Watson, 1919, p. viii). However, Wolpe legitimatized the investigation of covert processes within a behavioristic framework with systematic desensitization (1958). Since then a number of investigators who label themselves behavior therapists have developed techniques to modify behavior involving the manipulation of imagery events. These investigators have somewhat different conceptual models. Some label themselves as cognitive behavior modifiers (Meichenbaum, 1974; Lazarus, 1971; Mahoney, 1974; Goldfried and Davison, 1976). In this model, cognitions (such as talking to oneself, problem-solving, or imagery) are conceptualized as mediators of behaviors, and faulty cognitive patterns are assumed to be at least partly responsible for aberrant affect and behavior. In the cognitive model therapeutic improvement depends upon the alteration of such patterns.

Another group of investigators assume a learning theory base for covert processes. In contrast to the cognitive theorists, learning theor-

---

Joseph R. Cautela and Leigh McCullough • Department of Psychology, Boston College, Boston, Massachusetts 02109.

ists generally assume that private events can best be explained within a conditioning model, and they assume the functional equivalence of overt and covert behavior. Problem behaviors, overt as well as covert, are assumed to be subject to learning principles, and therapeutic improvement depends upon systematically manipulating specially constructed imagery according to learning principles to increase adaptive behaviors and to decrease those that are maladaptive.

Among the learning theorists there are several orientations in the use of private events. Some investigators operate within a respondent learning model, such as Wolpe's (1958) hierarchy of scenes presented in the imagination in systematic desensitization. Others are exponents of Mowrer's (1960) two-factor theory, such as Stampfl's (1961) prolonged presentation of aversive imagery in flooding. Still others assume an operant orientation, such as Homme's (1965) coverant control therapy, in which specific thoughts are made contingent upon the emission of target behaviors to be increased or decreased.

Covert conditioning assumes a learning-theory basis, and according to the conceptual scheme developed by Cautela, (1977a) follows an operant orientation. The purpose of this chapter is to present the covert conditioning assumptions and procedures. The chapter will also emphasize the necessity for thorough imagery development and practice, and will describe how covert processes can influence total organismic functioning.

2. Covert Conditioning Assumptions and Procedures

The term "covert conditioning" (Cautela, 1972a, 1977a) refers to a set of imagery-based procedures that alter response frequency by the manipulation of consequences. The techniques are specially designed and systematically presented to increase or decrease certain target behaviors. The assumption of covert conditioning is that covert behavior can be manipulated to cause an increase or decrease in other covert and overt behavior in a predictable manner. The rationale for these assumptions is outlined below.

2.1. A Learning-Theory Basis for Covert Conditioning

While conventional behaviorism dealt only with observable responses of the organism, covert conditioning acknowledges three general categories of behavior: covert psychological behavior (thoughts, feelings, and images), covert physiological behavior (heart rate, pulse, EEG, gastric secretions), and overt behavior. These categories are not viewed as isolated entities, but as interdependent and interacting processes. It is assumed that these processes obey the same laws of learning. It was formerly assumed that only overt behavior was subject to learning laws, but research is now indicating that both covert and overt behaviors interact with each other and obey similar laws (Cautela and Baron, 1977).

Regarding these three categories of behavior, the essential assumptions underlying the efficacy of the covert conditioning procedures are: (1) the homogeneity hypothesis, which states that all categories of behavior obey the same laws; i.e., empirical generalizations derived from overt behaviors can be applied to thoughts, images, or physiological processes such as heart rate or blood pressure, (2) the interaction hypothesis, which states that all categories of behavior interact with each other and with the environment; i.e., thoughts may influence feelings, blood pressure, or overt behaviors, and vice versa, and (3) that all categories of behavior respond similarly to the laws of learning; i.e., the heart rate, or galvanic skin response, or imagery may be reinforced or punished just as overt behavior may be reinforced or punished.

An operant learning framework was adopted because of evidence indicating that all three categories of behavior respond to operant conditioning techniques. This is not to say that certain covert behaviors may not be classically conditioned. King (1973) has described an image theory of classical conditioning, proposing that the conditioned response results from a conditioned stimulus image of the unconditioned stimulus. However, the homogeneity assumption within an operant framework is more parsimonious than ascribing different sets of laws to each different category of behavior. Further, the learning approach has the heuristic value of having so much data and speculation accumulated within the field in the past 50 years.

There is growing evidence in support of these assumptions. Neil Miller (1935) reported similar physiological responses to both saying the letter "t" and thinking the letter "t." Operant conditioning techniques have been used to modify covert physiological processes in biofeedback research (heart rate, Weiss and Engel, 1971; and Scott, Blanchard, Edmunson, and Young, 1973; blood pressure, Elder and Ruiz, 1973; and Benson, Shapiro, Tursky, and Schwartz, 1971; gastric secretions, Whitehead, Renault, and Goldiamond, 1975; and Welgan, 1974). Operant conditioning has also been demonstrated in the firing patterns of neurons in the CNS (Olds, Disterhoff, Segal, Kornblith, and Hirsh, 1972; Jasper and Shagass, 1941; Black-Cleworth, Woody, and Neiman, 1975). Covert psychological processes have been increased and decreased in frequency using covert operant techniques (Cautela,

1972b; Cautela, Walsh, and Wish, 1971; Cautela and Rosensteil, 1975; Asher and Cautela, 1972 and 1974). Research by Barlow and his colleagues in the treatment of sexual deviation supports both of the above assumptions, having demonstrated in many cases that covert psychological processes (maladaptive sexual imagery), covert physiological processes (penile volume), and overt behavior (pedophilia) all respond to learning laws and interact with each other in a predictable manner (Barlow and Agras, 1973; Barlow, Leitenburg, and Agras, 1969; Brownell and Barlow, 1978). Additional research that supports the homogeneity and interaction assumptions has used overt reinforcement to modify organic dysfunction such as migraine headaches (Friar and Beatty, 1976); tics (Hersen and Eisler, 1973); Tourette's syndrome (Rosen and Wesner, 1973); and epileptic seizures (Cautela, 1973b).

2.2. Covert Conditioning Procedures

The covert conditioning procedures include covert sensitization (Cautela, 1966, 1967), covert reinforcement (Cautela, 1970a), covert extinction (Cautela, 1971a), covert negative reinforcement (Cautela, 1970b), covert modeling (Cautela, 1971b) and covert response cost (Cautela, 1976a). As space does not permit a detailed description and experimental verification of each procedure, the reader is encouraged to refer to the original articles cited above. However, a brief description is necessary for a more comprehensive understanding of the chapter.

Essentially, covert conditioning assumes that covert behavior follows the same laws as overt behavior. Therefore, the probability of any covert behavior occurring again is influenced by the covert or overt behavior that follows it. For example, if an individual imagines he is about to take a drink of alcohol and then imagines that he vomits as he puts the drink to his mouth (covert sensitization), then the probability will decrease that he will want to drink alcohol. If he imagines that he drinks alcohol but it has no taste and it gives him no feeling (covert extinction), then the probability will decrease that he will want to take a drink. If the individual imagines that he avoids taking a drink and this provides an escape from an unpleasant thought, then the probability will increase that other drinks will be avoided (covert negative reinforcement). If he imagines someone else is about to take a drink and the model suffers certain consequences, then the nature of the consequences observed will influence the probability that the observer is going to drink again (covert modeling). Finally, if someone imagines a certain behavior, and then imagines that something of value is taken away from him (covert response cost), then he will be less apt to engage in that behavior again.

Of course, the important assumption underlying the above examples is that there is an interactive effect between covert and overt behaviors and they obey the same laws; i.e., a decrease in imagining a behavior will decrease the probability that the behavior will be performed overtly. If the covert conditioning assumptions and experimental evidence are valid, then it follows that any ongoing covert behavior influences the present and future overt and covert behaviors of the individual. Thus, the decrease in frequency of inappropriate alcohol-related imagery will decrease the probability of the individual taking a drink of alcohol, just as an increase in imagining positive sexual experiences will increase the likelihood of actual sexual encounters being pleasant.

Procedurally, in each of the covert conditioning techniques a person is asked to imagine a response to be modified and then is asked to immediately imagine a certain consequence. Experimental investigations of the covert conditioning procedures have been performed both with the response actually occurring, or presented in the imagination. The consequence, however, is always imagined. In the following paragraphs the procedures will be summarized and examples of scenes employed in covert conditioning will be presented.

2.2.1. Covert Sensitization (CS). Covert sensitization is based on the punishment paradigm in which an aversive stimulus is presented simultaneously with a response to be decreased. It is used to treat maladaptive approach behavior such as alcoholism, deviant behavior, obesity, and smoking. The procedure is labeled *covert* because neither the undesirable response nor the aversive stimulus are actually presented. These stimuli are presented in the imagination only. The word *sensitization* is used because the purpose of this procedure is to build up an avoidance to the undesirable response as, for example, in treating alcoholism:

> Just as you walk into a bar for a beer, you are suddenly overcome by a queasy feeling that begins in the pit of your stomach and increases until you are quite nauseous. You can taste a vile liquid as it comes up to the back of your throat, but you try to keep your mouth closed and swallow it back down. You reach for the beer to wash it down, but as soon as your hand touches the glass, you can no longer control the need to vomit. You open your mouth and puke all over the bar and the glass, and into the beer. You can see bits of food and mucous floating around in the beer. Snots and mucous come out of your nose. Everyone in the bar is looking at you, and you feel sick and embarrassed. Just turning away from the beer gives you some relief, and you run out of the bar into the fresh air and feel much better.

2.2.2. Covert Reinforcement (COR). The basic assumption of the covert reinforcement procedure is that a reinforcing stimulus presented in the imagination functions in a manner similar to an externally applied reinforcer. Covert reinforcement has been used to modify both maladaptive approach and maladaptive avoidance behaviors. The response to be modified is increased by being followed by a pleasant image. An example of such a pleasant image might be:

> Imagine that you are lying on a beach at the ocean. The warm sun is beating down upon you. You can feel that warmth penetrate your whole body. A gentle breeze brushes against your skin, you can hear the waves lapping on the shore, and as you lazily open your eyes, a beautiful seagull wings by. You feel totally peaceful and content.

A typical example of the use of this imagery is in the teaching of social skills. The client is instructed to imagine the pleasant scene whenever the therapist says, "reinforcement," represented by the symbol COR:

> Imagine that you are going to a party. (COR). As you arrive you greet the host with a smile and a friendly hello. (COR). As you are being introduced to people you smile, look them in the eye, and give a firm handshake. (COR). You make casual conversation with several people (COR) and think what an enjoyable time you are having. (COR).

2.2.3. Covert Negative Reinforcement (CNR). In cases where the client cannot think of anything pleasurable and aversive imagery is much more vivid and realistic, therapy may begin using escape from a noxious scene as a reinforcement for increasing certain behaviors. The paradigm for the procedure begins with imagining a noxious scene. When the scene is clear and the patient raises his finger, the therapist says, "Shift." The patient immediately erases the noxious scene and imagines the response to be increased. For example, to increase appropriate sexual behavior:

> Imagine that you are leaving a hockey game and are trapped in the middle of a pushing and shoving mob of people. People are yelling so that it hurts your ears. You can smell sweaty bodies all around you. You are being squeezed, your feet are being stepped on, and you see no way out.
> Shift.
> Now imagine lying in bed beside your wife. You are relaxed and comfortable and beginning to feel aroused.

2.2.4. Covert Extinction (CE). Covert extinction is based on the assumption that if a subject is instructed to imagine that reinforcing stimuli maintaining certain covert or overt behavior do not occur, then that behavior will decrease in probability. The procedure is labeled *covert extinction* since it involves the manipulation of imagery and is analogous to the experimental extinction paradigm.

In treating drug addiction:

> You are in your friend's apartment. The whole gang is there and you all shoot up. The guys are laughing and joking. You are sitting on the wooden floor with your legs crossed. John passes you a syringe as he has many times before. You feel the needle prick the skin of your left forearm and your right thumb presses down the plunger. You tense a moment and close your eyes, waiting for the rush, but it doesn't come. All your buddies are getting high and you are just sitting there feeling nothing at all. The injection has no effect whatsoever.

Covert sensitization might also be used in this case to decrease the desire to take drugs, and covert reinforcement would be applied to increase the occurrence of alternative behaviors.

2.2.5. Covert Modeling (CM). In covert modeling, the client is instructed to imagine observing a model behaving in various situations. Covert modeling is a procedure analogous to overt modeling (Bandura, 1970), and may be used both in increasing or decreasing specific responses.

In treating a client for depression:

> Imagine that you see a woman about your age in bed asleep. She is just beginning to awaken and as her eyelids flutter open, a smile comes over her face. She is thinking about the day ahead and how she is going to enjoy it.

In a complex problem such as depression, covert modeling might be only one of many treatment techniques that are used. Thought-stopping might be used to block depressive thoughts, and practice might be given in positively scanning the individual's environment. Covert reinforcement might be used to increase positive, nondepressive responses. Techniques such as the self-control triad and creative fantasy (to be described later) have also been beneficial in treating depression.

2.2.6. Covert Response Cost (CRC). In employing covert response cost (Cautela, 1976a) the client is instructed to imagine both the response to be reduced followed by the imaginary loss of a reinforcer, e.g., a watch, money, jewelry:

In the treatment of alcoholism:

> Imagine that you are walking to the liquor cabinet to pour yourself a drink. (Shift to CRC scene) Now imagine that your brand-new car that you worked so hard to buy has just been smashed into a tree. You are looking at it in shock. Imagine it as though it had happened and you are there. The entire front end is destroyed and your insurance will not replace it. You feel sweat come out on your brow and you feel a terrible sinking feeling in the pit of your stomach. You are bitterly disappointed.

In conclusion it should be emphasized that there is far more involved in successful application of the covert conditioning procedures than the simple presentation of scenes. The covert conditioning procedures are not used in isolation, but as a composite in treatment. Many factors contribute to effective treatment and these include a thorough and probing behavioral analysis, therapist experience, degree of relaxation, imagery development, amount of practice, presentation of the rationale, client motivation, and continual assessment of scene effectiveness. These issues will be addressed in the following section.

3. Imagery Development

Integral to the effective use of covert conditioning procedures is the ability of the client to achieve and perform appropriate imagery procedures. Factors such as the thoroughness of the behavioral analysis, image quality, emotional arousal, imagery assessment, and the amount of practice are all important contributors to therapeutic improvement. It is emphasized that each of these factors must be taken into consideration and carefully monitored for successful treatment to be expected.

3.1. Construction of Covert Scenes

The main goal in construction of imagery is to design scenes that are as clear as possible. It has been our clinical experience that the more the client is involved in the scene, the more effective it is in causing behavior change. This has recently been supported in research by Kozak and Lang (1976). This study points out that the more closely the therapist's imagery coincides with the client's, the greater the physiological change in the client and the greater the possibility of behavioral change. The usual procedure is to develop scenes based on the client's personal experiences. The therapist also describes the scenes in the client's own words. Of course, the imagery content depends upon the behavioral analysis of the target behavior.

For example, the problem of agoraphobia:

THERAPIST: Could you give me an example of the occasions when you *do* leave the house?
CLIENT: Yes, sometimes we do go to movies, but it terrifies me.
THERAPIST: Would you be able to go alone?
CLIENT: No! I could go only if my husband was with me.
THERAPIST: Would you have to sit in an aisle seat?
CLIENT: Absolutely.
THERAPIST: Would it matter whether you sat closer to the front of the theater or the back?
CLIENT: Oh, I don't know, does it matter?

THERAPIST: Yes, it matters very much to understand exactly the situations that are hardest for you, because it is from these descriptions that we construct the scenes that we later use in therapy.
CLIENT: All right, it does make a difference. I always feel safer the closer I am to an exit, so the back of the theater would be better.
THERAPIST: Would it matter if it were crowded?
CLIENT: Oh, yes, the more crowded it is the more afraid I am.

From this information, an example of a scene might be as follows using covert reinforcement (COR):

> You and your husband enthusiastically make plans to go to a movie. (COR). You get into the car with him and enjoy the drive to the theater. (COR). As you walk into the theater you proceed halfway down the aisle and find two seats on the end. (COR). It is crowded, but you don't mind. (COR). You sit down, watch the movie, and thoroughly enjoy it. (COR).

As indicated above, imagery development is reliant upon a thorough behavioral analysis. This includes determination of antecedents and consequences, and a detailed description of the maladaptive behavior.

The usual assessment procedure (Cautela and Upper, 1975) includes the administration of the Behavior Analysis History Questionnaire (Cautela, 1977b), the Fear Survey Schedule (FSS) (Wolpe and Lang, 1964), and the Reinforcement Survey Schedule (RSS) (Cautela and Kastenbaum, 1967). The FSS provides fear-provoking items to be used in systematic desensitization or COR, if that is prescribed. The RSS is a source of pleasurable items that may be used in COR. Of course, these questionnaires are supplemented by questioning of the patient by the therapist.

3.2. Development of Imagery Capacity

Once a covert conditioning technique is prescribed, the patient is instructed in the use of imagery and his clarity of imagery is assessed in the following manner:

> Now, sit back and relax and try to imagine the scene that I describe. Try to imagine that you are really there. Concentrate not only on seeing the image, but in imagining other senses as well. If you are imagining sitting in a chair, try to imagine that you can feel the chair against your legs and back. If you are imagining that you are in a store, try to imagine that you can hear people talking and cash registers ringing. You are not supposed to see yourself doing what I describe, but you are to try to feel as though you were actually present and experiencing the situation.
> First, let us imagine the scene clearly. Close your eyes and try to imagine everything I describe. Ready?

The client is asked if the scene was clear and how he felt about it.

If there is any difficulty, the scene is repeated by the therapist in greater detail.

When repetition is not effective enough, it is often necessary to improve a client's capacity to image through practice sessions. Whenever possible, imagery practice sessions are scheduled in addition to the weekly meetings. When there is difficulty in obtaining strong imagery, practice involves increasing relaxation, vividness, and controllability.

Relaxation training is sometimes useful because tension and anxiety may block concentration. Reduction in high arousal to moderate levels has been shown to correlate with greater clarity in imagery (Lang, 1977). The analogy explained to the client is that tension acts like a radar jam and only when that jamming is reduced may a clear signal be transmitted.

Imagery training is begun with a modified version of progressive relaxation (Jacobson, 1938) and is described in detail in our relaxation manual (Cautela and Grodin, 1977). Approximately 15 minutes are devoted to tensing and relaxing major muscle groups. This is followed by 5-10 minutes of relaxation imagery; i.e., lying on a beach in the sun, floating on a cloud, or sinking into a soft featherbed. At the end of each sequence the client is asked to rank the degree of relaxation obtained from 1 to 100 percent. (In cases where the client has great difficulty relaxing, the procedure may be enhanced at home while taking hot baths or showers.)

3.3. Training to Enhance Vividness and Controllability

3.3.1. Vividness.
A certain degree of vividness of imagery is essential to the effectiveness of the covert conditioning procedures. However, vividness must not be equated with solely visual imagery, for the greatest effectiveness is obtained when the client reports a vividness in all sense modalities. For example, if a client had trouble imagining or visualizing an airplane, the sound of the plane would be described, the kinesthetic feeling of the takeoff or the seatbelt, the physiological responses such as increased heartbeat or shortness of breath, and the appropriate affective state such as anxiety or exhilaration. It is emphasized that the client not simply imagine the scene, but try to feel that he is actually experiencing it. Recent research suggests that the largest and most consistent physiological responses occur in response to imagining somato-motor and visceral responses and to imagining "being there" rather than just imagining detailed descriptions without affective components (Lang, 1977).

In imagery training, the client is instructed to look at various objects in the office, close his eyes, and describe the object. This is repeated until the client is able to give a fairly accurate and detailed description of a newly presented object. The client is also encouraged to pay close attention to situations and objects outside the office and to describe an itemized reproduction of the scene, taking into consideration the sensations of taste, touch, sound, smell, and particularly affective responses, i.e., how the client feels about the situation or object.

In dealing with phobias, photographs of specific objects such as airplanes or pigeons are utilized. Using photographs has the advantage of being able to practice the imagery procedures many more times, since the client does not actually have to be at the location. The imagery training is not only used to increase the ability of imagining stimuli, but also increases the probability of achieving the affective state desired.

Clients are given homework assignments in which they are to write down certain experiences in as much detail as possible with as much realism as possible. In most cases the training described is sufficient to employ the covert conditioning procedures effectively. In fact, we have never witnessed a case where the subject was willing to cooperate in which imagery procedures could not be employed.

3.3.2. Controllability. Another problem mentioned above is that of imagery control. Development of controllability is an extremely important factor because, according to Richardson (1969), it directly influences therapeutic effectiveness. No matter how vivid the imagery, if the client lacks the ability to control the image, prospects for therapeutic improvement are poor. In fact, the most difficult state in which to cause behavioral change is one in which the client experiences intensely vivid imagery but cannot control or maintain adaptive thoughts and continues to revert to maladaptive images. (Thus, Kazdin's observation is correct that the client's report of the degree of vividness in imagery does not consistently correlate with behavior change; but controllability was not taken into consideration (Kazdin, 1977, p. 55). These two factors combined do correlate with behavioral change, according to Richardson, with the best combination being high levels of both vividness and controllability. The combination that correlates the least with behavioral change is high vividness and low controllability.

Clients with difficulty in controllability may not be able to switch easily from maladaptive images to adaptive ones. Many can begin positive scenes only to report that they are always interrupted by aversive thoughts. Some have great difficulty putting into use the covert procedures that they have been taught. Some examples of difficulty in controllability that have been reported are fantasy situations such as skiing down a hill and falling, stepping into a hot bath and slipping, continuous repetition of an upsetting image, or having every thought sequence end negatively. Clients have been successfully aided in controlling and redirecting such negative imagery in the following ways:

1. It is stressed that the fantasy is theirs, it belongs to them, they created it, and they are free to change it in any way they wish. We first ask the client to describe the scene again out loud, but with a positive outcome; i.e., they ski down the hill successfully, or they do not slip in the tub. Sometimes this is sufficient, but frequently the client remains unable to control his thoughts, and still envisions the negative consequences.

2. In such cases, the negative imagery is slowly modified by shaping. Attaining controllability often requires taking small steps toward the desired response. If the skiing imagery is used they may imagine falling down, but the fall does not hurt them. On repeated descriptions of the scene, they are encouraged to imagine themselves maintaining better balance, or stopping to rest if they imagine that they are going to fall.

3. Another process for facilitating controllability over imagery necessitates the client keeping a log of all the incidents in a week that cause anxiety, tension, or depression. This helps the client become aware of what situations elicit anxiety and is based on the rationale that thoughts recognized and interrupted at the onset are easier to control and eliminate. After a week of recording these incidents, clients become extremely cognizant of upsetting events. These lists then form the basis from which clients are trained to quickly identify tense situations and to relax and replace negative covert processes with more positive and adaptive ones where appropriate.

3.4. Imagery Practice

Once appropriate scenes are constructed and clarity is obtained, encouraging the client to do the homework scenes regularly and diligently becomes a crucial element of therapy. Clients are asked to practice daily the imagery sequences that have been developed during the therapy session. The amount of time required for practice varies for each client but an average schedule is performing the homework procedures three times a day for about 10–15 minutes each. It is stressed that many daily repetitions over many weeks are necessary for the technique to become a habit. An analogy is drawn between every practice session having some effect and driving a nail into a board with a hammer. Every practice session represents one strike of the hammer and the particular technique "sinks in" and becomes more effective with each "blow." Client practice can be increased by (1) writing down the homework procedures while in the therapy session so that the instructions are clear; (2) instructing the client to chart practice sessions in a notebook; (3) encouraging clients to discuss problems doing homework assignments, try to find solutions; (4) never criticizing the client for not practicing, but taking a supportive attitude to this problem (if the client is having difficulty we try to find the circumstances and situations that would facilitate the client performing the exercises); and (5) continually emphasizing how essential the practice sessions are to therapeutic improvement. It is pointed out that therapy will not be as successful if it involves only one hour per week. These procedures are somewhat successful with even the most recalcitrant clients.

3.5. Assessment of Imagery

The therapist must constantly assess the efficacy of the covert procedures being employed through behavioral feedback from the client, by directly observing the client, and by the client's self-report.

The capacity to obtain vivid and intense imagery and the ability to relax often vary from week to week and may quickly be spotted by having the client report a rating of clarity of imagery each week. Sometimes a client will rate clarity at 85 to 90 percent at one session and then report 40 to 50 percent at the next. At this point, the therapist and client must work together to determine what factors have contributed to this problem. If the difficulty is due to increased tension or anxiety, more emphasis on relaxation may be indicated. If the problem is due to depression or negative self-statements, then locating more reinforcers or positive scanning may be necessary. If the client is bored with the familiarity of the same scenes, the therapist and client cooperate to design new ones. It is the responsibility of the therapist to work with the client on maintaining a constant, high level of imagery vividness and affective intensity to better promote therapeutic effectiveness.

4. Application of Covert Processes to Overall Functioning

A learning theory basis for covert conditioning has been presented and the development of imagery has been discussed. Now various applications of these techniques will be considered. First, there will be a discussion of how imagery in a general sense may contribute to both adaptive behavior as well as maladaptive behavior. Second, the ways in which covert processes can influence specific classes of behaviors and their interactions will be examined.

4.1. Covert Processes and Maladaptive Behavior

Much faulty or abnormal behavior is developed and maintained due to covert processes. Singer acknowledges this "inherently tragic aspect" of thought patterns and suggests that our imagery (daydreams) may thus carry "the seeds of psychopathology" (1975, pp. 203-204).

It has repeatedly been observed in clinical practice that much maladaptive behavior is preceded by what are described as "urges" or desires to perform that behavior. For example, lighting a cigarette is preceded by some form of smoking imagery; either a self-statement such as "I sure would like a cigarette, right now," or feeling a sudden urge to smoke, or experiencing imagery depicting smoking.

Covert conditioning techniques would then be applied to those urges. Depending on the preference of the client for specific imagery (as determined by the various survey schedules) the procedures might involve imagining that cigarettes have maggots crawling all over them (covert sensitization), imagining that a cigarette was smoked but absolutely no pleasure was experienced (covert extinction), imagining that upon lighting a cigarette one lost one's wallet (covert response cost), or imagining that a model turned down an opportunity to smoke (covert modeling).

A similar composite of the covert conditioning procedures has been used in successfully decreasing maladaptive responding in such cases as overeating (Cautela, 1972b), self-injurious behavior of such severity that the patient's life was in danger (Cautela and Baron, 1973), sexual deviation (Cautela and Wisocki, 1971), and drug abuse (Cautela and Rosensteil, 1975).

In addition, there are less clearly defined behaviors such as depression or anxiety that are developed and maintained by multicovert processes, which have been treated successfully by imagery techniques. In this category it is quite common for therapists to encounter individuals who can be labeled "negative scanners." That is, almost everything is evaluated in a negative way, with the very worst consequences being imagined. Such people often label themselves as depressed. They negatively scan the mistakes of their past and present life and negatively scan their future. This is most often done covertly. For example, if a "negative scanner" were going to move into a new house, he would imagine unlimited varieties of terrible events that might befall him: plumbing failures, a leaking roof, or the neighborhood going downhill. Another example could involve an individual thinking over the next day's scheduling, considering how boring (or upsetting) it was going to be and becoming extremely "depressed." Negative scanners also bring the same viewpoint into therapy where they invariably negatively scan their own progress. If one approaches any situation with such framework, there will always be something that could be interpreted in a negative way. The opportunity to positively scan for good things in the situation will be ignored and a negative experience will be reported. This behavior can maintain other depressive and pathological behavior patterns.

It is very important to train such clients to try to positively scan their environment and to modify the negative scanning behaviors with the covert conditioning procedures. Examples of this might include following every positive self-statement with a pleasant scene (covert reinforcement), imagining a model with a very positive outlook surveying a situation (covert modeling), or imagining losing a valuable piece of jewelry following every negative or depressive thought (covert response cost). Positive scanning is also enhanced by having the client keep a journal in which all positive events or thoughts are recorded.

A number of maladaptive behaviors involve anticipated behaviors. These might involve imagining giving a speech, forgetting one's notes, and making a fool of oneself. Another incident of this sort would be imagining being on a plane and developing a panic attack or being on top of a high building, becoming dizzy, and being afraid of falling. All these behaviors are apt to be maladaptive in that they increase the probability that the individual is going to develop phobic behavior. According to the covert conditioning assumptions, the more one thinks of being in an elevator and becoming panicky or being in a plane and a crash occurring, the greater the probability that the individual will engage in avoidance behavior concerning that particular object. If someone were to imagine that in making a phone call he would stutter when the other person answers, the probability increases that if he makes the call, he will stutter.

The assumption is that many phobic behaviors, as well as many depressive behaviors, are probably developed and maintained by multicovert processes.

4.2. Behavioral Hygiene and Therapeutic Measures

In addition to decreasing maladaptive behaviors, covert conditioning procedures are employed to increase adaptive responding. Both approaches are essential to the total treatment success. Thus, when severely self-injurious behavior was eliminated in a hospitalized patient (Cautela and Baron, 1973), techniques such as covert reinforcement and covert modeling were used to increase behaviors that would contribute to more optimal functioning. In similar fashion, these techniques have been used to increase social skills with the opposite sex (Cautela and Baron, 1973), or to improve a sexual relationship with a spouse in the treatment of cases of sexual deviation (Cautela and Wisocki, 1971).

In a general sense, behavioral hygiene consists of trying to train a child or an individual to employ covert processes that are adaptive; i.e., processes that will not hinder the optimal performance of the individual. Therefore, in a situation in which a child thinks negatively and expresses it overtly, the parent might set about, by story or example, to lead the child toward more positive covert imagery. This is true of adults as well, who are encouraged in therapy to positively scan their environment. Clients are asked to describe the good things that happen during the week. They are taught thought-stopping (Cautela and Wisocki, 1977), on anticipatory maladaptive imagery, and covert reinforcement for positively reinforcing positive imagery. For instance, when an individual is facing an operation, rather than thinking that they are surely to die, they are encouraged to make positive statements to themselves. Examples of these might be "The chances are good that I will live through this and I should continue to think in this way." Then the client is instructed to imagine a pleasant scene (covert reinforcement), as has been developed in imagery training sessions. It is emphasized that this is *not* a "hide your head in the sand" approach. A realistic appraisal of each situation is essential and is encouraged. Yet, beyond that point, there is nothing that can be gained and much damage that might be done in thinking or worrying about negative consequences.

4.2.1. The Self-Control Triad. The senior author recently developed a behavioral-hygiene technique utilizing three behavioral procedures: thought-stopping, relaxation, and covert reinforcement. This appears an effective procedure in clinical practice. It has enabled clients to reduce or eliminate negative thought processes by replacing them with positive, adaptive imagery. This procedure is labeled the self-control triad.

Since a response sequence is more easily interrupted at its onset than after it has been allowed to proceed, the triad is taught as a response to the initial cue of the *onset* of anxiety, temptation, or negative imagery. As discussed in the section on imagery development, extensive training is given in becoming aware of these internal cues.

At the first sign of any maladaptive covert event, clients are instructed to immediately perform the following: (1) thought-stopping (distraction and interruption of any maladaptive thoughts by imagining the word "Stop" being yelled loudly and visualizing a big, red stop sign), immediately followed by (2) deep breathing while relaxing and covertly saying the word "Relax," and then followed by (3) covert reinforcement, imagining a pleasant scene. These three components of the procedure are taught separately, practiced thoroughly until the imagery is experienced vividly and intensely and, only then, are placed in sequence.

The procedure may be applied at any time and anywhere (eyes open or closed) that anxiety or negative thoughts occur, e.g., while driving in heavy traffic, in a heated discussion, prior to giving a speech, or even when tempted to make a maladaptive approach response such as overeating, taking drugs, or performing deviant sexual behavior.

5. Application of Covert Processes to Specific Classes of Behavior

We are presently beginning to employ covert procedures for the overall well-being of the individual. Some of the areas are discussed below.

5.1. Covert Behavior and Daydreaming

As is the case with the nature of private events, daydreaming has been a difficult concept to adequately define. According to Singer, daydreaming represents a shift of attention away from external environment and toward an "unfolding sequence of private responses made to some internal stimulus" (1975, p. 3). Similarly, daydreaming can be conceptualized as covert behavior that is not directly related to the present environmental conditions, and that represents a form of elaboration on a story or theme.

The important point for the purpose of this discussion is to understand that daydreaming is very influential in forming and controlling an individual's behavior. For instance, if an individual daydreams of raping someone and enjoys this sensation, the probability will increase that he will daydream about raping someone again. Furthermore, the more the individual daydreams about committing rape, the more probable it is that he will perform that behavior. If someone daydreams about committing suicide and imagines the reinforcing consequences (such as freedom from pain or having friends mourn him), it will increase the probability that he will try to perform this ultimate escape behavior. If daydreaming involves a fantasy concerning drugtaking or aggressive behavior with positive reinforcing emotions, the probability will increase that not only will these daydreams increase, but so might the corresponding overt behaviors.

Therefore, it is a very important assumption of covert conditioning that daydreaming as well as other covert processes are very influential in forming the behavioral repertoire and predicting future behavior. There are creative kinds of daydreaming where an individual may imagine feeling relaxed and performing well on an exam, a type of desensitization. There are creative daydreams in which one imagines solving a problem, thus seeking new ways to improve life. There are also the creative daydreams of children imagining playing with friendly animals or interacting with other children in a reinforcing and adaptive way. Not only is conditioning taking place, but they are beginning their own cognitive input.

5.1.1. **Creative Fantasy.** For clients who are negative scanners or who label themselves depressive or who say they can find nothing to replace negative thoughts, a technique called creative fantasy has been developed. This procedure uses imagery in a positive and creative way as in covert reinforcement, but expands it into a pleasant daydream. An excellent example of creative fantasy was presented by Singer when he described such a process in his own childhood involving elaborate and recurrent fantasies of a baseball team with scores, players, a world series, and a main figure called Poppy Ott (1975, pp. 17-28). In employing creative fantasy, clients are reassured that they are not going to go "schizy" or begin living in a fantasy world; but will be taught to use daydreaming as a means to stop negative thinking, to decrease boredom, or to reduce a feeling of depression, and even to become more creative.

The procedure for creative fantasy involves the client picking a plot, a theme, or a story—possibly something indicated on the Reinforcement Survey Schedule such as love of the out-of-doors. The client is then asked to close his eyes, imagine the scene, and then describe it aloud. An example used by one client involved having a cabin up in the mountains beside a stream. He would imagine spending the weekend there, doing simple tasks like chopping wood for the fireplace. Sometimes he would imagine walking in the woods with someone special beside him. Birds would flutter by and occasionally a small animal would dart through the underbrush. Once he imagined coming upon a beautiful little waterfall flowing into a cool, refreshing pond, so he decided to jump in and go for a swim. Particular attention was given to the feelings of contentment and well-being experienced during the fantasy.

After the client has related the constructive fantasy and has described it, the therapist reinforces the adaptive responses that were made. If some negative imagery is mentioned, the therapist and client work together on how to modify that imagery in a more positive direction. The purpose of creative fantasy is to increase the general level of reinforcement at any given time and to act as a replacement for undesirable covert behaviors.

Clients are told that it is not relevant whether or not they will be able to actually achieve the behavior of the fantasy. It is stressed that while they are having the fantasy, they should enjoy it as much as possible. Fantasy content should be eliminated whenever it involves a feeling of frustration or lack of fulfillment because the fantasy may not be realized. The purpose is *not* to build up expectations that will not be met. The point is solely to teach the client a positive and pleasant covert behavior that can serve as an enriching and adaptive resource in his life. Creative fantasy is often used to increase the general level of reinforcement in depressed individuals.

5.1.2. Covert Processes and Athletic Ability. A number of investigators have proposed that the use of imagery can enhance athletic performance (Corbin, 1972; Richardson, 1969). This involves covertly rehearsing a task with positive consequences for the specific intent of learning and has been labeled "mental practice" (Corbin, 1972). In the parlance of some athletes, this is called being "psyched-up," and we have all had the experience of imagining hitting a baseball or a golfball squarely and having it seem to aid better performance. Suinn used positive imagining with the Olympic Team and he claims promising results as a consequence of mental practice (Suinn, 1976). Therefore, if someone makes a bad golf swing, the worst thing that can be done is to imagine the poor swing the next time a swing is taken. What should occur is that the individual thought-stops on the bad swing and imagines only the correct swing. The same procedure would apply to making a free throw in basketball. If a basket is missed, the bad toss should never again be imagined and only the correct throw should be fantasized.

A rigorous review of the literature by Corbin reported over 75 investigations that gave support to the efficacy of mental practice. While Corbin feels that more rigorously controlled experiments are now in order, he states that there seems to be little doubt that "mental practice can positively affect skilled motor performance" (1972). Furthermore, covert reinforcement following the imagining of the successful performance of an athletic event should enhance performance.

Daydreaming can aid in problem-solving, relief from boredom, anticipation and memory, or assimilation of novel stimuli, but the actual function and evolutionary significance of daydreaming has not been ascertained. Some investigators consider it epiphenomenal and Singer suggests that it might be "just there" (1975, p. 115). The issue is one of how to put this process to use. The above examples represent just two attempts to harness this powerful mechanism for effecting behavior change. However, this is a relatively new concept and there is great potential for further exploration into the possibilities of utilizing daydreaming to change behavior.

5.2. Covert Behavior of Nocturnal Dreaming

Dream behavior has been traditionally of interest to the dynamically oriented therapist. But recently behavior modifiers have become interested in dreaming from a behavioral point of view.

Cautela's first experience in dealing with dream content developed from a clinical situation in which a client leaving the therapy session complained that she could not sleep due to terrible nightmares and therefore had trouble concentrating on her work the next day. The dream was essentially as follows:

> I am walking down a busy city street on a bright sunny day. I hear footsteps behind me and I turn and see a big, old-looking monster following me. I start running faster and faster and the monster keeps chasing me. No matter what I do, I can't get away from him. I find myself upon a roof, with the monster closing in on me. I finally jump off the roof and wake up in terror just before hitting the ground.

It was reasoned that the least that could be done would be to desensitize the client to the dream. She had already learned relaxation and desensitization and so she was asked to relax, close her eyes, and begin narrating the dream.

As she started talking about the part of the dream in which she heard footsteps, she would become frightened and cry out, "No, no, no. . . the thought of it terrifies me!" She would then be told, "Wait a minute, turn around, it's just a kind, elderly lady, so continue walking."

Gradually, as the scenes were continued, the elderly lady was transformed into a kind, elderly man, then into a man that looked a little gruesome and then finally into a monster. The most anxiety-provoking elements of the dream were repeated until the client was able to narrate the entire dream without anxiety. The client was highly motivated and agreed to practice this entire sequence five times each night before going to bed. At the next session, she cheerfully reported having the nightmare only once all week. The following week she continued the homework and never again has reported that particular nightmare or any other nightmare since that time.

This experience led Baron (1969) to do some experimental work on modifying nightmares. As a result it became apparent that it was relatively easy to eliminate nightmares with desensitization. No attempts were made to unbury important unconscious material, but no new nightmares were reported nor was any form of symptom substitution observed.

5.2.1. Dreams as Aids to Assessment. On a number of occasions in therapy, the senior author has noticed a correlation between treatment progress and the outcome of a dream. In one example, a firesetter reported that since he had begun covert sensitization procedures on his desires to start fires in fields, that he no longer had urges to set fires during the day, but that he still had dreams about setting fires. Therefore, covert sensitization was performed on the dream content itself that involved his shooting fire arrows at people and setting fires in fields. Thereafter, dreams concerning fire-setting were eliminated completely and he no longer reported urges during the day nor during dreams at night. Jurgela (1975) reported a case in which he was treating a child molester with covert sensitization. After receiving treatment for several sessions, the client volunteered the dream that when he took the boy into his room as usual to molest him, he now envisioned himself throwing garbage at the boy and found him quite disgusting.

Many similar reports of this nature have indicated that perhaps dreams have diagnostic value in terms of their efficacy in therapy. It often appears that dream content may be somewhat correlated with treatment progress. If the dream content indicates that the behavior is still occurring covertly while dreaming, the treatment is not complete even though the maladaptive responses are not occurring in overt or covert waking behavior. This assumption remains to be proved experimentally, but dream content is a factor that therapists from any discipline can refer to as indication of progress of the therapy.

When dream content indicates that maladaptive behavior is still occurring, the behavior therapist has two choices. Covert conditioning can be performed on the maladaptive behavior with the assumption that not enough conditioning has been done. Otherwise, conditioning may be performed on the dream content itself. Experiments are needed to determine which is the more efficacious procedure. Of course, there might be a question of whether the dream was actually eliminated or whether the individual simply no longer recalls the dream. This might be tested by experiments done in which the individual is awakened at various times during sleep and dream content is requested.

5.2.2. The Use of Dreaming as an Aid for Covert Conditioning.

As Freud observed, dream content "distinctly prefers impressions of the few days preceding" (1913, p. 138). We have noticed that when clients are practicing covert conditioning techniques, they are apt to have related imagery in their dreams. When these techniques are practiced just before going to sleep, clients often report dreams related to the scene just practiced. For example, when covert reinforcement is used to obtain self-control over eating, a scene would be described as follows:

> You walk into your kitchen and see a piece of pie. You want to eat it, but just as you do so, you think to yourself, "No! I don't want that pie. . .it will make me fat!" Then you are to imagine a pleasant reinforcing scene. (COR - One that had been rehearsed in therapy for vivid, controlled, positive imagery.)

The client is instructed to practice such a scene before going to sleep. As a result, very explicit dreams are often reported in which they were offered a piece of pie, and they refused it saying that it would make them fat. Likewise, there have been clients in therapy for drug addiction who have been practicing imagery in which they take heroin, but received no effect from it (covert extinction). Several such clients have reported dreaming of "shooting up" with some friends, but finding that they are the only ones that did not get high. Reports of these types have been consonant with improvement in therapy.

The process of practicing before falling asleep appears to have a two-fold advantage. The first is that the therapist is able to assess the effectiveness of the treatment technique by seeing if it enters the dream content. A second advantage may be that the dream content is offering another conditioning trial. Again, this relationship between dream content, diagnosis, and covert conditioning has to be explored in a systematic manner. But, in the meantime, we invite our behavioral colleagues to take note of the dream process of their clients.

5.3. The Use of Covert Conditioning in the Modification of Organic Dysfunction

As stated previously, all behavior can be conceptualized into three categories: covert psychological processes, covert physiological processes, and overt or observable behavior. Of course, all these behaviors are in fact organic behaviors. Each process has its distinct physiological component. The different covert psychological processes such as imagery, thinking, and feeling must, of course, be physiologically different from each other. A thought must have a different physiological concomitant from a feeling. And within these categories, thought A must necessarily be physiologically different from thought B. In like manner, overt psychological events (such as time out, overt punishment, overt reinforcement) necessarily involve different afferent stimulation. Ultimately, therefore, all behavioral processes are in fact organic processes. Outlined below are 10 essential assumptions involved in the conceptualization of covert conditioning and organic processes:

1. Psychological events are:
   a. Covert events
      (1) Thoughts (talking to oneself).
      (2) Images—responses similar to those made to external stimuli but external stimuli not present.
      (3) Feelings—internal sensations correlated with thoughts and images.
   b. External stimulation of sense modalities.
2. Psychological events are organic events.
3. Covert and overt psychological events obey the same laws.
4. Covert and overt events interact according to the same laws as covert events interacting with covert events (CE) and overt events interacting with overt events (OE).
5. Nonpsychological events of the organism obey the same laws as psychological events.
6. Psychological events interact with nonpsychological events according to the same laws as (CE × CE) (OE × OE) (CE × OE).
7. The laws governing organic events can best be described from theoretical speculations and established empirical relationships within the conditioning paradigm.
8. *All* organic dysfunctions are influenced by, or produced by, psychological events.
9. *All* organic dysfunctions should include the manipulation of psychological events.
10. Every diagnosis of organic dysfunction should include a behavioral analysis.

It follows from the above that when we use the label "psychosomatic" we are really describing how the categories of overt and covert psychological processes (organic events) influence other organic events. What we are really saying here is that organic events are influencing other organic events whenever we use the term "psychosomatic." From our point of view, it would do well to eliminate the term "psychosomatic" altogether, since all organic dysfunction is influenced by psychological processes that are organic events. There is no *a priori* way to decide what covert physiological events (and the related organic events) are influenced by psychological processes. For example, there is a growing belief by various investigators that psychological factors can influence the susceptibility and course of cancer (Cautela, 1976b; Pelletier, 1977; Greer and Morris, 1975; Seligman, 1975; Simonton and Simonton, 1975; Booth, 1973; Greene, 1969; Schmale and Iker, 1966; Neumann, 1959; LeShan and Worthington, 1956).

Our experience in dealing with organic dysfunction is to target that behavior as we would any psychological dysfunction and then do the appropriate behavioral analysis; i.e., the target behavior of epileptic seizures and the behavioral analysis consists in operationally defining the seizure, discovering the frequency, intensity, and duration of the seizures, and then identifying the antecedents and consequences.

Cautela has stated elsewhere that every organic dysfunction, regardless of its type, should involve *both a behavioral analysis and treatment, as well as a medical diagnosis and treatment* (1977). We have applied this approach to such dysfunctions as asthma, arthritis, pain, and ulcerative colitis. A growing body of research is indicating that stress and anxiety contribute to the occurrence, growth rate, and maintenance of malignancies (Kavetsky, Turkevich, and Balitsky, 1958, 1966; Goldfarb, Dreisen, and Cole, 1967; Corson, 1966; Ader and Friedman, 1965). Thus, we are in the process of conjointly treating a case of leukemia with the client's physician. Our behavioral analysis consisted of identifying stressful and anxiety-provoking antecedent conditions and consequences in the client's environment that may be contributing to, or reinforcing, the leukemic behavior. Our target behavior is the leukemia and the dependent variables that we measure are the platelets, white blood cell count, and number of myeloblasts. Treatment consists of a composite of the procedures described in this chapter (covert conditioning, self-control triad, relaxation, creative fantasy, plus assertive training and desensitization), systematically applied to increase the client's adaptive and coping responses to stressful stimuli and to reduce anxiety responses.

In summary then, our procedure in dealing with organic dysfunction involves a comprehensive approach that includes both medical treatment and the total package of behavioral procedures with an emphasis on covert conditioning.

References

Ader, R., and Freidman, S. B. Differential early experiences and susceptibility to transplanted tumor in the rat. *Journal of Comparative and Physiological Psychology,* 1965, 59, 361–364.

Anant, S. S. The use of verbal aversion (negative conditioning) with an alcoholic: A case report. *Behavior Research and Therapy,* 1968, 6, 395–396.

Ashem, B., and Donner, L. Covert sensitization with alcoholics: A controlled replication. *Behavior Research and Therapy*, 1966, *6*, 7-12.
Asher, L. M., and Cautela, J. R. Covert negative reinforcement. An experimental test. *Behavior Therapy and Experimental Psychiatry*, 1972, *1*, 1-5.
Asher, L. M., and Cautela, J. R. An experimental study of covert extinction. *Behavior Therapy and Experimental Psychiatry*, 1974, *5*, 233-238.
Bandura, A. Modeling theory: In W. S. Sahakian (Ed.), *Psychology of learning: Systems, models, and theories*. Chicago: Markham, 1970.
Barlow, D. H., and Agras, W. S. Fading to increase heterosexual responsiveness in homosexuals. *Journal of Applied Behavior Analysis*, 1973, *6*, 355-366.
Barlow, D. H., Leitenberg, H., and Agras, W. S. Experimental control of sexual deviation through manipulation of the noxious scene in covert sensitization. *Journal of Abnormal Psychology*, 1969, *74*, 569-601.
Baron, M. G. The relation between dreaming and learning. Unpublished master's thesis, Boston College, 1969.
Benson, M., Shapiro, D., Tursky, B., and Schwartz, G. E. Decreased systolic blood pressure through operant conditioning techniques in patients with essential hypertension. *Science*, 1971, *173*, 740-742.
Black-Cleworth, P., Woody, C. D., and Niemann, J. A conditioned eyeblink obtained by using electrical stimulation of the facial nerve as the unconditioned stimulus. *Brain Research*, 1975, *90*, 45-46.
Booth, B. Psychobiological aspects of "spontaneous" remission of cancer. *Journal of the American Academy of Psychoanalysis*, 1973, *1*, 303-317.
Brownell, K. D., and Barlow, D. H. Behavioral Treatment of Sexual Deviation. In E. Foa and A. Goldstein (Eds.), *The handbook of behavioral interventions*. New York: Wiley and Sons, 1978.
Cautela, J. R. Treatment of compulsive behavior by covert sensitization. *Psychological Record*, 1966, *16*, 33-41.
Cautela, J. R. Covert sensitization. *Psychological Reports*, 1967, *20*, 459-468.
Cautela, J. R. Behavior therapy and the need for behavioral assessment. *Psychotherapy: Theory, Research and Practice*, 1968, *5*, 175-179.
Cautela, J. R. Covert reinforcement. *Behavior Therapy*, 1970a, *1*, 33-50.
Cautela, J. R. Covert negative reinforcement. *Behavior Therapy and Experimental Psychiatry*, 1970b, *1*, 272-278.
Cautela, J. R. Treatment of smoking by covert sensitization. *Psychological Reports*, 1970c, *26*, 415-420.
Cautela, J. R. Covert extinction. *Behavior Therapy*, 1971a, *2*, 192-200.
Cautela, J. R. Covert modeling. Paper presented to the Association for the Advancement of Behavior Therapy, Washington, D.C. 1971b.
Cautela, J. R. Rationale and procedures for covert conditioning. In *Advances in behavior therapy*. New York: Academic Press, 1972a.
Cautela, J. R. The treatment of overeating by covert conditioning. *Psychotherapy: Theory, Research, and Practice*, 1972b, *9*, 211-216.
Cautela, J. R. Covert processes and behavior modification. *Journal of Nervous and Mental Disease*, 1973a, *1*, 157.
Cautela, J. R. Seizures; controlling the uncontrollable. *Journal of Rehabilitation*, 1973b, May-June, 34-40.
Cautela, J. R. Covert response cost. *Psychotherapy: Theory, Research and Practice*, 1976a, *13*, 397-404.
Cautela, J. R. Toward a Pavlovian theory of cancer. Paper presented at the Pavlovian Society, Louisville, Kentucky, November 13, 1976b.

Cautela, J. R. Covert conditioning: Assumptions and procedures. *Journal of Mental Imagery*, 1977a, *1*, 53-64.

Cautela, J. R. *Behavior analysis forms for clinical intervention.* Champaign, Illinois: Research Press, 1977b.

Cautela, J. R., and Baron, M. G. Multifaceted behavior therapy of self-injurious behavior. *Journal of Behavior Therapy and Experimental Psychiatry*, 1973, *4*, 125-131.

Cautela, J. R., and Baron, M. G. Pavlovian theory of dreaming. *Pavlovian Journal of Biological Science*, 1974, *9*, 104-121.

Cautela, J. R., and Baron, M. G. Covert conditioning: A theoretical analysis. *Behavior Modification*, 1977, *1*, 351-368.

Cautela, J. R., and Grodin, J. *Relaxation: A comprehensive manual.* Sponsored by the Rhode Island State Department of Education, Title III/IV. 1977.

Cautela, J. R., and Kastenbaum, R. A reinforcement survey schedule for use in therapy, training, and research. *Psychological Reports*, 1967, *20*, 1115-1130.

Cautela, J. R., and Rosensteil, A. K. The use of covert conditioning in the treatment of drug abuse. *The International Journal of the Addictions*, 1975, *10*, 277-303.

Cautela, J. R., and Upper, D. The process of individual behavior therapy. In M. Hersen and R. M. Eisler (Eds.), *Progress in behavior therapy.* New York: Academic Press, 1975.

Cautela, J. R. and Wisocki, P. A. Covert sensitization in the treatment of sexual deviation. *Psychological Record*, 1971, *21*, 37-48.

Cautela, J. R., and Wisocki, P. A. The thought-stopping procedure: description, application, and learning theory interpretations. *Psychological Record*, 1977, *2*, 255-264.

Cautela, J. R., Walsh, K., and Wish, P. The use of covert reinforcement in the modification of attitudes toward the mentally retarded. *Journal of Psychology*, 1971, *77*, 257-260.

Corbin, E. B. In W. P. Morgan (Ed.), *Ergogenic aids and muscular performance.* New York: Academic Press, 1972.

Corson, S. A. Psychological stress and target tissue. In E. M. Weyer and H. Hutchins (Eds.), *Psychophysiological aspects of cancer.* New York: New York Academy of Sciences, 1966.

Elder, S. T., and Ruiz, A. R. Instrumental conditioning of diastolic and systolic blood pressure in essential hypertensive patients. *Journal of Applied Behavior Analysis*, 1973, *6*, 377-382.

Fisher, S., and Greenberg, R. *The scientific credibility of Freud's theories and therapy.* New York: Basic Books, 1977.

Freud, S. *The Interpretation of Dreams.* Edinburgh: Ballantyne and Hanson, 1913.

Friar, L., and Beatty, J. Migraine: management by trained control of vasoconstriction. *Journal of Consulting and Clinical Psychology*, 1976, *4*, 46-53.

Goldfarb, C., Driesen, J., and Cole, D. Psychophysiologic aspects of malignancy. *American Journal of Psychiatry*, 1967, *123*.

Goldfried, M., and Davison, G. E. *Clinical behavior therapy.* New York: Holt, Rinehart, and Winston, 1976.

Greene, A. Psychological and somatic variables associated with development and course of monozygotic twins with discordant leukemia. *Annals of the New York Academy of Science*, 1969, *164*, 394-408.

Greer, S., and Morris, T. Psychological attributes of women who develop breast cancer. *Journal of Psychosomatic Research*, 1975, *19*, 147-153.

Hersen, M., and Eisler, R. M. Behavioral approach to study and treatment of psychogenic tics. *Genetic Psychology Monographs*, 1973, *87*, 289-312.

Homme, L. E. Perspectives in psychology: XXIV. Control of coverants: The operants of the mind. *Psychological Record*, 1965, *15*, 501-511.

Jacobson, E. *Progressive relaxation*. Chicago: University of Chicago Press, 1938.
Jasper, H. H., and Shagass, C. Conditioning of the occipital alpha rhythm in man. *Journal of Experimental Psychology*, 1941, 28, 373-388.
John, E. R. Contradiction of auditory and visual information by brain stimulation. *Science*, 1975, 187, 271-272.
Jurgela, A. Personal communication, 1975.
Kavetsky, R. E., Turkevich, N. M., and Balitsky, K. P. *Neoplastic process and the nervous system*. Kiev: State Medical Publishing House, 1958.
Kavetsky, R. E., Turkevich, N. M., and Balitsky, K. P. On the psychophysiological mechanism of the organism's resistance to tumor growth. *Annals of the New York Academy of Science*. 1966, 125, 933.
Kazdin, A. E., Research issues in covert conditioning. *Cognitive Therapy and Research*. 1977, 1, 45-58.
King, D. L. An image theory of classical conditioning. *Psychological Reports*, 1973, 33, 403-411.
Kozak, M. J., and Lang, P. J. The psychophysiology of emotional imagery: A structural analysis of image processing. Paper in preparation. Material presented as part of an address by the second author to the Netherlands Conference on Biofeedback, Amersfoot, Netherlands, November 25, 1976.
Lang, P. J. Imagery in therapy: An information processing analysis of fear. *Behavior Therapy*, 1977, 8, 862-886.
Lazarus, A. E. *Behavior therapy and beyond*. New York: McGraw-Hill, 1971.
LeShan, L. L., and Worthington, R. E. Personality as a factor in the pathogenesis of cancer. *British Journal of Medical Psychology*, 1956, 29, 49-56.
Mahoney, M. J. *Cognition and behavior modification*. Cambridge, Mass.: Ballinger Publishing Company, 1974.
Meichenbaum, D. *Cognitive behavior modification*. Morristown, N.J.: General Learning Press, 1974.
Miller, N. E. The influence of past experience upon the transfer of subsequent training. Unpublished doctoral dissertation, Yale University, 1935.
Mowrer, O. H. *Learning Theory and the Symbolic Processes*. New York: Wiley, 1960.
Neumann, C. Psychic peculiarities of female cancer patients. *Z. Psycho-Somatic Med.*, 1959, 5, 91-101.
Olds, J., Disterhoff, J. F., Segal, J., Kornblith, C. L., and Hirsh, R. Learning centers of the rat brain mapped by measuring latencies of conditioned unit responses. *Journal of Neurophysiology*, 1972, 35, 202-219.
Pelletier, K. R. *Mind as healer, mind as slayer: A holistic approach to preventing stress disorders*. New York: Dell Publishing Co., 1977.
Richardson, A. *Mental imagery*. New York: Springer, 1969.
Rosen, M., and Wesner, C. A behavioral approach to Tourette's syndrome. *Journal of Consulting and Clinical Psychology*. 1973, 41, 308-312.
Schmale, A., and Iker, H. The psychiatric setting of uterine cervical cancer. Annals of the New York Academy of *Science*, 1966, 125, 807-813.
Scott, R. W., Blanchard, E. B., Edmunson, E. D., and Young, L. D. A shaping procedure for heart rate control in chronic tachycardia. *Perceptual and Motor Skills*, 1973, 37, 327-338.
Seligman, M. E. *Helplessness: On depression, development and death*. San Francisco: W. H. Freeman, 1975.
Simonton, C., and Simonton, S. Belief systems and management of the emotional aspects of malignancy. *Journal of Transpersonal Psychology*, 1975, 7, 29-47.
Singer, J. R. *Imagery and daydream methods in psychotherapy and behavior modification*, New York: Academic Press, 1974.

Singer, J. R. *The inner world of daydreaming.* New York: Harper and Row, 1975.
Stampfl, T. G. Implosive therapy: A learning-theory derived psychodynamic therapeutic technique. In LeBarba and Dent (Eds.), *Critical issues in clinical psychology.* New York: Academic Press, 1961.
Suinn, R. M. Body thinking for Olympic champs. *Psychology Today,* 1976, *10,* 38-43.
Wachtel, P. *Psychoanalysis and behavior therapy.* New York: Basic Books, 1977.
Watson, J. B. *Psychology from the standpoint of a behaviorist.* Philadelphia: Lippincott, 1919.
Weiss, T., and Engel, B. T. Operant conditioning of heart rate in patients with premature ventricular contractions. *Psychosomatic Medicine,* 1971, *37,* 301-321.
Welgan, P. R. Learned control of gastric acid secretion in ulcer patients. *Psychosomatic Medicine,* 1974, *36,* 411-419.
Whitehead, W. E., Renault, P. F., and Goldiamond, I. Modification of human gastric secretion with operant conditioning procedures. *Journal of Applied Behavioral Analysis,* 1975, *8,* 147-156.
Wolpe, J. *Psychotherapy by reciprocal inhibition.* Stanford, California: Stanford Univ. Press, 1958.
Wolpe, J., and Lang, P. A fear survey schedule for use in behavior therapy. *Behavior Research and Therapy,* 1964, *2,* 27-30.

9

Covert Modeling: The Therapeutic Application of Imagined Rehearsal

Alan E. Kazdin

1. Introduction

In behavior therapy, a large number of techniques are based upon the use of imagery. In these techniques, clients are instructed to imagine carefully planned scenes to alter their behavior. The most well-investigated technique that fits this general description is systematic desensitization, in which a client usually imagines him- or herself engaging in various behaviors directed at overcoming anxiety (cf. Wolpe, 1958). Several techniques that are based upon imagery are referred to as covert conditioning and have been developed by Cautela (1971a, 1972). These techniques were derived from extrapolations of specific learning principles developed in laboratory research and include covert sensitization, covert positive reinforcement, covert negative reinforcement, covert extinction, covert punishment, and covert modeling (Cautela, 1966, 1967, 1970a, 1970b, 1971b, 1974, 1976b). Techniques such as covert reinforcement, punishment, and extinction are considered to be direct applications of the respective operant principles. Covert sensitization relies upon operant conditioning principles such as punishment and negative reinforcement as well as classical conditioning and aversion relief. Covert modeling derives from observational or vicarious learning. These techniques represent a major innovation in behavior therapy.

Alan E. Kazdin • Department of Psychology, The Pennsylvania State University, University Park, Pennsylvania 16802.

The covert conditioning techniques assume that imagined events influence behavior in a similar fashion to actual events. For example, in covert reinforcement, the client imagines himself performing a behavior he wishes to develop. After the behavior is performed in imagination, the client is immediately instructed to imagine some reinforcing (favorable) consequence. It is assumed that this sequence in imagination (i.e., imagined behavior followed by imagined consequences) exerts similar control over overt behavior as the direct operation of reinforcing consequences (i.e., overt behavior followed by the actual delivery of reinforcing consequences). The general assumption about the influence of imagined events has been very useful in generating specific treatment techniques. The viability of these techniques is attested to by the application they have enjoyed across a wide range of disorders. Covert conditioning techniques have been used to treat behaviors related to social inadequacy, fears, sexual deviance and dysfunctions, obsessions and compulsions, obesity, drug addiction, alcoholism, and other problems (Cautela, 1971a, 1972; Mahoney, 1974).

One of the more recently developed covert conditioning techniques is covert modeling. The purpose of the present chapter is to describe the practice of covert modeling and to evaluate the outcome literature pertaining to its efficacy and range of applicability. In addition, parameters of imagery that appear to influence the efficacy of treatment will be reviewed. Finally, methodological issues raised by studying covert modeling, and imagery-based treatments in general, and salient areas where additional research is needed also will be discussed.

2. Background and Implication of Covert Modeling

Covert modeling, first presented in 1971, is derived from the modeling or vicarious learning literature (Cautela, 1976).* Modeling refers to learning based primarily upon merely observing someone else (a model) perform a response. To acquire a response, an observer need not perform the response but only observe the response performance of a model. The effects of modeling have been well established both in laboratory research and clinical applications (see Bandura, 1970, 1971; Marlatt and Perry, 1975; Rachman, 1972, 1976; Rosenthal, 1976).

In general, several different interpretations of modeling effects are available. The most widely discussed interpretation has been proposed by Bandura (1970), who has accounted for observational learning on

---

* This published report of covert modeling was first presented as a paper delivered by Cautela to the Association for Advancement of Behavior Therapy, Washington, D.C., September, 1971.

the basis of covert coding processes on the part of the observer. Bandura has suggested that observing a live or film model conveys cues to the observer. These cues are symbolically coded through representational processes based upon imagery or verbalizations. Bandura (1970) has noted that observational learning refers primarily to the representational processes by which the modeled responses are coded rather than by the form in which these events are conveyed to the observer. Emphasizing the cognitive processes that account for performance of the observer suggests that viewing or observing a model are not essential ingredients for behavior change. Rather, altering the representational processes that guide behavior is responsible for behavior change.

Covert modeling represents a technique that may provide an alternative means of altering representational processes assumed to be important in live modeling. Rather than observing behavior, a client may imagine a model perform a behavior that the client wishes to develop. Thus, the modeling goes on covertly or in imagination. As usually conducted, covert modeling requires that a client imagine several situations in which someone other than himself performs behaviors that the client wishes to develop (see Cautela, 1971c). Scenes or situations are constructed in which the client can picture the behavior that is to be changed (e.g., approach toward some feared object, appropriate social interaction, etc.). For example, a client who is severely withdrawn would be asked to imagine a number of scenes in which a model engages in social interaction. Initially, the model would be described in scenes in which he or she performs relatively minimal social behaviors (e.g., perhaps merely greeting someone). Over the course of treatment, the scenes might illustrate behaviors that reflect more demanding interactions (e.g., maintaining a conversation, initiating an interaction at a party). The scenes are constructed in consultation with the client and focus upon the range of situations in which the behavior needs to be changed or developed.

Much of our own work has focused upon the use of covert modeling to develop assertive behavior in individuals who claim they have difficulty communicating their feelings to others or in sticking up for their rights.* Individuals who participate in the program receive covert modeling, or some variation, to develop their social skills across a wide range of situations. Treatment is administered by a therapist in indi-

---

* Assertive training encompasses teaching individuals to express themselves more effectively and may include both the expression of positive and negative feelings such as affection or anger. In our own work, the majority of client complaints pertain to refusing to comply with unreasonable demands, making demands of others, and, in general, sticking up for one's rights. Hence, this relatively narrow focus has served as the primary focus of treatment.

vidual sessions and usually is conducted over a period of two or three weeks.*

At the beginning of treatment, clients receive a rationale that describes the basis of modeling and covert conditioning treatment in general. Prior to actual treatment, clients receive practice in imagining various scenes and are instructed to focus on detail of the scenes. Also, clients practice imagining a model (someone other than themselves) who will be used in the treatment scenes. In light of research reviewed later in the present chapter, clients usually are instructed to imagine a model similar to themselves (e.g., in age and same sex). After practice in imagery, clients are given several scenes in which the model performs assertively.

Scenes are described by the therapist (or tape recorder). The client tries to imagine the material presented. When the image is clear, the client signals by raising a finger and maintaining his or her eyes closed. The client then is told to hold the image as best as possible until a predetermined time period has elapsed (e.g., 30 seconds). After the interval, the client is told to stop imagining the scene. The same scene is repeated or a new scene is presented. Treatment consists of traversing several scenes that elaborate diverse aspects of the behaviors the client wishes to develop. Three of the scenes that are used in the treatment of assertive behavior illustrate the general task provided for the client:

1. Imagine the person (model) in his (her) apartment around dinner time. The person has an important appointment later in the evening, but friends drop in for a visit. The friends have spent time there. They have finished their coffee but look like they are going to stay for some time. The person is getting somewhat bothered about the appointment and has to leave in a few minutes. While the friends are sitting there and everyone is chatting, the person breaks into the conversation and says: "Say, I'm really glad you dropped in but I have a meeting and have to leave. Perhaps we can get together sometime when we are both free."

2. Picture yourself at a concert with a friend. A few people in the row behind you are making a lot of noise and disturbing everyone. It seems they have a comment to make every few minutes that everyone can hear. A person sitting next to you (the model) turns around and says, "Will you people please be quiet?"

---

* The period of time of treatment does not necessarily attest for the rapid effects of covert modeling. Often the spacing of sessions and duration of treatment have been limited by the constraints of completing a large-scale research project.

3. Imagine the person (the model) is staying in a hotel. After one night there, he (she) notices that the bedsprings must be broken. The bed sags miserably and was very uncomfortable during the night. In the morning, the person goes to the clerk at the desk and says: "The bed in my room is quite uncomfortable. I believe it is broken. I wish you would replace the bed or change my room."

The above scenes and the manner of their presentation mentioned earlier should be taken only as illustrations for implementing covert modeling. Indeed, as shown later, adding features to the basic scenes can enhance treatment effects. Virtually all of the questions that might be asked about the practice of covert modeling remain to be answered by research. Thus, at present, there are no empirically based guidelines that dictate the importance of practicing imagery prior to treatment, the number of scenes that should be included in treatment, the duration that they are imagined by the client, the number and distribution of sessions, and so on. Yet, there has been some research that addresses the overall efficacy of covert modeling and the parameters that contribute to behavior change.

3. Efficacy of Covert Modeling

Evaluating the efficacy of covert modeling as a treatment technique raises at least two important questions. First, does the technique change behavior in therapy? Second, if the previous question can be answered affirmatively, with what therapeutic problems and populations does the technique work? At this stage in the research, neither of these questions can be answered unequivocally. As noted earlier, covert modeling as a therapy technique was only explicitly described in 1971. Thus, clinical applications and research have only begun to appear in the literature. Despite the paucity of reports on covert modeling, it is useful to review the current literature and to draw the conclusions that appear warranted at this time.

Initial applications of covert modeling consisted of a number of cases that were used to illustrate the procedure (Cautela, 1971c). Covert modeling was applied to individual therapy cases covering various maladaptive approach and avoidance responses and behavior deficits such as fear of blushing, social criticism, entering a homosexual bar, excessively consuming food, and responding assertively to others. In other case reports, covert modeling administered alone or in conjunction with other procedures has been shown to reduce agoraphobia, addiction to drugs, excessive consumption of alochol, and obsessive-compulsive behavior (Flannery, 1972a, 1972c; Hay, Hay, and Nelson, 1975). These case reports suggest the applicability of covert modeling across diverse disorders but, of course, do not empirically establish the efficacy of the technique.

A number of therapy outcome studies have evaluated covert modeling. The majority of these have been with relatively mild behavior problems of college students rather than with clinically debilitating disorders of patients. The mild problems have included subphobic levels of fear of rats or harmless snakes. In one of the first studies completed, Cautela, Flannery, and Hanley (1974) demonstrated that covert modeling was as effective as overt (film) modeling in reducing fear of rats in college students on behavioral and subjective measures of fear. Both overt and covert modeling groups were superior to a control group that merely discussed the nature of the fear that was treated. Subsequent studies also have demonstrated the efficacy of covert modeling in reducing subphobic levels of fear in college students (Kazdin, 1973a, 1974a, 1974b, 1974c; Thase and Moss, 1976).

Aside from the analogue fear studies, covert modeling has been investigated with a target problem and treatment population that more closely resembles clinical applications than do college students with mild animal fears. In separate projects, individuals recruited from a community for problems in asserting themselves have been solicited and screened on several criteria for severity of their problem to serve in an assertive training clinic (Kazdin, 1974d, 1975, 1976a). Clients who received covert modeling imagined a model engaged in assertive interactions in a variety of different scenes over four treatment sessions. These clients showed markedly greater improvement on behavioral and self-report measures of assertion skills immediately after treatment and at several months follow-up relative to subjects who imagined similar scenes without the modeling component or who receive no treatment. These results suggest that covert modeling leads to change and that these changes are not accounted for by the nonspecific effects associated with attending treatment *per se* or by the passage of time.

Applications of covert modeling at the case level suggest that the technique may have a wide applicability across clinical problems seen on an outpatient basis. However, empirical investigations have only looked at covert modeling with a narrow range of populations and behaviors. These investigations suggest that covert modeling does lead to therapeutic change both on behavioral measures of the target problem, psychological inventories, and self-report evaluation of improvement. Although the clinical literature suggests the applicability of the technique across problems and the research literature suggests that the technique can change behavior, this does not establish that covert modeling is an effective technique with clinical problems. The efficacy of the technique with problems in a clinical setting has not been rigorously tested.

It is quite possible, and perhaps in many cases likely, that the actual mechanisms responsible for change with a given therapeutic technique have little or no relation to those posited by the theory or principle upon which the technique is based (cf. Kazdin, 1977; Kazdin and Wilcoxon, 1976). In the case of covert modeling, treatment studies do not necessarily argue for the effects of modeling components of the procedure. As alluded to earlier, several studies have examined the importance of the model in the scenes that the clients imagine, both with the treatment of avoidance behavior and inassertiveness. Comparisons have been made to determine whether imagining a model is essential to behavior change. The results revealed that individuals who imagine a model engaged in the response that is to be developed tend to show behavior change whereas those who imagine the same scenes without the model engaging in the response do not (Kazdin, 1973a, 1974a, 1974b, 1974c, 1974d, 1975). These results support the importance of imagining rehearsal of the behavior that is to be changed.

4. Important Parameters of Covert Modeling

The basic covert modeling procedure requires that a client imagine a model perform the behavior he or she wishes to develop. In the case of much of the above research, the client imagines a model engage in assertive responses in several situations. Yet, this basic procedure allows for extensive variation. An important question that immediately arises is whether imagery might be varied in such a way as to enhance the effects of the basic covert modeling procedure. The question can be answered tentatively by drawing upon the findings from investigations on live and film modeling in the context of laboratory and therapy research (Bandura, 1970, 1971; Marlatt and Perry, 1975; Rachman, 1972, 1976; Rosenthal, 1976). A number of dimensions might be varied to enhance the efficacy of covert modeling. Many of these have been explored in analogue therapy research with fearful college students and remain to be explored in the context of clinical research.

4.1. Model–Client Similarity

The basic covert modeling paradigm requires that a client imagine a model but does not specify who the model is or the kind of model used. Research on live and film modeling suggests that the more similar the model and observer, the greater the effect of modeling on observer behavior (Bandura, 1971). This relationship has been found in several laboratory investigations that demonstrate that individuals informed that they share qualities in common with an unfamiliar model are more likely to imitate the model's responses than individuals who initially share no common qualities (e.g., Burstein, Stotland, and Zander, 1961; Stotland and Patchen, 1961; Stotland, Zander, and Natsoulas, 1961). Also, similarity of the model across age, sex, and socioeconomic and racial status have facilitated performance on the part of the observer (Bandura, 1971).

Similarity of the model and subject has been examined in the context of covert modeling in an analogue treatment study. In one project, subjects who feared harmless snakes participated in a covert modeling treatment study where similarity of the model and subject were manipulated along the dimensions of sex and age (Kazdin, 1974b). Subjects who were instructed to imagine a model similar to them in age and of the same sex showed a greater reduction in avoidance behavior and self-report anxiety than did subjects who were instructed to imagine a model who was much older and opposite sexed. Although this study suggests that similarity of the model and client are important in covert modeling, it did not indicate the specific dimension along which this similarity was important (e.g., sex or age alone or their combination). Research in film model has not always shown that model–observer similarity along the dimension of age consistently relates to behavior change (e.g., Bandura and Barab, 1973; Kornhaber and Schroeder, 1975).

Model similarity has been shown to be important along dimensions other than sex and age. In film modeling, research has shown that adult subjects who are anxious and avoidant in the presence of a particular stimulus are more likely to imitate models who initially display some anxiety and eventually overcome their anxiety than those who do not display any anxiety (Meichenbaum, 1971). [This relationship may differ with children (Kornhaber and Schroeder, 1975).] Similarly, in the area of covert modeling, fearful subjects who imagine models who initially are fearful (similar to themselves) but eventually overcome their anxiety perform more approach responses at the end of treatment than those who imagine nonanxious models (Kazdin, 1973a, 1974b).

At present, it appears that covert modeling is enhanced by increasing the similarity between the model and the client. Indeed, if the model and client are very dissimilar (e.g., differ in sex and approximate age), covert modeling may effect virtually no behavior change in the client (Kazdin, 1974b). The more dimensions along which the model and client are similar, the greater the behavior change (Kazdin, 1974b). Several questions about the influence of model–client similarity remain to be explored. The most salient question is determining the range of dimensions along which similarity may be important.

4.2. Model Identity

Another dimension that might be important in modeling is who the model is. The identity of the model may be confounded with similarity but presumably can be separated conceptually and empirically. One question that arises is whether the covert model should be the client himself or someone else. When covert modeling was initially posed as a treatment technique, it was defined as a procedure in which the client imagined someone other than himself (Cautela, 1971c). From a conceptual standpoint, there is no reason to maintain this distinction. Indeed, imagery-based procedures that rely upon imagining oneself rather than another individual have proven to be very effective. The best example of this is systematic desensitization where clients imagine themselves performing gradations of various behaviors they would like to develop in themselves. Because desensitization typically requires clients to imagine themselves performing responses, it might be viewed as a version of covert modeling, i.e., covert self-modeling. In two covert modeling investigations of fear reduction, imagining oneself as the model versus imagining someone else were compared (Kazdin, 1974c; Thase and Moss, 1976). The results revealed no differences in fear reduction after treatment. Subjects who imagined either themselves or someone else improved equally well in performing responses in a fear situation.

The above results suggest that whether one imagines oneself or someone else does not bear on the efficacy of covert modeling. As Cautela (1971c) suggested when initially describing the covert modeling procedure, the selection of the model might be determined by convenience. Some clients might find it easier to imagine either themselves or someone else performing the target behavior. In such cases, pragmatic considerations might dictate selection of the model with respect to model identity.

4.3. Multiple Models

In covert modeling, only a single model is required for the scenes. The client needs to imagine a given person engage in the response that is to be developed. Yet, research on covert modeling suggests that observing several models engage in the response that is to be developed is more effective in altering an observer's behavior than is observing only one model. This relationship was suggested by Bandura and Menlove (1968), who found that children who feared dogs showed greater reduction in fear after viewing several film models engage in fearless interactions with dogs than other children who viewed only a single model interaction with a dog. Other studies have shown that training with multiple models leads to higher levels of performance of observers and greater transfer of behavior across new stimulus conditions than does viewing a single model (Marburg, Houston, and Holmes, 1976).

The relationship of the number of models and behavior change has been examined in covert modeling studies. In the treatment of fear and inassertive behavior, studies have shown that clients who imagine several different models across treatment sessions show greater behavior change than those who imagine a single model across the sessions (Kazdin, 1974a, 1975, 1976b). In light of this evidence, covert modeling appears to be more effective when there are several models who are imagined by the client. Thus, over the course of treatment or from session to session the individual who is imagined should be varied.

It is unclear whether imagining several models is part of a larger dimension, namely, the extent to which the scenes that the client imagines vary. Possibly, the greater the variation of the scenes across several dimensions, the greater the behavior change. Imagining several different models may merely increase the diversity of cues across which the new responses are learned. If this is accurate, varying the types of scenes that are imagined also might enhance treatment.

4.4. Model Consequences

Modeling research has shown that observing behavior of a model is sufficient to learn a response. Yet, the learned response may not be performed until appropriate incentive conditions are available in the environment (Bandura, 1970, 1971). The incentive conditions refer either to the consequences that follow the model's performance or the response or to the observer's subsequent performance of the response after observing the model. As might be expected, individuals who observe a model receiving favorable or reinforcing consequences for performing a behavior tend to engage in the response more than individuals who observe the model receive aversive consequences or no consequences at all (Bandura, 1965).

Several studies outside of the context of covert modeling have explored the effects of imagined consequences on behavior. In laboratory and therapy studies, imagining positive or negative consequences following overt behavior increases or decreases subsequent performance of the behavior, respectively (e.g., Bellack, Glanz, and Simon, 1976; Weiner, 1965). These studies suggest that imagined consequences may influence overt behavior in the same way as do overt consequences.

In the area of covert modeling, a few studies have examined the influence of imagining positive consequences on behavior. Specifically, assertive training studies have compared the effects of imagining scenes with and without positive consequences following the model's assertive response (Kazdin, 1974d, 1975). In these studies some clients received covert modeling in which they imagined a model engage in assertive behavior across several situations. Other clients received covert modeling plus reinforcement in which they imagined situations with the addition of positive model consequences following behavior. For example, covert modeling clients might imagine a situation in which a model returns food that has been incorrectly prepared in a restaurant. Covert modeling plus reinforcement clients would imagine the same situation with an added consequence such as the final receipt of the correctly prepared food and an apology from the waiter. Throughout treatment the only differences were the imagination of consequences as part of the scenes. The results have tended to show that clients who imagined positive consequences performed more assertively at the end of treatment on self-report and behavioral measures than did those who imagined the scenes without the consequences. These results suggest the advisability of incorporating positive consequences into covert modeling scenes that are used to develop behaviors.

4.5. Unexplored Parameters

Although some initial work has been completed on parameters that influence the effect of covert modeling, extensive research is needed. This research can focus on the parameters outlined above or on several others that have yet to be explored. Extrapolations from the modeling literature using live and film models suggest some avenues for research. For example, in live and film modeling various characteristics of the subject (observer) influence the effects of modeling. Subjects who are low in self-esteem, highly dependent, or have a history of being rewarded for imitating a model tend to show higher levels of imitation than do those at the other end of these continua (Bandura, 1971). This research suggests that specific subject variables might be explored in the context of covert modeling.

An additional variable that has proven to be important in live and film modeling pertains to activities in which the observer engages to retain the behaviors that have been modeled. As noted earlier, modeling has been conceptualized as a process in which verbal and imaginal representational processes are altered through observation. Procedures that can enhance the coding of the observed stimuli will facilitate retention of the modeled material. Research has supported this by demonstrating that individuals who are instructed to symbolically code the model's performance, either through verbal summary labels or imagery, show higher levels of the model's behavior than individuals who are not instructed to engage in coding responses (Bandura, Grusec, and Menlove, 1966; Gerst, 1971). With a covert modeling, imagery already is used as part of the procedure and might not be easily added to enhance retention. However, it is possible to use verbal coding of imagined model performance to develop summaries of what the model has done. It would be expected that verbalization of the model's performance in a summary fashion would facilitate covert modeling in much the same way as it does with overt modeling. The effect of engaging in coding behaviors such as developing concise summary descriptions of the model's behavior remains to be investigated in the context of covert modeling.

Another dimension of interest is the source of the imagery used during covert modeling. In most of the investigations to date, specific scenes that the subject is to imagine are provided by the therapist or investigator. Possibly, situations and scenes that are self-generated rather than prescribed might be more effective. While no direct data can be brought to bear on this point, one study has shown that the extent to which subjects introduce their own elaborations into the scenes presented to them is related to behavior change. Clients who elaborated their scenes by introducing features not presented to them tended to show greater behavior change (Kazdin, 1975). These data are only correlational and do not suggest the causal relation between elaborations in imagery and behavior change. Yet, it would be worthwhile to directly study the effects of instructing clients to elaborate the scenes presented on behavior change.

In general, the specific parameters of imagery that influence behavior change have not been carefully elaborated. Yet, extrapolations from important dimensions in overt modeling have already suggested some important leads for maximizing the influence of imagery.

One difficulty of investigating the parameters of imagery and evaluating treatment outcome is ensuring that the parameters have been effectively manipulated. Essentially, ongoing client imagery needs to be assessed to determine whether specific dimensions were manipulated effectively. (The assessment of ongoing imagery will be discussed below.) Once methodological advances are made that permit the careful assessment of imagery, research can more easily explore specific parameters of the imagined scene.

5. Assessment of Imagery and the Mechanisms of Behavior Change

In covert conditioning techniques, clients are instructed to imagine specific scenes in which certain events take place in a carefully planned sequence. Presumably, select features of the scenes are essential to effect behavior change, as dictated by the specific techniques. For example, in covert modeling, the client must imagine the model perform the response that the client wishes to develop.

In the usual practice of covert modeling, the therapist describes the scene and allows the client a brief period to develop the image. Generally, it is assumed that the client's imagery adheres closely to the scene that the therapist describes. Yet, clients frequently have claimed that their imagery deviated from the scenes described by the therapist (e.g., Barrett, 1968; Davison and Wilson, 1973; Weinberg and Zaslove, 1963; Weitzman, 1967). The scene presented by the therapist occasionally is reported to initiate an ongoing movielike series of images that is not confined to the material presented.

The possibility that the client's imagery deviates from the scenes presented by the therapist has methodological, conceptual, and clinical implications. Methodological implications derive from the changes in imagery that clients make in treatment studies where variations of a given covert conditioning technique or different techniques are being compared. Clients may imagine similar scenes even when an investigator has intended to keep imagery somewhat distinct across groups. Methodological and conceptual implications derive from the possibility that "crucial" ingredients of a given technique may not be imagined consistently by the subject, which would bring into question precisely what the important ingredients are. Finally, clinical implications derive from uncovering those features of imagery that clients change that may contribute to or enhance treatment outcome. Indeed, several imagery-based techniques in wide use in Europe rely upon the flow of images on the part of the client after the therapist presents an initial theme or specific image to begin the process. In some ways, aspects of imagery that the behavior therapist might regard as deviations from the therapeutic scenes are viewed by others as essential components of imagery-based treatment (cf. Singer, 1974). In any case, to examine the importance of changes in imagery by the client from that which is presented by his therapist in changing behavior requires assessment of imagery content. The assessment of imagery needs to compare the scenes presented by the therapist with those actually imagined by the client.

In our work, assessment of imagery content has been accomplished by having clients narrate aloud the scenes that they are imagining during the treatment sessions (Kazdin, 1975, 1976a). After the scene is presented, the clients are allowed time to develop the imagery. When the scene is clear and while the image is still held, the client narrates the scene. These narrations are tape-recorded and subsequently evaluated to determine their similarity to the scenes presented.

This method of assessment has been used to evaluate imagery during covert modeling. In one project designed to develop assertive behavior, several covert modeling groups were compared (Kazdin, 1975). The importance of imagery assessment can be conveyed by examining only three of the groups. In a model-only group, clients received scenes that included a model who asserted him or herself. In a model-plus-reinforcement group, clients received scenes in which a model was assertive and where the assertive response was followed by favorable (possibly reinforcing) consequences. A scene-control group imagined assertion-relevant scenes in which an assertive response was appropriate but in which no assertive model was included. For clients in each group, imagery was assessed as the client narrated the scenes imagined during the four treatment sessions to determine whether the imagined scenes adhered to the scenes presented.

Interestingly, assessing imagery revealed that clients introduced features into their scenes that had not been presented. For example, clients in the model-only condition occasionally introduced favorable model consequences even though these ingredients had not been in the scenes presented. Essentially, these subjects had been assigned to the model-only group but had imagined an assertive model-plus-reinforcing consequence. Perhaps of even greater interest were the scene-control subjects who received scenes in which an assertive response was appropriate with no model performance. Some of these subjects imagined an assertive model as well as reinforcing consequences following the model's assertive behavior even though neither of these latter components had been presented in their scenes. Overall, the above study indicated that covert modeling subjects occasionally deviated from the scenes presented to them. Moreover, the deviations were systematic in that certain ingredients that are relevant to the efficacy of treatment (e.g., model consequences) were introduced.

The extent to which scene deviation occurs in imagery-based therapies needs to be assessed. The assessment of imagery may have important methodological implications for evaluating outcome research.

An investigator may wish to compare variations of a given imagery-based technique or to examine the active ingredients of treatment. For example, a covert reinforcement study might compare two groups, one of which imagines performing the target response followed by a pleasant scene (covert reinforcement) and the other which imagines performing the target response alone with no pleasant consequences (control). The groups may not differ in treatment outcome. The absence of differences between groups, assuming some improvement, does not necessarily impugn the effects of covert reinforcement or the importance of reinforcing consequences. Possibly, the actual imagery of the subjects may make the groups more homogeneous than originally intended by the experimenter. Essentially, subjects may imagine features that "alter" the treatment conditions to which they are assigned. In the above example, subjects in the control condition may well introduce pleasant consequences so that treatment might be covert reinforcement even though this was not the intended condition. Thus, some subjects in the control conditions would receive a procedure functionally similar to the actual treatment group. Comparison of control and treatment groups might even be more unclear if some subjects in the treatment group did not imagine the pleasant scenes that are intended to be reinforcing.

From a methodological standpoint, imagery assessment may be very important to ensure that the technique investigated actually is carried out by the clients. Imagery assessment provides a check on the experimental manipulation and can provide some assurance that the components of imagery the investigator intended to manipulate were in fact studied. Assessment of imagery would seem to be particularly informative in cases where experimental and control conditions or different treatment variations produce no differences in outcome. The failure to find group differences is significant only if there is some assurance that the treatment conditions were distinct (i.e., that the clients' scene deviations did not make treatments more homogeneous than intended) and that the essential components of treatment were imagined.

There are clinical implications that may follow from the assessment of imagery. Assessment might yield useful hypotheses about the mechanisms of behavior change and suggest variables that might be manipulated to enhance treatment effects. For example, one of the covert modeling studies mentioned earlier assessed the extent to which clients elaborated basic portions of the scenes (Kazdin, 1975). Elaboration of the scenes consisted of introducing additional descriptive material in the scenes over and above that which was provided. The elaborations pertained to aspects of the covert model's behavior or the consequences. As noted earlier, clients who tended to introduce more elaborations into their imagery showed greater improvement on outcome measures of assertion than did those who elaborated less or not at all. These results suggest that elaboration of scenes may play an important part in treatment effects.

Similarly, in another project, the extent to which clients described feelings of the model in the scenes was correlated with improvements in assertive responding (Kazdin, 1976a). Possibly clients might be instructed to intentionally focus on feelings (subjective states) of the model in the scenes as a method of enhancing treatment effects. Whether encouraging clients to elaborate the scenes presented by the therapist or to focus on particular aspects of the scene enhance treatment are only hypotheses that remain to be evaluated. Yet, these and similar hypotheses may be derived from assessing what clients imagine during treatment.

6. Imagery-Based Techniques versus Overt Behavior Rehearsal

Imagery-based techniques have been used extensively in behavior therapy. Part of the popularity of these techniques is accounted for by the advantages they provide over techniques where the actual stimuli are presented to the client who performs the behaviors in treatment. Presenting stimuli and consequences in imagery allows for more diversity and flexibility for a client than does the presentation of the actual events themselves. Also, having the client imagine performing various responses is more efficient in time and in arranging situations than having the client actually perform the response. In many situations, procedures based upon imagery or actual performance of the target subject might be equally applicable and the convenience of imagery-based procedures dictates its selection. An obvious question that arises is the relative effectiveness of procedures based upon imagery or upon actual client performance. Obviously, the advantage of convenience accorded imagery-based treatments might not be a major consideration if these treatments are less effective than an available *in vivo* counterpart.

The question of the relative efficacy of imagery-based versus *in vivo* techniques has not been well investigated in the area of modeling. However, comparisons have been made of imagery-based techniques and their *in vivo* counterpart in the area of systematic desensitization and flooding, two behavior-therapy techniques that have been highly effective in treating anxiety-based disorders. With *in vivo* desensitization, the client approaches the feared stimulus rather than merely imagining this performance. Research has shown that graduated exposure to the feared stimulus *in vivo* or overt rehearsal of the appropriate response leads to greater fear reduction on self-report and behavioral measures than does imagery-based desensitization (Crowe, Marks, Agras, and Leitenberg, 1972; Garfield, Darwin, Singer, and McBrearty, 1967; LoPiccolo, 1969; Sherman, 1972; Strahley, 1965). Flooding research also suggests that overt exposure and contact with the stimulus is superior to imaginal exposure (Crowe *et al.*, 1972; Marks, 1975; Watson and Marks, 1971).

Other studies suggest the superiority of treatments that require overt performance rather than those based upon imagined performance. For example, Bandura, Blanchard, and Ritter (1969) compared modeling with guided participation, which involves exposure to a live model plus graduated performance of the modeled behavior, with imagery-based desensitization and modeling (watching films) in the treatment of snake fear. While the latter two treatments led to greater fear reduction than did no treatment, the group that actually performed the behavior during treatment showed the greatest fear reduction. This study suggests that actually performing the target response in treatment led to greater fear reduction than did two different treatments that relied upon symbolic processes, i.e., imagery-based desensitization and symbolic modeling, where imaginal and verbal coding processes are assumed to be operative. Other research has demonstrated that treatments requiring actual performance on the part of the client are superior to desensitization or modeling in reducing fears and developing social skills (Blanchard, 1970; Crowe *et al.*, 1972; Friedman, 1971; Ritter, 1969; Roper, Rachman, and Marks, 1975; Wright, 1976.

There have been few comparisons of the covert conditioning techniques developed by Cautela with techniques involving overt client performance. Recently, Thase and Moss (1976) compared covert modeling where clients imagined either themselves or another individual as a model with participant modeling in reducing snake avoidance. Subjects who received participant modeling showed significantly greater reductions in fear on self-report and behavioral measures than did the covert modeling groups. In another study, Flannery (1972b) compared two variations of covert reinforcement to reduce fear of rats. In one variation, subjects imagined reinforcing scenes for actually approaching the fear stimulus; in the other variation, subjects imagined reinforcing scenes for approaching the fear stimulus in their imagination. The group with *in vivo* exposure showed greater fear-reduction on self-reported fear and on the behavioral test. Overt rehearsal of the behavior to be developed is not invariably superior to covert rehearsal.

McFall and his colleagues (McFall and Lillesand, 1971; McFall and Twentyman, 1973) found that rehearsing a response covertly or overtly (verbally) were equally effective in developing assertive behavior. Possibly, verbally stating a response in simulated situations is somewhat distinct from rehearsing the requisite behaviors (e.g., verbal and nonverbal) that might be performed in actual situations.

Overall, the above studies suggest that overt behavioral practice of behavior leads to greater behavior change than covert rehearsal. These results have been obtained across different techniques. If this conclusion is warranted from the literature, certainly a major question is the priority of using covert conditioning techniques in treatment. Until additional evidence is available, it appears that whenever possible a therapist would do well to emphasize overt behavioral rehearsal. Unless covert techniques can be demonstrated to offer clear treatment gains, they might be reserved for those situations in which live exposure and rehearsal cannot be incorporated into treatment. Even when clients cannot rehearse overt behavior in the actual situation in which behavior is to be developed, it still may be wise to revert to overt rehearsal in simulated situations in treatment rather than to use imagery. Certainly, extensive research is needed to evaluate the relative effects of imagery-based and overt behavior-change procedures. The main question raised here is whether covert conditioning techniques are the treatment of choice in cases where overt behavioral practice can be used.

Aside from contrasting imagery-based therapy with overt rehearsal and advancing one over the other, the techniques may be useful when used in conjunction. For example, in the treatment of anxiety, various authors have suggested that imagery-based treatment might be used initially to help overcome anxiety to the point that the client can begin to perform the anxiety-provoking responses *in vivo* (Bandura, 1969; Marks, 1975). The *in vivo* portion of treatment presumably might provide the greater therapeutic gains in terms of magnitude of behavior change and generality of change across stimuli. In this sense, imagery-based treatment may provide an initial preparatory step for overt practice of the behavior in actual situations (e.g., Watson and Marks, 1971). At present, there is no clear empirical basis to endorse the combination of overt and covert techniques. To endorse this option, evidence would need to show that overt rehearsal of the behavior is less effective than overt and covert rehearsal combined. Certainly, research needs to address the contribution of covert processes to behavior change and the relative effectiveness of different combinations of covert and overt techniques.

7. Conclusions and Implications

Research in the area of covert modeling, and perhaps covert conditioning in general, might profit from focusing on at least four related questions. These include the overall efficacy of the technique and the problems to which the technique is well suited, the conceptualization of the technique, the imagery reported by the clients, and the relative efficacy of imagery-based techniques and their overt counterpart.

As noted earlier, very little research currently is available that attests to the effectiveness of covert modeling with clinical populations or problems. The bulk of the research has focused upon college students with mild fears. The amenability of the behavior of college students to change may make much of the current research have little or no bearing upon the ultimate efficacy of the technique with clinical problems. Indeed, some authors have commented upon the relative ease with which behavior change can be demonstrated and the influence of nontreatment factors in effecting change in college students (e.g., Bernstein and Paul, 1971; Kazdin, 1973b). A few case applications of covert modeling have been reported to effect important clinical changes. However, the inability to attribute behavior changes in these reports to covert modeling per se must be acknowledged. In general, the efficacy of covert modeling has not been convincingly established. Only a few outcome studies exist, which, at this point, are not sufficient to serve as a strong basis for endorsing widespread clinical application. Certainly, a major task for subsequent research is to complete additional outcome studies.

The conceptualization of covert modeling, and other covert conditioning techniques, also requires additional research. Originally, covert techniques have been derived from extrapolations of principles of learning developed in laboratory research. While such a derivation has an obvious heuristic value, research has suggested that the mechanisms of change in imagery-based therapy may not be consistent with the theoretical rationale. For example, imagining performance of some behavior followed by favorable consequences has been referred to as covert reinforcement. Yet, several studies have suggested that many variations of the procedure, including variations inconsistent with a "reinforcement" interpretation, work equally well (Blanchard and Draper, 1973; Hurley, 1976; Ladouceur, 1974; Marshall, Boutilier, and Minnes, 1974). Findings with other imagery-based techniques also have raised questions about the conceptual basis for their efficacy (cf. Kazdin, 1977). This research does not impugn the efficacy of various techniques but does raise questions about the mechanism responsible for change. Additional models and conceptualizations of imagery-based techniques need to be posed and empirically evaluated.

The imagery of the clients in treatment warrants scrutiny. The scenes that the clients actually imagine and report, as distinguished from those that are presented to them, bear directly upon the conceptualization of imagery-based techniques and the mechanisms of change. It may be premature to discuss important ingredients of treatment until there is clear evidence that clients include these ingredients in their imagery and do not systematically add other features that might plausibly account for behavior change. Also, assessment of imagery is likely to suggest variables that correlate with therapeutic change. The correlates may suggest variables that can be directly manipulated to enhance therapy outcome. Several studies have suggested that self-report of the qualitative aspects of imagery (e.g., vividness, clarity) do not consistently correlate with behavior change (e.g., Davis, McLemore, and London, 1970; Kazdin, 1974b; McLemore, 1972). Perhaps attention should focus on the content of imagery, especially since there is evidence that this varies systematically in treatment (Kazdin, 1975).

The relative effectiveness of "covert" and "overt" techniques needs to be determined. In the areas of desensitization, modeling, and flooding, research suggests relatively consistently that overt presentation of stimuli and overt client performance lead to greater therapeutic change than do imagery-based treatments (Bandura, 1969; Marks, 1975). The comparisons between *in vivo* and imaginal treatment have not been made across the diverse imagery-based techniques. The few reports available with modeling suggest that imaginal procedures may be less effective than overt counterparts (e.g., Bandura et al., 1969; Thase and Moss, 1976). Basic comparative research is essential to determine the priority that covert conditioning techniques are to be accorded when selecting a therapy technique. Overt performance may not be feasible to handle some problems that are treated in therapy. Yet, whether covert conditioning techniques should serve as a prime treatment modality or as a technique to be used when overt performance is not readily available remains to be determined.

ACKNOWLEDGMENT

This chapter was completed while the author was a Fellow at the Center for Advanced Study in the Behavioral Sciences. The author is grateful to the Center staff for assistance in preparing the manuscript.

References

Bandura, A. Influence of model's reinforcement contingencies on the acquisition of imitative responses. *Journal of Personality and Social Psychology*, 1965, 1, 589-595.
Bandura, A. *Principles of behavior modification*. New York: Holt, Rinehart, and Winston, 1969.
Bandura, A. Modeling theory. In W. S. Sahakian (Ed.), *Psychology of learning: Systems, models, and theories*. Chicago: Markham, 1970.
Bandura, A. Psychotherapy based upon modeling principles. In A. E. Bergin and S. L. Garfield (Eds.), *Handbook of psychotherapy and behavior change*. New York: Wiley, 1971.
Bandura, A., and Barab, P. G. Processes governing disinhibitory effects through symbolic modeling. *Journal of Abnormal Psychology*, 1973, 82, 1-9.
Bandura, A., Blanchard, E. G., and Ritter, B. Relative efficacy of desensitization and modeling approaches for inducing behavioral affective, and attitudinal changes. *Journal of Personality and Social Psychology*, 1969, 13, 173-199.
Bandura, A., Grusec, J. E., and Menlove, F. L. Observational learning as a function of symbolization and incentive set. *Child Development*, 1966, 37, 499-506.
Bandura, A., and Menlove, F. L. Factors determining vicarious extinction of avoidance behavior through symbolic modeling. *Journal of Personality and Social Psychology*, 1968, 8, 99-108.
Barrett, C. L. "Runaway imagery" in systematic desensitization therapy and implosive therapy. *Psychotherapy: Theory, Research and Practice*, 1968, 7, 233-235.
Bellack, A. S., Glanz, L. M., and Simon, R. Self-reinforcement style and covert imagery in the treatment of obesity. *Journal of Consulting and Clinical Psychology*, 1976, 44, 490-491.
Bernstein, D. A., and Paul, G. L. Some comments on therapy analogue research with small animal "phobias." *Journal of Behavior Therapy and Experimental Psychiatry*, 1971, 2, 225-237.
Blanchard, E. B. Relative contributions of modeling, informational influence, and physical contact in extinction of phobic behavior. *Journal of Abnormal Psychology*, 1970, 76, 55-61.
Blanchard, E. B., and Draper, D. O. Treatment of a rodent phobia by covert reinforcement: A single subject experiment. *Behavior Therapy*, 1973, 4, 559-564.
Burstein, E., Stotland, E., and Zander, A. Similarity to a model and self-evaluation. *Journal of Abnormal and Social Psychology*, 1961, 62, 257-264.
Cautela, J. R. A behavior therapy treatment of pervasive anxiety. *Behaviour Research and Therapy*, 1966, 4, 99-109.
Cautela, J. R. Covert sensitization. *Psychological Record*, 1967, 20, 459-468.
Cautela, J. R. Covert negative reinforcement. *Journal of Behavior Therapy and Experimental Psychiatry*, 1970a, 1, 273-278.
Cautela, J. R. Covert reinforcement. *Behavior Therapy*, 1970b, 1, 33-50.
Cautela, J. R. Covert conditioning. In A. Jacobs and L. B. Sachs (Eds.), *The psychology of private events: Perspectives on covert response systems*. New York: Academic Press, 1971a.
Cautela, J. R. Covert extinction. *Behavior Therapy*, 1971b, 2, 192-200.
Cautela, J. R. Covert modeling. Paper presented at the fifth annual meeting of the Association for Advancement of Behavior Therapy, Washington, D.C., September 1971c.
Cautela, J. R. Rationale and procedures for covert conditioning. In R. D. Rubin, H.

Fensterheim, J. D. Henderson, and L. P. Ullmann (Eds.), *Advances in behavior therapy.* New York: Academic Press, 1972.

Cautela, J. R. Covert response cost. Unpublished manuscript. Boston College, 1974.

Cautela, J. R., Flannery, R., and Hanley, E. Covert modeling: An experimental test. *Behavior Therapy,* 1974, *5,* 494-502.

Crowe, M. J., Marks, I. M., Agras, W. S., and Leitenberg, H. Time-limited desensitization, implosion and shaping for phobic patients: A crossover study. *Behaviour Research and Therapy,* 1972, *10,* 319-328.

Davis, D., McLemore, C. W., and London, P. The role of visual imagery in desensitization. *Behaviour Research and Therapy,* 1970, *8,* 11-13.

Davison, G. C., and Wilson, G. T. Processes of fear-reduction in systematic desensitization: Cognitive and social reinforcement factors in humans. *Behavior Therapy,* 1973, *4,* 1-21.

Flannery, R. B. Covert conditioning in the behavioral treatment of an agoraphobic. *Psychotherapy: Theory, Research and Practice,* 1972a, *9,* 217-220.

Flannery, R. B. A laboratory analogue of two covert reinforcement procedures. *Journal of Behavior Therapy and Experimental Psychiatry,* 1972b, *3,* 171-177.

Flannery, R. B. Use of covert conditioning in the behavioral treatment of a drug-dependent college dropout. *Journal of Counseling Psychology,* 1972c, *19,* 547-550.

Friedman, P. H. The effects of modeling and role-playing on assertive behavior. In R. D. Rubin, H. Fensterheim, A. A. Lazarus, and C. M. Franks (Eds.), *Advances in behavior therapy.* New York: Academic Press, 1971.

Garfield, Z. H., Darwin, P. L., Singer, B. A., and McBrearty, J. F. Effects of "in vivo" training on experimental desensitization of a phobia. *Psychological Reports,* 1967, *20,* 515-519.

Gerst, M. S. Symbolic coding processes in observational learning. *Journal of Personality and Social Psychology,* 1971, *19,* 7-17.

Hay, W. M., Hay, L. R., and Nelson, R. O. The adaptation of covert modeling procedures to the treatment of chronic alcoholism and obsessive-compulsive behavior. Paper presented at meeting of the Association for Advancement of Behavior Therapy, Washington, D.C., December, 1975.

Hurley, A. D. Covert reinforcement: The contribution of the reinforcing stimulus to treatment outcome. *Behavior Therapy,* 1976, *7,* 347-378.

Kazdin, A. E. Covert modeling and the reduction of avoidance behavior. *Journal of Abnormal Psychology,* 1973a, *81,* 87-95.

Kazdin, A. E. The effect of suggestion and pretesting on avoidance reduction in fearful college students. *Journal of Behavior Therapy and Experimental Psychiatry,* 1973b, *4,* 213-221.

Kazdin, A. E. Comparative effects of some variations of covert modeling. *Journal of Behavior Therapy and Experimental Psychiatry,* 1974a, *5,* 225-231.

Kazdin, A. E. Covert modeling, model similarity, and reduction of avoidance behavior. *Behavior Therapy,* 1974b, *5,* 325-340.

Kazdin, A. E. The effect of model identity and fear-relevant similarity on covert modeling. *Behavior Therapy,* 1974c, *5,* 624-635.

Kazdin, A. E. Effects of covert modeling and model reinforcement on assertive behavior. *Journal of Abnormal Psychology,* 1974d, *83,* 240-252.

Kazdin, A. E. Covert modeling, imagery assessment, and assertive behavior. *Journal of Consulting and Clinical Psychology,* 1975, *43,* 716-724.

Kazdin, A. E. Assessment of imagery during covert modeling treatment of assertive behavior. *Journal of Behavior Therapy and Experimental Psychiatry,* 1976a, *7,* 213-219.

Kazdin, A. E. Effects of covert modeling, multiple models, and model reinforcement on assertive behavior. *Behavior Therapy*, 1976b, 7, 211-222.
Kazdin, A. E. Research issues in covert conditioning. *Cognitive Therapy and Research*, 1977, 1, 45-58.
Kazdin, A. E., and Wilcoxon, L. A. Systematic desensitization and nonspecific treatment effects: A methodological evaluation. *Psychological Bulletin*, 1976, 83, 729-758.
Kornhaber, R. C., and Schroeder, H. E. Importance of model similarity on extinction of avoidance behavior in children. *Journal of Consulting and Clinical Psychology*, 1975, 43, 601-607.
Ladouceur, R. An experimental test of the learning paradigm of covert positive reinforcement in deconditioning anxiety. *Journal of Behavior Therapy and Experimental Psychiatry*, 1974, 5, 3-6.
LoPiccolo, J. Effective components of systematic desensitization. Unpublished doctoral dissertation. Yale University, 1969.
Mahoney, M. J. *Cognition and behavior modification.* Cambridge, Mass.: Ballinger, 1974.
Marburg, C. C., Houston, B. K., and Holmes, D. S. Influence of multiple models on the behavior of institutionalized retarded children: Increased generalization to other models and behaviors. *Journal of Consulting and Clinical Psychology*, 1976, 44, 514-519.
Marks, I. M. Behavioral treatments of phobic and obsessive-compulsive disorders: A critical appraisal. In M. Hersen, R. M. Eisler, and P. M. Miller (Eds.), *Progress in behavior modification.* Vol. 1. New York: Academic Press, 1975.
Marlatt, G. A., and Perry, M. A. Modeling methods. In F. H. Kanfer and A. P. Goldstein (Eds.), *Helping people change: A textbook of methods.* New York: Pergamon, 1975.
Marshall, W. L., Boutilier, J., and Minnes, P. The modification of phobic behavior by covert reinforcement. *Behavior Therapy*, 1974, 5, 469-480.
McFall, R. M., and Lillesand, D. Behavior rehearsal with modeling and coaching in assertion training. *Journal of Abnormal Psychology*, 1971, 77, 313-323.
McFall, R. M., and Twentyman, C. T. Four experiments on the relative contributions of rehearsal, modeling, and coaching to assertion training. *Journal of Abnormal Psychology*, 1973, 81, 199-218.
McLemore, C. W. Imagery in desensitization. *Behaviour Research and Therapy*, 1972, 10, 51-57.
Meichenbaum, D. H. Examination of model characteristics in reducing avoidance behavior. *Journal of Personality and Social Psychology*, 1971, 17, 298-307.
Rachman, S. Clinical applications of observational learning, imitation, and modeling. *Behavior Therapy*, 1972, 3, 379-397.
Rachman, S. J. Observational learning and therapeutic modelling. In M. P. Feldman and A. Broadhurst (Eds.), *Theoretical and empirical bases of the behaviour therapies.* London: Wiley, 1976.
Ritter, B. The use of contact desensitization, demonstration-plus-participation, and demonstration alone in the treatment of acrophobia. *Behaviour Research and Therapy*, 1969, 7, 157-164.
Roper, G., Rachman, S., and Marks, I. Passive and participant modelling in exposure treatment of obsessive-compulsive neurotics. *Behaviour Research and Therapy*, 1975, 13, 271-279.
Rosenthal, T. L. Modeling therapies. In M. Hersen, R. M. Eisler, and P. M. Miller (Eds.), *Progress in behavior modification.* Vol. 2. New York: Academic Press, 1976.
Sherman, A. R. Real-life exposure as a primary therapeutic factor in the desensitization treatment of fear. *Journal of Abnormal Psychology*. 1972, 79, 19-28.

Singer, J. L. *Imagery and daydream methods in psychotherapy and behavior modification.* New York: Academic Press, 1974.
Stotland, E., and Patchen, M. Identification and changes in prejudice and authoritarianism. *Journal of Abnormal and Social Psychology,* 1961, 62, 265-274.
Stotland, E., Zander, A., and Natsoulas, T. The generalization of interpersonal similarity. *Journal of Abnormal and Social Psychology,* 1961, 62, 250-256.
Strahley, D. F. Systematic desensitization and counterphobic treatment of an irrational fear of snakes. Unpublished doctoral dissertation. University of Tennessee, 1965.
Thase, M. E., and Moss, M. K. The relative efficacy of covert modeling procedures and guided participant modeling on the reduction of avoidance behavior. *Journal of Behavior Therapy and Experimental Psychiatry,* 1976, 7, 7-12.
Watson, J. P., and Marks, I. M. Relevant and irrelevant fear in flooding—A crossover study of phobic patients. *Behavior Therapy,* 1971, 2, 275-293.
Weinberg, N. H., and Zaslove, M. "Resistance" to systematic desensitization of phobias. *Journal of Clinical Psychology,* 1963, 19, 179-181.
Weiner, H. Real and imagined cost effects upon human fixed-interval responding. *Psychological Reports,* 1965, 17, 659-662.
Weitzman, B. Behavior therapy and psychotherapy. *Psychological Review,* 1967, 74, 300-317.
Wolep, J. *Psychotherapy by reciprocal inhibition.* Stanford: Stanford University Press, 1958.
Wolpe, J. *The practice of behavior therapy.* New York: Pergamon, 1969.
Wright, J. C. A comparison of systematic desensitization and social skill acquisition in the modification of a social fear. *Behavior Therapy,* 1976, 7, 205-210.

PART V

Broader Applications of Imagery

Introduction

The section that follows includes chapters that point up applications of the imagery and fantasy procedures to problems that go beyond the traditional client–patient procedure. The studies by Schultz and by Frank also exemplify quite specific and carefully designed and executed experimental investigations. They point to the exciting research possibilities of the study of imagery in relation to behavior and cognitive or affective change. These chapters also indicate that theoretical orientations that reflect psychodynamic or cognitive-affective assumptions can to some degree be coordinated with focused change efforts.

Schultz's study is important in suggesting an approach to mood change in chronic depressives, thus making them more accessible for psychotherapy. It also points to the necessity of understanding different depressive styles and other personality predispositions. Imagery approaches may be more effective when related to such specific orientations that are increasingly accessible to assessment.

Frank's study also points to specificity of effects in relationship to particular goals, affective empathy, or behavioral prediction. It also points to very wide-ranging possibilities of preventive approaches, training rather than treatment for normal young adults. These procedures have been repeated and studied further by Dr. Frank in work carried out during the past year.

The final chapter of this section brings the body back into relationship with our imagery capacities. Dr. Geller's primary orientation is ego-psychoanalytic but he seeks to show how linkages between the imaginal processes that dominate classical psychoanalytic psychotherapy and the more action, bodily oriented emphases of Gestalt and Encounter or Bioenergetic therapies can be forged. This wide-ranging chapter also moves beyond the traditional therapeutic client–patient setting and points toward broader treatment modalities or preventive approaches.

10

Imagery and the Control of Depression

K. David Schultz

1. Introduction

Recently, the scientific study of the function of daydreaming, fantasy, and imagery has enjoyed renewed popularity. The past decade in particular has witnessed a remarkable expansion of interest in this area. Particularly in the short time since the appearance in 1966 of Singer's book, *Daydreaming: An introduction to the experimental study of inner experience,* imaginal processes are increasingly being viewed as a constructive activity rather than as a mere storehouse of sensations (Neisser, 1972). A new appreciation has been gained regarding the role of imaginal processes in learning (Paivio, 1971), memory (Paivio, 1971), and perception (Segal, 1971). The clinical implications of imaginal processes are especially emphasized in Singer's (1971, 1974) discussion of numerous imagery and daydream techniques that have been utilized to augment the treatment of various psychiatric syndromes.

As Singer (1974) indicated, there currently exists a growing body of literature with a lengthy historical tradition indicating that induced fantasy and imagery techniques may play an important role in stimulating behavioral change. Unfortunately, however, no systematic research has been employed to evaluate the effects of particular imagery conditions on the mood and general clinical symptomatology of patients representative of a specific psychiatric syndrome. Therefore,

---

K. David Schultz • Division of Psychiatry, Waterbury Hospital Health Center, Waterbury, Connecticut 06720.

Schultz (1976) recently conducted a study designed to investigate the short-term effects of specific imagery content on a group of depressed psychiatric patients.

2. Imagery in the Treatment of Depression: A Research Strategy

After conducting an extensive review of fantasy and imagery techniques in the treatment of depression, Schultz (1975) suggested that some type of focused imagery might either (a) distract an individual from his depressed mood state; or (b) help him to contact and discharge suppressed affect leading to a reduction in conflict and a corresponding decrease in level of depression. Several types of imagery conditions were considered particularly relevant to depression. The "hostility-directed-inward" hypothesis of depression (Abraham, 1911; Freud, 1917; Rado, 1928) in conjunction with a catharsis model suggests that angry or aggressive imagery may break through the depressive cycle (Lazarus, 1968). If, however, depression is not "hostility-directed-inward" but related more to dependency, then encouraging a patient to develop socially gratifying imagery (Beck, 1967, 1970) might combat the patient's sense of inadequacy and deprivation (Abraham, 1924; Freud, 1923) by recalling in pictorial form certain past successes or gratifications. If there are at least two types of depression, as mounting research suggests (Blatt, 1974; Blatt, D'Afflitti, and Quinlan, 1976), then certain kinds of imagery may work better for one type of depressive than for another. Furthermore, if any kind of focused imagery can distract the individual from his depressed mood, then reminiscence or anticipation of familiar positive scenes, such as positive imagery of a nature scene, may be useful in changing mood during periods of fear, depression, or boredom (Singer, 1971). If the distraction hypothesis is correct, then all three of these imagery conditions may be equally useful in alleviating depression, as suggested by Lazarus (1968), who discussed an affective expression model of depression that posits that the deliberate stimulation of feelings of anger, amusement, affection, sexual excitement, or even anxiety may disrupt the depressive cycle. If, however, merely producing free-flowing, ongoing thought and imagery of any kind is the crucial variable, then a nondirected free imagery condition (Freud, 1954; Rychlak, 1973) might be just as useful as the other three directed imagery conditions in alleviating depression.

Thus, Schultz (1976) designed and conducted a study that investigated the following questions:

1. Is directed imagery more beneficial than nondirected unfocused imagery among depressed male psychiatric patients?

2. Does the content of directed imagery affect the degree of benefit?

3. Do patterns of daydreaming and depressive experiences affect the degree of benefit?

4. What implications do the answers to these questions have regarding the relationship among imagery, affect, and overt behavioral change?

2.1. Methodology

Presently a brief acquaintance with the essential research methodology is in order.* Subjects were 60 white male veterans who met the following very stringent criteria of depression: (a) diagnosis of depression by the admitting psychiatrist; (b) presence of dysphoric mood; (c) presence of four or more neurovegetative signs of depression; and (d) diagnosis of a psychiatric illness of at least one week's duration with no present indication of schizophrenia, organic brain syndrome, alcoholism or drug addiction, mental retardation, or life-threatening medical illness. It is, therefore, to be noted that at the time of their participation in this study these subjects were quite seriously depressed and frequently were experiencing a marked decrease in their previous level of functioning. Furthermore, of all subjects who met the above criteria 90% voluntarily agreed to participate in the study, suggesting that this sample may be relatively closely representative of a seriously depressed male psychiatric population.

Each subject was seen individually by the experimenter within the first week after either inpatient or outpatient psychiatric treatment was begun. Initially, each was assigned according to a stratified randomization procedure to either the aggressive, socially gratifying, positive, or free-imagery groups with subjects in each group being matched on age, educational level, and severity of depression. Each subject was initially encouraged to regard the use of imagery as a skill procedure that can be learned. After being instructed to get as comfortable as possible, he was then asked to close his eyes or focus his gaze at a point. Next, the subject was instructed to follow one of the four imagery procedures by visualizing the entire experience in his "mind's eye" in as great detail as possible: (a) *aggressive imagery*, to recall someone saying or doing something to him that angered him; (b) *socially gratifying imagery*, to recall someone saying or doing something that made him feel very pleased; (c) *positive imagery*, to recall a place in nature he used to visit in order to relax; or (d) *free imagery*, to report all images, thoughts, fantasies, and ideas that occurred to him without consciously

---

* Those readers who wish additional methodological details are referred to Schultz (1976).

trying to direct his mental experience. After participating in the imagery induction procedure (which lasted about 10 minutes), each subject was instructed to complete in the following order a series of cognitive, affective, and perceptual measures that have been shown to be related to one's level of depression:

1. The *apparent horizon* measures a person's localization of gaze and was administered as described by Wapner, Werner, and Kris (1957). Downward localization has been found after experimentally induced states of depression (Blatt, Quinlan, and D'Afflitti, 1972).

2. *Time productions*. Subjects were asked to produce their judgments of 15-, 30-, 20-, and 40-second time intervals as outlined by Blatt et al. (1972), who reported that in depression time appears to move more slowly.

3. *Self-esteem*. Subjects were administered the Quinlan-Janis Self-Esteem Scale as outlined by Quinlan and Janis (1976), who used the scale to measure self-esteem enhancement with women in a diet clinic.

4. The *Differential Emotions Scale* consists of 10 emotion categories (interest, joy, surprise, distress, disgust, anger, guilt, shyness, fear, and contempt), which subjects were asked to complete as described by Izard (1971).

5. *Dream*. Subjects were asked to create a dream as descriptively or as simply as they wished. These "dreams" were later rated on number of words, time (latency, total, and net), and emotional tone (inter-rater reliability, $r = .91$).

6. *Mirth response*. Subjects were shown each of three cartoons and were asked to rate the degree of funniness of each cartoon as outlined by Zillmann and Cantor (1972).

7. *Reactions to study*. Subjects were asked to rate their liking of the study, degree of success, likelihood of participating again, degree of liking the experimenter, and degree of viewing other subjects as more successful.

2.2. Results

As indicated in Tables I and II, when comparing directed (aggressive, socially gratifying, and positive) with free imagery, subjects were found after directed imagery to produce significantly lower levels of depression (as inferred from the previously mentioned dependent measures). Furthermore, a comparison of the four imagery groups along a linear continuum of degree of "social" or interpersonal involvement (aggressive highest, socially gratifying second, positive third,

Table I. Comparison of Fantasy Groups on the Dependent Measures: Means and Significant F-Tests

Variable	Fantasy group means				F^a
	1 Aggressive	2 Social-Grat	3 Positive	4 Free	
Time productions	58.43	68.60	88.43	85.73	3.96^c
Mood					
Distress	8.87	8.13	8.53	12.27	4.10^c
Anger	3.93	7.60	4.53	7.67	8.19^e
Fear	10.33	6.60	9.47	11.33	4.02^c
Contempt	5.80	6.13	5.20	8.53	5.32^d
Dream					
Total time	107.33	128.73	148.27	193.60	2.90^c
Net time	99.67	110.60	132.00	184.80	3.28^c
Number words	91.53	85.60	101.40	135.20	2.23^b
Mirth response					
Self-ratings					
Cartoon 1	50.13	52.40	45.73	25.40	2.27^b
Cartoon 3	58.13	31.53	64.33	50.07	3.43^c
Reactions to study					
Liked study	6.60	5.80	4.53	5.13	3.18^c
Sum participate	12.07	11.07	9.07	10.20	2.79^c

$^a df = 3,56$.
$^b p \leq .10$.
$^c p \leq .05$.
$^d p \leq .01$.
$^e p \leq .001$.

and free lowest)* revealed, as noted in Table III, the significant linear trend of subjects producing lower levels of depression after imagery of a more socially oriented nature. These statements are somewhat oversimplified, however, because when considering the more complex effect on particular emotions among these depressed patients, positive imagery plays a crucial role in reducing distress, anger, and contempt

---

* This ordering along a continuum of social involvement was derived on the basis of the subjects' behavior during the various imagery sessions. Aggressive imagery was ranked highest on social involvement since subjects in this group seemed to show the greatest amount of object relatedness by generating a great intensity of affect while appearing to be involved with and recognize the other person as an individual separate from themselves. Socially gratifying imagery was ranked second since subjects in this group all recalled incidents involving another person, but focused on this person in a more narcissistic, almost symbiotic manner as the source of supplies. Positive imagery was ranked third because subjects often associated significant people with the scenes in nature that were recalled. Free imagery was ranked lowest because although subjects may have occasionally mentioned significant people during the free-imagery session, these references were usually fleeting and seldom brought up again.

Table II. Comparison of Fantasy Groups on the Dependent Measures: Tukey Multiple Range Tests[a]

Variable	Mean difference comparison[a]							
	1 vs. 2	1 vs. 3	1 vs. 4	2 vs. 3	2 vs. 4	3 vs. 4	A vs. B	C vs. 4
Time productions	−10.17	−30.00[c]	−27.30[c]	−19.83	−17.13	2.70	−23.56[d]	−13.91
Mood								
Distress	0.78	0.34	−3.40[b]	−0.40	−4.14[c]	−3.74[c]	−1.90	−3.76[d]
Anger	−3.67[d]	−1.60	−3.74[d]	3.07[c]	−0.07	−3.14[c]	0.33	−2.32[c]
Fear	3.73	0.86	−1.00	−2.87	−4.73[d]	−1.86	−1.93	−2.53
Contempt	−0.33	0.60	−2.73[c]	0.93	−2.40[c]	−3.33[d]	−0.90	−2.52[d]
Dream								
Total time	−21.40	−40.94	−86.27[c]	−19.54	−64.87	−45.33	−52.80	−65.49[b]
Net time	−10.93	−32.33	−85.13[c]	−21.40	−74.20	−52.80	−53.27	−70.71[c]
Mirth response								
Self-ratings								
Cartoon 3	26.34	−24.73	19.87	−51.07[c]	−6.47	44.60	−15.40	−19.33
Reactions to study								
Liked study	0.20	1.47[c]	0.87	1.27	0.67	−0.60	1.07[c]	0.31
Sum part.	1.00	3.00[c]	1.87	2.00	0.87	−1.13	1.94	0.53

[a] A = Groups 1 and 2 combined; B = Groups 3 and 4 combined; and C = Groups 1, 2, and 3 combined. N = 15 in each Group.
[b] $p \leq .10$.
[c] $p \leq .05$.
[d] $p \leq .01$.

and increasing mirth. However, positive imagery seems to have little impact on such measures as localization of gaze, subjective experience of time, and self-esteem and therefore does not influence the composite cognitive, affective, and perceptual measures in a manner consonant with a general reduction in level of depression. Finally, subjects representative of different patterns of daydreaming and depressive experiences reported differential levels of depression after the various imagery conditions. For example, as shown in Figure 1, those subjects whose depression was characterized by themes of dependency produced lower levels of depression after aggressive and socially gratifying

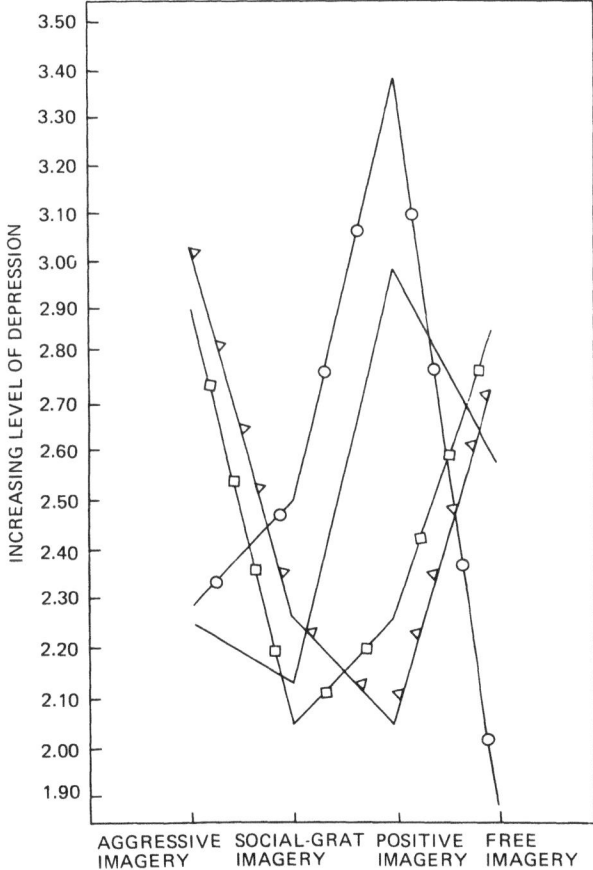

Figure 1. Comparison of levels of depression reported by subjects representative of different patterns of daydreaming and depressive experiences according to content of imagery stimulated. Dependency ———; self criticism △———; positive-vivid daydreaming □———; guilty-dysphoric daydreaming ○———.

Table III. Linear, Nonlinear, Quadratic, and Cubic Trend Analyses on the Dependent Measures: F-Tests

Variable	Linear[a]	Nonlinear[b]	Quadratic[a]	Cubic[a]
Apparent horizon	5.04[c]	0.22		
Time productions	10.07[d]	0.91		
Self-esteem	4.05[c]	0.89		
Mood				
Distress	6.38[c]	2.97		
Anger	6.92[c]	8.82[e]	0.15	17.49[e]
Fear	1.66	5.19[d]	7.59[d]	2.80
Contempt	6.56[c]	4.69[c]	5.59[c]	3.80
Dream				
Total time	8.30[d]	0.20		
Net time	8.79[d]	0.53		
No. words	4.90[c]	0.90		
Mirth response				
Exp. ratings				
Cartoon 1	2.31	9.76[e]	16.00[e]	3.53
Cartoon 2	0.43	4.66[c]	9.13[d]	0.18
Cartoon sum	0.04	5.33[d]	10.66[d]	0.00
Self-ratings				
Cartoon 1	4.88[c]	0.96		
Cartoon 3	0.06	5.11[d]	0.64	9.58[d]
Reactions to study				
Liked study	5.33[c]	2.10		
Others' success	4.51[c]	0.55		
Sum part.	4.96[c]	1.71		

[a] $df = 1,56$.
[b] $df = 2,56$.
[c] $p \leq .05$.
[d] $p \leq .01$.
[e] $p \leq .001$.

imagery, whereas those depressives who tended to be more self-critical reported fewer signs of depression after socially gratifying and positive imagery. Similarly, those subjects whose daydreaming was positively oriented showed lower levels of depression after socially gratifying and positive imagery while those subjects who tended toward guilty-dysphoric themes in their daydreaming indicated more signs of depression after positive imagery than after the other imagery conditions.

2.3. Discussion

How do we understand these findings? Central to clarifying the differences between subjects who participated in directed imagery, particularly more socially oriented directed imagery, and those who participated in nondirected free imagery, is the issue of what the depressed subjects are doing during the different imagery sessions. This is not merely an issue of the presence or absence of imagery since a similar percentage (approximately 75-80%) of subjects in each of the four groups were able to produce some imagery. Rather, the two critical issues appear to be (a) the directedness or focusing of imagery contact and (b) the socially relevant content of imagery and its effects on affective arousal.

2.4. Directedness of Imagery

The difference in level of depression among subjects after directed as compared with subjects after nondirected, free imagery may reflect the fact that although subjects in the free-imagery condition made use of imagery that focused on positive wishes and generated positive, productive fantasy, this positive imagery was repeatedly interfered with by the intrusion of thoughts concerning present life problems. After the intrusion of such thoughts the subject was often unable to regain his focus on the preceding positive imagery, became preoccupied with his current problems, and frequently produced negative imagery often involving visualization of unpleasant life events that apparently lead to an even greater intensification of unpleasant feelings. Thus, it appears that subjects in the free-imagery group, although potentially able to generate positive, productive fantasy and imagery were in fact unable to maintain such fantasy and imagery. This inability seems to be a corollary of the nondirected nature of the free imagery task (i.e., report all of the thoughts, fantasies, images, and ideas that come to mind). Thus, the situation was not structured so that subjects are encouraged to block the intrusion of thoughts regarding current life problems. Once these negative thoughts and concerns were given attention, the subject appeared unable to check their impact on his awareness and gradually began to generate negative imagery that seemed to further exacerbate his negative feeling state.

In contrast, the task orientation of the directed imagery instructions encouraged the subject to attend to events in specific content areas (i.e., the recollection of an aggressive, socially gratifying, or positive nature scene event) that directed his attention from preoccupation with his present negative thoughts, concerns, and problems as well as all of the unpleasant affects and discomforting behaviors associated with them. The degree to which subjects were able to maintain the directedness of their imagery (and the thoughts associated with these specific content areas), while avoiding their usual negative preoccupations and brooding, appears to be directly related to the degree to which they were able to experience positive changes in their affective state, as indicated by the generally lower levels of depression reported by subjects after directed imagery. Such an interpretation of the present findings is highly consonant with a cognitive-affective "circular feedback" model of depression suggested by Feshbach (in Beck, 1967) and Beck (1967). However, there remains the finding that it was not simply subjects after directed imagery who produced lower levels of depression but that subjects who experienced directed imagery of a more social or interpersonal nature produced even lower levels.

2.5. Interpersonal Significance of Imagery

Both aggressive and socially gratifying imagery involved a focus on an interpersonal interaction between the subject and a significant person in his life. This interaction often generated strong affective arousal during the imagery session as evidenced by subjects' frequent verbal and nonverbal expressions of anger, frustration, and hostility during aggressive imagery and smiles, pleasure, contentment, and pride during socially gratifying imagery. It appears that the more socially oriented imagery may have helped subjects to generate greater affective arousal due to its psychological meaningfulness to the subject. In contrast, affect generated among subjects during positive imagery of a nature scene often involved a sense of relaxation and relief that did *not* appear to parallel the intensity of anger aroused among subjects during aggressive imagery or the intensity of pleasant affect generated among subjects during socially gratifying imagery. Nevertheless, it is noteworthy that although subjects after experiencing positive imagery of a nature scene did not report a composite pattern on the cognitive, affective, and perceptual measures consistent with a general reduction in level of depression, they did report a reduction in such discrete emotion categories as distress, anger, and contempt and an increase in mirth. Thus, among a group of seriously depressed psychiatric patients positive imagery has less impact on the overall level of depression but instead has a greater influence in stimulating a brief reduction in unpleasant discrete emotions such as distress, anger, and contempt. These findings are in keeping with Lazarus's (1968) "affective expression" model of depression, which posits that the deliberate stimulation of strong feelings of anger, amusement, affection, sexual excitement, or even anxiety may disrupt the depressive cycle.

It is important to recognize, however, that the stability or duration of the lowered level of depression after directed imagery (as inferred from the dependent measures) is relatively brief, possibly lasting for no more than 30 minutes to one hour after the imagery session. Nevertheless, these findings suggest that the use of imagery in the disruption of the depressive cycle may involve a two-fold process: (a) the generation of strong affects that disrupt or break through the depressive cycle of negative thought leading to increased negative feeling leading to further negative thinking; and (b) the maintenance of strong affect through the directedness of an imagery procedure that shifts the subject from perseverating and brooding over current negative thoughts, concerns, and problems. Such a two-fold conceptualization is consonant with several conceptualizations of depression, the "affective expression" model suggested by Lazarus (1968) and the "circular feedback" model suggested by Feshback (in Beck, 1967) and Beck (1967).

3. Alternative Models

The circular feedback model posits a mutually reinforcing interaction between cognition and affect suggesting that thoughts not only influence feelings but that feelings can influence thought content. Traynor (1974) reported that with increasing levels of depressive affect college males change their attitudes about their fantasies and focus more on negative topics. Similar findings reported among high school males (Rychlak, 1973), general male psychiatric patients (Starker and Singer, 1975), and depressed male psychiatric patients (Schultz, 1976) also support the Feshbach and Beck notion that affects can indeed influence thought content. This position is further strengthened by the findings reported earlier that in a nondirected, free imagery situation depressed male psychiatric patients continue to be preoccupied with their current negative life concerns, which often generate negative imagery apparently leading to maintenance or even exacerbation of the depressed mood levels that brought about the negative thinking. The extent to which the depressed male's thinking and imagery is not meaningfully directed away from his current problems and negative life concerns is the extent to which he is permitted to reinforce continually his depressive mood. Thus, the circular feedback cycle between cognitions and affects repeats itself almost like a computer reverberating through an infinite loop.

In a study of attention and recall using college students, Klinger, Barta, and Mahoney (1976) found that subjects were (a) more likely to notice and attend to concern-related material than nonconcern related material; and (b) that they were more than twice as likely to recall it and reflect it in their spontaneous thoughts. Other preliminary data suggested that the most influential concerns are those that are affectively most important, those about which there is the greatest urgency, and those that are most jeopardized. Recently, Klinger (1975) further elaborated the cognitive-affective circular feedback mechanism when he emphasized that "fantasy *normally* steers away from overtly threatening content because of the integrated responses to negative affective feedback; but when presented with unmistakable fear and guilt-related cues (as appears to be the case almost constantly with severely depressed people), the patient's fantasy will reflect the relevant concerns" (p. 11). Thus, in an unstructured situation the severely depressed person seems to generate his own fear- and guilt-related cues, which lead to a self-perpetuation and exacerbation of his depressive state.

Klinger (1975) also suggested that rehearsing certain daydream themes or stories (i.e., life scripts in terms of the transactional-analysts such as Berne) makes them integrated components of *people's inner reality:* "The subjective sense that something is "real" depends on the idea of the thing having had a chance to become integrated. Thus, there is here a potent source of distortion, delusion, and clinical error which it is important to take into account" (Klinger, 1975, p. 12). Klinger's ideas provide a framework for the formulation that depressives (particularly males) rehearse negative experience in their fantasy, imagery, and daydreams, perhaps even as attempts toward mastery and self-control (Meichenbaum, 1975). However, these attempts toward mastery unfortunately appear abortive in that the depressive who feels "lousy" about himself develops negative fantasies and negative images about himself, rehearses these negative self-images in his fantasies and daydreams, and gradually develops a subjective sense of the "reality" of his negative self-image. Figure 2 indicates this process pictorially.

In a recent study of depressed male psychiatric patients Schultz (1976) reported that undesirable recent life events (e.g., changes in sleep pattern, personal injury or illness, financial problems, troubles with spouse, sexual problems, etc.) occurred more frequently and were more likely to be continuous than were desirable events. Moreover, previous research (Paykel, Myers, Dienelt, Klerman, Lindenthal, and Pepper, 1969) had indicated a higher incidence of undesirable recent life events among depressives as compared with the general popula-

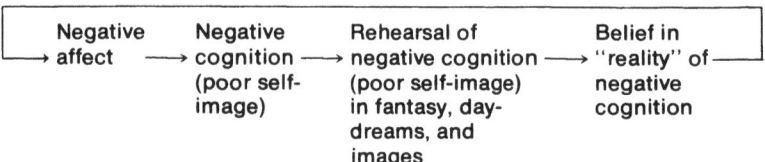

Figure 2. Aspects of the cognitive-affective circular feedback process.

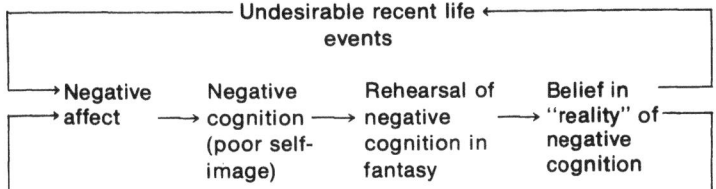

Figure 3. Aspects of the cognitive-affective circular feedback process incorporating recent life events.

tion. Taken together, these findings suggest that undesirable life event factors may contribute to the depressive cycle in depressed patients. This would be incorporated into the previous diagram as follows (Figure 3):

Carrying this theoretical conceptualization a bit further, once undesirable life events are introduced into this model, the individual's belief in his negative self-image and world could (a) lead him to indeed precipitate more undesirable life events through carelessness and apprehension; and/or (b) cause him to interpret or attribute a greater degree of undesirability to his recent life experiences than he might otherwise or ordinarily do. However, Schultz (1976) also found that severity of depression and undesirable life events are positively but only marginally significantly correlated, suggesting that although negative or undesirable recent life experiences may contribute to initiating the depressive cycle in patients vulnerable to depression, recent life event factors may play only a minor role in influencing present mood states. Indeed, this finding taken into consideration with Klinger's (1975) research suggests as indicated in Figure 4 that undesirable recent life events may serve as cues to previously more traumatic life events from the individual's past experience, which may then further exacerbate the negative self-image, leading to increased belief in the "reality" of the negative cognition.

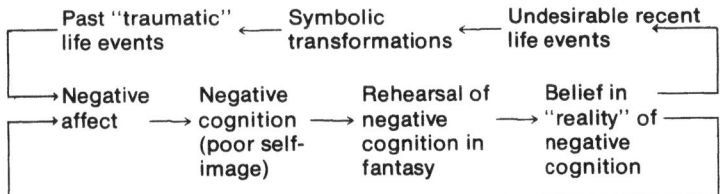

Figure 4. Aspects of the cognitive-affective circular feedback process incorporating recent life events as cues to previous more traumatic life events in the etiology of depression.

Schultz (1976) also reported a positive relationship between undesirable recent life events and Positive-Vivid Daydreaming on the Imaginal Processes Inventory (Singer and Antrobus, 1972), suggesting that a higher degree of unpleasant external experience may lead to a greater reliance on positive internal fantasy experience. Moreover, Schultz also found a positive relationship between poor adjustment to undesirable recent life events and Fear of Failure in Daydreaming. Although interpretation is tentative because the data are correlational, these findings may suggest that the depressed individual may seek refuge from unpleasant external experience by attempting to immerse himself in positive fantasies. This may represent both an attempt toward mastery of the unpleasant life experiences as well as an avoidance of or withdrawal from a pervasive fear-of-failure. However, it is postulated that this beneficial use of fantasy may only be temporary as the capacity to make spontaneous use of positive fantasy as an escape from negative external as well as internal experience may be quite tenuous, perhaps being inversely related to the level of negative or depressive affect. It could be argued that should there be an increase in further undesirable life experiences and/or an internal negative change in attitude and/or a spontaneous lowering in the level of physiological functioning either through fatigue or illness, the individual's negative-depressive affect may be exacerbated to the point where the individual can no longer spontaneously take refuge in positive fantasies and imagery. As mentioned earlier, some support for such reasoning is derived from research with college males (Traynor, 1974), general male psychiatric patients (Starker and Singer, 1975), and depressed male psychiatric patients (Schultz, 1976), which noted that increasing depressive affect is accompanied by increased negative fantasy content and increased negative attitudes toward daydreaming.

Taken together, these findings suggest that mildly depressed males may indeed be able spontaneously to take refuge from negative life experiences for a while by immersing themselves in positive fantasy. However, should some event occur that might even briefly increase their depression to a moderate or severe level they may not only find themselves unable to take refuge spontaneously in positive fantasy but also unable to avoid rehearsal of negative cognitions through negative fantasy and imagery. To take an example from physics, it may be that the mildly depressed individual who experiences an added quantum of "depressive" energy is similar to the electron that, exposed to an added quantum of kinetic energy, "jumps" into a higher orbital level and continues to move about the nucleus of the atom until some other change in energy might occur. A mildly depressed individual who experiences an added quantum of "depressive" energy may "jump" into a moderate or even severe level of depression that may not only make it impossible for him to make spontaneous use of the beneficial aspects of positive fantasy and imagery but may indeed "leave" him to "cycle" continuously through an increasingly "vicious circle" of negative affect → negative cognition → rehearsal of negative cognitions in fantasy → belief in "reality" of negative conditions → increased negative affect.

Of particular interest, however, is the fact that the findings reported earlier (Schultz, 1976) suggest that if someone directs the moderately or severely depressed male from thinking about his present life concerns by having him focus his imagery on particular kinds of significant life experiences (aggressive, socially gratifying, positive nature scene), he may be helped to disrupt for a brief period of time the cognitive-affective circular feedback cycle (something that he may no longer be able to do spontaneously or of his own volition, especially while his level of depression is elevated). Moreover, as noted earlier, the more socially oriented directed imagery conditions seem to offer some advantages over those with little or no social involvement. Furthermore, although positive nature-scene imagery seems to have less impact in reducing the overall level of depression, it seems to play a more crucial role in influencing discrete emotions. And finally, not only do the various imagery conditions seem to have a differential effectiveness in temporarily alleviating depression, but also such personality characteristics as depressive experiences and daydreaming patterns seem to influence what type of imagery condition will be more effective for a particular individual.

4. Patterns of Depressive Experiences

There was some evidence indicating that the four imagery conditions produced a differential effect on level of depression among subjects representative of the various types of depressive experiences. Findings indicated that those high on the Dependency factor of depressive experiences reported significantly fewer signs of depression after aggressive and socially gratifying imagery than after positive and free imagery. This supports the conclusions of Blatt, D'Afflitti, and Quinlan (1976) that high scores on Dependency are indicative of intense concerns regarding feelings of abandonment, loneliness, and dependency with a strong externally directed focus on interpersonal relationships. Of the four imagery conditions, aggressive and socially gratifying are oriented toward greater social and interpersonal involvement. Thus, it seems that those depressed subjects whose concerns center around vulnerability in interpersonal relationships produce lower levels of depression after socially oriented directed imagery than after nonsocial directed imagery or nondirected free imagery. Apparently socially gratifying imagery may help to meet some of the neediness as well as alleviate the fears of abandonment and rejection of those high on Dependency. Since apprehension regarding the management of interpersonal anger and aggression seem to be predominant concerns for those high on Dependency, the lower levels of depression after aggressive imagery suggest that expression of anger and aggression in a relatively "safe" and "accepting" setting may help to reduce the subject's fears about the possible negative repercussions of the expression of anger (e.g., the subjects' intense fears of losing others after the expression of anger may be reduced for at least a brief period of time). This finding lends some support for the appropriateness of the "catharsis" model (Feshbach, 1955) for this subgroup of depressed patients but suggests that the "hostility-directed-inward" hypothesis of depression (Abraham, 1911; Freud, 1917; Rado, 1928) may have more relationship to dependency among depressives than to the formation of guilt.

In summary, it appears the expression of aggression may lead to a reduction in level of depression, primarily for those subjects scoring high on Dependency.

Those high on the Self-Criticism factor of depressive experiences produced significantly lower levels of depression after socially gratifying and positive imagery than after aggressive and free imagery. High scores on Self-Criticism involve a generally internally oriented focus reflecting feelings of guilt, unworthiness, failure to meet one's standards and ideals, and a critical attitude toward oneself. Clearly, these findings do not support the simple hydraulic "hostility-directed-inward" hypothesis of depression.* Of the four imagery conditions, socially gratifying and positive imagery are more specifically oriented toward the recollection and rehearsal of positive, pleasant, and comfort-producing memories. Thus, depressed subjects whose concerns focus on a pervasive self-critical attitude seem to report fewer signs of depression after directed imagery with a more pleasant, positive content.

---

* However, it is possible that this group of veterans may be more truly representative of the passive-dependent type of person than depressed psychiatric patients in a private hospital who may more closely represent the self-criticism type of depressive. Thus, there may be a need for a group showing higher self-criticism to study further the "hostility-directed-inward" hypothesis of depression and its relation to the development of guilt and self-criticism.

Perhaps socially gratifying imagery, which focuses on recalling and rehearsing a past event in which someone said or did something that helped the subject to feel very good and pleased about himself, reduces the subject's self-critical attitude by reminding him of past accomplishments and previous appreciation that others have felt toward him. These findings also suggest that socially gratifying imagery may even help the subject to *identify* with the less harsh superego of a significant person in his life and thereby reduce the self-critical attitude of his own superego for a period of time. Since those high on Self-Criticism seem to be almost constantly preoccupied with their negative self-evaluation, the lower levels of depression after positive nature-scene imagery suggest that having people recall and rehearse their memories of a place in nature where they used to go to relax, "unwind," and feel "really comfortable" may help direct subjects away from self-critical thinking and remind them of times when they were able to forget their cares, gain some distance and mastery over uncomfortable feelings, and actually relax and "unwind" for a while.

In summary, the present findings indicate that different kinds of imagery stimulation produce a differential effect on the depressive symptomatology of subjects representative of different factors of depressive experiences. This finding supports the suggestion (Blatt *et al.*, 1976) that types of depressive experiences may be a useful and simple way to distinguish among those depressives who may benefit more from one particular treatment modality as opposed to another. Clearly, further research is needed to determine whether depressive experiences can be predictive of long-term as well as short-term changes in level of depression among various treatment approaches.

5. Daydreaming Patterns

Some evidence indicative of the various imagery conditions having a differential effect on level of depression among subjects representative of the two types of daydreaming patterns was found. Findings indicated that those high on the Positive-Vivid Daydreaming pattern reported significantly fewer signs of depression after socially gratifying and positive imagery than after aggressive and free imagery. High scores on Positive-Vivid Daydreaming are indicative of high acceptance of daydreaming, positive content in daydreaming, and visual imagery in daydreaming, reflecting a general stylistic pattern associated with a more constructive and positive orientation to daydreaming. Of the four imagery conditions, socially gratifying and positive imagery consist of more positively oriented content. Apparently, socially gratifying and positive imagery correspond with, reinforce, and further enhance the constructive and positive characteristics of those subjects who maintain a positive orientation to daydreaming, and thereby reduce depression.

Those subjects high on Guilty-Dysphoric Daydreaming produced significantly higher levels of depression after positive imagery than after aggressive, socially gratifying, and free imagery.* High scores on the Guilty-Dysphoric Daydreaming pattern are characteristic of frequent guilt daydreams, fear of failure daydreams, and hostile-aggressive daydreams, reflecting a general stylistic pattern focusing around doubt, guilt, self-punishment, failure, and aggression in daydreaming. Of the four imagery conditions, positive and socially gratifying imagery are oriented more specifically toward the recollection and rehearsal of positive, pleasant, and comfort-producing memories. Although somewhat speculative, it appears that subjects high on Guilty-Dysphoric Daydreaming may find it disconcerting to produce positive imagery. It is possible that these subjects may experience an uplift in mood during positively oriented imagery but may not be able to sustain this beneficial effect afterward due to the predominance of their Guilty-Dysphoric Daydreaming pattern. Thus, the contrast between brief pleasure and relaxation followed by the resumption of unpleasant daydreaming may lead to a further exacerbation of dysphoric mood.

In summary, findings indicate that imagery stimulation produces a differential effect on depressive symptomatology among subjects representative of these two types of daydreaming patterns. This finding supports Singer's (1971) suggestion that imagery and daydreaming patterns may provide a useful and simple procedure to determine those patients who may be more likely to benefit from imagery and daydreaming methods in psychotherapy. Such a diagnostic procedure would not only make for more efficient patient selection, but would also (a) offer patients greater awareness of what is actually involved in the dimension of imagery and daydreaming; and (b) suggest specific avenues that imagery training may follow. Such a procedure has as yet been little used in connection with daydreaming and imagery training in psychotherapy.

6. Conclusions

Findings indicate that depressed psychiatric patients who experience directed imagery, particularly of a more socially oriented nature,

---

* It is noteworthy, however, that subjects high on Guilty-Dysphoric Daydreaming produced the second highest level of depression after socially gratifying imagery.

produce fewer factors associated with depression than those patients who experience a free imagery situation. Thus, directed imagery may be more suitable in reducing a depressed patient's level of depression for a brief period of time than free imagery. Finally, the four imagery conditions produced a differential effect on the level of depression reported by depressed psychiatric patients who were representative of different patterns of daydreaming and depressive experiences.

7. The Nature of the Psychotherapeutic Process

Essential to examining the implications of the psychotherapeutic uses of imagery is an understanding of one's view of the psychotherapeutic process. Of particular relevance is the position held by Singer (1974), Strupp (1970), Meichenbaum (1975), and Klinger (1975) who contend that the primary purpose of psychotherapy is the development of self-awareness, self-control, competence, and autonomy. Furthermore, they suggest that most neurotic symptoms can be shown to be guided by central mediating processes such as beliefs and self-attitudes that can be implicit and may have evolved from symbolic transformations. Taking the position that psychotherapy is essentially a technology to produce personality and behavior change, they regard the function of the therapist as centering around making a person's problem(s) increasingly specific so that it can be focused upon with some degree of precision through the use of available psychological knowledge and technique. Thus, the objective of psychotherapy is to present the client in a reasonably systematic manner methods for handling his own behavior that he can take with him after leaving the consultant's office.

Although emphasizing the therapist's skilled technology, Singer (1974) and Strupp (1970) also stress the importance of the humanity of the therapist-client interaction and the necessity for development of the client's trust in the therapist as crucial initial components for establishing an atmosphere of mutual cooperation. Considering the psychotherapeutic use of imagery techniques within this framework may lead to a more meaningful understanding of the various components present in these methods.

8. Imagery, Daydreaming, and a Cognitive Theory of Self-Control

Conducting research designed to bring together the clinical concerns of semantic, or cognitive, therapists and the technology of behavior therapy, Meichenbaum (1975) and his colleagues have found promising evidence, in terms of generalization and persistence of treatment effects, that follow from the inclusion of self-instructional and imagery processes into "standard" behavior-therapy procedures. These findings lead Meichenbaum to emphasize a "cognitive theory of self-control" by which he attempts to explain why modifying the client's internal dialogue (i.e., his self-statements and images) leads to behavioral change.

Meichenbaum considers therapeutic change to come about by means of a three-stage sequential, mediating process in which (a) the client becomes an observer of his behavior and physiological responses, (b) this self-recognition becomes the cue to emit incompatible cognitions and behaviors, and, finally, (c) what the client says to himself (i.e., his appraisals, attributions, self-statements, and images), following change influences the generalization and persistence of treatment effects. Meichenbaum's three-stage sequential, mediating process not only offers a more detailed description of the training or skills-acquisition phase of cognitive-behavioral therapy, but seems to begin during an initial conceptualization phase and continue through a final transfer phase as well. Meichenbaum notes, however, that these latter two phases have often received little attention in behavioral therapy literature.

9. The Conscious Control of Consciousness: The Use of Imagery in Alleviating Depression

A consideration of Meichenbaum's three-phase theory of cognitive-behavior therapy in conjunction with the previous description of the cognitive-affective circular feedback processes involved in the etiology of depression provides an interesting framework for understanding the psychotherapeutic use of imagery in helping an individual to develop conscious control of his consciousness and thereby alleviate depressive symptomatology. Although such a conceptualization as indicated earlier in Figure 4 is still tentative, depression can be viewed as coming about in the following manner. The occurrence of undesirable recent life events (e.g., changes in sleeping pattern, personal injury or illness, financial problems, troubles with spouse, sexual problems, etc.) may serve as cues through implicit symbolic transformations to previous more "traumatic" life events, which may then exacerbate negative affect, which in turn leads to further negative cognitions (poor self-image) followed by a rehearsal of these negative cognitions through fantasy, which finally culminates in a belief in the "reality" of the negative cognition or poor self-image. Once this process has started and a level of moderate to severe depression has been reached, the process appears to take on more autonomous functioning such that the moderately or severely depressed individual is no longer able spontaneously to direct his thinking and thereby take refuge in positive fantasies or imagery that could alleviate depressive symptomatology.

If the etiology of depression is regarded from this point of view, how does the therapist make psychotherapeutic use of imagery in helping the depressed client to develop conscious control of his consciousness and thereby alleviate depression? A detailed examination of Schultz's (1976) research findings offers some tentative suggestions. As Meichenbaum (1975) has emphasized, the initial conceptualization phase of psychotherapy, though often receiving little attention in the literature, is crucial in providing the framework within which the client can develop greater self-awareness, self-control, mastery, and autonomy of his consciousness. During this initial conceptualization phase, Schultz's (1976) imagery procedure and research findings suggest the importance of meeting individually with the depressed client in order to gather information about him (diagnostic assessment) as well as to provide the client with verbal and sometimes written information regarding the manner in which the psychotherapist plans to help the client gain increasing mastery over his depression. Thus, during this initial conceptualization phase the therapist-client interaction is crucial in furthering diagnostic assessment, fostering the client's motivation, developing the humanity of the therapist-client relationship, and furthering the development of the client's trust in the therapist (Singer, 1974; Strupp, 1970). Furthermore, this process of fostering the client's trust, motivation, and understanding when begun initially can more readily continue throughout the skills acquisition and final transfer phases of psychotherapy. And finally, although continued research is needed to determine further the diagnostic and prognostic usefulness of differences in patterns of daydreaming and depressive experiences, such information may (a) provide an efficient procedure to determine which type of imagery condition might be most effective for a particular depressed client; and (b) suggest specific areas that treatment may focus on.

The imagery procedure utilized in Schultz's (1976) research provides numerous suggestions for the incorporation of imagery into the training or skills-acquisition phase of psychotherapy. Elaboration and discussion of initial imagery instructions can help the client focus on his use of imagery as a skill procedure that can be learned and improved through practice. Suggestions to relax and either close his eyes or stare off at a point can establish conditions (e.g., increased concentration and reduced external stimulation) that enhance attention to internal processes and augment the vividness and autonomic effects of fantasy and imagery (Singer, 1974). Such a series of instructions and suggestions can help the depressed client to become a better observer of the specific behaviors and physiological processes that form his depressive symptomatology.

The use of specific directed imagery instructions can encourage the depressed client to develop and rehearse through imagery a particular memory that can produce affects, cognitions, and behaviors (e.g., increased affective arousal and altered self-statements) incompatible with his depressive symptomatology. The directedness of the imagery instructions can serve as a cue to maintain these altered affects, cognitions, and behaviors.

Finally, what the client says to himself following these changes can influence the persistence of the treatment effects. For example, in the aggressive-imagery condition the disavowal of counteraggression (i.e., "I only thought about revenge") may help the client to accept and feel comfortable with his imagery experience and thereby maintain his altered affects, cognitions, and behaviors. Likewise, in the socially gratifying and positive imagery conditions similar self-statements (e.g., "I feel better about myself" or "I am more relaxed and comfortable") may help alter the client's view of himself (improve his poor self-image), provide him with some sense of mastery and control, and thereby maintain a set of affects, cognitions, and behaviors incompatible with depressive symptoms. This in turn can help the client to develop increased belief in the "reality" of an improved self-image that can lead to an increase in positive affect.

Finally, regarding the generalization of imagery training during the final transfer phase of psychotherapy, Schultz's (1976) procedure and findings suggest the importance after each imagery session of encouraging the client to ask questions and make comments regarding his participation in the imagery training. During this discussion period the client may mention having tried to direct his thinking in the past and having actually been able to do so prior to becoming increasingly depressed (as did many of Schultz's depressed psychiatric patients). The client can then be encouraged to continue practicing the imagery training procedure between formal imagery training sessions in the psychotherapist's office, thus helping the client to begin in a gradual step-wise fashion to generalize transfer of benefit to his everyday life (as did a number of Schultz's depressed psychiatric patients who indeed met with some sustained success through continued practice on their own accord of the imagery training procedure). However, the usefulness of such suggested repeated imagery training is very tentative since Schultz's (1976) study assessed only the short-term effects of particular imagery content on depressive symptomatology. Thus, further research is clearly necessary to determine (a) the long-term effects of repeated imagery training; and b) the degree of transfer of benefit from clinically managed fantasy and imagery to extraclinical behavior.

10. Psychotherapeutic Uses of Imagery

10.1. Clinical Illustrations

The reader may be wondering how one might utilize specific imagery techniques in the psychotherapeutic treatment of his or her own clients. How and in what manner may imagery techniques be incorporated into conventional psychotherapy while still paying attention to important intrapersonal and interpersonal dynamics? The following brief clinical vignette illustrates how imagery techniques enhanced the psychoanalytically oriented treatment of a seriously disturbed man.

> The client, Mr. Y., a thirty-three year-old married male, father of four children, was hospitalized with a diagnosis of schizoaffective schizophrenia. He had a one-year history of depression and suicide attempts and an 11-year history of marital discord. He was seen three times per week in hour-long individual, psychoanalytically oriented psychotherapy. Among other things, Mr. Y. initially complained of disturbing "hallucinations." After further exploration, however, it became apparent that Mr. Y. was no longer hallucinating but was instead describing very vivid and very frightening visual imagery of being "trapped in blazing tall buildings," "falling off the World Trade Center," or "jumping off a highway overpass." On one occasion, Mr. Y. began talking about fears of jumping from his upstairs window. Gradually, he closed his eyes as he continued talking and vividly experienced imagery of jumping. As he did so, he perched on the edge of his chair and then actually jumped the few inches to the floor, at which point he opened his eyes. Mr. Y. was very frightened and mentioned that his heart was pounding. Despite his distress, he was able to understand the difference between the vivid but frightening internal imagery and the actual external event. With encouragement, Mr. Y. was able to rehearse the imagery several times and thereby learned to recognize it as fantasy and vivid imagery that he could control. Over time Mr. Y. became less frightened of it; and as his anxiety decreased, he was actually able to substitute more pleasant imagery and fantasy for the previously frightening images. Mr. Y., with the help of his psychotherapist, was then able to examine in a way that was "safe" for him the basis of his fantasies of self-destruction (i.e., their relationship to the guilt and need for punishment he felt due to having wished for his wife's death and the death of his eldest child).

The next clinical summary indicates how imagery techniques were incorporated into the structurally oriented treatment of a seriously dysfunctional marital relationship.

The clients, Mr. and Mrs. A. were each fifty-five and fifty-two years old respectively, had been married for 23 years, and had three adolescent daughters. Although they had a 20-year history of marital discord, their relationship had remained relatively stable and unchanged despite Mrs. A.'s threats to leave and her demands that Mr. A. become involved in treatment. At the time treatment began, Mrs. A. "wanted" a divorce while Mr. A. "hoped" for a reconciliation of the marriage. They were seen once per week in hour-long structurally oriented couples treatment with the specific function of providing them a place to talk about their interests and differences. The therapist emphasized that he had no vested interest in their remaining together or separating and that neither he nor they could be completely certain of the specific outcome of treatment except that they both might feel better about whatever they ultimately decided to do. Early in the treatment it became apparent that the children were closely triangulated into Mr. and Mrs. A.'s marital discord. Practically all verbal interaction focused around arguments over the children with the pattern emerging of Mr. A. being the "worrier" and Mrs. A. the "protector." Finally, in an attempt both to avoid this habitual ingrained verbal pattern while at the same time to bring them more closely in contact with their feelings and to experience their relationship more vividly, the therapist described in detail to them a family-scultping technique developed by Papp (1973). Briefly, each was asked to make up a dream that depicts the present state of their relationship, particularly emphasizing their problems. Within this made-up dream, each was to depict the spouse as some object, plant, animal, or person in costume and then to picture him or herself in a similar manner. Finally within this made-up dream each was to imagine some action or movement between them that illustrates their present difficulties. After doing this silently, both were encouraged to tell each other their made-up dream and to act it out. After acting it out, both were asked how they had dealt with the acted-out problem, followed by being encouraged to do something different when acting out the problem a second time. In Mrs. A.'s made-up dream she "saw" Mr. A. as a "lion tamer with a whip" and herself as a "caged lioness with her paws over her eyes." As Mr. A. continued to "crack the whip," she wanted to walk away but remained "cowering in fear beneath him." In Mr. A.'s made-up dream he viewed Mrs. A. as "an object, a woman" he's reaching out to who "keeps pushing him away." As Mrs. A. continued to "block his advances," he wanted to be "closer" but maintained his intrusive manner of "reaching out" to her. As a result of this imagery technique, both were brought into vivid contact with their feelings regarding their relationship and were able to recognize for the first time through their imagery the self-defeating manner in which they were relating to each other. Thus, Mrs. A. was encouraged to walk away from her husband when she felt intimidated, and Mr. A. was encouraged to explore new ways of being "tender" and "supportive" rather than so intrusive with his wife. Throughout the remaining treatment sessions this imagery served not only as an impetus for developing new patterns of interaction but also as a vivid reminder of their maladaptive relationship, arising wherever old patterns of interaction remained.

Thus, given the careful consideration of such clinical issues as the therapist's level of expertise, the timing of the intervention, the therapeutic context within which the intervention takes place, and the client's conceptual openness to the procedure, it appears that imagery techniques can be integrated into the treatment of very seriously disturbed clients regardless of whether the therapy is of a psychoanalytically oriented nature or whether the client is an individual, couple, or family system.

10.2. An Overview

Regarding the use of imagery in the control of depression, Schultz's (1976) findings indicated (a) that the affective state of depressed psychiatric patients can be modified for a brief period of time through various imagery approaches; and (b) that this modification in affective state is specifically related to certain aspects of the depressed patient's personality structure (i.e., his patterns of daydreaming and depressive experiences). These findings, however, also have some general implications for the use of imagery in psychotherapy regardless of the client's diagnosis.

To begin with, Singer (1974) and others have noted that the client who seeks psychotherapy brings with him generally the same basic capacity for imagery as all human beings. Often, however, the awareness of or sustained attention to fantasy and imagery shows wide individual differences among the general population. Thus, a first step in the use of imagery in therapy is that the therapist (a) calls attention to inner experience and imaginal processes; and (b) notes the possibility of using imagery as a resource in treatment. This not only opens up a dimension that has been given little attention by many clients in the past but also offers a means for increased mastery and self-control. Secondly, the emphasis on imagery and fantasy encourages the client to become aware that many of the thoughts, fantasies, expectations, and judgments about people and situations represent distorted and poorly integrated childhood experiences that no longer correspond appropriately with his current life situation. Furthermore, imagery and fantasy in psychotherapy can also serve to increase the client's awareness that he has stored many more experiences than he ordinarily recognized (Singer, 1974). Of particular importance to the client is the discovery that his capacity for using specific imagery to generate positive affect or to shift away from certain negative affective patterns is a valuable skill that can be learned. And finally, the immediacy and parallel processing aspects of imagery have been useful in minimizing the client's resistance (Reyher, 1963) and thereby facilitating the psychotherapeutic process.

References

Abraham, K. Notes on the psychoanalytic investigation and treatment of manic-depressive insanity and allied conditions. In *Selected papers of Karl Abraham*. London: Hogarth, 1948. (Originally published 1911.)

Abraham, K. A short study of the development of libido. In *Selected papers of Karl Abraham*. London: Hogarth, 1948. (Originally published 1924.)

Beck, A. T. *Depression: Causes and treatment.* Philadelphia: University of Pennsylvania Press, 1967.

Beck, A. T. Role of fantasies in psychotherapy and psychopathology. *Journal of Nervous and Mental Disease,* 1970, *150*(1), 3-17.

Blatt, S. J. Levels of object representation in anaclitic and introjective depression. *Psychoanalytic Study of the Child,* 1974, *29,* 107-157.

Blatt, S. J., Quinlan, D. M., and D'Afflitti, J. Magnification and diminishing of image size and their effects on psychological states. *Journal of Abnormal Psychology,* 1972, *80*(2), 168-175.

Blatt, S. J., D'Afflitti, J. P., and Quinlan, D. M. Experiences of depression in normal young adults. *Journal of Abnormal Psychology,* 1976, *85*(3), 383-389.

Feshbach, S. The drive-reducing function of fantasy behavior. *Journal of Abnormal and Social Psychology,* 1955, *50,* 3-11.

Feshbach, S. Personal communication with A. T. Beck. In. A. T. Beck, *Depression: Causes and treatment.* Philadelphia: University of Pennsylvania Press, 1967.

Freud, S. Mourning and melancholia. In *Collected papers.* Vol. IV. New York: Basic Books, 1959, 52-170 (Originally published 1917.)

Freud. S. *The ego and the id.* New York: Norton, 1960. (Originally published 1923.)

Freud, S. *The origins of psychoanalysis, letters to Wilhelm Fliess, drafts and notes: 1887-1902.* New York: Basic Books, 1954.

Izard, C. E. *The face of emotion.* New York: Appleton-Century-Crofts, 1971.

Klinger, E. the nature of fantasy and its clinical uses. In J. L. Singer (Chair) *Imagery approaches to psychotherapy.* Symposium presented at the meeting of the American Psychological Association, Chicago, August, 1975.

Klinger, E., Barta, S. G., and Mahoney, T. W. Motivation, mood, and mental events: Patterns and implications for adaptive processes. In G. Serban (Ed.), *Psychopathology of human adaptation.* New York: Plenum, 1976.

Lazarus, A. A. Learning theory and the treatment of depression. *Behavior Research and Therapy,* 1968, *6,* 83-89.

Meichenbaum, D. Toward a cognitive theory of self-control. In G. Schwartz and D. Shapiro (Eds.), *Consciousness and self-regulation: Advances in research.* New York: Plenum Press, 1975.

Neisser, U. Changing conceptions of imagery. In P. Sheehan (Ed.), *The function and nature of imagery.* New York: Academic Press, 1972.

Paivio, A. *Imagery and verbal processes.* New York: Holt, Rinehart, and Winston, 1971.

Papp, P. Sculpting the family. *Family Process,* 1973, *11,* 44-48.

Paykel, E. S., Myers, J. K., Dienelt, M. N., Klerman, G. L., Lindenthal, J. J., and Pepper, M. P. Life events and depression: A controlled study. *Archives of General Psychiatry,* 1969, *21,* 753-760.

Quinlan, D. M., and Janis, I. L. State self-esteem measure. In Janis, I. L. (Ed.), *Counseling on personal decisions: Theory and field research on helping relationships.* New Haven: Yale University Press, in press.

Rado, S. Problem of melancholia. *International Journal of Psychoanalysis,* 1928, *9,* 420-438.

Reyher, J. Free imagery: An uncovering procedure. *Journal of Clinical Psychology,* 1963, *19,* 454-459.

Rychlak, J. Time orientation in the positive and negative free phantasies of mildly abnormal versus normal high school males. *Journal of Consulting and Clinical Psychology,* 1973, *41,* 175-180.

Schultz, K. D. Directed fantasies in the treatment of depression: A review of the literature. Unpublished manuscript and major area paper, Yale University, 1975.

Schultz, K. D. Fantasy stimulation in depression: Direct intervention and correlational studies. Unpublished doctoral dissertation, Yale University, 1976.
Segal, S. J. (Ed.) *Imagery: Current cognitive approaches*. New York: Academic Press, 1971.
Singer, J. L. *Daydreaming*. New York: Random House, 1966.
Singer, J. L. Imagery and daydream techniques employed in psychotherapy: Some practical and theoretical implications. In C. Spielberger (Ed.), *Current topics in clinical and community psychology*. Vol. 3. New York: Academic Press, 1971.
Singer, J. L. *Imagery and daydream methods in psychotherapy and behavior modification*. New York: Academic Press, 1974.
Singer, J. L., and Antrobus, J. S. *Daydreams, imaginal processes, and* personality: A normative study. In P. W. Sheehan (Ed.), *The function and nature of imagery*. New York: Academic Press, 1972.
Starker, S., and Singer, J. L. Daydream patterns of self-awareness in psychiatric patients. *Journal of Nervous and Mental Disease*, 1975, 313-317.
Strupp, A. Specific vs. nonspecific factors in psychology and the problem of control. *Archives of General Psychology*, 1970, *23*, 393-401.
Traynor, T. D. Patterns of daydreaming and their relationships to depressive affect. Unpublished masters thesis, Miami University, Oxford, Ohio, 1974.
Wapner, S., Werner, H., and Kris, D. M. The effect of success and failure on space localization. *Journal of Personality*, 1957, *25*, 752-756.
Zillmann, D., and Cantor, J. R. Directionality of transitory dominance as a communication variable affecting humor appreciation. *Journal of Personality and Social Psychology*, 1972, *24*(2), 191-198.

11

Just Imagine How I Feel: How to Improve Empathy Through Training in Imagination

Susan J. Frank

1. Introduction

Most of us probably spend some part of our day musing about real or imaginary people. In dismissing these activities as "mere fantasies," most research psychologists (e.g., Shrauger and Altrocchi, 1964) have ignored the contention of an insistent few (Horowitz, 1972; Singer, 1966, 1974b) that daydream experiences have adaptive (and demonstrable) implications for the way persons acquire knowledge about other persons. While my own experience as a clinical psychologist and avid daydreamer led me to side with the latter point of view, the scarcity of empirical evidence made it a difficult position to substantiate. Accordingly, I designed a study that proposed to teach individuals to put their fantasies to work in order to increase their empathic abilities. This study—the theoretical considerations from which it developed, its research design and procedures, and the implications of its findings for theory, practice, and further research—is the subject of the present chapter.

Susan J. Frank • Department of Psychology, University of Maryland, College Park, Maryland 20740.

2. Theoretical Background: Three Levels of Empathy

The development of training procedures and hypotheses in the present study stemmed from a conceptual analysis of the process of empathy and a review of the relevant literature. This investigation indicated the necessity of approaching the notion of empathy (most broadly defined as the way people know about or understand other people) from three different levels of analysis, including a *behavioral*, a *subjective*, and a *cognitive-structural* level. The possibility that imaginative skills facilitate learning about others needs to be considered at each level.

2.1. The Behavioral Level of Empathy

In dealing with other people it is essential to be able to predict their future behaviors with a fair degree of accuracy. Hence, for a number of years psychologists (e.g., Dymond, 1948, 1949; Taft, 1955) focused their attention on the behavioral level of empathy, i.e., on the ability to acquire knowledge about and predict another person's overt behaviors. In fact, they often treated the notion of empathy as if it were synonymous with predictive accuracy.

One of the earliest psychologists to study empathy in this behavioral sense referred to imagination in defining her construct. According to Dymond (1950), empathy refers to the "imaginative transposing of oneself into the thinking, feeling, and acting of another" (p. 343). However, further research suggested that the behavior prediction paradigm she popularized as an operational definition of empathy has relatively little to do with imaginative processes (Shrauger and Altrocchi, 1964).

In behavior-prediction experiments, the observer typically is assessed for his or her ability to predict another person's self-descriptive responses to a personality inventory or attitudes questionnaire following a brief encounter. Cline (1964) has demonstrated a positive relationship between accurate predictions of self-descriptive behaviors and accurate postdictions of a person's characteristic behaviors in real-life situations. Moreover, his research suggests that, at least in public, people generally guide their behaviors according to social expectations and stereotypes; hence, reference to these stereotypes enables an observer to predict these behaviors with a fair amount of accuracy.

Studies by Bronfenbrenner, Harding, and Gallwey (1958) as well as by Cline (1964) demonstrate that accurate behavioral predictions are largely mediated by deductive reasoning based upon knowledge and use of social stereotypes, and by behavioral observation. Presumably, observations of a person's behavior enable the observer to distinguish between and select among alternative stereotypes with which to characterize a particular individual.

Careful behavioral observation and more refined, as opposed to global, stereotypes appear to be most important when predicting behaviors for a relatively homogeneous population (Bronfenbrenner et al., 1958). This is the case for studies that ask college students to predict behaviors for other college students. For example, while a college student is probably more likely to report a special interest in intellectual activities compared to a blue-collar worker of the same age, relative differences in intellectual interests between two college students are often more subtle. The observer who takes care to note and distinguish between the behaviors of the "grind," who reports that he stayed up all night studying for a test, and the "partier," who is hung over from the same night's celebrations, will probably make more accurate predictions about their respective responses to achievement items on a personality questionnaire than an observer who exclusively bases his or her judgments on the stereotypical notion that college students are intellectually motivated.

From this duscussion it may be inferred that college students trained to increase their skills in behavioral observation and social inference should be superior to those who do not receive this training in predicting another student's self-descriptive behaviors. On the other hand, discussions of research reported in the literature suggest that training directed at increasing fantasy behaviors should have little or no effect on empathic skills at the behavioral level.

For example, in a review of the behavior-prediction literature, Shrauger and Altrocchi (1964) point out that prediction paradigms involve a set to be "accurate or realistic" rather than a set "which emphasizes imagination and fantasy." They go on to conclude that a realistic set "is more relevant (than an imaginative set) for understanding the ways in which people characteristically perceive others in real life situations" (p. 290). The difficulty with their conclusion is that, in equating the processes presumed to underlie behavioral prediction paradigms with "the ways in which people characteristically perceive others," they fail to consider other levels of empathy where fantasy may play a more important role.

2.2. The Subjective Level of Empathy

Psychologists interested in a more subjective level of empathy have focused on the acquisition of knowledge about the private meaning of behavior (Harty, 1972; Kohut, 1959) rather than on its prediction. At this level of empathy, the ability to understand another person's subjective experience presumably requires the ability to reflect upon one's own private reality (Blatt, 1963; Greenson, 1960; Kohut, 1959); hence, these theorists have underscored the role of the observer's images and fantasies in "intuiting" the implicit or symbolic meaning of another person's overt behaviors.

For example, Gordon (1972), Horowitz (1972), and Piaget (1962) have noted the close association between mental images, feelings, and highly personalized or symbolic meanings of experience. The use of mental images and fantasies presumably allows the observer to more vividly capture and share in the emotional and symbolic meaning of a seemingly ordinary verbal communication. For example, the statement, "My mother and I like to keep in touch," may elicit an image of a little child connected to a giant "super-mom" via a huge umbilical cord. This image captures a subjective dimension not inherent in the manifest verbal communication.

Nonverbal cues help to explain the usefulness of intuitive images and fantasies in alerting the observer to a seemingly private and yet presumably valid aspect of another person's experience. In proposing an "information processing" model as an alternative to more mystical notions of intuition (cf. Westcott, 1968), Beres and Arlow (1974), and also Berne (1953) hypothesize that latent nonverbal messages, (e.g., tone of voice or body movements) are more revealing of a person's private reality than manifest verbal communications. Furthermore, they propose that unconscious or preconscious fantasy activity acts as a kind of cognitive filter or "mental set" against which these nonverbal cues are "selectively perceived, inhibited, disregarded, or transformed" (Beres and Arlow, 1974, p. 44). Incoming nonverbal data, in turn, has a modifying effect on the observer's initial set, i.e., on preconscious images and fantasies.

Presumably, information from latent nonverbal cues and preexisting preconscious images and fantasies is synthesized and emerges into awareness in the form of a visual image or conscious fantasy, which is in turn associated with an emotional experience. Elicited images, fantasies, and emotions appear to provide the intuitive observer with a clue as to the implied or symbolic meaning of the original communication. A number of writers (Beres and Arlow, 1974; Berne, 1949; Reik, 1937) have underscored the association between the appearance of intuitive images and fantasies in awareness and a relatively passive mode of attention.* This passive and nonanalytic mode of attention

---

* Miller (1972) has empirically demonstrated an association between image modes of mentation and passive, nondirected attention.

differs sharply from the directed, reality-oriented kind of mentation presumed to be associated with acurate prediction of overt behaviors (Shrauger and Altrocchi, 1964).

In sum, this model suggests that training individuals to suspend analtyic, directed modes of attention and to increase their use of fantasy and images in response to interpersonal communications should best increase their capacity to intuit accurately another's subjective experience. Moreover, it implies an association between the capacity to attend to and interpret accurately nonverbal cues and the ability to intuit another's subjective experience, as well as between the ability to intuit another's subjective experience and imaginative skills.

2.2.1. **Identification of Nonverbal Cues.** The arguments presented so far suggest that intuitive images are partially mediated by an ability to attend to and interpret accurately nonverbal cues. However, it does not necessarily follow that a general capacity to identify nonverbal cues correctly is facilitated by imaginative skills. In predicting the effect of fantasy training, on accurate identification of nonverbal cues, it is necessary to consider whether there is any advantage to encoding the original nonverbal data in the form of an image as opposed to a verbal identifier.

The greater amount of information retained in a sensory image (e.g., a mental picture of a scowling face) as opposed to a verbal identifier (e.g., an "angry man") argues for its superiority as a mode of processing nonverbal cues (Sheehan, 1972). By holding on to the "concrete data" in a fleeting nonverbal communication, mental images allow the observer extra time to reevaulate an initial interpretation. Furthermore, because of the association of visual images with "simultaneous" as opposed to "sequential" processing (Horowitz, 1970), the meaning of a particular cue can be more easily considered in terms of its relationship to other (sensory) data. The additional information provided by this other data may be additive (as, for example, when hostility conveyed in a tightly pursed lip is confirmed by an image of a clasped fist); or may change qualitatively the apparent meaning of a particular cue (e.g., a pursed lip in conjunction with an image of a shaky hand may convey anxiety, rather than hostility).

The capacity of images to represent large amounts of information simultaneously may be particularly advantageous in subjective empathy since (a) latent nonverbal messages provide information not contained in the verbal communication; and (b) the implicit meaning of a communication is often dependent upon a total configuration of information rather than an isolated cue. In sum, these arguments reiterate the proposed association between nonverbal cues, subjective empathy, and imaginative processes. Furthermore, they suggest that increasing a person's ability to represent interpersonal events in the form of images should increase his capacity to identify accurately the meaning of nonverbal communications.

2.3. The Psychoanalytic Notion of Empathy

A conceptual bridge between behavioral and subjective levels of empathy discussed above and a cognitive-structural level of empathy, to be discussed below, is readily provided by the psychoanalytic notion of empathy. A number of psychoanalytic writers (Fleiss, 1942; Reik, 1937; Schafer, 1959), have proposed that the acquisition of interpersonal knowledge includes both the observation of the behaviors of others and of one's own private experiences. These writers describe empathy as a two-phase process. The first phase is experiential and imaginative and is characterized by a temporary and partial suspension of reality-oriented thought. Fleiss (1942) refers to the use of fantasy in empathy during this first phase as "conditioned daydreaming." The term "conditioned" is used to underscore the idea that the observer's fantasies and images are initially elicited and constrained by ongoing behavioral observations and previous knowledge of another person.

The emphasis in the second phase is on objective-logical processes. This phase is reflective and reality-oriented and is characterized by the activation of higher-order cognitive role-taking schemes. These structures are active in the validation of "intuitions" and hypotheses from the previous stage against further directed behavioral observations. Furthermore, they serve to integrate interpersonal images and abstract concepts into more complete notions of persons and relationships (Selman, 1974, 1976). Hence, in bridging its behavioral and subjective components, this two-phase psychoanalytic notion of empathy also provides the framework for cognitive-structural integration.

2.4. The Cognitive-Structural Level of Empathy

The notion of cognitive role-taking structures defines the third level of empathy that needs to be considered in relation to imaginative skills. These structures refer to ways of making logical sense of psychosocial reality. Selman (1974, 1976) has described the development of such role-taking schema in terms of an invariant sequence of developmental stages.*

---

* Selman (1976) has demonstrated an isomorphic relationship between social-reasoning stages and logical stages as the latter have been described by Jean Piaget (and Inhelder, 1969).

Selman's stages are abstracted from empirical observations of the way in which persons of different ages resolve interpersonal dilemmas. The relative degree of integration of subjective and objective perspectives into unified and differentiated constructs of persons and relations is presumed to be in large part dependent upon the observer's level of role-taking abilities.

Selman's work (1974, 1976) suggests that the early adolescent confuses subjective realities with shared meanings imputed to behaviors by social expectations and stereotypes. Thus, at what he refers to as a "generalized other" (or stage 3) level of perspective-taking, frequent overabstract and stereotyped references to persons as "selfish," "kind," or "considerate" fail to consider more complex behaviors and levels of experience. In contrast, the middle or late adolescent reasoning at the "qualitative systems" (or stage 4) level of perspective-taking comes to recognize and understand the notion of unconscious processes. Private individualized systems of meaning are now seen as alternatives to, but are not yet integrated with objective behavioral events and shared social realities (e.g., "He doesn't realize his flattery is really a cover for his hostile feelings"). Finally, those late adolescents and young adults who adopt a relativistic (or stage 5) social perspective recognize the reciprocal or mutually interdependent relationship between subjective perspectives and objective social behaviors. For example, in describing her best friend, a relativistic college student remarked: "My roommate knows who I am, knows what I am about, knows what I am doing . . . our interchange feels good to me . . . *she perceives how I perceive myself and doesn't reject that."* These developments have particular relevance for the present study since participants were all late adolescents.

Throughout adolescence, experienced contradictions between subjective and objective social perspectives presumably motivate cognitive restructuring of interpersonal schemas in the direction of a new, more mature integration. In fact, integrated social perspective-taking may be construed as a product of the moderating effect of objective behavioral observation on interpersonal fantasies, and the enriching effect of interpersonal fantasies on objective observations and stereotypical expectations. Overattentiveness to either subjective or objective realities may lead to failure to experience their contradictions and, hence, failure to reevaluate existing schemas. Alternatively, learning to shift attention flexibly between imaginative experiences and objective behaviors and social concerns should highlight these contradictions and lead to more differentiated and integrated cognitive role-taking structures.

So far, in emphasizing the importance of imaginative activities in the development of social perspective-taking, I have stressed the presumed advantages, if not the necessity of attending to both subjective and objective social realities. However, this discussion would not be complete without mention of a number of specific structural properties of images and daydreams that argue for their particular adpativeness in social-cognitive development. These include (a) their association with symbolic meanings and affective experiences; (b) their ability to provide the individual with a means of achieving increased psychological distance from interpersonal events; and (c) their efficiency in simultaneously representing multiple perspectives.

The association between symbolic and implied meanings of experience and interpersonal images and fantasies (Gordon, 1972; Horowitz, 1972; Piaget, 1962) becomes especially significant in the middle or late adolescent's discovery of a multidimensional intrapsychic self. This discovery is characteristic of the transition between a (stage 3) "generalized other" and a (stage 4) "systemic" concept of personality.

An individual employing stereotypical notions of social reality may have difficulty in cognitively assimilating unacknowledged feelings and latent symbolic meanings associated with a particular encounter. Images and fantasies connected to this event and reexperienced in the context of a daydream may be retrospectively "understood" on an emotional level without yet being readily identified or integrated into appropriately complex interpersonal categories (Horowitz, 1972). Experienced contradictions between the initial social perception and the more symbolic daydream experience gradually may lead to an attempt to reflect on and integrate these diverse perspectives into a multilevel dynamic construct of motivation and personality.

For example, unpleasant daydreams of being "killed with kindness" associated with memories of a seemingly amicable social exchange may alert an introspective observer to anxieties about closeness of which he was previously unaware. In addition to its specific content, this discovery potentially includes a growing awareness of the relation of dynamic concerns to behaviors and a notion of unconscious processes.

Daydreaming behaviors also offer an individual an opportunity to gain increased psychological distance from particularly stressful or complex interpersonal events. In an ongoing interpersonal event, a high degree of involvement on the part of each of the actors may make it difficult to stand back and reflect on the nature of the interaction, or on one's own or the other's point of view. Retrospective daydreaming allows the individual to practice her role-taking skills by "replaying" the event repeatedly in a more "muted" (Sarbin, 1972) or neutral context. The capacity of images and fantasies to elicit emotions (Horowitz, 1972), combined with the skillful daydreamer's ability to regulate these emotions by modifying or shifting from a particular image (Singer,

1974a), allows her to reexperience the feelings associated with the interaction without being overwhelmed by their intensity. Gradually, she is able to assimilate the event through modification of her interpersonal schema.

The third property of images that makes them especially adaptive modes of interpersonal representation is their association with simultaneous processing of information (Horowitz, 1972; Singer, 1974b). In a general sense, the development of social reasoning is defined by an increasing ability to consider multiple and alternative perspectives simultaneously. It then follows that the capacity of images as opposed to words (a) to represent self and other and the relationship between self and other simultaneously; and (b) to condense multiple meanings into a "single image format" (Horowitz, 1972, p. 300) makes an image mode of representation especially adaptive in facilitating this development. Because of simultaneous representations interpersonal images facilitate the individual's ability to shift flexibly between alternative perspectives and to momentarily own and experience each (Horowitz, 1972). In brief, experiencing, reflecting on, and attempting to integrate contradictions between alternative points of view represented in interpersonal images and fantasies should lead to cognitive reorganization and to the development of more differentiated and integrated role-taking schema.

2.5. Implications for Empathy Training

To summarize, the notion of empathy may be approached from three different levels of analysis: a behavioral, a subjective, and a cognitive-structural level. These three levels appear to be differentially related to imaginative as opposed to more reality-oriented kinds of processes. Accordingly, from a description of each, it is possible to hypothesize about the type of intervention required to facilitate empathic abilities at all three levels.

At the behavioral level of empathy, accurate predictions of another person's self-descriptive behaviors appear to be mediated by directed behavioral observations and social inferences. Hence, behavioral rather than imaginative kinds of training techniques should be most effective in facilitating empathy at this level.

At the subjective level, intuitive images and fantasies associated with a relatively passive mode of attention seem to provide important clues to the symbolic or implicit meaning of another person's verbal communications. Hence, training individuals to attend to and experience vividly interpersonal images and fantasies in response to interpersonal communications should enhance empathic abilities at the subjective level. Because intuitive images appear to be elicited by nonverbal cues, it may also be hypothesized that the ability to identify implied meanings in verbal communications is positively associated with the ability to accurately identify nonverbal cues. Moreover, the capacity of sensory images to capture and retain information contained in the communicator's nonverbal behaviors implies that interpersonal fantasy training can also increase accurate identification of nonverbal cues.

At the cognitive-structural level, the development of more mature stages of social reasoning appears to involve both behavioral and imaginative modes of observation. The increasing differentiation and integration of subjective and objective perspectives characteristic of the later stages suggests that cognitive-structural development may be facilitated by training in engaging in and reflecting on interpersonal fantasy experiences, and in relating these experiences to objective behavioral observations and social concerns.

3. Research Procedures

3.1. Overview of the Research Plan

The study to be described was designed to test hypotheses about training at each level of empathy. Accordingly, college freshmen at Yale University were randomly assigned to three empathy training conditions: a *behavioral;* an *experiential fantasy;* and a *fantasy-discussion* condition. Two other groups (a naturalistic *fantasy-interest* group consisting of students involved in theater and other fantasy-related activities; and a *comparison* group) provided no treatment controls. Approximately 21 students were in each of the five conditions.

Table I summarizes the training procedures in each training condition, the level of empathy they were designed to facilitate, and the outcome measures used to assess each level. Results were used to test the following hypotheses:

3.2. Hypotheses

1. Training in the *behavioral* and the *fantasy-discussion* conditions in objective behavioral observation and social inference will facilitate accurate prediction of self-descriptive behaviors in response to a personality inventory.

Table I. Training Procedures, Levels of Empathy, and Empathy Measures

Empathy training conditions	Empathy training procedures	Level of empathy	Operational definition	Empathy measure
Behavioral	Training in describing interpersonal events and goals in behavioral terms; applying behavioral principles to bring about behavioral change	Behavioral	Accurate predictions of another student's self-descriptive responses to a personality inventory	Accurate Predictions of Attitudes Test
Experiential fantasy	Training in free-association and vivid imagery techniques; experiencing interpersonal fantasies in response to social communications	Subjective	Accurate identification of implied meanings in 40 taped verbal messages	Test of Implied Meanings
		Nonverbal sensitivity	Accurate identification of visual and auditory nonverbal cues in a 45-minute film	Profile of Nonverbal Sensitivity
Fantasy discussion	Same as experiential fantasy plus training in reflecting on and relating fantasies to objective perspectives and behavioral events	Cognitive-structural	Use of mature levels of social reasoning in resolving a hypothetical interpersonal dilemma	Social Reasoning Interview
		(Behavioral, subjective, nonverbal sensitivity)[a]	(Same as above)	(Same as above)

[a] Because the fantasy-discussion condition included both an objective-behavioral and an imaginative component, it was expected to facilitate empathy at the behavioral and subjective as well as at the cognitive structural level.

2. Training in the *experiential-fantasy* condition and the *fantasy-discussion* condition in interpersonal experiential-fantasy techniques will facilitate identification of implied meanings in verbal communications. The fantasy-related activities of members of the *fantasy-interest* group, most analogous to those in the experiential-fantasy condition, will also facilitate this skill.

3. Training in the *fantasy-discussion* condition in experiencing and reflecting on interpersonal fantasy experiences and in relating these fantasy experiences to objective reality events will facilitate the development of more differentiated and integrated levels of social reasoning in resolving a hypothetical interpersonal dilemma.

4. Training in the *experiential-fantasy*, *fantasy-discussion*, and *fantasy-interest* conditions in interpersonal experiential-fantasy techniques will facilitate accurate identification of nonverbal auditory and visual communications. Moreover, persons skilled in identifying accurately implied meanings in verbal communications should also be skilled in identifying accurately nonverbal cues.

Differential effects of training on the content and structure of daydreaming behaviors were also explored by means of a posttreatment daydreaming log. While not in the form of a formal hypothesis, fantasy training was expected in some way to effect self-reported daydreaming patterns.

3.3. Empathy Training Conditions

Each training condition included five small training groups with approximately four students in each. Two 2-hour followed by eight 1-hour training sessions were conducted over a five-week period. The seven advanced undergraduate women who led the training groups all had some academic and clinical training in psychology. Training group leaders were assigned to conditions in such a way as to provide a means for statistically assessing possible confounding effects due to differences in leader effectiveness or degree of leader blindness (cf. Frank, 1977).*

3.3.1. Behavioral Training Condition. The behavioral training condition was designed to teach participants to make detailed behavioral observations and to apply behavioral principles in modifying peer interactions. Training began with a gradated series of exercises that introduced students to behavioral constructs and principles† and

---

* Each of six leaders ran two training groups within the same or different conditions. Of these, three were blind for two of the three training conditions and three were blind for one of the three training conditions. The experimenter ran one group in each of the three training conditions.

† Adapted from Patterson (1971).

taught them to break down real-life events and interpersonal goals into detailed verbal and nonverbal behaviors. Participants were then instructed how to fill out a "behavior problem solving sheet." This sheet was used to record actual behaviors in an interpersonal interaction with a peer and to plan new behaviors that would respectively elicit or decrease desired or undesired responses. Learning to choose appropriate reinforcements and to shape peer behaviors required students to make accurate, behaviorally based inferences about the other person in order to predict his or her response correctly.

Following the initial training session, students were presented each week with a different interpersonal situation with which to apply the behavioral procedures that they had learned. These situations consisted of a general description of a social interaction with peers (e.g., "trying to help a troubled friend") for which they were asked to provide a recent example from their own experiences.

Treatment hours were divided into two alternating segments. Three 15-minute "social problem solving" segments were used to apply the behavioral worksheet procedure to an interpersonal situation. During each of these segments, a different student was selected to act as "speaker" and was asked to describe a personal example of the week's interpersonal situation to the group. With help from other group members, speakers used the behavior problem solving sheet to analyze their own and their peer's behaviors and to develop a program for modifying the interaction in the direction of their interpersonal goals.

Three five-minute "cognitive problem solving segments" provided a change of pace while preventing any further discussion between the social segments. During these shorter segments, students worked on a timed cognitive task consisting of visual-spatial analogy problems.

3.3.2. Experiential Fantasy Training Condition.

This condition was designed to teach participants to attend to and experience vividly interpersonal images and fantasies in response to interpersonal communications. Following a brief introduction to relaxation procedures (Lazarus, 1971), initial training began with a gradated series of practice exercises designed to teach participants to attend to and experience vividly interpersonal images and to allow their images and fantasies to flow in a free-associative, undirected way.

Treatment hours were again divided into two alternating segments. In a 15-minute "fantasy segment," participants were relaxed on the floor and asked to visualize the week's "scene." Scenes were identical to the social-problem situations in the behavioral condition. After encouraging participants to let their minds wander to images and fantasies elicited by the scene, the leader selected a "speaker" to give a detailed description of his or her fantasy to the group. Speakers were asked to describe the behaviors, thoughts, and feelings of the persons in their fantasies; to imagine themselves as each person in the scene; and to describe the interaction from each person's point of view. While each spoke, other members were told to imagine what the speaker was "seeing" and "feeling." This procedure was followed by a five-minute cognitive segment identical to that used in the behavioral condition.

3.3.3. Fantasy-Discussion Training Condition.
This condition was designed to teach participants to engage in and to reflect on interpersonal fantasy experiences, and to relate these experiences to real-life behaviors and social concerns. Initial training procedures were identical to those in the experiential-fantasy condition with one important exception. Participants in the fantasy-discussion condition were trained to use a "fantasy analysis questionnaire" to reflect on their fantasy experiences. A series of open-ended questions (e.g., "How was your friend's behavior different in your fantasy than in real life?") helped students to explore contradictions between real-life interactions and imaginary events; and between their own fantasy experiences and those of other group members. Leaders in this condition were trained not to provide responses nor to probe nor interpret responses of participants. Members, however, were free to engage in the discussion at any level. Training sessions in this condition were divided into alternating 10-minute fantasy and 10-minute discussion segments.

3.4. Outcome Measures

3.4.1. Empathy Measures.
Following training, participants in all five conditions were assessed for their empathic abilities at the behavioral, subjective, and cognitive-structural levels, and for their ability to identify accurately nonverbal cues. The relation of empathy measures to levels of empathy, and to experimental predictions is illustrated in Table I (p. 319).

The behavioral level of empathy was assessed by the Accurate Predictions of Attitudes Measure. This measure is comprised of a 50-item true-false attitudes questionnaire*; students were required to predict another student's self-descriptive response to each of the 50 items following an initial 15-minute encounter.

---

* Items were selected from nine scales of the Personality Research Form (PRF, Form A, Jackson, 1965). These scales were chosen because of their relative effectiveness in differentiating between a large group of Yale students in a previous study. The choice of differentiating items was designed to increase the range of actual differences between students in their responses to the inventory, such that accurate predictions of these responses could not rest predominantly on a global stereotype of the "Yale student," and would instead have to be responsive to behavioral indicators of these differences.

The subjective level of empathy was assessed by the Test of Implied Meanings (Sundberg, 1966), a 20-minute test consisting of 40 taped verbal messages, 20 spoken by a male and 20 spoken by a female. The listener is instructed to mark one of four choices indicating possible implicit meanings.

The cognitive-structural level of empathy was measured by the Test of Social Reasoning (Selman, 1974, 1976). This measure uses an interview format to assess an individual's level of social reasoning in resolving a hypothetical dilemma, in this case a conflict between the achievement needs of two friends in a competitive situation.

Accuracy in identifying nonverbal cues was measured by the Profile of Nonverbal Sensitivity (Rosenthal, Archer, DiMatteo, Koivumaki, and Rogers, 1976) a 45-minute sound black and white motion picture made up of 220 two-second nonverbal messages. The observer has to choose for each message which of two alternative situations, (e.g. talking to a lost child versus returning an item to a store) correctly matches the nonverbal message. A total of 20 interpersonal situations are portrayed, all by the same young woman. Each is represented in 11 different channels, including three pure visual channels (face, body, and face and body), two pure audio channels, (pitch and intensity without sequence, and sequence and rhythm with muffled pitch) and six compound channels, (combinations of each audio with each video channel). The 20 situations are also categorized by four types of content including positive-dominant, positive-submissive, negative-dominant, and negative-submissive messages.

3.4.2. Daydreaming Log. Participants in the three experimental and fantasy-interest groups also completed a posttreatment daydreaming log, a procedure for keeping a week-long record of their fantasy experiences. Fantasy was broadly defined as any "stimulus independent thought" (Antrobus, Singer, Goldstein, and Fortgang, 1970), i.e., any thought that is not directly related to the activity (such as solving a math problem or driving a car) in which the observer is presently engaged.

By way of written instructions, participants were taught to "sample" their three most vivid fantasies at six different times during the day; samples were to be taken during social interactions as well as solitary moments. A printed index card provided students with a model to rate each of their fantasies on a series of scaled descriptive categories. Dimensions included a brief description of the content, a five-point rating of vividness, and an indication of mode(s), including visual, auditory, and/or bodily concerns. Eight affects were also rated for each fantasy on a five-point scale (fear, distress, surprise, interest, shame, joy, contempt, and anger).

324   Susan J. Frank

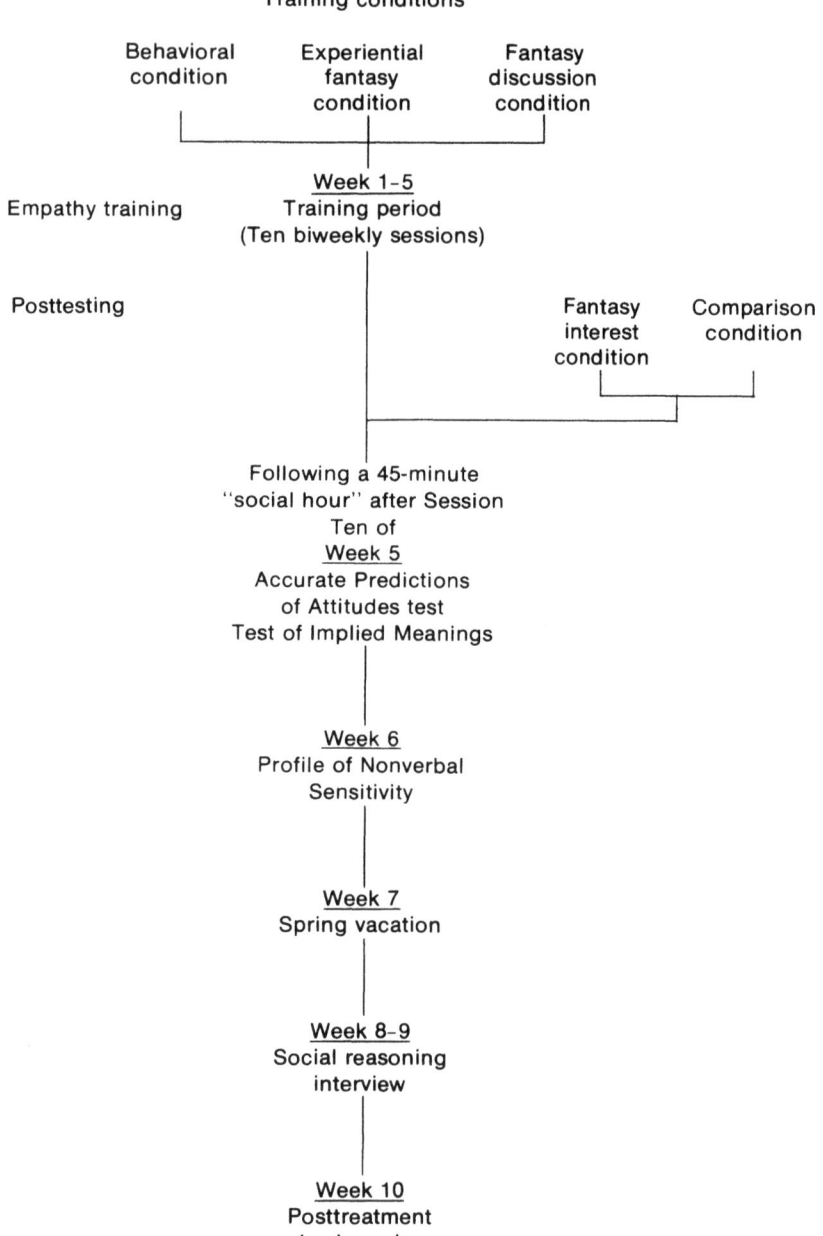

Figure 1. Sequence and timing of the empathy training and administration of outcome measures.

3.4.3. Administration and Scoring Procedures.

A flow chart illustrating the sequence and timing of the empathy training and administration of the outcome measures is provided in Figure 1. Since the Accurate Predictions of Attitudes Measure and the Test of Implied Meanings were administered in the same evening, it was necessary to control for a possible order effect. Hence, 46 students completed the behavior-prediction test before the implied meanings test, while 61 students completed these measures in reverse order.

With the exception of the experimenter, three other interviewers who conducted the social-reasoning interviews were blind for treatment conditions of the interviewees. Careful probing of responses was to ensure against the possibility that sophisticated verbal skills would camouflage lower-stage reasoning through the use of seemingly higher-stage phrases.

Scoring for the Accurate Predictions of Attitudes test and the Test of Implied Meanings was based on number of correct responses. For the Profile of Nonverbal Sensitivity, participants received a score for the number of correct responses in each of the 11 audio and visual channels and four content areas, as well as a total score for all 220 items. Stage scores for the social-reasoning interview were based on descriptions provided by Selman (1974) of each of the five developmental stages of social reasoning.* Protocols were scored blind by the investigator.

4. Results of the Study

Results of the four empathy measures were analyzed by analysis of variance procedures using a Sex × Treatment (× Order) design. To control for intelligence, SAT scores were covaried with treatment effects when appropriate.† These variance analyses treated participants as individuals rather than as members of particular subgroups.‡

---

* Since research up until now has focused primarily on younger children, the investigator worked with Selman to determine a set of specific criteria for scoring the higher stages.
† No significant differences between conditions on any of the SAT measures of intelligence were found. Verbal SAT scores correlated significantly with accuracy in identifying implied meanings in verbal communications ($r = .30, p > .001$) and with level of social reasoning ($r = .22, p > .01$). Math SAT scores were related to total sensitivity on the Profile of Nonverbal Sensitivity ($r = .19, p > .05$).
‡ With the exception of the social-reasoning data, effects for subgroups within treatments were not significant ($p > .10$; cf. Winer (1971)). Additional analyses to explore possible confounding effects due to differences in degree of leader blindness or leader effectiveness indicated that other variables (sex, order, treatment) could better account for the findings. A more detailed discussion of these issues can be found in Frank (1976).

Table II. Analysis of Covariance for Accuracy Scores for the Accurate Predictions of Attitudes Test

Source	df	MS	F
Main effects	6		.91[a]
Treatment	4	80.33	4.31
Sex	1	17.01	.69[b]
Order	1	142.32	8
Two-way interactions			.94
T × S	4	31.72	1.06
T × O	4	17.42	1.01
S × O	1	.128	
Three-way interactions			.19
T × S × O	4	35.95	2
Within cells	87	16.37	
Total	106	20.58	

[a] $p < .01$.
[b] $p < .001$.

4.1. Major Findings

Findings supported predicted effects of empathy training for both the behavioral and cognitive-structural levels. Predictions for the subjective level were partially supported. Specifically, tests of the major hypotheses (Tables II–V) showed the following:

4.1.1. Behavioral Predictions. As predicted, participants in the behavioral- and fantasy-discussion conditions made more accurate predictions of their partner's self-descriptive behaviors on the Accurate Predictions of Attitudes personality inventory than participants in the experiential-fantasy, fantasy-interest, or comparison conditions ($t = 3.35$, $df = 102$; cf. $p < .001$, Table II, Figure 2). Hence, training in objective reality-oriented observation and social inference seems to facilitate empathy at the behavioral level. An unexpected order effect also shows that persons who took the attitude-prediction measure before rather than after the Test of Implied Meanings made more accurate behavioral predictions ($p < .01$).

4.1.2. Identification of Implied Meanings. Predictions for the Test of Implied Meanings (Table III, Figure 3), a measure of subjective empathy, were partially confirmed by the data. The facilitating role of fantasy training in identifying implicit meanings in verbal communications was supported by the performance of participants in the experiential-fantasy and fantasy-interest* groups but not by that of par-

---

* This finding corroborates that of Sundberg (1966), who reports that acting experience facilitates performance on the Test of Implied Meanings.

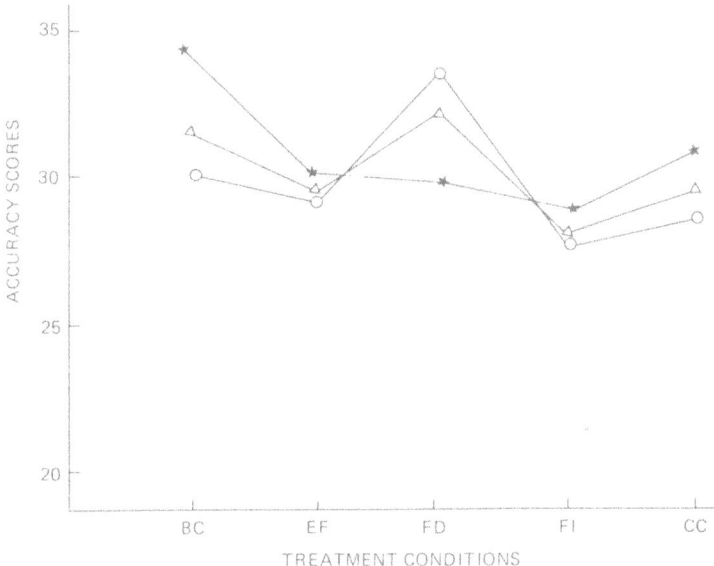

Figure 2. Plotted accuracy scores for the Accurate Predictions of Attitudes test for condition and sex. BC = behavioral condition; EF = experiential fantasy condition; FD = fantasy discussion condition; FI = fantasy interest condition; CC = comparison condition. Males ○———; females ★———; total △———.

Table III. Analysis of Covariance for Accuracy Scores for the Test of Implied Meanings

Source	df	MS	F
Covariates			
Verbal SAT	1	211.44	13.44
Main Effects			
Treatment	4	59.52	3.78[a]
Sex	1	238.12	15.14[b]
Order	1	.36	.02
Two-way interactions			
T × S	4	23.19	1.47
T × O	4	11.71	.74
S × O	1	25.87	1.64
Three-way interactions			
T × S × O	4	1.36	.09
Within cells	86	15.73	
Total	106	21.71	

[a] $p < .01$.
[b] $p < .001$.

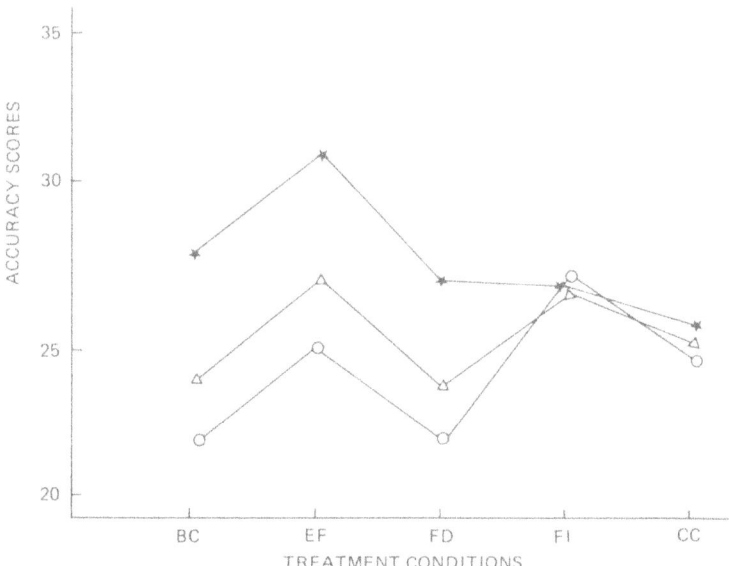

Figure 3. Plotted accuracy scores for the Test of Implied Meanings. BC = behavioral condition; EF = experiential fantasy condition; FD = fantasy discussion condition; FI = fantasy interest condition; CC = comparison condition. Males ○———; females ★———; total △———.

ticipants in the fantasy-discussion condition ($t = 3.05$, df = 102, $p < .01$).* In effect, when training in experiential modes of fantasy was combined with training in more reflective and analytic processes, accuracy appeared to suffer. A strong overall superiority for women in identifying implied meanings ($p < .001$) is consistent with the general belief that women are more "intuitive" than men.

4.1.3. Levels of Social Reasoning. Analysis of the data from the social-reasoning interview, a cognitive-structural measure of empathy, supported the hypothesis that training in experiencing and reflecting on fantasy experiences and in relating these experiences to objective events would facilitate the use of more differentiated and integrated stages of social reasoning in resolving a hypothetical interpersonal dilemma. As predicted, participants in the fantasy discussion group used higher levels of social reasoning than participants in other training conditions ($t = 3.75$, df = 100, $p < .001$; Table IV, Figure 4).† Moreover,

---

* This comparison of the experiential-fantasy and fantasy-interest groups versus the fantasy-discussion, behavioral, and comparison groups was unplanned.

† Reliability for 20 randomly selected protocols rescored by Selman was quite satisfactory ($r = .91$, $p > .001$).

Empathy Through Training in Imagination

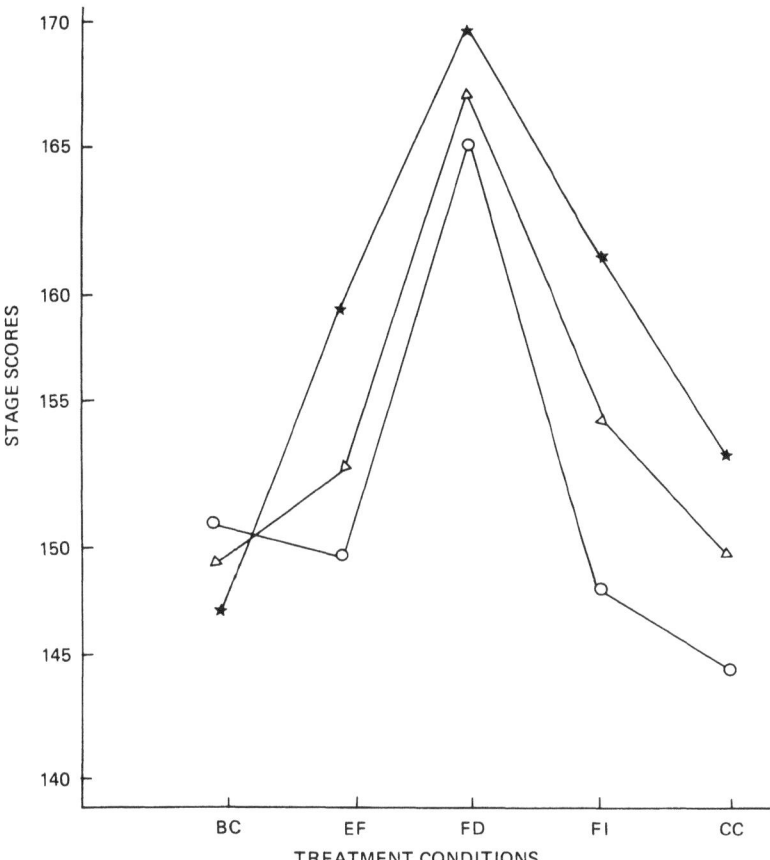

Figure 4. Plotted stage scores for the Test of Social Reasoning for condition and sex. BC = behavioral condition; EF = experiential fantasy condition; FD = fantasy discussion condition; FI = fantasy interest condition; CC = comparison condition. Males ○———; females ★———; total △———.

these participants tended to show more frequent awareness of Stage 5 psychological relativism in reasoning about interpersonal dilemmas ($x = 35.53, p < .001$, Table V).

Findings for the social-reasoning data were qualified by the sharply deviant performance of one subgroup in the fantasy-discussion condition. The mean for this subgroup was in the opposite direction of what was predicted.* A discussion of this issue will be taken up in the section that follows.

---

* Because a significant subgroup within treatment effect ($F = 2.61, df = 12,35, p < .05$) was a function of this one very deviant group, the data were analyzed as planned, based on the individual within treatment error term.

4.1.4. Identification of Nonverbal Cues.

As predicted, accuracy in identifying nonverbal cues was positively correlated with accuracy in identifying implicit meanings in verbal communications ($r = .44$, $p < .001$). However, results for the total score on the Profile of Nonverbal Sensitivity test did not support the hypothesis that training in experiential interpersonal fantasy techniques would facilitate accurate identification of nonverbal cues. While for the total sample women were found to be more sensitive than men ($p < .01$), an overall treatment effect for the total score was not significant (Table VI; Figure 5). However, some unexpected findings to be reported below provide tentative support for the original hypothesis.

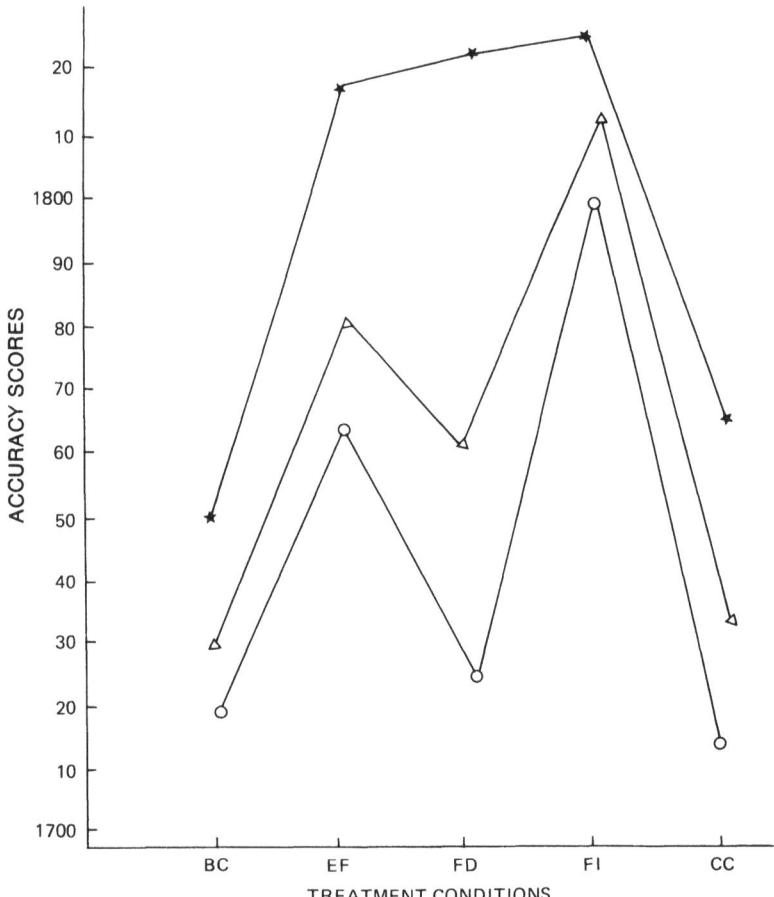

Figure 5. Plotted total accuracy scores for the Profile of Nonverbal Sensitivity test for condition and sex. BC = behavioral condition; EF = experiential fantasy condition; FD = fantasy discussion condition; FI = fantasy interest condition; CC = comparison condition. Males ○——; females ★——; total △——.

Table IV. Analysis of Covariance for Stage Score[b] for the Test of Social Reasoning

Source	df	MS	F
Covariates			
Verbal SAT	1	16.54	5.51[a]
Main Effects			
Treatment	4	10.35	3.44[b]
Sex	1	8.82	2.94
Two-way interactions			
T × S	4	2.51	.84
Within cells	94	3.00	
Total	104	3.45	

[a] $p < .05$.
[b] A weighted scoring system was used to translate full and transitional stage scores into ordinal data.

4.2. Additional Findings

Three sets of additional findings serve to clarify—and also qualify—the original predictions:

4.2.1. Sex Differences.
Differences in overall performance and in effects of training for males as opposed to female participants on a number of empathy measures were not predicted. These differences include the following:

1. Females were superior to males in accurately identifying implied meanings in verbal communications and in accurately identifying nonverbal communications; hence, females may be more skilled than males in adopting a passive, imaginative mode of attention presumed to enhance performance on these two tasks.

Table V. Frequency Distributions of Social-Reasoning Stage for Each Condition

	Social-reasoning stage			
Treatment condition	Stage 3[a]	Stage 3/4	Stage 4[b]	Stage 4/5 and 5[c]
Behavioral	0	11	10	2
Experiential fantasy	0	5	16	0
Fantasy discussion	1	4	6	10
Fantasy interest	3	4	10	3
Comparison	1	10	6	3

[a] Stage 3 refers to a "generalized other" level of perspective-taking.
[b] Stage 4 refers to a "qualitative-systems" level of perspective-taking.
[c] Stage 5 refers to a "relativistic" level of perspective-taking.

2. Though not significant, females in the three fantasy-related conditions were visibly (Figure 5) more accurate in identifying nonverbal cues than males and females in other conditions.

3. In making accurate behavioral predictions, females trained in objective behavioral observation and males trained in reflective fantasy techniques tended to benefit most from the interventions (Figure 2).

4. In identifying implicit meanings in verbal communications (Figure 3) females tended to benefit most from training in experiential interpersonal fantasy techniques; whereas males tended to be negatively effected by the two treatment procedures that included analytic reality-oriented modes of observation.

4.2.2. Compound versus Pure Nonverbal Messages.

In addition to the suggestive findings for females in the fantasy-related conditions (see 2, above), a separate study of results for "compound" as opposed to "pure" channels for the Profile of Nonverbal Sensitivity provided some further support for the original hypothesis that training in imaginative skills would facilitate accurate identification of nonverbal cues. Specifically, training in the three fantasy-related conditions was found to have enhanced sensitivity to nonverbal stimuli when messages included *both* audio and visual channels ($p < .05$, $F = 2.47$, $df = 4,105$; Figure 6) but not when they included only sound or visual channels.

This finding is as intriguing as it is unexpected. It may be that visual and verbal representations are equally efficient in identifying single channel communications. The superiority of visual images in facilitating identification of "compound" messages could be explained by the association of mental pictures with simultaneous processing; this association would enable the trained observer to take advantage of the added information in multichannel communications.

Table VI. Analysis of Covariance for Total Accuracy Scores for the Profile of Nonverbal Sensitivity

Source	df	MS	F
Covariates			
Math SAT	1	7492.39	4.24[a]
Main effects			
Treatment	4	17953.24	1.60
Sex	1	97108.34	8.67[b]
Two-way interactions			
T × S	4	3027.49	.27
Within cells	105	12455.27	

[a] $p < .05$.
[b] $p < .01$.

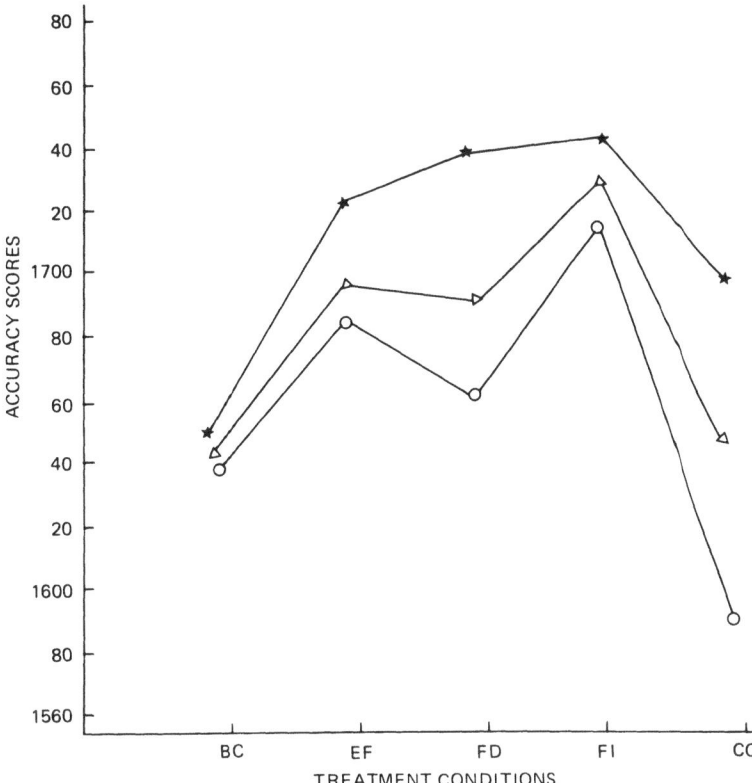

Figure 6. Plotted accuracy scores for identification of nonverbal communications in video and audio (compound) channels for the Profile of Nonverbal Sensitivity. BC = behavioral condition; EF = experiential fantasy condition; FD = fantasy discussion condition; FI = fantasy interest condition; CC = comparison condition. Males ○———; females ★———; total △———.

4.2.3. Daydreaming Log. The data from the daydreaming log provided a third set of additional findings. While no specific predictions were made, it was assumed that the fantasy interventions would have an effect on the structure and content of subsequent daydreams. To explore this hypothesis, mean scores for each of the daydreaming dimensions were correlated with "membership" in a treatment condition.*

---

* Conditions were coded as "dummy" variables such that each could be correlated with mean scores for each of the daydreaming dimensions. Means were based on the total number of fantasies recorded. Seventy-eight of the 86 participants in the three experimental and fantasy-interest conditions submitted daydreaming logs. Because of the small N and the low magnitude of the correlations, this data must be treated as exploratory.

Table VII. Daydreaming Variables: Significant Correlations with Treatment Conditions[a]

	Treatments			
Daydreaming variable	Behavioral	Experiential fantasy	Fantasy discussion	Fantasy interest
Vividness		−.27[c]		
Future		.24[b]		
Complexity of interpersonal interaction			.29[c]	
Distress–anguish			.20[b]	
Contempt–disgust				−.25[b]
Surprise–startle			.28[c]	
Number of affects				−.25[b]
Achievement		.20[b]		
Failure		.24[b]		
Guilt		−.26[c]	.19[b]	
Romantic			.23[b]	
Adventure				.18[b]
Immediate bodily concerns	.27[c]	−.19[b]	−.19[b]	
Social–political			.22[b]	
Loneliness		.37[c]		
Mystical			.24[c]	−.19[b]
Self as subject			−.21[b]	
Boyfriend–girl friend			.19[b]	

[a] $N = 78$. For a more complete list of variables the reader is referred to Frank (1976).
[b] $p < .05$.
[c] $p < .01$.

The major findings are summarized in Table VII. The most interesting of these are for students in the fantasy discussion condition. Post-treatment daydreams for participants in this condition were characterized by more anguish and surprise; by a diversity of content, including themes relating to guilt, but also to social-political, romantic, and mystical concerns; and most important, by more complex interpersonal interactions. In general, training in reflecting on daydream experiences appears to be associated with a later increased use of these experiences for working through and assimilating interpersonal conflicts and concerns.

The subsequent fantasies of individuals in the experiential-fantasy condition tended to be more concerned with self, (e.g., personal achievement and failure) than with relationships with others.* For participants in both fantasy-training conditions, daydreams following

---

* The negative relationship between vividness and membership in this condition may be due to labeling effects. After the intense fantasy experiences in the training sessions, ordinary daydreams may have seemed pale.

Table VIII. Correlations between Image Modality in Daydreams and Three Measures of Empathy[g]

	Empathy measure		
Image modality	PONS[d] (nonverbal sensitivity)	TIM[e] (sensitivity to implied meanings)	APA[f] (behavioral prediction)
Visual	.21[b]	.26[a]	.18
Auditory	−.05	−.01	−.18
Physicalistic	−.15	−.16	−.20[c]

[a] $p < .01$.
[b] $p < .05$.
[c] $p < .10$.
[d] PONS = Profile of Nonverbal Sensitivity Test.
[e] TIM = Test of Implied Meanings.
[f] APA = Accurate Predictions of Attitudes Test.
[g] $N = 78$.

the training periods were unlikely to include immediate bodily concerns. The reverse is true for the behavioral condition in which a positive relationship to bodily concerns was accompanied by a tendency to be more situation-bound ($r = .18, p < .06$). Thus, compared to persons who received training in fantasy, those trained in behavioral observation seemed less able to distance their thought activity from immediate incoming stimuli from their own bodies or from the immediate environment.

Two additional analyses of the relationship between some of the daydreaming variables and particular empathic abilities are especially relevant to the present discussion. These results are presented in Tables VIII and IX. The significant relationship between visual images re-

Table IX. Significant Correlations between Positive and Negative Content in Daydreams about Self and Other and Sensitivity to Positive and Negative Content in Nonverbal Communications[c]

	Fantasy content			
Nonverbal content	Positive-self	Positive-other	Negative-self	Negative-other
Positive submissive		.27[b]		
Positive dominant		.25[a]		−.25[a]
Negative submissive				−.31[b]
Negative dominant				
Total PONS score		.21[a]		−.26[b]

[a] $p < .05$.
[b] $p < .01$.
[c] $N = 78$.

ported in subsequent daydream experiences and accurate identification of implicit and nonverbal communications suggests the possibility that this type of mentation facilitates empathy. While visual images appear to play a facilitating role, both physicalist and auditory images seem to interfere with or be unrelated to empathy.

The findings that daydreaming about positive experiences with others is associated with accurate identification of positive nonverbal communications supports the notion that daydreams provide an opportunity to practice empathic skills. The negative relationship between nonverbal sensitivity and negative interpersonal content in daydreams is consistent with findings by Gould (1972) that showed that hostile fantasy content in small children is associated with a deficit of empathic abilities.

5. Discussion

5.1. Review of the Findings: Some "Ifs," "Ands," and "Buts"

When viewed as a whole, the empirical evidence solidly supports the general hypothesis that individuals can be trained to harness their imaginative activities in order to increase their empathic abilities. Support for the original hypotheses was strongest for empathy at the behavioral and cognitive-structural levels. More moderate support was also found for predictions at the subjective level. On the other hand, for each of the three levels of empathy, the predicted effects of training were more or less qualified by some unexpected "ifs", "ands," and "buts." Of these, I have chosen three: (a) the differential effects of training for male versus female participants, (b) the significant "order" effect for behavioral and subjective measures of empathy, and (c) the vulnerability of the fantasy discussion training procedures to differences in group process, as topics for further discussion.

5.1.1. Sex Differences at the Behavioral and Subjective Levels.
At both the behavioral and subjective levels of empathy, training appeared to have a differential effect for male versus female participants. In making behavioral predictions, females in the behavioral condition and males in the fantasy-discussion condition tended to benefit more from treatment procedures than members of the opposite sex. This finding suggests that fantasy may in part mediate accurate empathy even at the behavioral level, and that each sex may have gained a skill that they did not initially have. Females, usually found to be more fanciful and to have more vivid fantasies and images than males (e.g.,

Marks, 1972), presumably increased their skills in reality-oriented modes of observation as a result of training in behavioral techniques. Males who typically interpret their experience in a more analytic and reality-oriented way, through training in reflective daydreaming, probably became more skilled in imaginative modes of observation. It is possible that having recourse to both modes is more effective than recourse to only one in making accurate predictions.

In contrast, at the subjective level of empathy, training in more reality-oriented modes of observation in two of the three empathy training conditions appeared to have a negative effect on the empathic abilities of male participants. Males in both the fantasy discussion and behavioral conditions tended to have decreased in their ability to identify accurately implicit meanings in verbal communications as compared to males and females in other conditions. This finding supports the position of Berne (1953) and others that directed, analytic, and reality-oriented modes of interpersonal observation interfere with intuitive processes, and furthermore suggests that males are specially vulnerable to this interference. However, if, as has been proposed above, the superior performance of the males in the fantasy-discussion condition in predicting overt self-descriptive behaviors can be accounted for by the incorporation of imaginative modes of observation into more habitual analytic and reality-oriented patterns, the question arises as to what prevented them from using these newly learned modes in acquiring more subjective kinds of interpersonal knowledge.

A possible cognitive explanation proposes a complex interaction between training procedures in the fantasy-discussion condition, the participants' habitual mode of observation, and the nature of the empathy task. Learning to shift between two radically different levels of interpersonal observation made the training procedures in the fantasy-discussion condition especially difficult. Moreover, it is conceivable that the requirement to alternate between a habitual active reality-oriented mode and a less familiar passive imaginative mode was more difficult, confusing, and even anxiety-producing for the males in this condition than the requirement to shift between a habitual imaginative and a more reality-oriented mode for the females in the same condition.

For the males, lack of experience with more passive imaginative modes of experiencing may have resulted in a related inability to regulate comfortably the intrusion of newly acquired, and therefore unstable imagery experiences into more familiar forms of mentation and social perception. Hence, overactivation of an inhibition factor, observed and described by Miller (1972), that suppresses the intrusion of image modes of representation in abstract directed thought may in part account for their particularly poor performance on a task that presumably required and pulled for a passive imaginative form of mentation.*

The pull of the Test of Implied Meanings for a predominantly passive imaginative mode of observation can be contrasted with that of the Accurate Predictions of Attitudes test. In the behavior-prediction task participants focus on reality-oriented concerns and actively engage in a discussion with a partner, while in the implied meanings task they listen silently to a series of taped messages in a relatively subdued setting. Under the former conditions the males in the fantasy-discussion condition may have been more comfortable and, in fact, especially skilled in using their newly acquired fantasy skills in the context of a structured interaction. In this context, images of themselves in the place of their partners hiking in the mountains during spring vacation or spending their time finishing overdue term papers may have aided them in developing more differentiated stereotypes, more careful social inferences, and hence more accurate behavioral predictions.

5.1.2. Interference of an Induced "Implied Meanings" Set on Predictive Accuracy.

The relatively poor performance of students who took the behavior-prediction measure after rather than before the Test of Implied Meanings provides a related though somewhat different example of decreased performance associated with difficulty in shifting cognitive set. This finding is probably a result of the specific set elicited by the Test of Implied Meanings, i.e., by the instructions to look for implied meanings, and the subdued, fantasy-inducing ambience of the testing situation. A focus on implicit meanings may easily have resulted in confusion between intended and unintended meanings. This confusion presumably interfered with predictive accuracy when judging the way another person would describe himself to a relative stranger in a testing situation.

Failure to differentiate implicit from manifest communications neglects the demands of reality and/or defensive processes. A similar phenomenon is often observed in clinical-psychology training programs. As first-year students become increasingly attuned to underlying dynamic meanings in interpersonal communications, they frequently are observed to forget the warning in an anecdote about Sigmund Freud. When questioned about the "dynamic meaning" of his penchant for smoking cigars, the analyst is said to have replied "sometimes a cigar is just a cigar."

---

* Dynamic conflict surrounding issues of activity-passivity and, relatedly, an association between fantasy and feminization may also have been contributing factors for the males.

5.1.3. The Effect of Group Process on Training at the Cognitive-Structural Level.
The hypothesis that training in experiencing and objectively reflecting on fantasy experiences would facilitate empathy at the cognitive-structural level was qualified somewhat by the deviant and negative findings for one subgroup in the fantasy-discussion condition. In special cases, training procedures appear to be vulnerable to the effects of individual differences on group process. Some anecdotal evidence describing the interaction in this group will help to explain the apparent ineffectiveness of training procedures on the social-reasoning stages of the participants and, more important, will also provide some insight into the way in which these procedures were effective, when they were effective, in leading to cognitive restructuring in the four other subgroups.

The subgroup in question was led by the experimenter and included four males and one female. Tensions in the group derived from a number of different sources, in particular a high degree of defensiveness among all the participants; radically different and often clashing personalities; and a tendency to withdraw on the part of three of the participants who might have offered a more positive balance to the negativistic stance toward the treatment procedures adopted by the two more aggressive members of the group. Furthermore, the presence of the experimenter, who was seen as having special status and authority in a group in which power and control were salient issues, could only have increased the tensions already present. A brief consideration of the personality of each member, inferred both from their fantasies and the ensuing discussion, will serve to clarify the nature of some of these difficulties.

One male in the group was a black student from the South who was struggling to find a place for himself in a white Anglo-Saxon Protestant Ivy League university and whose *modus operandi* for dealing with other white students was to withdraw into a sullen silence. A second male was a highly intellectualized, obsessive young man who thought, and said, that "psychology is a lot of bull," and that behavior has basically one clear-cut meaning. A third male, the only person in the study demonstrating no sign of an intrapsychic (stage 4) perspective, was a somewhat obstreperous, externally oriented individual who could easily be engaged in a warm and friendly discussion about sports, but had real difficulty looking at his thoughts and feelings. His fantasies almost invariably included themes of power and control in which he as the underdog secretly pulled the strings of seemingly powerful puppet dictators. He and the intellectual student were informal leaders for approximately two-thirds of the training sessions. The fourth male, like the black student, tended to withdraw from the interaction. During the fantasy segment he became very absorbed in his experiences and at times seemed to slip away into his own world, often having difficulty reporting what he was experiencing. Finally, the only woman in the group, already isolated by her sex, also physically as well as socially set herself apart from other members of the group.

Not surprisingly, the discussion segments in this group often involved little interaction. Questions posed from the fantasy-analysis questionnaire were frequently responded to with brief negative replies: "My fantasy doesn't tell me anything," or "My friend is just the way I saw him in my daydream." Furthermore the two male leaders in the group often tried to make the situation into a humorous joke, while the black student looked angry but said little, and the two other members withdrew.

Considering this state of affairs, what was interesting about this group was that any movement occurred at all. Yet, largely, it seemed, as a result of the experiential fantasy aspect, gradual movement began to take place. For some of the group, insight into others' experiences seemed to precede insights into their own. For example, the intellectual young man suddenly noted that the woman's fantasies always included some sort of architectural structures in which she surrounded herself, and that these self-imposed boundaries seemed somehow related to where she usually sat in the room.

The most impressive change, however, came from the black student who seemed to develop an increasing capacity for insight.* In response to a scene in which he was to imagine himself "alone in a crowd of people," this student saw himself at a party. He was sitting in a corner on a black luggage trunk, disdainfully watching the movements of a popular white student. From his own perspective he described the white student as a snob who could never consider talking to a black southern peon like himself. However, in placing himself in the white student's shoes and describing himself through this student's eyes, he spoke about the white student's perspective of himself as a snob who was too taken with himself to join the group and probably "hated white people, anyway." The look of surprise and wonder on the black student's face at the end of the daydreaming segment was a statement without words of the meaning for him of the fantasy experience. The other students were also visibly moved and during the discussion actively engaged in an exchange about the alternative ways in which they each saw the various participants in the fantasy. In the two remaining sessions, the black student became a leader in the group

---

* This student's posttreatment level of social reasoning, reflective of a clear transition from a third-person dyadic to a qualitative systems (intrapersonal) perspective, was possibly an outcome of training.

discussions and helped to create a real shift in the overall feelings members had about each other. With more training sessions the insights into alternative perspectives that the students finally appeared to be gaining might have been integrated into more differentiated perspective-taking structures.

The experience in this group described in this set of anecdotes raises an important question. It may be that for persons who (a) were characterized by a high degree of defensiveness, and (b) were not yet able to think in terms of coterminous objective and subjective meanings of experience, the experiential fantasy training group might have been a less threatening and a more growth-producing experience.* However, for the one student who became overabsorbed in his fantasies, the behavioral condition might actually have helped him in considering more objective aspects of his social reality and in giving them their due. Interestingly enough, this student was the only member of the group to demonstrate clear stage 4 (qualitative systems) reasoning. A glimpse from his fantasies of some of the interpersonal stresses in his life suggested that an overemphasis on subjective perspectives was leaving him feeling rejected, deeply wounded, and especially vulnerable to the slightest hint of hostility in passing remarks from significant others. As Loevinger and Wessler (1970) have pointed out, structural development does not necessarily mean that persons have fewer problems, but rather that the way in which persons define and cope with interpersonal problems is qualitatively different at different stages.

5.2. Further Implications for Research and Practice

In any research endeavor, the questions raised are as important as those that seem to be answered. Further attempts at refinement of the present research design and the relationships found among the major variables will have to consider the strength and stability of the treatment procedures, and the generalizability and clinical applications of the findings. Two specific issues in this regard will be posed here.

Firstly, those factors in real life that influence the ways in which individuals construe what it means at a particular point in time or in a particular place to be "empathic" need to be explored. In this regard, the fact that predictive accuracy on a behavioral task decreased when persons were led to believe from a previous task that empathy referred to identifying implied meanings in an individual's communications indicates that situational factors very much influence the way in which

---

* The relatively large number of participants in the experiential-fantasy group reasoning at stage 4 (76%, see Table VIII) suggests participants in this condition, to a lesser extent, may have benefited from the training.

an empathic task is defined. For example, it is unclear to what extent persons spontaneously attend to implicit meanings without an externally imposed set, and what situational variables induce them to do so. Moreover, it is important to understand the effect on a dyadic relationship when individuals agree or disagree in their respective definitions of empathy, i.e., when one person focuses on subjective meanings and the other person on objective meanings of what is communicated. If each participant is viewed as an "information processor" (Berne, 1953) it is conceivable that discordance in an interaction might arise when one individual's "noise" is another individual's "information."

Secondly, research is needed to clarify the implications of the present findings for clinical practice. Despite an extensive concern with evaluating the empathic skills of psychotherapists (cf. Bachrach, 1976; Kagan, 1975; Truax and Carkhuff, 1967), clinical psychologists have neglected the implications of their treatment techniques for improving the empathic abilities of their clients (cf. Fox and Goldin, 1964). Choice of treatment techniques in psychotherapy is a process that should include decisions as to the level of empathy to be addressed.

Data from the present study suggest that behavioral techniques address themselves to behavioral levels of empathy but may not improve the client's ability to reason about his or her relationships nor to get in touch with richer and more private aspects of his or her own and others' experiences. Alternatively, as in many of the increasingly popular imaginative therapies (Singer, 1974a), overabsorption in fantasy and too great a focus on implied and symbolic meanings may lead to distorted expectations for the way in which others will behave, and may not provide sufficient opportunities for cognitive restructuring of interpersonal events. While analytic therapies include both free associative techniques and active reflection on both objective and subjective events, they have to cope with the apparent difficulty of many individuals in shifting between a reality-oriented and an imaginative mode of observation. Therapies that expect this kind of flexibility without providing any formal training may confuse the client and lead to a rigid attempt to hold on to habitual modes of experiencing. The cognitive basis for this rigidity is easily missed in exclusively dynamic interpretations of "resistance."

5.3. Theoretical Implications: The Fourth Level of Empathy

5.3.1. Relationships between Levels of Empathy. One of the important questions that still remains to be discussed is the relationship between different levels of empathy. The expected relationship between empathic abilities at the subjective level and the ability to identify nonverbal cues supports the contention that "intuition is never a sensory deprived experience" (Guiora, Bolin, Dutton, and Meer, 1965, p. 120), i.e., that it is mediated by objective empirical observations. However, no other relationships were found between the different empathy measures. Hence, behavioral, subjective, and cognitive-structural levels of empathy appear to be defined by statistically independent abilities. Nonetheless, the larger theoretical question that remains is whether one can really talk about empathy in a complete sense without considering all three levels.

For example, an individual who is a good predictor of stereotyped behaviors, but fails to recognize the special meanings of these behaviors to another individual may fail to make accurate predictions when it really matters. Stereotyped predictions are based on the assumption that most people behave in a particular way most of the time and there is no reason to believe that in any one case they will behave differently (Chein, 1945). Hence, a person's chronic submission to authority, when mistaken for willful conformity, may take the observer completely by surprise when that person suddenly reveals his anger in the form of unmasked rage. On the other hand, in addition to distorted behavioral predictions, overabsorption in fantasy leaves persons vulnerable to implicit levels of meaning and "half-truths" that when taken out of context may lead to negative and/or disproportionate evaluations of self and other.

Social perspective-taking, i.e., the way in which persons cognitively structure their social experiences, provides a conceptual bridge between behavioral and subjective levels of empathy. More mature levels of social reasoning are defined by an increasing capacity to integrate subjective and objective perspectives. Nonetheless, the capacity to differentiate conceptually between these two levels of meanings does not necessarily predict how sensitive individuals will actually be to another person's implicit communications or how able they will be to make accurate behavioral predictions. It may be that empathic abilities at the behavioral or subjective levels are skills that need to be practiced and that individuals at any level of development differ in the degree to which they have cultivated these skills. On the other hand, the way in which the knowledge acquired through the use of these skills is understood will depend on the individual's ability to differentiate clearly and integrate subjective and objective levels of meaning from a number of different perspectives.

In sum, as psychologists we find ourselves in the positions of the persons whom we study. In hoping to understand how persons understand persons we have to differentiate between and acquire knowledge about empathy at a number of different levels. If we wish to study (a) what it is about others that people are able to report that they know (a behavioral level of observation), we must also consider ways in which to study (b) the meaning that they impart to what they know (a subjective level of observation) and (c) the way in which they organize and integrate this knowledge with other knowledge that they acquire about the nature of persons and relations (a cognitive-structural level of observation).

5.3.2. **The Fourth Level of Empathy.** More specifically, as clinicians, as researchers, and as theoreticians we need to draw upon our own abilities to empathize with the empathizer's experience. This task may be construed as a "fourth level of empathy," by which I mean the capacity to know which level of empathy is most appropriately addressed at a particular point in time with a particular individual. As psychotherapists we need to develop clearer guidelines for determining at what point it is appropriate to encourage our clients to become more deeply immersed in their private worlds of fantasies; at what point it is helpful to direct their gaze to more socially shared realities; and at what point it is useful to ask them to step outside their experience and consider the ways in which they perceive their social environment. As researchers, we must ask ourselves whether our measures assess the level of empathy most appropriate for our particular intervention; and as theoreticians, we need to consider and evaluate our own assumptions about the nature of empathy. In all three endeavors, our ability to imagine ourselves in the place of the persons whom we study may help us to clarify the nature of their empathic experiences. In this regard, the power of our own imaginations may turn out to be one of our most important resources.

References

Antrobus, J. S., Singer, J. L., Goldstein, S. L., and Fortgang, M. Mind-wandering and cognitive structure. *Translations of the New York Academy of Science*, 1970, 32, 242-252.

Bachrach, H. M. Empathy: We know what we mean, but what do we measure? *Archives of General Psychiatry*, 1976, 33, 35-38.

Beres, D., and Arlow, J. A. Fantasy and identification in empathy. *Psychoanalytic Quarterly*, 1974, 43, 26-50.

Berne, E. The nature of intuition. *Psychiatric Quarterly*, 1949, 23, 203-226.

Berne, E. Concerning the nature of communication. *Psychiatric Quarterly*, 1953, 27, 185-198.

Blatt, S. J. The objective and subjective modes: Some considerations in the teaching of clinical skills. *Journal of Projective Techniques and Personality Assessment*, 1963, 27, 151-157.

Bronfenbrenner, U., Harding, J., and Gallwey, M. The measurement of skill in social

perception. In D. C. McClellan, A. L. Baldwin, U. Bronfenbrenner, and F. L. Strodtbeck (Eds.), *Talent and society*. Princeton: Van Nostrand, 1958, 29-111.
Chein, J. The logic of prediction: Some observations on Dr. Sarbin's exposition. *Psychological Review*, 1945, 52, 175-179.
Cline, V. G. Interpersonal perception. In B. Maher (Ed.), *Progress in Experimental Personality Research VI*. New York: Academic Press, 1964, 221-281.
Dymond, R. F. A preliminary investigation of the relation of insight and empathy. *Journal of Consulting Psychology*, 1948, 12, 228-233.
Dymond, R. F. A scale for the measurement of empathic ability. *Journal of Consulting Psychology*, 1949, 13, 127-133.
Dymond, R. F. Personality and empathy. *Journal of Consulting Psychology*, 1950, 14, 343-350.
Fleiss, R. The metapsychology of the analyst. *Psychoanalytic Quarterly*, 1942, 11, 211-227.
Fox, R. E., and Goldin, P. C. The empathic process in psychotherapy: A survey of theory and research. *Journal of Nervous and Mental Diseases*, 1964, 138, 323-331.
Frank, S. J. The facilitation of empathy through training in imagination. Unpublished dissertation, Yale University, 1977.
Gordon, R. A very private world. In P. W. Sheehan (Ed.), *The function and nature of imagery*. New York: Academic Press, 1972, 63-80.
Gould, R. *Child studies through fantasy*. New York: Quadrangle Books, 1972.
Greenson, R. Empathy and its vicissitudes. *International Journal of Psychoanalysis*, 1960, 41, 418-424.
Guiora, A. Z., Bolin, R. K., Dutton, C. E., and Meer, B. Intuition: A preliminary statement. *Psychoanalytic Quarterly Supplement*, 1965, 39, 110-122.
Harty, M. K. Studies of clinical judgment, Part II. *Bulletin of the Menninger Clinic*, 1972, 36, 279-301.
Horowitz, M. J. *Image formation and cognition*. New York: Appleton-Century-Crofts, 1970.
Horowitz, M. J. Image formation: Clinical observations and a cognitive model. In P. W. Sheehan (Ed.), *The function and nature of imagery*. New York: Academic Press, 1972, 281-309.
Jackson, D. N. *Personality Research Form*. Goshen, New York: Research Psychologist Press, 1965.
Kagan, N. Influencing human interaction - Eleven years with IPR. *Canadian Counsellor*, 1975, 9, 74-97.
Kohut, H. Introspection, empathy and psychoanalysis. *Journal of the American Psychoanalytic Association*, 1959, 7, 459-483.
Lazarus, A. *Behavior therapy and beyond*. New York: McGraw-Hill Book Company, 1971.
Loevinger, J., and Wessler, R. *Measuring ego development construction and use of a sentence completion test*. New York: Jossey-Bass, 1970.
Marks, D. E. Individual differences in the vividness of visual imagery and their effect on function. In P. W. Sheehan (Ed.), *The function and nature of imagery*. New York: Academic Press, 1972, 83-108.
Miller, T. Some characteristics of two different ways of listening. Unpublished doctoral dissertation, New York University, 1972.
Patterson, G. R. *Families*. Champagne, Illinois: Research Press, 1971.
Piaget, J. *Play, dreams, and imitation in childhood*. New York: W. W. Norton and Company, Inc., 1962.
Piaget, J., and Inhelder, B. *The psychology of the child*. New York: Basic Books, 1969.
Reik, T. *Surprise and the psychoanalyst*. New York: E. P. Dutton and Company, 1937.
Rosenthal, R., Archer, D., DiMatteo, M. R., Koivumaki, H. H., and Rogers, P. L. Measuring sensitivity to nonverbal communication: The PONS test. Unpublished manuscript, Harvard University, 1976.

Sarbin, T. R. Imagining as muted role-taking: A historical-linguistic analysis. In P. W. Sheehan (Ed.), *The function and nature of imagery*. New York: Academic Press, 1972, 333-354.

Schafer, R. Generative empathy in the treatment situation. *Psychoanalytic Quarterly*, 1959, *28*, 342-373.

Selman, R. The development of conceptions of interpersonal relations: A structural analysis and procedures for the assessment of levels of interpersonal reasoning based on levels of social perspective-taking. Unpublished manuscript, Harvard-Judge Baker Social Reasoning Project, Harvard University, 1974.

Selman, R. Toward a structural analysis of developing interpersonal relationship concepts: Research with normal and disturbed preadolescent boys. In A. Pick (Ed.), *X Annual Minnesota Symposia on Child Psychology*. Minneapolis: University of Minnesota Press, 1976.

Sheehan, P. W. A functional analysis of the role of visual imagery in unexpected recall. In P. W. Sheehan (Ed.), *The function and nature of imagery*. New York: Academic Press, 1972, 149-174.

Shrauger, S. E., and Altrocchi, J. The personality of the perceiver as a factor in person perception. *Psychological Bulletin*, 1964, *62*, 289-307.

Singer, J. L. *Daydreaming: An Introduction to the experimental study of inner experience*. New York: Random House, 1966.

Singer, J. L. *Imagery and daydream methods in psychotherapy and behavior modification*. New York: Academic Press, 1974a.

Singer, J. L. Daydreaming and the stream of thought. *American Scientist*, 1974b, *2*, 417-425.

Sundberg, N. D. A method for studying sensitivity to implied meanings. *Gawein* (Journal of Psychology in Nijmegen University, Netherlands) 1966, *15*, 1-8.

Taft, R. The ability to judge people. *Psychological Bulletin*, 1955, *52*, 1-23.

Traux, C., and Carkhuff, R. *Toward effective counseling and psychotherapy*. Chicago: Aldine Press, 1967.

Westcott, M. R. *Toward a contemporary psychology of intuition: A historical, theoretical, and empirical inquiry*. New York: Holt, Rinehart and Winston, 1968.

Winer, B. J. Statistical principles in experimental design. New York: McGraw-Hill, 1971.

12

The Body, Expressive Movement, and Physical Contact in Psychotherapy

Jesse D. Geller

> And blest are those whose blood and
> judgement are so well commingled that
> they are not a pipe for fortune's
> finger to sound what stop she please.
> —Shakespeare, *Hamlet*

1. Introduction

An overview of the current "therapeutic marketplace" (Frank, 1972) reveals the proliferation, and increasing popularity, of a wide range of body- or movement-oriented therapies, e.g., orgone therapy (Reich, 1949), bioenergetic analysis (Lowen, 1967), postural-relearning (Feldenkrais, 1949), Rolf structural integration (Rolf, 1963), psychomotor-training (Pesso, 1969), the Alexander technique (Alexander, 1974), and the various forms of dance-movement therapy (e.g., Chace, 1953; Schoop, 1971; Siegel, 1973; Bartenieff, 1972), etc. These approaches do not share a common vocabulary, a standardized repertoire of techniques, nor are they unified by a comprehensive theory of psychopathology and behavior change. They evolved to meet the needs of different types of patient populations. They are practiced in a wide variety of institutional contexts and their practitioners come from diverse disciplinary backgrounds. Feldenkrais was originally a physicist, Rolf a biochemist, Alexander an actor. The pioneers in the scientific

---

Jesse D. Geller • Department of Psychiatry, Yale University School of Medicine, New Haven, Connecticut 06520.

rediscovery of the "art" of movement as a mode of therapy were dancers.

What unifies these divergent approaches is a fundamental belief in the functional identity of personality and the physical appearance of the body at rest and in movement. They all share the belief that our capacity for growth, feeling, and change is limited by our capacity for body awareness, and that our capacity for body awareness is limited by our capacity for movement. Body-movement therapists make no clear dichotomy, whether psychodynamically or experientially, between mental and bodily events. Moreover, in contrast to the so-called "talking cure"* they all primarily deal with psychopathology as manifested in movement and body structure, and attempt to effect therapeutic changes by working exclusively or primarily on this level.

The basic operational premise guiding the work of body-movement therapists is that changes in personality can be brought about directly by modifying the body structure and its functional motility. This work may or may not involve an ongoing discussion of "therapeutic" material. Ida Rolf (1963) claims that systematic realignment of the body structure at the neuromuscular level ("Rolfing") alone is sufficient to produce greater self-awareness, new suppleness and flexibility, greater ease in handling interpersonal relations, a decrease in the physical tension found in chronically contracted muscles, and an increased reservoir of energy. Borrowing ideas from sources as disparate as the martial arts, Yoga, and the twirling dances of the Sufi's, Feldenkrais (1949) has developed a regimen of delicate body exercises to alter patterns of thinking and feeling. Orgone therapists (Reich, 1949) blend characterological and biophysical techniques in proportions that vary from patient to patient and from time to time with a particular patient. Bioenergetic therapists (Lowen, 1967) similarly supplement analytic procedures with expressive movement exercises, physical manipulation of the skeletal musculature, and deep-breathing exercises. Dance therapy originated as an adjunctive therapy for hospitalized psychiatric patients. The American Dance Therapy Association (1972) defines it as "the psychotherapeutic use of movement as a process which furthers the emotional and physical integration of the individ-

---

* Gestalt (Perls, 1971) and primal therapy (Janov, 1970) prominently include body-oriented practices, but for our purposes are more appropriately regarded as occupying an intermediate position between the so-called verbal and body therapies. As Brown (1973) notes, Gestalt techniques are far more awareness centered than body centered. Janov's highly channelized objective is premised on the assumption that the essence of neurosis consists in the encapsulation of pain within both the psyche and body. Techniques that rely on electronic sensing devices to gain control over internal states (e.g., biofeedback) will not be considered in this paper.

ual" (p. 1). In dance therapy, patients are given the opportunity to move freely in space, to discover or rediscover what it means to play, to discover what it feels like to have sensations in different body parts, to risk abandoning themselves to compelling musical rhythms, to become a member of a cohesive group, to participate in rituals, to spontaneously express or dramatize emotions, to shout or attach concrete images and metaphors to their actions, to touch and be touched by others, etc. Trudi Schoop (1971), a pioneer dance therapist summarized this orientation when she wrote:

> If I am correct in assuming that mind and body are interactive, I feel a problem of mental disturbance can be influenced from either side. When psychoanalysis brings about change in the mental attitude, there should be a corresponding physical change. And when dance therapy brings about a change in the body behavior, there should be a corresponding change in the mind. The approach of dance therapy is through body-mind. Both methods want to change the total being, mind and body. (p. 5)

From antiquity, the two dimensions of human existence, the body and the mind, have been the focus of controversy between competing approaches to education and therapeutics. In this paper we shall examine some of the contemporary manifestations of this controversy, especially as it is reflected in psychotherapists' attitudes toward the body, expressive movement, and physical contact with patients. Our aim is not to enter the debate as to whether "acting-it-out" is therapeutically more efficacious than "talking-it-out." With respect to the question of outcome in psychotherapy, we believe that it is most heuristic, following Bergin (1971), to ask the question, What treatment in the hands of which therapist is most effective for this individual with that problem and under which set of circumstances? We are, moreover, in agreement with Frank's (1972) hypothesis that the relative popularity of any mode of therapy grows not out of its demonstrable superiority but rather out of its congruence with prevailing values and life-styles. We are also more impressed with the common denominators that unify all forms of psychotherapy. The approaches discussed here all share the common features that Frank regards as the universal components of any healing relationship:

> . . .a confiding, emotionally charged relationship between the patient and a help-giving individual or group; a special setting containing symbols of healing; a rationale; and a set of activities prescribed by the rationale involving both patient and therapist. The fact that rationales and procedures differ so widely does not negate the necessity of both. No form of psychotherapy can exist without them. (p. 31)

As Lévi-Strauss (1967) has argued, this is no less true for shamanistic practices than it is for the academically trained psychotherapist.

Within this framework we shall discuss the biases and assumptions underlying the body-movement therapies and the implications that follow from attempts to translate the kaleidoscopic multiplicity of human experience into verbal and nonverbal channels of communication. This paper focuses on the changing status of the body in the quest for self-realization, the habitual distinction between style and content, the concept of unconscious mental representation, and the roles of insight, interpretation, and physical contact in promoting a genuinely communicative relationship. In pursuing these goals, we shall contrast body-movement therapies and psychoanalytically oriented therapy. All therapies must come to terms with their relationship to psychoanalytic therapy just as all therapists must come to terms with their "transference" to Freud. As Auden (1957) observed in his memorial poem to Freud: "To us he is no more a person now but a whole climate of opinion, under whom we conduct our differing lives" (p. 57).

2. The Democratization of the Relationship of the Mind and the Body

Movement and body therapies are challenging views that are deeply embedded in our philosophical and cultural heritage: the tendency to value the intangible, spiritual, metaphysical more than the tangible and the seen; and the Cartesian view of the body as a machine directed by the soul. From classical antiquity, the body has been conceptualized as either antithetical to the objectives of the soul, the primary obstacle in man's pursuit of self-realization, or merely "inferior" to the soul. In the West as in the East, bodily needs have traditionally been subordinated to mental, moral, and spiritual development. The emphasis has been on subordinating and controlling the body as a prerequisite for spiritual advancement. Even the classical Greek educational ideal of a "sound mind in a sound body" emanates from a belief (Friedlander, 1964) in the soul's superiority over the body. In the teachings of Hatha Yoga, the body is similarly important as a means, not as an end. Although in modern times the concept of self has gradually replaced the concept of soul, the former is still haunted by its philosophical heritage. Thus, many use the concept of self as if it referred to an invisible, intangible something that "animates" the body without physical agency and "inhabits" it without being in any place (Langer, 1942).

It is only gradually that modern psychotherapeutic practices have been liberated from these values and implications. In this regard, the psychoanalytic tradition represents a historical link and critical point of departure for the new body-movement therapies.

Freud (1923) regarded the body as the source of all consciousness and the body image as the nucleus of the ego. Although he viewed personality as "a democracy of opposing predispositions," he clearly advocated "the primacy of the intellect." For Freud (1913), the secondary processes represented "a higher level of mental representation." He viewed primary-process thought as tied to archaic levels of the development of language and methods of representation that dominated the conscious thought of children and "primitive" people (1923). There have always been advocates of a "poetic" approach to psychoanalysis (e.g., Reik, 1949) but the ideal image of the analyst has been that of a "detached scientist." Loewald (1960) believes that Freud considered "scientific man . . . as the most advanced form of human development" (p. 10). As Sontag (1966) notes, Freud is also heir to the Platonic tradition in two paramount and related ways: his acceptance of the view that sexuality is "lower" and the sublimations in art, science, culture "higher," and his acceptance of the self-evident value (both practical and theoretical) of self-awareness. The so-called Freudian "analytic attitude" encourages a lack of piety toward the "higher" things, a respectful interest in the "lower," and, as Reiff (1963) claims, a detachment from both.

Freud was not a champion of libidinal expressiveness. According to Tillich (1962), the concept of sublimation is Freud's most puritanical belief. Although psychoanalytic therapies are premised on the value that we must accept our bodily needs, Freud was convinced of the fundamental antagonism between the individual's need for instinctual gratification and the oppressive but inevitable demands of civilization. The ascetic ideals of self-reliance and personal achievement are discernible in the Freudian outlook. Reiff (1963) states that Freudian pedagogy teaches the patient-student "to develop an informed (i.e., healthy) respect for the sovereign and unresolvable basic contradictions that galvanize him into the singularly complicated human being that he is" (p. 17). Psychoanalytic therapeutic reeducation thus encourages a stance of reasoned disillusionment, a tolerance of ambiguities, a deeply searching yet impartial responsiveness to the paradoxes and absurdities of existence. Ever mindful of the inescapable conflict between passion and duty, psychoanalytic therapists have renounced the concept of cure. Psychological rebirth from the analytic perspective is an illusion, and for Freud the permanence of analytic gains depends crucially on whether the patient after analysis is spared "too searching a fate." Thus, despite its melioristic orientation and positive attitude toward wordly gratification, the Freudian perspective is deeply shaped by what Schafer (1970) has called the tragic and ironic visions of reality.

3. The Romantic Vision of the Body-Movement Therapies

A romantic vision seems to be a particularly distinctive feature of the body-movement therapies. They are romantic to the extent that they view therapy as an archetypal quest for "naturalness," a lost golden age, "a second innocence," or as an attempt to achieve the elusive goal of self-actualization. The goals of body-movement therapists vary in accord with the restraints imposed by time, severity of pathology, finances, etc. Yet, they also entertain the utopian possibility of reconciling seamlessly the split between the mind and the body. The new body-movement therapies are repudiating rationalistic biases, the dichotomy between objective reality and subjective fantasy, and the assumption that the scientific approach to the self is the highest and most mature evolutionary stage of development. They do not see adult, objective, impersonal cognition as the baseline and implicit model for all thought processes, nor do they regard an impersonal, scientific construction of reality as the absolute, fixed standard of "objectivity." External reality is not portrayed as a constraining frustrating power in eternal opposition to the individual seeking unlimited expression of his drives. The emphasis is upon such values as expressiveness, direct immediate experience, and spontaneity.

Whereas some body-movement therapists eschew the hierarchical structuring of the personality into pejoratively toned "higher" and "lower" categories, others are in the tradition of Nietzsche (1954), who proclaimed: "But the awakened and knowing say body am I entirely and nothing else, and soul is only a word for something about the body. . . . There is more reason in your body than in your best wisdom" (p. 146). According to Brown (1973), the new body therapies are "id affirmative" rather than "ego affirmative."

From a moral point of view, this shift is potentially revolutionary. For Rieff (1961), "Health at the expense of morality" (p. 25) is a potentially dangerous by-product of this new freedom for natural biological urges. Other intellectuals deplore the life-style and values underlying the so-called consciousness movement. Marin (1976) dismisses it as "the new narcissism" that encourages "deification of the isolated self."

The body-movement therapies do not necessarily repudiate the value of consciousness or reflectiveness. Their work is not unmindful of Gendlin's (1962) assertion that "feeling without symbolization is blind, symbolization without feeling is empty" (p. 5). Nevertheless, the new body and movement therapies would seem to believe, along with Norman O. Brown (1959), that what is needed is not Appolonian (or sublimation) consciousness, but Dionysian (or body) consciousness. For example, Perls's (1971) invitation to "lose your mind so that you can come to your senses" (p. 25) contrasts starkly with Freud's description of psychoanalysis as the instrument that would progressively conquer the id. Despite the emphasis on expressiveness, body-movement therapists recognize that the implementation of their values requires the cultivation of a very special kind of perceptual awareness.

4. Obstacles to the Development of Body-Awareness

Listening to and attending to the wisdom of one's body is a highly refined and sophisticated act of consciousness. It should not be confused with maintaining physical fitness and sound health. Brown (1973) has aptly noted that energetic, physically fit, action-oriented people (e.g., dancers, athletes), "may be emotionally crippled because they perceive their bodies as objects-of-use to be coerced into submission" (p. 100).

A respectful attitude toward one's body, an accurate body image, and a pleasurable sense of being "a body" appear to be heroic achievements in our culture. Difficulty in accurately reading and using adaptively the messages of the body is not limited to the psychiatrically disabled. There are many reasons why people, in general, have formidable blind spots in their knowledge of their bodies. Visual inspection of important body sectors (e.g., the vagina, the anus) is extremely limited, and it is impossible to examine visually the interior of the body. Careful and extended inspection of the body geography is discouraged by those religious and moralistic systems that view the body as a source of sin. This theme still flourishes, according to Fisher (1973), in doctrines that emphasize rationality and intellectuality. Socialization practices that emphasize that action must be based on rational "reasons" rather than body feelings, and the tendency to regard body arousal (e.g., emotionality) as misleading or as introducing irrationality into decision-making blunt our skill in interpreting body experiences. Because we lack publicly stated norms against which we can match our own body experiences, it is difficult for the average individual to judge what the body should "feel" like. Careful analysis of the body and body sensations is intimately enmeshed with the diagnosis of disease and associated with internalized prohibitions against being dirty or unattractive. The image of the body-as-commodity has replaced the image of the body-as-tool in our technologically dominated society. In the wake of this shift, the cosmetics and fashion industries, unrealistic standards of beauty and physique, and the denigration of aging insure that few individuals will develop and sustain a loving and respectful attitude toward the physicality of the body.

Becker (1973) maintains that the essence of man resides in his efforts to reconcile "the existential contradiction between a symbolic self, that seems to give man infinite worth in a timeless scheme of things, and a body that is worth about 98¢" (p. 28). He has termed this paradox the "tragedy of man's dualism."* For Becker we are "gods with anuses." This dilemma underscores the most powerful and ubiquitous resistances to knowing the body. According to Fisher (1973), looking directly and naively at the body is resisted because in so doing" its properties as a *concrete* object becomes too painfully *obvious*" (p. 7). Fisher goes on to say:

> There is comfort in thinking of your body not as a mere physical object, which, as such, would be subject to all of the vicissitudes and happenings that befall ordinary objects in the universe. But if an individual inspects his body without reservation he must necessarily perceive that it is basically a biological phenomenon like all other biological organisms. Ultimately, it is a collection of matter, regardless of how complex the values and meanings ascribed to it. To become aware of this fact is to open the door to intimations of mortality and other forms of vulnerability. It is probably important defensively to most people to conceptualize their bodies within an elaborate framework of psychological meaning that functions almost like a halo or protective armoring—denying that the body is, after all, an aggregate of molecules not much different from those occurring widely in nature. It is difficult for man to accept that his body is not "above it all." (p. 8)

5. Communication in Psychotherapy

In seeking to implement their goals, psychotherapists of whatever persuasion must deal with several interrelated and inescapable problems of communication. Communication, irrespective of the medium through which it is accomplished, requires the translation of internal psychologic reality into external, social reality. Since human experience in any one moment of conscious time is both plural and voluminous, any attempt to communicate this variegated experience entails simplifications and distortions. Paraphrasing McLuhan (1964), the capacity of any given medium to reproduce the full variety of the original experience depends on the number of sensory channels that it calls into action when working properly. The larger the number of senses

---

* The reflected appraisals that constitute the body image include the information conveyed by mirrors. Lacan (1968) has emphasized that this source of knowledge of our physical and physiologic self—"external," "disembodied"—contributes an "otherness" to the experience of one's body. Lacan would therefore agree with Becker that the split between the symbolic self and the body can never be reconciled seamlessly.

involved, the better the chance of transmitting a reliable copy of the sender's emotional state.

McLuhan (1964) believes that the spoken word answers these requirements more faithfully than any other medium or sense modality, because spoken language arouses collateral experiences, accommodates a more fully representative range of sensory experiences than any other type of human communication, and is typically modulated by acoustic, visual, tactile, and olfactory cues.

But is spoken language the best medium for "embodying" the sources of gain in psychotherapy? Spoken language may provide us with our most faithful and indispensable picture of human experience, but the "primacy of language" as a therapeutic medium of exchange must be considered in the light of other critical issues. Preverbal and psychotic experiences do not lend themselves to the linear arrangement of ideas. The primary medium through which information is exchanged in a relationship shapes the form of the relationship that evolves. Any mode of communication imposes characteristic features upon the messages passing through them. McLuhan contrasts the hesitant creativity of speech with the dull regimentation of written language. Moreover, therapeutic skill requires a refined receptiveness and sensitivity toward "nongenuine" communication. One of the most firmly rooted psychotherapeutic assumptions is that psychopathology, to a large extent, results from and is perpetuated by distorted and inadequate communication. Despite conscious willingness, patients in psychotherapy flee from spontaneous and candid self-disclosure.

Contemporary reexaminations of the concept of insight (Schafer, 1973) have emphasized that it is not expanding awareness or the cathartic effect of becoming conscious *per se* that facilitates change, but rather the experience of discovering oneself in the medium of communicating with another person. Schafer concludes that

> It is precisely this discovery in a medium of relationship that every patient, each in his own way and for his own reasons, has grown to feel helpless about. He anticipates that the discovery will be unbearable and the disclosure of it either intolerable in itself or intolerable as the certain cause of a forthcoming traumatic response by the other person, the therapist. (p. 144)

In the wake of such fears and resistances, there are apt to emerge discrepancies between self-reports and expressive behavior observable to the therapist. The activity of speaking, moreover, during the early stages of therapy, is used primarily to appeal to the therapist to do something or to respond in some way, e.g., imploring, commanding, forbidding, seducing (Loewenstein, 1956). Paraphrasing Paul (1973), free association is the goal rather than the method of psychoanalytic psychotherapy. Rarely are patients capable of establishing a "genuinely communicative relationship" from the outset of treatment.

6. Form and Content in Psychotherapy

In general, psychopathological modes of communication are characterized by disjunctions between that which we have learned to call "content" and that which we have learned to call "form." The idea of content typically refers to the subject matter of a therapeutic dialogue (e.g., "What X is saying is. . .," "What X is trying to say is. . .,"etc.) The formal aspects of a patient's self-presentation are comprised primarily of those expressive activities that are observable to the therapist, e.g., individual variations in speech, gait, posture, gestures, dress, manner, etc. Despite theoretical affirmations of the indissolubility of form and content in producing an individual's unique style, in the practice of all contemporary psychotherapies reductionistic biases persist. Neither the psychoanalytic approach nor the new body-movement therapies have integrated fully these conceptually distinguishable components of a person's style, character, or mode of relating into their working clinical models.

Wilhelm Reich (1949) was the first psychoanalyst to draw systematic attention to the possibility that an overemphasis on the idea of content as essential and of form as decorative or accessory was responsible for many therapeutic failures. He observed that the "subject matter" of a therapy hour *per se* did not define the experience of growth-inspiring self-disclosure. He argued that what had been talked about during the course of therapy did not necessarily provide an accurate barometer of the depth of intimacy or productivity of the relationship, and concluded that, especially during the early stages of treatment, the form of expression was far more important than ideational content in defining the unique nature of a patient's resistances and transference. This aspect of Reich's work led to a growing appreciation, among traditional therapists, of the formal aspects of a patient's mode of relating. Nevertheless, according to Horowitz (1972), in the psychoanalytic situation the emphasis is on thought content and control rather than on thought form. Expressive behaviors, although regarded as integral aspects of communication, are usually viewed as ancillary or alternative conveyors of content. Whereas in psychoanalytic practice content comes first, for the body-movement therapists the formal aspects of communication are primary. The innovative practices of the new body-movement therapies have tended to be experiments with form at the expense of content. Like systems analysts, they prefer to neglect the significance of what is said in favor of a study of the structures through which it is transmitted.

To discuss this and other issues, it is necessary to introduce the concept of "representation." Horowitz (1972) defines representation as "an organization of information in a form that can be part of conscious experience" (p. 797). In discussion the course of cognitive growth, Bruner (1964) has written:

> If we are to benefit from contact with recurrent regularities in the environment, we must represent them in some manner. To dismiss this problem as "mere memory" is to misunderstand it. For the most important thing about memory is not storage of past experience, but rather the retrieval of what is relevant in some usable form. This depends upon how past experience is coded and processed so that it may indeed be relevant and usable in the present when needed. The end product of such a system of coding and processing is what we may speak of as "representation." (p. 2)

Both Bruner and Horowitz distinguish three systems of processing information by which human beings construct models of their world: through action, through imagery, and through language. Following Horowitz, we shall refer to these three categories as the enactive, image, and lexical modes of representation.

7. The Role of Language in Psychoanalytic Therapy

The preeminence of language in traditional psychotherapy is obvious. With verbally accessible adults, private experiences are transformed and externalized primarily through the medium of syntactically articulated speech. For Merleau-Ponty (1962), "Speech in the speaker does not translate ready-made thought, but accomplishes it" (p. 178). Thus, the patient's task is to transform simultaneously occurring emotional, sensory, and cognitive events into language capable of being made comprehensible to the therapist. In psychoanalytic therapy patients promise "absolute honesty" (Freud, 1913), and the psychoanalytic method seeks to eliminate resistances to "talking about" issues that are being communicated or revealed through actions. Moreover, psychoanalytically oriented therapists tend to share the belief that little in a patient changes or grows effectively that has not come within the range of competence of language and discourse.

Psychoanalytic psychotherapy, however, has never been anchored exclusively in language. This misconception underlies many of the pseudoclashes between the body-movement therapies and traditional therapy. Speech is not merely a substitute for action in traditional therapy. Thus, Loewenstein (1956) has written, "Indeed speaking involves motor discharge by means of the vocal organs and in this respect plays a role in the therapeutic action of psychoanalysis" (p. 462). Despite the primacy that Freud accorded to language, he early recognized that crucial therapeutic material was inaccessible to imagistic or lexical modes of representation. The hypothesis that patients express in action what they are reluctant to discuss or cannot remember is a fundamental canon of psychoanalytic practice.

To begin with, Freud believed that nonverbal behavior, being under less conscious control than speech and therefore more likely to escape efforts at concealment, could provide information that patients were hesitant or unable to discuss verbally. Thus, in 1905 he wrote: "He that has eyes to see and ears to hear may convince himself that no mortal can keep a secret. If his lips are silent, he chatters with his fingertips; betrayal oozes out of him at every pore" (p. 94). Subsequent psychoanalysts have been primarily concerned with decoding the meaning or symbolism of nonverbal behaviors (e.g., Deutsch, 1952; Feldman, 1959).

Secondly, Freud designed the psychoanalytic situation so that during their sessions patients would relive and reenact rather than "just talk about" their lives. He noted (1949) that in the transference "the patient produces before us with plastic clarity an important part of his life history, of which he could otherwise have given us only an unsatisfactory account. It is as though he were acting it in front of us instead of reporting it to us" (p. 194). Anna Freud (1968) has similarly written: "This 'forgotten past,' so far as it refers to the pre-verbal period, has never entered the ego organization in the strict sense of the term, i.e., is under primary not secondary repression and, therefore, is not recoverable in memory, only apt to be relived (repeated, acted out, in behavior)" (p. 167).

Thirdly, "motility" or enactive modes of representation have never been prohibited in the psychoanalytic situation. Khan (1974) has argued that often growth-promoting experiences" in the analytic situation can have no means of symbolic and/or concrete actualization if motility is rigidly tabooed. Self-experience is intimately related to body-ego" (p. 297). Balint (1968) reported the following event, which occurred during the second year of an "arduous analysis," with a young woman whose presenting complaint was an inability to achieve anything:

> Apparently the most important thing for her was to keep her head safely up, with both feet firmly planted on the ground. In response, she mentioned that ever since her earliest childhood she could never do a somersault, although at various periods, she tried desperately to do one. I then said:

"What about it now?"—whereupon she got up from the couch and, to her great amazement, did a perfect somersault without any difficulty. This proved to be a real breakthrough. Many changes followed, in her emotional, social and professional life, all towards greater freedom and elasticity. (p. 50)

Such anecdotes appear rarely in the case reports of psychoanalytic therapists. By contrast "acting-out" with the therapist as witness and accomplice is a commonplace occurrence in the body-movement therapies. Concomitantly, although there is widespread agreement that therapeutic progress is facilitated, nurtured, rendered possible by therapist contributions that significantly transcend verbal utterances, the therapists' nonlexical contributions to the psychotherapeutic relationship have been given scant attention in the traditional psychotherapy literature. This issue, particularly as it is reflected in the concept of countertransference and in the role of physical contact between patient and therapist, will be focused upon in a subsequent section of the paper. At this point we will examine what Sontag (1966) has termed "the never consummated project of interpretation" (p. 17).

In pursuing this goal we have relied on the conceptual distinction between the "experiential" and "meaning" aspects of therapeutic interaction. Following Gendlin (1962), we believe that the "creation of meaning" and "experiencing" are intimately associated, and required of all psychotherapeutic work. Schacter's (1964) research compellingly demonstrates that a state of physiological arousal alone is not sufficient to induce an emotion, and that cognitions exert a strong steering function in helping a person "decide" what he is feeling. In a series of experiments to determine which cues permit a person to identify his own emotional state, Schacter discovered that it was possible to lead subjects who were "experiencing" precisely the same chemically induced state of physiological arousal to believe that they were feeling angry, or euphoric, or merely showing the physical side effects of the chemical agent. These findings indicate that patients must be given the opportunity to correctly label, discuss, and differentiate the ambiguous and often unfamiliar sensations (i.e., "feelings") that are aroused in therapy. Otherwise, they are likely to confuse, distort, or find it impossible to "get in touch with" feelings that for them may be uninterpretable in terms of past experience. For example, according to Lowen (1958), patients who fear being punished for "good feelings" tend to react to genital excitation with exaggerated alarm. Thus, although pleasure demands a loosening of restraints, mere realigning of these patients' body structures might result in increased anxiety rather than greater emotional freedom.

8. The Search for Meaning

Every therapist seeks to understand or "make sense" of his patients' communications, be they verbal or nonverbal. Freud's original clinical investigations, as Rosen (1969) points out, "were an attempt to find meaning in the meaningless" (p. 197). Indeed, psychoanalytic therapy is premised fundamentally upon the view that emotionally intensified understanding of covert or unconscious cognitive processes is antecedent to and causative of changes in overt behavior. To understand, in this tradition, is to seek indices of content and experiences that are not being verbalized. To this end, the analytically oriented therapist listens to the content of the patient's associations and/or observes the manner in which a patient speaks. As previously noted, the formal aspects of a patient's communications are primarily regarded as ancillary conveyors of content. Moreover, all observable phenomena are bracketed, in Freud's terminology, as *manifest content*. This manifest content must be interpreted in order to find the true meaning—the *latent content*—beneath. Neurotic symptoms, slips of the tongues, dreams, nonverbal gestures, are all treated as occasions for interpretation. Sontag (1966) has concluded that for Freud, "these events only *seem* to be intelligible. Actually, they have no meaning without interpretation. To understand *is* to interpret. And to interpret is to restate the phenomenon, in effect to find an equivalent for it" (p. 7).

From the psychoanalytic perspective, everything that is available to consciousness should be communicable through consensually shared verbal forms, and anything that is not available to consciousness (i.e., anything being defended against) will be evident only in a form in which the patient himself could not recognize the content; that is, the material is in symbolic form. The clinical basis of these assumptions is directly related to the view of neurotic symptoms as substitutes (i.e., symbolic equivalents) for repressed memories of past traumatic events. The Freudian style of interpretation, therefore, digs "behind" the patient's utterances and nonverbal behavior to find a subtext that is the "true" one. In other words, the ultimate hope, as Rosen (1961) has written, of the psychoanalytically oriented therapist "is to understand those aspects of the patient's unconscious mental contents which produce his symptoms" (p. 450).

Because we do not know in what form unconscious memories or processes, as such, exist within our patients, we must describe them by analogy. The unconscious is first and foremost a hypothetical construct. Freud (1940) states it this way:

> We have discovered technical methods of filling up the gaps in the phenomena of our consciousness, and we make use of those methods just as

a physicist makes use of experiment. In this manner we infer a number of processes which are in themselves "unknowable" and interpolate them in those that are conscious to us. And if, for instance, we say: "At this point an unconscious memory intervened," what that means is: "At this point something occurred of which we are totally unable to form a conception, but which, if it had entered our consciousness, could only have been described in such and such a way." (pp. 196–7)

At a theoretical level, Freud stated that the unconscious was much broader than the repressed. However, according to Schimek (1975), Freud's working clinical model of the unconscious, was that "the primary and original form of the unconscious is an ideational one, namely contents of memories or fantasies which by acquiring drive cathexis become causal agents of behavior" (p. 182). Freud's model of cognitive growth, additionally, presumes the existence of "mental" representations from the beginning of development. From the psychoanalytic perspective ideation invariably precedes action. Taken together, these views led Freud to describe unconscious memories, within the clinical psychoanalytic situation, in terms of the content they would have if they were conscious and verbalized.

9. The Unconscious in the Body-Movement Therapies

The new body-movement therapies are premised, either explicitly or implicitly, on an alternative view of the relationship between cognition and action. The assumption that the attitude of activity interferes with or is an incompatible alternative to remembering is deeply rooted in the psychoanalytic tradition (Schachtel, 1959). In the body-movement therapies, movement presumably facilitates rather than endangers the evocation of unconscious memories, fantasies, and primitive ways of coping with traumatic experiences. The emphasis on direct body work, moreover, necessitates an expanded or modified view of unconscious mental representation. It is generally accepted that as individual psychomotor patterns are learned, they become so internalized with repetition that their specifics recede below consciousness, usually never to emerge again. What adult can explain or even be aware of the precise series of habitual actions employed in walking, dressing, eating? Body-movement therapists further assume that specific gaps, avoidances, and tensions in our movement patterns are rendered unconscious. Siegel (1975) writes: "The instinctive withdrawal or tightening by which we once protected ourselves from some specific threat becomes fixed in our body's repertoire and continues to govern the way we move long after the initial reason for it is gone" (p. 8). This view is consistent with Sharpe's (1938) hypothesis that the body is a carrier of explicit memories localized in its various parts, and Deutsch's (1952) assumption that certain body parts become invested with unconscious symbolic meaning according to their structure and function.

Most importantly, body-movement therapies presume the "existence" of what Piaget (1951) has called a "pre-representational level of concrete action-schemes." Piaget maintains that during the "sensorimotor" period of development (i.e., approximately the first 18 months of life), the infant does not have representations or mental images by which he can evoke persons or objects in their absence. But, in the process of accommodating his innate behavioral repertoire and spontaneous movements to the demands of reality, the child presumably develops "cognitive substructures" or a complex system of "action-schemes." For Piaget and Inhelder (1969), "A scheme is a structure or organization of actions as they are transferred or generalized by repetition in similar or analogous circumstances" (p. 13). By means of a sensorimotor coordination of these action-schemes, without the intervention of symbolic representation or thought, the child, according to Piaget, begins to construct and organize his reality. That is, well before the formation of the first mental images the child gradually discovers means to achieve different ends. He develops a logic of action. Although prerepresentational, these broad categories of action (e.g., intentional grasping) and affective reactions (e.g., smiling) imply the attribution of meaning.

It will be recalled that Freud's model of cognitive development presumes the "existence" of "mental representations" from the beginning of development, and that he hypothesized that the primary and original form of the unconscious is ideational (i.e., contents of memories or fantasies.) The change from random motor movements to adaptive action requires, for Freud, a cognitive representation of the goal prior to the action. For Freud, action is originally the enactment of a wishful fantasy. According to Schimek (1975), the data and concepts of contemporary developmental psychology, and of Piaget in particular, indicate: "The view of the unconscious as a storage container of specific images and memories may no longer be tenable or even necessary," and that it is legitimate to infer "unconscious sensorimotor organizers of action at a pre-ideational, as well as a preverbal level, without postulating that *behind* the various observable manifestations of an inferred unconscious motive lies an unconscious image or fantasy" (p. 182).

From another perspective, Schachtel (1959) has pointed to the fact that even the most profound and prolonged psychoanalysis does not lead to an extensive recovery of childhood memory. For Schachtel, the progressive repression of infantile sexuality and the censorship of objectionable material is insufficient to account for gaps in and the impoverishment of autobiographical memory. For Schachtel the quality of memory and the conditions of forgetting are closely related to the mode of prior learning and attention. He believes that the categories (or schemata) of adult memory are not suitable receptacles for early childhood experiences and therefore not fit to preserve these experiences and enable their recall. According to Schachtel, "Our minds are not capable of accommodating childhood experiences. More often than not, adults are not even capable of imagining what the child experiences" (p. 314). Schachtel further argues that although the memory of one's more recent personal past is fairly continuous, this formal continuity in time is offset by barrenness in content. During the course of development, experience becomes increasingly cliché-ridden and conventionalized. Experiences are replaced by pseudoexperiences, we see and hear what we are taught to expect, and we tend to rationalize our memories, rendering them acceptable and comfortable.

These findings and speculations are likely to have a profound effect on the theory and practice of all therapies. They argue for the value of "educative"- or "growth"-oriented therapeutic opportunities to overcome "normal amnesia" (Schachtel, 1959). They lend credence to those approaches that seek to realign the body so that movement and the postural organization of the body are restructured at a neuromuscular level (i.e., Alexander technique, Rolfing). They suggest that dance therapy, with its emphasis on enactive modes of representation, may be ideally suited to those forms of psychopathology that may be caused by vicissitudes occurring at a precognitive level of organization. They support the hypothesis that the past is continually presented to the world in the form of the individual's personal style of moving.

10. Movements Are Expressive

A review of the literature on expressive movements indicates that any given movement has been considered by different investigators, or by one investigator at different times, as an indicator of momentary affective states, enduring personality characteristics, "role" or group membership, or as an indicator of "unconsciously" motivated communication. The only unifying concept in the literature on body movement is the tenet, often explicitly stated, "Movements are expressive."

The early investigators of this hypothesis (e.g., Allport and Vernon, 1933; Wolff, 1943) were concerned with intraindividual consistencies in psychomotor behavior patterns. Their research was designed to show that many different behaviors of an individual (e.g., his gait, his posture, the tonal quality of his voice, his handwriting) are "manifestations" of underlying personality characteristics. As used by these investigators, the hypothesis "movements are expressive" seemed to be derived from the more general belief that, in principle, under specified conditions, everything a person does, every action or movement he makes, can be used by a knowledgeable and sensitive observer as a basis (either from the behaviors themselves or from inferences based on these behaviors) for understanding the individual. Nevertheless, there is a lack of clarity in their use of hypothesis; it is unclear whether they believed that the behaviors in question were derived from the underlying personality characteristics (i.e., genotypes) or were behaviors consistent with the posited genotype.

Another source of confusion in the literature on so-called body language is the widespread failure to distinguish between movements that are *informative* to an observer from those that are *communicative* in motivation. As Scheflen (1964) has aptly noted:

> All too often research into the meaning of "nonverbal" elements of communication has consisted merely of isolating a fragment, counting its frequency, and then free associating or asking subjects to free associate about its meaning, as if elements of behavior carried meaning in and of themselves. (p. 319)

With few exceptions (Mahl, 1968; Birdwhistell, 1970) efforts to decode the meaning of nonverbal behaviors have blurred the distinction between movements as "signs" and movements as "communications." Although signs and communications may be equally valid data sources, particularly when trying to understand an individual, they differ in several important respects. Any behavior may be taken as a "sign" of something else. The concept of a sign implies only an observer making an inference or assigning significance to an event or behavior. It does not suggest an act of transmission of information from one person to another; that is, the concept does not imply a subject who is actively making his experience public to another person. The concept of "communication," on the other hand, implies a socially shared signal system, that is, a code, an encoder who makes something public via that code, and a decoder who responds systematically to that code (Wiener, Devoe, Rubinow, and Geller, 1972).

A collapsing of the sign-communication distinction may be inherent in any approach that is primarily concerned with decoding the meaning of nonverbal behavior. Even if a therapist distinguishes theoretically between movements as signs and movements as communications, within the context of a therapy hour, it is difficult, if not impossible, to know whether one is decoding a communication encoded by an individual or whether one is drawing an inference from his behavior. This issue is a matter of relative indifference to the therapist for whom nonverbal behavior is an ancillary mode of communication, especially when trying to understand a particular individual. However, the failure to distinguish movements as signs and movements as communications has retarded the development of a comprehensive notational system to study nonverbal behavior as an independent channel of communication. Moreover, because movement events, within the psychoanalytic situation, acquire full significance only in the context of the verbal utterances that they either precede or follow, the sensorium of the psychoanalytic therapist is likely to be biased in favor of audition. For example, although Sullivan (1954) emphasized the importance of gestural and behavioral cues in communicating empathy, he asserted that "The psychiatric interview is primarily a matter of vocal communication, and it would be quite a serious error to presume that communication is primarily verbal. The sound accompaniment suggests what is to be made of the verbal propositions stated" (p. 32).

Body-movement therapists do not share this auditory bias. Expressive movements are viewed as an alternative mode of communication, rather than accessory to or preliminary to spoken language. There are a variety of implications that follow from the contrasting observational bases of the psychoanalytic and body-movement oriented therapies.

Horowitz (1972) maintains that the focus on thought content and control rather than upon thought form in the psychoanalytic situation encouraged the tendency to blur the distinction between qualities of thought form and qualities of thought organization. The frequent concurrence of visual images, for example, with regressive content during psychoanalytic hours, led, according to Horowitz, to such assumptions as: "(1) primary process thought is represented in images and secondary process thought is represented in words; (2) thought in images is more primitive than thought in words; or (3) thought in images is concretistic, and thought in words is abstract" (p. 794). These assumptions are clearly unwarranted. Although the enactive, imagistic and lexical modes of representations sequentially emerge during the course of development, they each can vary in their degree of complexity, subtlety, and articulation.

Psychotherapeutic modes of representing experience are different, not hierarchically ordered. A nonutilitarian view of symbolism represents yet another challenge to the tendency to hierarchically order human functions. Theorists such as Langer (1942) have reasoned that the need or propensity to symbolically transform experience is a biological "given," i.e., an intrinsic characteristic of the human animal. Langer writes:

> Despite the fact that his need gives rise to almost everything we commonly assign to the "higher" life, it is not itself a "higher" form of some "lower" need; it is quite essential, imperious, and general, and may be called "high" only in the sense that it belongs exclusively (I think) to a very complex and perhaps recent genus. (p. 40)

If the process of symbolic transformation of experience is as basic an activity as, for example, eating, suppression of the symbol-making function may have a disruptive effect on the integrity of the personality. If it is further assumed that full realization of the brain's capacity for symbolization is realized to the extent that the enactive, imagistic, and lexical modes of representation are called into play, then underutilization, for whatever reason, of any of these modes should be given therapeutic attention.

11. Against Interpretation

The emphasis on insight as the crucial therapeutic ingredient in psychoanalytically oriented therapy follows from the assumption that changes in overt behavior are dependent upon and follow changes in the structure and content of covert cognitive processes. It is this broader assumption, and the correlated emphasis on interpreting hidden meanings, that are being questioned by body-movement therapists.

This anti-interpretive trend derives, in part, from the concern with what Sontag (1966) has identified as "the hypertrophy of the intellect at the expense of energy and sensuality in our culture" (p. 17). Critiques of the psychoanalytic method authored by body-movement therapists do not emphasize that any individual's life can accommodate a multiplicity of equally plausible interpretations. Rather, they are guided by view, expressed most cogently by Sontag (1966):

> Interpretation must itself be evaluated within a historical view of human consciousness. In some cultural contexts, interpretation is a liberating act. It is a means of revising, of transvaluing, of escaping the dead past. In other cultural contexts, it is reactionary, impertinent, cowardly, stifling. (p. 7)

The body-movement therapists believe we are living in such a time. Interpretations typically take the sensory experience of an event for granted, and proceed from there. Sharpness of sensory experience cannot be taken for granted in our culture. All of the conditions of modern life conspire to dull the senses. Overproduction of material goods, media bombardment, overcrowding, noise pollution, the accelerating rate of social change, bureaucratization, etc., are all believed to be contributing to a massive sensory anesthesia. Moreover, as society has become more "psychologized," man, according to several theorists, has become increasingly disembodied. Rieff (1963) claims that the Freudian "analytic attitude" predisposes contemporary man to focus more on the determinants of action than on the action itself. May (1969) has asserted that the schizoid condition is a general tendency in our culture. This trend is reflected in the changing ecology of psychopathology. The experience of inner emptiness, boredom, inauthenticity, apathy, dread of intimacy, protective shallowness, pseudoinsightfulness, hypochondriasis, and an unappeasable hunger for exciting experiences to fill the sense of inner void have become increasingly common manifestations of psychopathology in our time (Kernberg, 1975). Psychotherapists are being confronted, in increasing numbers, with patients who "act out" their conflicts instead of sublimating or repressing them, and/or with patients who are suffering from characterological problems highlighted by schizoid or narcissistic detachment. (Guntrip, 1969; Kernberg, 1975). The chief block to therapy presented by such patients is emotional inaccesibility. Purportedly, the search for hidden meanings with such patients further depletes or reinforces their already impoverished ability to participate in the pure, untranslatable, sensuous immediacy of concrete experiences. The Polsters' (1974) claim that the emphasis placed on the transferential or "as-if" aspects of the Freudian therapeutic relationship clouded the basic issue of direct experience. Shapiro (1975) similarly argues that a preoccupation with listening for interpretable derivatives or clues to unconscious neurotic conflicts can give rise to a discrediting of the process of conscious self-direction.

In contemporary psychoanalytic thinking, consciousness is no longer assigned a passive and innocuous role in guiding behavior (Schafer, 1976). Moreover, in the practice of psychoanalytic therapy "what we do" does not count less than "why we do it." Interpretations are often essential to removing those resistances that interfere with "authentic experiencing" or "being." With schizoid and obsessional patients, in particular, psychoanalytic therapists make use of interpretations in order to delimit and curtail mentation in the lexical mode so as to make available simple, direct bodily experiences. In other words, interpretations are not merely "explanations"; they can be used to widen the range of sensory channels that are excited by experience. Self-knowledge has never been regarded, by traditional therapists, as an end in itself.*

---

* Psychoanalysts (e.g., Schimek, 1975) have recently acknowledged the possibility that insight might follow rather than precede personality change.

In any case, the emphasis in the body-movement therapies is upon helping patients become aware of *how* they behave the way they do rather than *why*. Each approach, states Brown (1973), has developed its own techniques to help the patient "reclaim in immediate awareness his largely desensitized sensorimotor-affective modalities by making the patient actively attend to them" (p. 99). Implicit in this view is the hypothesis that the emotional experience of overcoming a resistance is necessary and sufficient to bring about changes in personality.

Emphasis on the immediacy of concrete experience rather than upon the interpretation of experience does not necessarily reflect a new species of anti-intellectualism (as has often been charged). Contemporary art, as well, is concerned primarily with the analysis and extension of sensations. McLuhan (1964) calls contemporary artists "experts in sensory awareness." For Sontag (1966):

> Transparence is the highest, most liberating value in art—and in criticism—today. Transparence means experiencing the luminousness of the thing itself, of things being what they are. . . . The function of criticism should be to show *how it is what it is,* even *that it is what it is* rather than to show *what it means.* . . . In place of hermeneutics we need an erotics of art. (p. 14)

It would appear as if art, psychological forms, and social forms all reflect each other and change with each other. From this perspective, the innovative practices of the body-movement therapies can be seen as an evolutionary phase in the history of psychoanalytically enlightened therapy.

12. Overcoming Resistances: The Reichian Influence

As previously noted, the divergent forms of body-movement therapy do not question the need to make inferences about unconscious mental process and/or repressed memories of past traumatic events. Body-movement therapies additionally share with traditional practitioners the view that the making conscious of the unconscious does not take place directly, but rather by the gradual elimination of resistance to consciousness. Loewald (1960) has written, "In sculpturing, the figure to be created comes into being by taking away from the material; in painting, by adding something to the canvas" (p. 12). He maintains that in analysis, as in sculpting, the "true form" (of the patient) comes into being by chiseling away the transference distortions and resistances, and that, as in sculpture:

> . . .we must have, if only in rudiments, an image of that which needs to be brought into its own. The patient, by revealing himself to the analyst, provides rudiments of such an image through all the distortions—an image

which the analyst has to focus in his mind, thus holding it in safe keeping for the patient to whom it is mainly lost. (p. 12)

Body-movement therapists emphasize such images as thawing out, softening, dissolving, loosening muscular rigidity to describe the process of overcoming resistances. Using the elbow, as well as the hands, the Rolfer digs deeply into the patient's muscles, moving them to unlock supporting tissue. The Rolfer stretches, tones, and repositions the body musculature to establish natural alignment with the forces of gravity.

In general, the body-movement therapists would appear to be resurrecting and selectively emphasizing the more ill-fated psychoanalytically inspired writings of Wilhelm Reich (1949). For Freud, the somatic correlate of a psychic disorder manifested itself in a specific fashion (e.g., paralysis or loss of feeling in the extremities). The overall impairment of an individual's predominant action patterns in everyday life remained rather peripheral in comparison to the search for the repressed, unconscious determinants of symptomatic acts and their ideational manifestations. Reich extended and somaticized the insights of Freud. In his practice, he worked at dissolving muscular rigidity as well as psychic resistances. From this work Reich (1961) states:

The loosening of the rigid muscular attitudes resulted in peculiar somatic sensations, involuntary trembling, jerking of muscles . . . and the somatic perception of anxiety, anger, and pleasure. . . . These manifestations were not the "result," the "causes," or the "accompaniment" of "psychic" processes; they were simply *these processes in themselves in the somatic sphere.* (p. 242)

Reich further maintained that if the psyche and the body express themselves concurrently and identically, then, "Character attitudes may be dissolved by the dissolution of the muscular armor; and conversely, muscular attitudes by the dissolution of character peculiarities" (1961, p. 293). Within the mainstream of psychoanalytic tradition, the second half of Reich's conclusion has not been given extensive attention. By contrast, body-movement therapies are premised fundamentally on the assumption that changes in personality can be brought about directly by modifying the body structure and its functional motility.

Whereas psychoanalytic therapists (e.g., Mahl, 1968) are apt to view autistic gestures (i.e., movements that are not substitutable for verbal utterances) as a sign that something important but not yet present is forthcoming, dance-movement therapists fully exploit the communicative (rather than informative) function of idiosyncratic expressive movements. By reinforcing partial manifestations of a movement, dance therapists can guide their patients, via successive approximation, toward the full realization of that movement with its accompanying emotional and attitudinal equivalents. Moreover, whereas bioenergetic exercises emphasize the repetitive performance of single acts (e.g., hitting, kicking, breathing) and ritualized stress positions to invoke release, patients in dance therapy are invited to move freely. The term "dance therapy," unfortunately, implies the highly specialized, patterned activity that is dance. In dance therapy, movement is a "free" use of the body, free in the sense that many choices are possible, but not in the sense of indiscriminate, undiscriminating action (Siegel, 1975). Movement should also not be confused with the misleading term, "body language." "Body language" implies that there is a universal set of gestures by which, if we "read" them properly, we can ferret out the hidden meanings in people's behavior.*

In response to their need for a vocabulary of movement, body-movement therapists have explored more highly conscious and organized uses of systems being developed to describe aspects of nonverbal behavior, e.g., Birdwhistell (1970); Davis (1972); Ekman and Friesen (1969); Mehrabian (1972); Wiener et al. (1972); Spiegel and Machotka (1974). Many dance therapists believe that the effort-shape system originally developed by Laban (1960) represents the most promising model for describing systematically the richness and variation in quality of the ongoing stream of human movement. Just as a play's script is an impoverished version of the actual "performance," a description of movement, no matter how detailed, when limited to the action itself, yields little information about how the mover really moved. You know what he did but you don't know how he did it. Effort-shape analysis describes the variations in how people move in any part of the body regardless of what they are doing; it does not deal directly with the semantic or symbolic meaning of gestures. The effort-shape analyst looks at the flow of movement; at tension and relaxation, strength and lightness, suddenness and sustainment, directness and indirectness, and at the forms the body makes in space. The system describes both how a person relates to the outside world (space) and how he or she discharges and modifies energy (effort). Because it focuses on quality apart from "content" or what is done, it can be used to describe,

---

* The symbolization involved in gestures is not the same as that which obtains between verbal symbols and their referents. Whereas words bear a logical or purely arbitrary relation to the subjective experiences they "mean," the movements of the body present the existence of subjective experiences. They do not consist of a system of distinctive signs corresponding to distinct ideas. The movements of the body are, moreover, not systematically coordinated by rules governing their organization and combination (i.e., grammar, syntax) Therefore, we may speak of communication by bodily signs, but there can be no such thing as "body language."

measure, and classify all human movement. (Bartenieff and Davis, 1965).

13. Styles of Exercising Authority

Ever since Freud abandoned his efforts to stimulate reverie by putting his hands on the patient's forehead, the emphasis in the psychoanalytic literature has been upon the hazards associated with physical contact between patient and therapist.

A few scattered references indicate that psychoanalytic therapists believe that the "laying on of hands" can have potential benefits in the treatment of children and severely regressed adults. Marmor (1972) suggests:

> In an anaclitic therapeutic approach to seriously ill psychosomatic patients, such as those with ulcerative colitis, or status asthmaticus, a "maternal" holding or stroking of hands may be both helpful and justified. Similar behavior may be indicated with regressed psychotic patients. Non-erotic holding or hugging of pre-adolescent children, especially autistic and withdrawn ones, may even be essential to their therapy. (p. 8)

Fromm-Reichman (1950) similarly acknowledges that "at times it may be wise and indicated to shake hands with a patient, or, in the case of a very disturbed person, to touch him reassuringly or not to refuse his gesture of seeking affection or closeness" (p. 69). Both Marmor and Fromm-Reichman, nevertheless, have urged therapists to be extremely thrifty in their physical contacts with patients with neurotic and personality disorders, especially if there is the slightest possibility that they might be interpreted or responded to as erotic.

Psychoanalytic conservatism regarding physical contact between patient and therapist derives fundamentally from Freud's (1919) belief that structural (i.e., permanent) changes in the personality could only be brought about by conducting therapy" as far as is possible, under privation—in a state of abstinence; and that as far as his relations with the physician are concerned, the patient must have unfulfilled wishes in abundance" (p. 396). Thus, depending on the clinical needs of the moment and the long-term goals of the treatment effort, psychoanalytically oriented therapists strive, through an examination of the patient's problems in the therapeutic relationship, to promote self-understanding rather than gratify, spurn, or manipulate their patients' love, demands, insults, or misperceptions. By transforming intrapsychic problems into an interpersonal struggle, the psychoanalytic therapist seeks to demonstrate compellingly, in the here and now, to their patients the ways in which they unwarrantedly, stereotypically, and habitually structure relationships in a self-defeating manner. In so doing, the patient is forced to come forth, to move toward the therapist. The psychoanalytic situation thus stimulates yet frustrates the development of an intense, intimate "real" relationship. Concomitantly, by bringing the patient's authority conflicts into the therapy, the psychoanalytic therapist gradually democratizes the relationship. By judiciously withholding gratifications and by generally refraining from exercising various leadership functions that inhere in their authority positions (e.g., recommending courses of action, and vouching for the rightness or success of actions taken), psychoanalytic therapists provoke dilemmas for their patients, the resolution of which strengthen capacities for autonomous self-direction as well as for mutuality. A patient's readiness to participate fully in an egalitarian relationship has come to be seen as an important index of readiness to terminate psychoanalytic therapy (Hurn, 1971).

Many of the innovative practices of the new body-movement therapies can be understood as value-based modifications of the psychoanalytic style of exercising authority. The term "authority" is used here in Etzioni's (1968) sense of "legitimate power," i.e., power that is used in accordance with the subject's values and under conditions that he views as proper. Because they have not been fully sanctioned or legitimized by the medical and academic communities, the new body-movement therapies are often practiced in "alternative institutions," the so-called growth centers.* The ecumenical pragmatic atmosphere of these "antiestablishment" settings encourages participation in a variety of modern Western therapies and the ancient disciplines of the East. Body-movement therapists, themselves, tend to be pluralistic in approach. The combined use of Gestalt, bioenergetic, and Rolfing techniques is not atypical. Moreover, in their efforts to direct and/or influence their patients, body-movement therapists assume either an egalitarian or a benignly authoritarian stance. The division of labor, in Rolfing, is such that the patient is a passive recipient of the procedures that are done to him. Other body-movement therapists attenuate the inherently asymmetrical structure of the "doctor-patient" relationship by expanding their expressive options. Therapist self-disclosure is central to the practice of many of the body-movement therapies. Moreover, they have repudiated taboos against physical expressions of intimacy between therapist and patient. In so doing, body-movement therapists

---

* Recent evidence (Lieberman and Gardner, 1976) suggests that growth centers may not be an alternative to traditional psychotherapy, but rather an addition. Eighty percent of the individuals using the facilities of growth centers, in Lieberman and Gardner's sample, had previous or current psychotherapeutic experience.

can provide schizophrenic patients with direct evidence that their body boundaries are firm and definite, rather than brittle and easily violated. On the other hand, the immediacy and intensity of touch can break through the emotional inaccessibility of patients whose bodily limits are excessively defined. Therapeutic discussion of the disclaimers and qualifying signals that typically accompany physical contact can also help patients identify when a communication is not to be taken literally, e.g., as a seduction or as a hostile attack.

As yet, the countertransference implications of this permissive orientation have not been subjected to careful scrutiny by the body-movement therapists. By contrast, traditional psychotherapists have emphasized the dangers and ethical responsibilities posed by the erotic transference. Undoubtedly, there are therapists who rationalize various forms of erotic interplay with their patients on the grounds of offering restitutive emotional experiences. McCartney (1966) used Reich's ideas to justify sexual intercourse with his female patients. No theory, however, is immune to distorted exploitation. Freud's fearful expectation of this possibility is revealed in his warning to Ferenczi, who sought to combat parental unkindness by acting the part of a loving parent, including the showing of physical affection. In a letter dated December 13, 1931, Freud wrote:

> You have not made a secret of the fact that you kiss your patients and let them kiss you. . . . Now picture what will be the result of publishing your technique. There is no revolutionary who is not driven out of the field by a still more radical one. A number of independent thinkers in matters of technique will say to themselves: Why stop at a kiss? Certainly one gets further when one adopts "pawing" as well, which after all doesn't make a baby. And then bolder ones will come along who will go further, to peeping and showing—and soon we shall have accepted in the technique of analysis the whole repertoire of demi-viergerie and petting parties, resulting in an enormous increase of interest in psychoanalysis among both analysts and patients. The new adherent, however, will easily claim too much of this interest for himself; the younger of our colleagues will find it hard to stop at the point they originally intended, and God the Father Ferenczi, gazing at the lively scene he has created, will perhaps say to himself: Maybe after all I should have halted in my technique of motherly affection before the kiss. (Jones, 1957, pp. 163-4)

14. Changing Conceptions of Countertransference

The psychotherapist's ethical responsibilities are "sacred." Yet, Freud's concerns about protecting the integrity of psychoanalysis, taken together with the "rule of abstinence," may have promoted a restrictive attitude toward the psychoanalytic therapist's expressive options and emotional reactivity. This trend is reflected in what Tower (1956) has termed the psychoanalyst's "countertransference anxieties." The classical definition of countertransference is, according to Kernberg (1975), "the unconscious reaction of the psychoanalyst to the patient's transference" (p. 50). Kernberg believes that this orientation carries with it the implication that neurotic conflicts of the analyst are the main source of the countertransference, and follows from Freud's recommendation that the analyst "overcome" his countertransference. Although this conception of the therapist's role does not necessarily imply loss of spontaneity or detached coolness, its implementation does require disciplined motoric inhibition. Szasz (1957) has suggested that it is much easier to work in this mode if one is of an ascetic temperament. This point of view poses for the therapist, as a theoretical ideal, achieving a state of "desirelessness" vis-à-vis patients. Annie Reich (1950), a proponent of the "classical" conception of countertransference, maintained that any reluctance on the part of the analyst to give up the relationship with the patient indicated unresolved countertransference problems. Searles (1965) emphasized the courage it required for him to publish the hypothesis that genital excitation during analytic hours as well as erotic and romantic dreams about patients might signal the imminent successful termination of the treatment. In general, the antilibidinal pressures exerted by this professional climate may have inhibited the systematic investigation of the therapist's bodily experiences. Havens (1974) has similarly concluded that "psychoanalysis directs attention to misuses of the therapist's self, through the discovery and management of countertransference phenomena. It has not made comparable contributions to the *uses* of the self" (p. 1).

To counteract this imbalance, growing numbers of psychoanalytically oriented therapists have advocated the use of what Kernberg (1975) has deemed the "totalistic" conception of countertransference. From this perspective, countertransference is defined by Kernberg as "the total emotional reaction of the psychoanalyst to the patient in the treatment situation" (p. 76). Exponents of this point of view have not necessarily relaxed taboos against touching, nor do they agree on the circumstances under which "emotional reactions" might be verbally communicated to a patient. However, they have all fostered a more open exploration of the ways in which psychotherapists emotionally experience and acquire knowledge about their patients. Consequently, the image of the therapist as "blank screen" or mirror onto which the patient projects his transference is being replaced by the notion of the therapist as "resonating chamber." Modell (1976), for example, hypothesizes that the diagnosis of the narcissistic character disorder is aided by a particular form of the countertransference response, that is, boredom and sleepiness as a result of the patient's state of nonrelatedness. Grossman (1965) suggests that the absence of sexual feelings and impulses in the therapist toward an attractive patient, after they have been working together for a sufficiently long period of time, can be a noteworthy signal for deeper investigation of a patient's fears about appearing attractive. Heimann (1956) maintains that, whatever our feelings and reactions, however neurotic, in a patient's presence, they are in part, at least, a response to some need of the patient. These revisions, growing out of cautious self-scrutiny, argue for "disciplined subjectivity" rather than "objectivity" on the part of the therapist. As Khan (1974) has argued, experiencing another person can never be a neutralized stance of relating. Moreover, although a therapist might never touch or hold a patient in actuality, all intimacy, even when it is purely verbal, retains its original sense of involving body closeness. This notion is contained in Winnicott's (1965) metaphorical concept of the "holding environment." The term derives from the parental function of holding the infant but more broadly implies the provision of safety and protection from dangers. It is only by providing such a background of safety that the therapist can help his patient come to the liberating recognition that the "mind is the body."

References

Alexander, F. M. *The resurrection of the body.* New York: Delta, 1974.
Allport, G. W., and Vernon, P. *Studies in expressive behavior.* New York: The Macmillan Co., 1933.
American Dance Therapy Association. What is dance therapy really? *Proceedings of the 1972 American Dance Therapy Association.*
Auden, W. H. *Selected poetry of W. H. Auden.* New York: The Modern Library, 1957.
Balint, M. *The basic fault: Therapeutic aspects of regression.* London: Tavistock, 1968.
Bartenieff, I. Dance therapy: A new profession or a rediscovery of an ancient role of the dance? *Dance Scope,* 1972, 7, 6-19.
Bartenieff, I., and Davis M. *Effort-shape analysis of movement: The unity of function and expression.* New York: Albert Einstein College of Medicine, 1965.
Becker, E. *The denial of death.* New York: The Free Press, 1973.
Bergin, A. Some Implications of psychotherapy research for psychotherapeutic practice. *Journal of Abnormal Psychology,* 1971, 71, 235-246.
Birdwhistell, R. L. *Kinesics and context.* New York: Ballantine Books, 1970.
Brown, M. The new body psychotherapies. *Psychotherapy: Theory, research, and practice,* 1973, 10, 98-116.
Brown, N. O. *Life against death.* Middletown, Connecticut: Wesleyan University Press, 1959.
Bruner, J. S. The course of cognitive growth. *American Psychologist,* 1964, 19, 1-15.
Chace, M. Dance as an adjunctive therapy with hospitalized mental patients. *Bulletin of the Menninger Clinic,* 1953, 17, 14-19.

Davis, M. *Understanding body movements: An annotated bibliography.* New York: Arno Press, 1972.
Dell, C. *A primer for movement description.* New York: Dance Notation Bureau, Inc., 1970.
Deutsch, F. Analytic posturology. *Psychoanalytic Quarterly,* 1952, *21,* 196-214.
Ekman, P., and Friesen, W. V. Nonverbal leakage and clues to deception. *Psychiatry,* 1969, *32,* 88-106.
Etizioni, A. *The active society.* New York: The Free Press of Glencoe, 1968.
Feldenkrais, M. *Body and mature behavior.* New York: International Universities Press, 1949.
Feldman, S. S. *Mannerisms of speech and gesture in everyday life.* New York: International Universities Press, 1959.
Fisher, S. *Body consciousness.* Englewood Cliffs, New Jersey: Prentice-Hall, 1973.
Frank, J. D. The bewildering world of psychotherapy. *The Journal of Social Issues,* 1972, *28,* 27-43.
Freud, A. Acting out. *International Journal of Psychoanalysis,* 1968, *49,* 165-170.
Freud, S. Fragment of an analysis of a case of hysteria. (1905) *Collected Papers.* Vol. 2. New York Basic Books, 1959.
Freud, S. Further recommendations in the technique of psychoanalysis. (1913) *Collected Papers.* Vol. 2. New York: Basic Books, 1959.
Freud, S. Totem and taboo. In J. Strachey (Ed.), *The standard edition of the complete works of Sigmund Freud.* Vol. 13. London: Hogarth, 1958 (originally published, 1913).
Freud, S. Remembering, repeating and working through. In J. Strachey (Ed.), *The standard edition of the complete psychological works of Sigmund Freud.* Vol. 12. London: Hogarth, 1958 (originally published, 1914).
Freud, S. Turnings in the ways of psychoanalytic therapy. (1919) *Collected papers.* Vol. 2. New York: Basic Books, 1959.
Freud, S. *The ego and the id.* (1923) New York: W. W. Norton, 1962.
Freud, S. *An outline of psychoanalysis.* New York: W. W. Norton, 1949.
Friedlander, P. *Plato.* New York: Pantheon Books, 1964.
Fromm-Reichmann, F. *Principles of intensive psychotherapy.* Chicago: University of Chicago Press, 1950.
Gendlin, E. T. *Experiencing and the creation of meaning.* New York: Free Press of Glencoe, 1962.
Grossman, C. M. Transference, countertransference and being in love. *Psychoanalytic Quarterly,* 1965, *34,* 249-256.
Guntrip, H. *Schizoid phenomena, object relations and the self.* New York: International Universities Press, 1969.
Havens, L. L. The existential use of self. *The American Journal of Psychiatry,* 1974, *131,* 1-10.
Heimann, P. On counter-transference: *International Journal of Psychoanalysis,* 1956, *31,* 81-84.
Horowitz, M. J. Modes of representation of thought. *Journal of the American Psychoanalytic Association,* 1972, *20,* 793-819.
Hurn, H. T. Toward a paradigm of the terminal phase. *Journal of the American Psychoanalytic Association,* 1971, *19,* 332-348.
Janov, A. *The primal scream.* New York: Dell, 1970.
Jones, E. *Life and work of Sigmund Freud.* Vol. 3. New York: Basic Books, 1957.
Kernberg, O. *Borderline conditions and pathological narcissism.* New York: Jacob Aronson, Inc., 1975.
Khan, M. M. R. *The privacy of the self.* New York: International Universities Press, 1974.
Laban, R. *The mastery of movement.* London: MacDonald and Evans, 1960.

Lacan, J. The mirror phase. *New Left Review*, 1968, *51*, 71-78.
Laing, R. D. *The divided self*. Baltimore: Pelican Books, 1965.
Langer, S. K. *Philosophy in a new key*. Cambridge, Harvard University Press, 1942.
Lévi-Strauss, C. *Structural anthropology*. New York: Anchor, 1967.
Lieberman, M. A., and Gardner, J. R. Institutional alternatives to psychotherapy. *Archives of General Psychiatry*, 1976, *33*, 157-162.
Loewald, H. On the therapeutic action of psychoanalysis. *International Journal of Psychoanalysis*, 1960, *41*, 1-18.
Loewenstein, R. M. Some remarks on the role of speech in psychoanalytic, technique. *International Journal of Psychoanalysis*, 1956, *37*, 460-468.
Lowen, A. *Physical dynamics of character structure*. New York: Grune and Stratton, 1958.
Lowen, A. *The betrayal of the body*. London: Collier, 1967.
McCartney, J. Overt transference. *Journal of Sex Research*, 1966, *2*, 227-237.
McLuhan, M. *Understanding media: The extensions of man*. New York: Signet Books, 1964.
Mahl, G. F. Gestures and body movements in interviews. In J. Shlien (Ed.), *Research in psychotherapy*. Vol. 3. Washington, D. C.: American Psychological Association, 1968.
Marin, P. The new narcissism. *Reflections*, 1976, *11*, 1-16.
Marmor, J. Sexual acting-out in psychotherapy. *The American Journal of Psychoanalysis*, 1972, *32*, 3-8.
May, R. *Love and will*. New York: W. W. Norton, 1969.
Mehrabian, A. *Nonverbal communications*. Chicago: Aldine-Atherton, 1972.
Merleau-Ponty, M. *Phenomenology of perception*. New York: Humanities Press, 1962.
Modell, A. "The holding environment" and the therapeutic action of psychoanalysis. *Journal of the American Psychoanalytic Association*, 1976, *24*, 285-309.
Nietzsche, F. Thus spoke Zarathustra. In W. Kaufman (Ed.), *The portable Nietzsche*. New York: The Viking Press, 1954.
Paul, I. H. *Letters to Simon*. New York: International Universities Press, 1973.
Perls, F. *Gestalt therapy verbatim*. New York: Bantam Books, 1971.
Pesso, A. *Movement in psychotherapy: Psychomotor techniques and training*. New York: University Press, 1969.
Piaget, J. *The origins of intelligence in children*. New York: International Universities Press, 1951.
Piaget, J., and Inhelder, B. *The psychology of the child*. New York: Basic Books, 1969.
Polster, E., and Polster, M. *Gestalt therapy integrated*. New York: Vintage Books, 1974.
Reich, A. On the termination of analysis. *International Journal of Psychoanalysis*, 1950, *31*, 179-183.
Reich, W. *Character analysis*. New York: Orgone Institute Press, 1949.
Reich, W. *Function of the orgasm*. New York: Farrar, Straus, and Giroux, 1961.
Reik, T. *Fragment of a great confession*. New York: Farrar and Strauss, 1949.
Rieff, P. *Freud: The mind of the moralist*. New York: Doubleday, 1961.
Rieff, P. *Freud: Therapy and technique*. New York: Collier Books, 1963.
Rolf, I. P. Structural integration. *Systematics*, 1963, *1*, 66-83.
Rosen, V. The relevance of "style" to certain aspects of defense and the synthetic function of the ego. *International Journal of Psychoanalysis*, 1961, *42*, 447-457.
Rosen, V. Sign phenomena and their relationship to unconscious meaning. *International Journal of Psychoanalysis*, 1969, *50*, 197-207.
Schachtel, E. *Metamorphosis*. New York: Basic Books, 1959.
Schachter, S. The interaction of cognitive and physiological determinants of emotional state. In L. Berkowitz (Ed.), *Advances in experimental social psychology*. New York: Academic Press, 1964.

Schafer, R. The psychoanalytic vision of reality. *International Journal of Psychoanalysis,* 1970, *51,* 279-297.
Schafer, R. The termination of brief psychoanalytic psychotherapy. *International Journal of Psychoanalytic Psychotherapy.* 1973, *2,* 135-148.
Schafer, R. *A new language for psychoanalysis.* New Haven: Yale University Press, 1976.
Scheflen, A. E. The significance of posture in communication systems. *Psychiatry,* 1964, *27,* 316-331.
Schimek, J. G. A critical re-examination of Freud's concept of unconscious mental representation. *International Review of Psychoanalysis,* 1975, *2,* 1971-186.
Schoop, T. Philosophy and practice. *American Dance Therapy Newsletter,* 1971, *5,* 3-5.
Searles, H. F. Oedipal love in the countertransference. In *Collected papers on schizophrenia and related subjects.* New York: International Universities Press, 1965.
Siegel, E. V. Movement therapy as a psychotherapeutic tool. *Journal of the American Psychoanalytic Association,* 1973, *21,* 333-343.
Siegel, M. B. *Please run on the playground.* Hartford: Connecticut Commission on the Arts, 1975.
Shapiro, D. Dynamic and holistic ideas of neurosis and psychotherapy. *Psychiatry,* 1975, *33,* 218-226.
Sharpe, E. F. *Dream analysis: A practical handbook for psychoanalysis.* New York: W. W. Norton, 1938.
Sontag, S. *Against Interpretation.* New York: Delta, 1966.
Spiegel, J., and Machotka, P. *Messages of the body.* New York: The Free Press, 1974.
Sullivan, H. S. *The psychiatric interview.* New York: W. W. Norton, 1954.
Szasz, T. On the experiences of the analyst in the psychoanalytic situation. *Journal of the American Psychoanalytic Association,* 1957, *4,* 197-223.
Tillich, P. *Psychoanalysis and existentialism.* Conference of the American Association of Existential Psychology and Psychiatry, February, 1962.
Tower, L. E. Countertransference. *Journal of the American Psychoanalytic Association,* 1956, *4,* 224-255.
Wiener, M., Devoe, S., Rubinow, S., and Geller, J. D. Nonverbal behavior and nonverbal communication. *Psychological Review,* 1972, *79,* 185-214.
Winnicott, D. *The maturational process and the facilitating environment.* New York: International Universities Press, 1965.
Wolff, W. *The expression of personality,* New York: Harper and Brothers, 1943.

PART VI

Conclusion

Introduction

Our concluding chapter by Dr. Meichenbaum takes a hard look at various approaches using imagery and asks the simple question, Why should they work? It would be premature to assert that we are anywhere near an answer to that question. Indeed, despite the anecdotal reports of success that all participants in this volume can match, we have little systematic evidence of the degree to which some approaches work better than others and little evidence of differential effectiveness for different kinds of clients or different patterns of presenting complaints or symptoms. Meichenbaum's chapter, written from the perspective of an innovative worker in the area of cognitive-behavior modification, poses some significant possibilities, however. The effort at integration and clarification will be a welcome one to the reader after the long route traversed in this volume.

Some readers and indeed our contributors may find some of Meichenbaum's comments or suggested argument for therapeutic effects overly simplified. Indeed, considering the elaborate superstructure of theory in the various procedures described, one may feel that Meichenbaum has given short shrift to subtleties of theory generally. At the same time it can be argued that psychotherapeutic work beginning with psychoanalysis carried too heavy a burden of elaborate theory that could not be easily reconciled to the actual operations performed by therapists. A boldly simple statement of the type with which we conclude this volume puts the burden on the specific imagery therapists to show why the subtleties of their theory are essential to explain the psychological effects of their treatments. The formulation by Meichenbaum also has the advantage of pointing the way toward some useful research approaches.

We have somewhat ambitiously called this book *The Power of*

Human Imagination and the testimony of our contributors, all responsible scholars, supports that emphasis. At the same time, since we work within the scientific domain we must be on guard to look for stronger evidence and also to recognize (as Kazdin's chapter suggests) the limitations of human imagery. Because psychologists, especially through more than half of this century, tended to ignore imagery as a possibly adaptive and researchable psychological function, we have tried herein to stress the positive implications of this basic human capacity. Time and much more scientific hard work will tell whether our emphasis carries us too far into the realms of fantasy or whether imagery truly represents a relatively untapped reservoir for the effective amelioration of maladjustment or for greater personal development.

13

Why Does Using Imagery in Psychotherapy Lead to Change?

Donald Meichenbaum

1. The Need for an Integrative Orientation

Desensitization, emotive imagery, aversive images, implosive images, covert modeling, "depth" images, psychosynthesis, eidetic therapy, guided affective images. . . one could continue conservatively to index over 20 ways images have been used in psychotherapy. Success is claimed for each procedure. By now, you may be impressed, if not overwhelmed, by the plethora of imagery techniques used in psychotherapy. It is almost as if we had given psychotherapists a creativity task and asked them to answer the following item: "What are all of the unusual uses of imagery in psychotherapy?" Only the therapist's imagination and degree of *chutzpa* seem to restrict what he asks his client to imagine under the so-called rationale of psychotherapy.* Assagioli (1965) asked patients to imagine that their bodies were being consumed in flames in order to experience a degree of freedom and a sense of "spiritual essence." Luenar (1969) (see chap. 5) requested clients to imagine scenes involving meadows, mountains, and brooks. Wolpe

---

* Rosten (1968) defines the Yiddish word "chutzpa" as gall, brazen nerve, presumption-plus-arrogance, such as no other word and no other language can do justice to. Chutzpa is that quality enshrined in a man who, having killed his mother and father, throws himself on the mercy of the court because he is an orphan.

Donald Meichenbaum • Department of Psychology, University of Waterloo, Waterloo, Ontario, Canada. The theory presented in this chapter was based on research supported by a grant from the Ontario Mental Health Foundation, Grant Number 551-75B.

(1958) had clients imagine phobic scenes along a graded hierarchy. In all of its varieties, imagery has been embraced as a psychotherapeutic tool with a fervor that bears critical evaluation. Birk (1974) called such fervor "furor therapeutics," that is, an unbridled therapeutic optimism, with accompanying signs of a frenzy of publications unconstrained by careful empirical evaluation. Although Birk was using "furor therapeutics" to refer to biofeedback therapy, it seems equally applicable to the burgeoning use of imagery in psychotherapy.

The purpose of this chapter is *not* to dampen a sense of optimism, but rather to impose a critical analysis on the host of imagery techniques and to examine how imagery procedures "fit" in the broader context of psychotherapy. The goal is to offer a conceptual framework that will help us understand why and how a client's therapeutic images contribute to change. At present the number of proposed mechanisms underlying imagery therapy seem to be no fewer than the number of techniques available. Concepts of extinction, adaptation, catharsis, mental rehearsal, changed self-image, self-reinforcement, cognitive restructuring, unconscious unfolding, circumventing patient resistance, and so on, have all been offered to explain the value of imagery. The lexicon reflects the breadth of the psychological litany, whether derived from Freud, Jung, Perls, Wolpe, etc. Wilkins (1974) has indicated that in the absence of an empirically based unified theory of imagery, the psychotherapy literature attempts to account for improvement primarily by borrowing theoretical constructs from other psychological areas (e.g., conditioning, Hullian theory, psychoanalytic formulations, etc.):

> These theories not only may have generated theoretical inconsistencies, but may also have fostered the inclusion of unnecessary procedural elements in the practice of psychotherapy. (Wilkins, 1974, p. 163)

Perhaps we can "cut (or shovel) through" the different imagery techniques and their accompanying rationales, noting elements in common. An examination of these similarities will help elucidate the nature of the psychological mechanisms involved in behavioral change. The field of psychotherapy is in urgent need of such theoretical speculations, for without them we will merely witness the fecundity of imagination—and a flood of empirical studies. This research will essentially be concerned with the relative efficacy of one imagery procedure versus another for some particular clinical population or the sequential examination of the components of a particular imagery therapy procedure. Not that "engineering" questions are unimportant, but perhaps we can short-circuit some tedious and expensive comparisons by theorizing a bit, searching for common elements, and examining where imagery fits within the larger context of psychotherapy.

2. Imagery and the Context of Psychotherapy

An examination of a particular therapy procedure, such as imagery, usually fails to place that particular technique within the larger psychotherapeutic context. Prior to the use of any particular treatment intervention(s) there is an initial phase of psychotherapy that involves (1) the client's describing symptoms or reasons for coming to therapy; (2) a historical and usually a situational analysis of the presenting problem; and (3) the therapist's offering a description of the treatment and providing the client with some rationale for his problems and the proposed therapy. The therapy rationale may not be offered in an explicit didactic fashion, but may emerge implicitly out of the therapist–client interactions. The types of questions the therapist asks, the tests he gives, the homework he assigns, each contribute to the emerging rationale.

Therapists have usually subsumed this initial phase of psychotherapy under such terms as *nonspecific factors*. Rarely are the events prior to the use of a particular imagery technique discussed. We are usually provided with specific details of the nature, contents, duration of the specific images, but little or no mention is made of the client's conceptualization of his problem(s), his expectations about treatment, and so forth.

Following the use of a particular imagery procedure, a transfer phase ensues during which the client employs the skills he has acquired in nonclinical settings. Indeed, the client's success in implementing the cognitive and behavioral coping skills he has acquired in therapy will influence the maintenance and generalization of the effects of imagery-based therapy.

Thus, the more than 20 imagery therapy procedures must be viewed in the context of a flow of events. Such an observation may appear quite obvious and commonsensical, but its recognition serves as a prelude to a cognitive theory of behavior change that will elucidate the psychological processes that underlie imagery techniques.

3. Cognitive Theory of Behavior Change

Elsewhere (Meichenbaum, 1977) I have provided a detailed presentation of the sequence of cognitive mediating events that accounts for behavioral change following from psychotherapeutic interventions. For now, an encapsulated summary will suffice.

My cognitive theory postulates a three-phase process that can describe behavior change resulting from diverse types of clinical intervention. These three phases form a flexible sequence (not a lock-step progression) in which various psychological processes and environmental events interact in contributing to change.

3.1. Self-Awareness

The first step in the change process involves the client's becoming an observer of his own behavior. If behavioral change is to result from psychotherapy, then the client through heightened awareness and deliberate attention must monitor his thoughts, feelings, physiological reactions, and/or interpersonal behaviors with increased sensitivity. With practice, the client will begin to notice earlier and earlier signs of the onset of his maladaptive reactions, noting low-intensity incipient cues. The cues may be *intra*personal in nature, such as the client's physiological reactions, thoughts, images, feelings, and/or they may be *inter*personal, the situational context or behavioral reactions of others. This process of *heightened awareness* or "raised consciousness" is facilitated in the course of therapy by means of the conceptualization, or translation process, that evolves between the client and therapist.

When the client enters therapy, he usually conveys a sense of helplessness, hopelessness, a fear of "losing one's mind," a sense of demoralization, all of which have been described by Frank (1974), Meichenbaum (1977), Raimy (1975), and Strupp (1970). This is reflected not only in the client's comments to the therapist, but also in the content of his internal dialogue (i.e., the set of automatic thoughts and images that precede, accompany, and follow his maladaptive behavior).

In the same way that the therapist attempts to make sense of the client's problems, the client also is attempting to construct some meaning for his behavior. The conceptualization system that emerges between the client and therapist serves the function of providing this necessary "meaning." The language system of the conceptualization process will be influenced by the therapist's orientation, client's expectations, and goals of treatment.

The exact behaviors upon which the client will focus are influenced by the conceptualization process that evolves during therapy. Whereas the client usually enters therapy with some conceptualization of his problems (as well as expectations concerning therapy and the role of the therapist), the client's conceptualization of his problem must undergo change if he is to alter his behavior. As a result of the translation process that occurs in therapy, the client develops a new way to view his maladaptive behaviors or symptoms. Attending to maladaptive behaviors now takes on a different meaning. This is important because one of the things that already characterizes some clients prior

… to therapy is a heightened awareness, a self-preoccupation. Prior to therapy the client's internal dialogue about his maladaptive behaviors is likely to be delimited, repetitive, and unproductive, contributing to a sense of helplessness and despair. In order to change, the client must come to view his thoughts, images, feelings, and behaviors differently. The conceptualization process that is inherent in all therapies facilitates this translation process.

For example, a female client who entered therapy with obsessive-compulsive behaviors may be seen in conjoint therapy with her husband in order to examine the interpersonal meaning and function of her symptoms. In this way the therapist is helping "translate" the meaning, or what the client says to herself, about her presenting problems. Rather than the client's symptoms being a reflection of "her" problem, over the course of therapy, the problem now becomes viewed from a different conceptualization or language system. The language system gives rise to particular intervention steps, and the focusing or increased awareness of specific behaviors. It is proposed that such a translation process occurs in every therapeutic approach and, as we will see, one function of imagery exercises in therapy is to facilitate and reinforce this translation process.

The initial phase of the cognitive theory of behavior change is concerned with the increased awareness that evolves from the translation process; but more must occur if change is to then take place.

3.2. Generating Adaptive New Thoughts and Responses

As the client's self-observations become attuned to incipient low-intensity aspects of his maladaptive behavior, the client learns to omit adaptive coping cognitions and behaviors that interfere with the maladaptive ones in the second theoretical phase of behavior change. The self-observation signals the opportunity for producing adaptive thoughts and behaviors. The content of what the client learns to do when he notices his maladaptive behaviors will vary with the conceptualization that emerges in therapy. However, if the client's behavior is to change, then what he says to himself and/or imagines must initiate a new behavioral chain, one that is incompatible with his maladaptive behaviors. Behavior therapy procedures are particularly valuable in aiding in the acquisition of such skills.

Thus, the process of self-observation acts as a stimulus for the client to emit incompatible thoughts, images, and behaviors that he has discussed, learned, and rehearsed in therapy. It is important to indicate that the processes of self-observation and the accompanying act of engaging in an internal dialogue interrupt the sequence of maladaptive behaviors. Habitual acts (i.e., not premeditated) will now be "deautomatized," that is, preceded by deliberate cognitions. Such "forced mediation" increases the likelihood of interrupting a chain of events that would otherwise lead to maladaptive responses.

3.3. *In Vivo* Practice

This leads us to the third phase of the change process, which focuses on the client coping *in vivo*, and on what he says to himself and imagines about the outcomes of these "personal experiments." Persistence and generalization of treatment effects are determined by the client's internal dialogue and images concerning his own behavior change. What the client says to himself and/or imagines (e.g., his appraisals, attributions, self-evaluations) about both his behavior and the reactions of others to his behavior will influence the amount of transfer of treatment that occurs. The third phase of the cognitive theory of behavior change is concerned with the process of the client's producing adaptive behaviors in his everyday world and how he assesses the behavioral outcomes.

This three-phase description of the client's mediational processes can help explain the changes that result from imagery-based therapies, as well as other forms of psychotherapy.

4. Imagery-Based Therapies

The many different imagery-based therapy procedures can be conceptualized and clustered in numerous ways. We could focus on the different theoretical systems that have been used to explain the respective approaches, whether deriving from a learning, Jungian, psychoanalytic, and/or Gestalt orientation. On the other hand, we could disregard the so-called theories in which each of the procedures is couched, its "scientific trappings," and examine procedural similarities between procedures. Wilkins (1974) employed this approach. The present plan is to determine the psychological processes that are common to the variety of imagery therapies and then to examine the respective imagery-based therapies in terms of the three-phase cognitive theory of behavior change. In this way we can consider how a particular imagery therapy procedure will in turn influence (1) the specific aspects of the client's own behavior to which he attends; (2) what he then says to himself and images when he notices the maladaptive behaviors; (3) what new adaptive behaviors he is likely to produce and how he will assess and react to the consequences that follow his attempt at engaging in the adaptive acts. Imagery-based therapy procedures influence the behavioral change process at each of these phases, with some imagery techniques focusing a bit more on one phase than another.

5. Psychological Processes Underlying Imagery-Based Therapies

The first point to be emphasized is that fantasy of spontaneous imagery is prevalent in the normal population. As Singer and McCraven (1961) reported, 96% of the respondents to a daydreaming questionnaire reported that they daily engage in some form of daydreaming. Their daydreams took the form of fairly clear images of people, objects, or events. Daydreaming dealing with planning future actions and particularly interpersonal contacts were in high frequency, with the largest percentage of daydreams involving fairly practical immediate concerns. For most of the respondents, daydreaming was *not* a matter of wish-fulfillment ideation, but rather attempts to explore the future through positing a variety of alternatives, not specifically involving satisfactory outcomes.

Given the widespread occurrence of imagery behavior, it is not surprising to find that a number of imagery-based and cognitive therapists assign a central role to spontaneous fantasies in contributing to clients' maladaptive behavior. For example, Beck (1970) reported that anxiety patients offered reports of having experienced repeated daydreams with a content of personal danger. Interestingly, these same patients had not reported these daydreams to physicians who had previously interviewed them. The physicians had not deemed it important to query about the contribution of images to the clients' maladaptive behavior. Beck reported that in one case a woman with a fear of walking alone found that her spells of anxiety followed images of her having a heart attack and being left helpless. In a second case, a college student discovered that her anxiety at leaving the dormitory was triggered by visual fantasies of being attacked. Such idiosyncratic cognitions (whether pictorial or verbal) are usually very rapid and often contain an elaborate idea compressed into a few seconds. Beck pointed out that these cognitions are experienced as though they were automatic and involuntary, and that they usually possess the quality of appearing plausible, rather than unrealistic. Singer and Antrobus (1972) described factor patterns based on large-scale studies of daydreaming that indicated that anxious-distractible or guilty-dysphoric styles of daydreaming were more likely to be associated with emotional disturbance.

Feather and Rhoads (1972) have also highlighted the role imagery plays in contributing to maladaptive behavior. For example, they illustrate this in the case of the phobic by eliciting the client's fantasy as related to the phobic situation. The therapist gets at the client's fantasy by pursuing the question, What is the *worst* thing that could happen if the client were confronted by the phobic stimulus event? A speech-anxious client reported the fantasy of getting so angry with himself and the audience that he loses control and hurts someone. Feather and Rhoads desensitized the client to the fantasy underlying the anxiety. The desensitization treatment is based on the notion that in many instances the client is afraid of his own thoughts, and that much of the client's behavior is a learned avoidance of having such thoughts.

In both the Beck and Feather-Rhoads examples the therapy operates by having the clients become aware of the role their images play in contributing to their maladaptive feelings and behavior. Almost all of the imagery-based therapies attempt to assess the role that the client's imagery plays in contributing to his presenting problems. Note that whether such images actually account for the occurrence of the maladaptive behavior is less important than that both the client and therapist believe that is the case. So long as the client is willing to entertain the notion that such images contribute to his problems, then he will more likely accept the therapy rationale and the consequential intervention steps. In other words, we do not know whether nonclinical cases or nonpatients have similar imagery experiences. Do low speech-anxious individuals, for example, also have fantasies similar to those in the Feather-Rhoads example, but perhaps with the same set of images having—for reasons unknown—adaptive rather than maladaptive consequences? What about Beck's case of the undergraduate female and her images of being attacked? When does such imagery lead to adaptive appropriate precautions and when does it lead to debilitating anxiety and clinical symptomatology? Singer (1975) has proposed that while most people have some frightening or destructive fantasies, only those persons whose fantasies are predominantly fearful or dysphoric are likely to show neurotic or psychotic trends. Normal individuals show a variety of fantasy, including many playful, positive, or fanciful wishful daydreams.

In short, two points need to be underscored. First, it is a mistake to infer the causative role of particular images in psychopathology without exploring their occurrence in "normal" populations. Secondly, and more relevant to the concerns of the present chapter, the client-therapist belief that certain images are causative serves an important therapeutic function. Whether or not such images actually contribute to the client's maladaptive behaviors is less important for purposes of explaining change than is the client's emerging conceptualization of his problems in terms that involve imagery.

Recall that my goal is to put forth an explanatory system that will explain behavior change following from diverse imagery-based therapies. Once the therapist and client begin to focus on the client's imagery (either in terms of daydreams, dreams, and/or the set of automatic images that precede, accompany, and follow the maladaptive act), they are beginning to evolve an explanatory system, a conceptualization, for inducing change.

A number of hypotheses have been offered to explain the therapeutic importance of focusing on the client's images. Therapists have argued that focusing on the client's images will:

1. Help clarify or pinpoint the nature of the client's current problem
2. Reduce unpleasant affect through repetition of the fantasy
3. Teach the client to distinguish between reality and fantasy
4. Teach the client to make ever finer discriminations among impulsive, motivational, cognitive, and behavioral aspects of his problem
5. Teach the client to control the fantasy scene
6. Increase the client's ability to recognize the irrationality of his beliefs
7. Decrease expectancy of disastrous consequences and increase realistic appraisal of external problems
8. Make the client's unconscious conscious

Central to many of these hypotheses is the notion that the imagery-based cognitive therapies operate by teaching clients, or giving clients the sense that they *can control their images*, in terms of content, frequency, duration, and functional impact on other ongoing streams of behavior, such as affect, physiological reactions, interpersonal behavior. Prior to therapy many clients express the feeling that they are "victims" of the thoughts, images, and feelings they experience. A sense of helplessness with regard to one's internal life is an important component of many presenting problems. Common to each of the imagery-based therapies is the teaching of imagery control. Many different therapeutic techniques are employed to achieve the goal of self-control. These vary from monitoring maladaptive images to instructing clients to intentionally increase the frequency of the maladaptive images, to bringing the image under some particular stimulus control both within the therapy setting and *in situ*, to trying to alter the meaning of a particular set of images by such techniques as imagery blow-up.*

Thus, it is proposed that imagery-based therapies contribute to change because they (1) "seduce," convince, teach the client to entertain the notion that his imagery contributes to his maladaptive behavior; (2) teach the client to become aware of and monitor his images and note their occurrence within the maladaptive behavioral chain, with the consequence of interrupting that maladaptive chain; and (3) alter what the client says to himself, and does, when he experiences images. The consequence of these processes is that they convey to the client a sense of control over his images and "inner life" and in turn overt interpersonal behavior.

The changing of the meaning that particular images hold for the client bears comment. Pylyshyn (1973) has noted that when we discuss mental imagery we usually rely heavily on a "picture metaphor":

> The whole vocabulary of imagery uses a language appropriate for describing pictures and the process of perceiving pictures. We speak of clarity and vividness of images, of scanning images, of seeing new patterns in images, and of naming objects or properties depicted in images. (Pylyshyn, 1973, p. 8)

The problem with the "picture metaphor" is that it fails to take into consideration the meaning system in which the image is couched. The mental representation or cognitive structures that generate and contribute to the image are overlooked. Within the domain of psychotherapy literature the language of the picture metaphor has given rise to a false distinction between so-called "imagery" therapies as compared to "verbal" therapies. Each time we ask our clients to engage in certain imagery exercises we are also affecting his internal dialogue, what he says to himself about the image, the meaning system surrounding the image and his maladaptive behaviors. It is proposed that each of the imagery therapies described in this book operates by influencing the client's internal dialgoue and his cognitive structures (e.g., beliefs) about his maladaptive behavior. Focusing our attention only on the parameters involving the image (such as duration, frequency, content of the image) will blind us to the larger impact of such imagery exercises. Whether we consider the imagery employed by a behavior therapist, or a Gestalt therapist, or a Jungian therapist, in each case the respective conceptualization of the client's problems will be con-

---

* Blow-up is an imagery procedure whereby the therapist has the client imagine in an exaggerated fashion the presenting problem. It is similar to implosion and paradoxical intention techniques (see Lazarus, 1971 for a description).

veyed in therapy. Insofar as the client comes to view his problems from that perspective, insofar as a translation process occurs, behavior change follows. Each technique operates by reinforcing in the client a new conceptualization of his problem. The adoption of this conceptualization leads to an alteration in the meaning of the client's maladaptive behavior. This changed meaning is evident in the internal dialogue in which the client engages, or what he says to himself, when he notices his maladaptive behavior.

Thus, it is proposed that imagery-based therapies operate by (1) conveying to the client a sense of control over his imagery and other behaviors and (2) by changing for the client the meaning of his maladaptive behavior. I have argued elsewhere (Meichenbaum, 1977) that it is not the occurrence of "maladaptive" images or irrational beliefs per se that accounts for psychopathological behavior. Rather, I proposed that one's behavior is influenced by the nature of the coping mechanisms that the individual calls into play when he notices that he has engaged in a set of maladaptive or task-inappropriate images, thoughts, feelings, and/or behaviors. A consideration of these coping mechanisms leads us to a discussion of the third psychological process that is required to explain the contribution of imagery-based therapies to behavior change. This is the process of mental preparation or covert modeling rehearsal. A number of different terms have been used to describe this psychological process, including "mental practice" (Richardson, 1967a, b), "work of worrying" (Janis, 1958; Marmor, 1958), and "muted role playing" (Sarbin, 1972). For example, the value of imagery rehearsal has been underscored in the mental-practice literature, in which various motor skills are taught by means of having subjects imagine engaging in the particular activity prior to its performance. Richardson (1967a) reports that the more familiar a task has become, the greater the relative gain that can be expected from mental practice. Other variables that have been implicated as important to mental rehearsal are accuracy of anticipated outcomes, clarity and control of imagery, degree of proficiency on the task, length of time provided for imagery, and the alternation of mental and physical practice. In the area of "work of worrying," the research on covert modeling has also shed light on how imagery-based therapies contribute to behavior change. A variable that has been explored is the distinction between *coping* and *mastery* modeling. The mastery model is one who demonstrates a flawless performance without any sign of hesitation, emotional distress, or self-doubt. On the other hand, the coping model displays initial performance anxieties, makes mistakes, but copes with his falterings, demonstrating the cognitive and behavioral strategies required for controlling and coping with diverse obstacles. Kazdin (1973, 1974) demonstrated that when clients are asked to imagine overcoming their fears and anxieties by means of mental rehearsal or covert modeling, a coping model is more effective than a mastery model. These results are consistent with other modeling studies by Meichenbaum (1971) and Sarason (1975), who have also found a coping model more effective than a mastery model. In other words, insofar as imagery-based therapies provide the client with opportunities to mentally rehearse, or to engage in mental problem-solving, the therapy will contribute to behavior change. The research on coping versus mastery modeling suggests that when we ask clients to engage in images, as in desensitization treatment, we are providing them with an opportunity to provide themselves with a model. The closer the model is to the real-life experience the more effective it is likely to be. One other byproduct of employing such coping models within imagery treatment should be noted. By using a coping model, the therapist is teaching the client to notice his maladaptive behavior, and this recognition is to be the cue, the reminder, to use the coping techniques he has learned and rehearsed in therapy. The client's own symptoms become the signal or discriminative stimulus for the generalization of treatment. Whereas prior to therapy the client's symptom might have been the harbinger for further deterioration, as a result of therapy, maladaptive behavior takes on a new meaning, namely, it is the reminder to use the coping techniques that he has mentally rehearsed in therapy.

In fine, the three psychological processes that have been proposed to explain why imagery-based therapies contribute to change are:

1. The sense of control that the client develops because of the monitoring and rehearsing of various images both in therapy and *in vivo*.

2. The changed meaning or altered internal dialogue that precedes, accompanies, and follows instances of maladaptive behavior. The imagery exercises couched within particular conceptualization contribute to this altered meaning or translation process.

3. The mental rehearsal of behavioral alternatives that contribute to the development of coping skills.

Each of these psychological processes influences the various phases of behavior change that have been previously described: The sense of control, altered meaning, and mental rehearsal influence what behaviors the client will attend to, what he says to himself or images when he notices instances of his maladaptive behaviors, what adaptive behaviors he emits, and finally, his evaluations of the consequences of trying the new behaviors.

Earlier, I spoke of *chutzpa* required in generating and using the host of imagery techniques in therapy. Perhaps some of this energy and "gall" should be directed at generating theories that explain why therapies contribute to change. The present chapter was designed to begin this process. By the way, no one ever suggested I was short on *chutzpa*.

ACKNOWLEDGMENTS

The author is grateful to Sandra Bates and Myles Genest for their editorial comments.

References

Assagioli, R. *Psychosynthesis: A collection of basic writings.* New York: Viking, 1965.
Beck, A. Role of fantasies in psychotherapy and psychopathology. *Journal of Nervous and Mental Disease*, 1970, *150*, 3-17.
Birk, L. Biofeedback: Behavioral medicine. *Seminars in Psychiatry*, 1974, *4*, 361-367.
Feather, B., and Rhoads, J. Psychodynamic behavior therapy: Theory and rationale. *Archives of General Psychiatry*, 1972, *26*, 496-506.
Frank, J. *Persuasion and healing.* Baltimore: Johns Hopkins Press, 1974.
Janis, I. *Psychological stress.* New York: John Wiley and Sons, 1958.
Kazdin, A. Covert modeling and the reduction of avoidance behavior. *Journal of Abnormal Psychology*, 1973, *81*, 87-95.
Kazdin, A. Covert modeling, model similarity, and reduction of avoidance behavior. *Behavior Therapy*, 1974, *5*, 325-340.
Lazarus, A. *Behavior therapy and beyond.* New York: McGraw Hill, 1971.
Leunar, H. Guided affective imagery: A method of intensive psychotherapy. *American Journal of Psychotherapy*, 1969, *23*, 4-22.
Marmor, J. The psychodynamics of realistic worry. *Psychoanalysis and Social Science*, 1958, *5*, 155-163.
Meichenbaum, D. Examination of model characteristics in reducing avoidance behavior. *Journal of Personality and Social Psychology*, 1971, *17*, 298-307.
Meichenbaum, D. *Cognitive-behavior modification: An integrative approach.* Plenum Press, 1977.
Pylyshyn, Z. What the mind's eye tells the mind's brain: A critique of mental imagery. *Psychological Bulletin*, 1973, *80*, 1-24.
Raimy, V. *Misunderstanding of the self: Cognitive psychotherapy and the misconception hypothesis.* San Francisco: Josey Bass, 1975.
Richardson, A. Mental practice: A review and discussion. Part I. *Research Quarterly*, 1967a, *38*, 95-107.
Richardson, A. Mental practice: A review and discussion. Part II. *Research Quarterly*, 1967b, *38*, 263-273.
Rosten, L. *The joys of Yiddish.* New York: McGraw Hill, 1968.
Sarason, I. Test anxiety and the self-disclosing coping model. *Journal of Consulting and Clinical Psychology*, 1975, *43*, 148-153.
Sarbin, T. Imagining as muted role-taking: A historical-linguistic analysis. In P. Sheehan (Ed.), *The function and nature of imagery.* New York: Academic Press, 1972.

Singer, J. L. *The inner world of daydreaming*. New York: Harper and Row, Colophon, 1975.
Singer, J. L., and Antrobus, J. S. Daydreaming, imaginal processes and personality: A normative study. In P. Sheehan (Ed.), *The function and nature of imagery*. New York: Academic Press, 1972.
Singer, J. L., and McCraven, V. Some characteristics of adult daydreaming. *Journal of Psychology*, 1961, 51, 151-164.
Strupp, H. Specific vs. non-specific factors in psychotherapy and the problem of control. *Archives of General Psychiatry*, 1970, 23, 393-401.
Wilkins, W. Parameters of therapeutic imagery: Directions from case studies. *Psychotherapy: Theory, Research and Practice*, 1974, 11, 163-171.
Wolpe, J. *Psychotherapy by reciprocal inhibition*. Stanford: Stanford University Press, 1958.

Author Index

Abraham, K., 282, 296, 305
Abralsam, G., 163
Adelsson, U., 157, 163
Ader, R., 250
Ashen, A., 123, 197, 198,
    200n, 201, 202, 203,
    204, 205, 206, 207,
    208, 209, 210, 212,
    213, 214, 215, 216,
    217, 218, 219, 220,
    221, 222
Alexander, F. M., 347, 375
Allport, G. W., 363, 375
Anant, S. S., 250
Antrobus, J. S., 323, 344
Arnheim, R., 189, 190,
    191, 195
Ashem, B., 251
Asher, L. M., 230, 251
Assagioli, R., 381, 393
Attneave, F., 187, 188,
    191, 195
Auden W. H., 350, 375

Bachrach, H. M., 342, 344
Balint, M., 159, 163, 358,
    375
Bandura, A., 26, 27, 28, 32,
    233, 251, 256, 261,
    262, 264, 265, 266,
    271, 272, 274, 275
Barber, T. X., 172, 195
Barlow, D. H., 230, 251

Barolin, G., 140, 163
Baron, M. G., 247, 251
Barrett, C. L., 267, 275
Bartenieff, I., 347, 371,
    375
Bateson, G., 190, 195
Beck, A. T., 28, 32, 46, 48,
    282, 290, 291, 306,
    387, 393
Becker E., 354, 375
Bellack, A. S., 265, 277
Benedetti, G., 145, 163
Benson, M., 229, 251
Beres, D., 312, 344
Bergin, A., 349, 375
Berne, E., 312, 337, 342,
    344
Bernstein, D. A., 273, 275
Biller, H. B., 219, 222
Birdwhistell, R. L., 364,
    370, 375
Birk, L., 382, 393
Black-Cleworth, P., 229,
    251
Blanchard, E. B., 271, 273,
    275
Blatt, S. J., 282, 284, 295,
    297, 306, 312, 344
Bogen, J. E., 6, 32
Booth, B., 250, 251
Bourne, L. E., 3, 32
Brengelmann, J. C., 151,
    154, 159, 163
Bronfenbrenner, U., 310,
    311, 344

Brown, M., 348n, 352, 353,
    368, 375
Brown, N. O., 352, 375
Brownell, K. D., 230, 251
Bruner, J. S., 9, 32, 357,
    375
Bühler, C., 145, 163
Burns, B., 65, 84, 87, 92
Burstein, E., 262, 275

Capra, F., 171, 190, 191,
    193, 194, 195
Cautela, J. R., 7, **227–250**,
    228, 229, 230, 233,
    235, 236, 240, 242,
    246, 250, 251, 252,
    255, 256, 257, 259,
    260, 263, 271, 275,
    276
Casey, E. S., 185, 186, 195
Chace, M., 347, 375
Chaitin, G. J., 192, 195
Chang, C.-Y., 182, 195
Chein, J., 343, 345
Cline, V. G., 310, 345
Corbin, E. B., 245, 252
Corson, S. A., 250, 252
Crowe, M. J., 271, 276

Dahlgren, H., 155, 163
Davé, R., 91, 92
Davidson, G. C., 267, 276
Davis, D., 274, 276

Davis, M., 370, 376
Dell, C., 376
Desoille, R., 7, 120, 123, 126, 163, 214, 222
Deutsch, F., 358, 362, 376
Dolan, A. T., 207, 211, 219, 221, 222
Douglas, M., 193, 195
Dymond, R. F. A., 310, 345

Eisenstein, S., 4, 32
Ekman, P., 370, 376
Elder, S. T., 229, 252
Eliade, M., 181, 182, 183, 184, 185, 195
Ellis, A., 25, 27, 32
Erickson, M., 169, 171, 173
Escalona, S. K., 99, 120
Etzioni, A., 372, 376
Evans-Wertz, W. Y., 179, 185, 195
Eysenck, H. J., 152, 164

Feather, B., 388, 393
Feldenkrais, M., 348, 376
Feldman, S. S., 358, 376
Ferenczi, S., 14, 373
Feshbach, S., 290, 291, 296, 306
Fisher, S., 120, 225, 252, 353, 354, 376
Flannery, R. B., 260, 271, 276
Fleiss, R., 314, 345
Fox, R. E., 342, 345
Frank, J. D., 347, 349, 376, 384, 393
Frank, L., 126, 164
Frank, S. J., 25, 279, **309–344**, 320, 325n, 345
Frazer, J. G., 184, 195
Freiwald, M., 141, 164
Fretigny, R., 214, 223
Freud, A., 358, 376
Freud, S., 5, 8, 14, 17, 32, 35, 40, 48, 52, 74, 79, 81, 85, 87, 88, 89, 91, 92, 120, 126, 127, 135, 137, 138, 145, 158,

Freud, S. (cont.)
159, 160, 161, 164, 183, 248, 252, 282, 296, 306, 351, 357, 358, 360, 362, 369, 371, 373, 376
Friar, L., 231, 252
Friedman, P. H., 271, 276
Fromm, E., 96, 120
Fromm-Reichmann, F., 371, 376

Ganz, L., 85, 92
Gardner, H., 186, 191, 195
Garfield, Z. H., 271, 276
Garrity, B., 221, 223
Gazzaniga, H. S., 6, 32
Geller, J. D., 7, 8, 279, **347–375**
Gendlin, E. T., 352, 359, 376
Gerst, M. S., 267, 276
Gill, M., 5, 32
Ginott, H., 175, 195
Goldfarb, C., 250, 252
Goldfried, M., 227, 252
Gordon, R., 312, 316, 345
Gordon, W. J., 90, 92
Gould, R., 336, 345
Gray, C. R., 201, 223
Greene, A., 250, 252
Greenleaf, E., 123, **167–195**, 160, 170, 173, 175, 186, 188, 191, 195
Greenson, R., 312, 345
Greer, S., 250, 252
Grossman, C. M., 375, 376
Guggenbuhl-Craig, A., 167, 195
Guiora, A. Z., 343, 345
Guntrip, H., 97, 120, 367, 376
Gur, R. E., 91, 92
Gur, R. L., 88, 92

Haggard, E. A., 40, 49
Haley, J., 169, 171, 173, 176, 182, 194, 195
Hammer, M., 109, 120

Happich, C., 126, 164
Hariton, E. B., 25, 33
Haronian, F., 164, 222, 223
Harty, M. K., 311, 345
Havens, L. L., 374, 376
Hay, W. M., 260, 276
Heimann, P., 375, 376
Henle, I., 157, 164
Hersen, M., 230, 252
Hillman, J. A., 196
Holfeld, H., 157, 164
Homme, L. E., 228, 252
Horney, K., 74, 77, 92
Horowitz, M. J., 7, 8, 10, 12, 13, 33, 35, **37–48**, 38, 40, 44, 49, 101, 120, 226, 309, 312, 313, 316, 317, 345, 356, 357, 365, 376
Hull, R. F. C., 180, 196
Hurley, A. D., 273, 276
Hurn, H. T., 372, 376

Jackson, D. N., 322n, 345
Jacobson, E., 126, 164, 236, 253
Jaensch, E. R., 201, 223
James, W., 4, 33
Janis, I. L., 24, 33, 391, 393
Janov, A., 348n, 376
Jasper, H. H., 229, 253
Jaynes, J., 8n, 33
Jellinek, A., 100, 120
Jerison, H. J., 188, 189, 191, 196
John, E. R., 253
Johnson, D. M., 3, 33
Jones, E., 373, 376
Jordan, S., 221, 223
Jung, C. G., 40, 49, 76, 123, 136, 158, 161, 164, 180, 181, 182, 183, 184, 185, 186, 191, 196
Jurgela, A., 247, 253

Kagan, N., 342, 345
Kanzer, M., 40, 49
Kaplan, H. S., 25, 33
Katzenstein, A., 222, 223

Author Index

Kavetsky, R. E., 250, 253
Kazdin, A. E., 7, 23, 24, **225–274**, 226, 237, 253, 260, 261, 262, 263, 264, 265, 266, 268, 269, 270, 273, 274, 276, 277, 380, 391, 393
Kepecs, J. G., 40, 49, 198, 223
Kernberg, O., 367, 374, 376
Khan, M. M. R., 358, 375, 376
King, D. L., 229, 253
Klinger, E., 291, 292, 293, 299, 306
Koch, W., 157, 164
Kohut, H., 311, 312, 345
Kornadt, H.-J., 134, 164
Kornhaber, R. C., 262, 277
Kosbab, F. P., 139, 157, 164
Kozak, M. J., 234, 253
Kreische, R., 143, 164
Kretschmer, E., 126, 164
Kreutzer, G., 160, 164
Kris, E., 6, 33
Krojanker, R. J., 125, 164
Kubie, L., 207, 223
Kulessa, C., 148, 152, 153, 155, 159, 164

Laban, R., 370, 376
Lacan, J., 354n, 377
Ladouceur, R., 273, 277
Laing, R. D., 95, 120, 377
Landau, E., 139, 164
Lang, P. J., 236, 253
Langer, S. K., 350, 365, 366, 377
Lazarus, A., 25, 33, 198, 222, 223, 227, 253, 282, 290, 291, 306, 321, 345, 390n, 393
LeBaron, S., 63, 92
LeShan, L. L., 250, 253
Leuner, H., 22, 109, 120, 123, **125–163**, 125, 126, 128, 131, 139, 140, 141, 142, 143,

Leuner, H. (cont.)
145, 146, 149, 157, 158, 160, 161, 165, 214, 223, 381, 393
Lévi-Strauss, C., 349, 377
Lewin, K., 26, 33
Lieberman, M. A., 372n, 377
Lipkin, S., 198, 223
Loevinger, J., 341, 345
Loewald, H., 351, 368, 376
Loewenstein, R. M., 355, 357, 377
LoPiccolo, J., 271, 277
Lowen, A., 348, 359, 377
Luce, R. A., 197, 222, 223
Lynn, D. B., 219, 223

McCartney, J., 373, 377
McCullough, L. S., **227–250**
McFall, R. M., 272, 277
McLemore, C. W., 274, 277
McLuhan, M., 354, 355, 368, 377
Mahl, G. F., 364, 369, 377
Mahoney, M. J., 227, 253, 256, 277
Maier, H. W., 125, 165
Marburg, C. C., 264, 277
Marin, P., 352, 377
Marks, D. E., 336, 337, 345
Marks, I. M., 271, 272, 274, 277
Marlatt, G. A., 256, 257, 261, 277
Marmor, J., 371, 377, 391, 393
Marshall, W. L., 273, 277
Martin, D. G., 207, 209, 223
Masters, W. H., 149, 166
May, R., 367, 377
Mehrabian, A., 370, 377
Meichenbaum, D., 22, 24, 33, 226, 227, 253, 262, 277, 292, 299, 300, 306, 379, **381–393**, 383, 384, 391, 392, 393

Merleau-Ponty, M., 357, 377
Miller, N., 229, 253
Miller, T., 312n, 337, 345
Mischel, W., 3, 33
Modell, A., 374, 377
Morishige, H. H., 67, 72, 84, 85, 87, 88, 91, 92
Mowrer, O. H., 228, 253
Murphy, G., 110, 120

Neisser, U., 281, 306
Nerenz, K., 143, 166
Neumann, C., 250, 253
Nietzsche, F., 352, 377
Norman, D. A., 201, 223

Odier, C., 196
Old, J., 229, 253
Orne, M., 183, 196

Paige, S., 7
Paivio, A., 4, 8, 33, 281, 306
Panagiotou, N., 203, 208, 209, 212, 216, 223
Patterson, G. R., 320n, 345
Paul, I. H., 355, 377
Pavlov, I. P., 197, 223
Paykel, E. S., 292, 306
Pelletier, K. R., 250, 253
Penfield, W., 205, 206, 207, 223
Perky, C. W., 199, 223
Perls, F., 11, 33, 196, 348, 352, 377
Pesso, A., 347, 377
Piaget, J., 192, 193, 194, 196, 312, 314n, 316, 345, 362, 377
Piers, E., 222, 223
Plaum, G., 143, 166
Polster, E., 367, 377
Pope, K. S., **3–32**, 6, 16, 33, 226
Popplewell, J. F., 219, 224
Posner, M. I., 96, 120
Prindull, E., 134, 166
Pylyshyn, Z., 390, 393

Quinlan, D. M., 284, 295, 306

Rachman, S., 256, 261, 277
Rado, S., 282, 296, 306
Raimy, V., 384, 393
Rapaport, D., 5, 33, 85, 91, 92
Rechenberger, H. G., 157, 166
Redlich, F. C., 161, 166
Reich, A., 374, 377
Reich, W., 14, 33, 347, 348, 356, 369, 377
Reik, T., 312, 314, 345, 351, 377
Reyher, J., 14, 17, 33, 35, **51–92**, 67, 69, 72, 74, 79, 84, 85, 88, 90, 92, 93, 305, 306
Richardson, A., 31, 33, 198, 199, 201, 224, 237, 245, 253, 391, 393
Rieff, P., 351, 352, 367, 377
Ritter, B., 271, 277
Rizley, R. C., 28, 33
Rock, I., 85, 93
Rodin, J., 6, 33
Rogers, C. R., 160, 166
Rokeach, M., 77, 79, 81, 93
Rolf, I. P., 347, 348, 377
Roper, G., 271, 277
Rosen, M., 230, 253
Rosen, V., 360, 377
Rosenthal, R., 323, 345
Rosenthal, T. L., 256, 261, 277
Rosten, L., 381n, 393
Roth, J. W., 141, 149, 150, 166
Rychlak, J., 282, 291, 306

Sachsse, U., 143, 166
Salber, W., 130, 166
Salzman, L., 47, 49
Sarason, I., 392, 393
Sarbin, T. R., 316, 346, 391, 393
Sarmousakis, G., 221, 222, 224

Schachtel, E., 10, 33, 361, 362, 363, 377
Schacter, S., 359, 361, 377
Schafer, R., 314, 346, 351, 355, 367, 378
Scheflen, A. E., 364, 378
Schimek, J. G., 361, 362, 367n, 378
Schmale, A., 250, 253
Schneck, J. M. G., 140, 166
Schofield, L. J., 88, 93
Schoop, T., 347, 349, 378
Schultz, J. H., 123, 126, 166
Schultz, K. D., 25, 279, **281–305**, 282, 283n, 291, 292, 293, 294, 295, 301, 302, 303, 305, 306, 307
Schwartz, G., 4, 29, 31, 33, 34
Schwartz, G. E., 6, 34
Scobie, G. E. W., 222, 224
Scott, R. W., 229, 253
Searles, H. F., 374, 378
Sechehaye, M., 196
Segal, S. J., 199, 224, 281, 307
Seidman, J. M., 3, 34
Seligman, M. E. P., 28, 34, 250, 253
Selman, R., 314, 315, 323, 325, 328n, 346
Shapiro, D., 367, 378
Sharpe, E. F., 362, 378
Sheehan, P. W., 90, 93, 120, 313, 346
Sheikh, A. A., 21, 123, **197–222**, 198, 206, 212, 219, 221, 224
Shepard, R., 187
Sherman, A. R., 271, 277
Shorr, J. E., 22, 35, **95–120**, 98n, 120, 121
Shrauger, S. E., 309, 310, 311, 313, 346
Siegel, E. V., 347, 378
Siegel, M. B., 361, 370, 378
Silberer, H., 126, 166
Silverman, L. H., 71, 93
Simonton, C., 176, 196, 250, 253
Simonton, O. C., 4, 34

Simpson, O. J., 31, 34
Singer, J. L., **3–32**, 6, 7, 8, 10, 12, 13, 14, 17, 23, 24, 25, 26, 29, 34, 37, 49, 98, 121, 126, 136, 166, 167, 173, 196, 198, 224, 226, 240, 243, 246, 253, 254, 267, 278, 281, 282, 284, 298, 299, 301, 302, 305, 307, 309, 317, 342, 346, 387, 388, 394
Sommerschield, H., 79, 93
Sontag, S., 351, 359, 360, 366, 368, 378
Sperry, R., 6, 34
Spiegel, J., 370, 378
Spitz, R., 160, 166
Stampfl, T. G., 229, 254
Stanislavski, C., 172, 196
Starker, S., 28, 34, 291, 294, 307
Stern, D. B., 62, 63, 64, 65, 84, 93
Stern, R., 196
Stewart, K., 170, 196
Stierlin, A., 144, 166
Stotland, E., 262, 278
Strahley, D. F., 271, 278
Strupp, H. H., 30, 34, 299, 301, 307, 384, 394
Suinn, R. M., 4, 31, 34, 245, 254
Sullivan, H. S., 52, 53, 54, 74, 78, 81, 83, 87, 88, 89, 91, 93, 95, 101, 120, 171, 175, 196, 365, 378
Sundberg, N. D., 323, 328n, 346
Swartley, W., 128, 138, 166
Swedenborg, S. W., 184, 196
Szasz, T., 374, 378

Taft, R., 310, 346
Tauber, E. S. 18, 34
Taylor, J. A., 151, 154, 159, 166

Author Index

Thase, M. E., 260, 263, 271, 274, 278
Thom, R., 193, 194, 195
Tillich, P., 351, 378
Tomkins, S., 9, 34
Tower, L. E., 374, 378
Traynor, T. D., 291, 294, 307
Truax, C., 342, 346
Turk, D., 25, 34

Ulam, S. M., 9, 34
Urbantschitsch, V., 201, 224

Volkan, V. D., 158, 166
Von Franz, M.-L., 179, 180, 181, 183, 186, 196

Wachtel, P., 225, 226, 254
Wächter, H.-M., 148, 150, 151, 152, 154, 156, 157, 166,
Wallen, R. W., 54, 93
Wapner, S., 284, 307
Watson, J. B., 227, 254
Watson, J. P., 271, 272, 278
Watzlawick, P., 176, 190, 192, 196
Weaver, R., 175, 186, 196
Weinberg, N. H., 267, 278
Weiner, H., 265, 278
Weiss, T., 229, 254
Weitzman, B., 267, 278
Welgan, P. R., 229, 254
Werner, H., 78, 85, 89, 90, 93, 145, 166
Westcott, M. R., 312, 346
Whitehead, W. E., 229, 254
Whorf, R. L., 191, 196
Wiener, M., 364, 370, 378
Wilkins, W., 382, 386, 394

Wilson, E., 4, 34
Winer, B. J., 346
Winnicott, D., 375, 378
Wiseman, R. J., 91, 93
Witkin, H. A., 27, 34
Wittgenstein, L., 186, 188, 196
Wolff, W., 363, 378
Woolf, V., 4, 34
Wolpe, J., 23, 227, 228, 235, 254, 255, 278, 381, 382, 394
Wright, J. C., 271, 278

Zaidi, S. M. H., 222, 224
Zeeman, E. C., 193, 194, 196
Zepf, S., 131, 166
Zillmann, D., 284, 307
Zimmer, H., 181, 196
Zucker, H., 172, 186, 196

Subject Index

Accurate Predictions of Attitudes Measure, 322, 325–327, 338
Actor Prepares, An (Stanislavski), 172
Age Projection Test, 210–212, 220
American Dance Therapy Association defines dance therapy, 348–349
Anxiety
  daydreams related to, 387
  and dystonia, 80–81
  self-disclosure related to, 52–67

Biofeedback in covert conditioning, 7, 25, 30–31, 177, 229–230, 248–250
Behavior Analysis History Questionnaire, 235
Behavior modification movements' influence on psychotherapy, 225–228

Catastrophy theory, 193–194
Change (Watzlawick, Weakland, and Fisch), 192
C-I-G. *See* Consciousness-Imagery-Gap
Cognition and expression
  interrelated modes of representation in, 8–13, 38–48
Colitis Ulcerosa (Freiwald, Liedtke, and Zepf), 141
Concepts vs. percepts, 85, 190
Consciousness-Imagery-Gap (C-I-G), 218–219
Consciousness movement, 352
Countertransference, 18–19, 45, 87, 359, 373–375

Daydreaming: An Introduction to the Experimental Study of Inner Experience (Singer), 281
Daydreams
  and active imagining therapy, 167, 171
  anxiety related to, 387
  covert influences of, 243–246
  and depression, 287, 292, 294, 295, 297–298, 301
  and empathy, 309, 316–317, 323, 333–336
  and GAI, 125–163
  image modality of, 8, 68
  logging of, 243–246, 333–336
  See also Dreams
Depression
  circular feedback cycle of, 290, 292–295, 300
  covert conditioning for, 233, 240–241, 244
  daydream pattern of, 287, 292, 294, 295, 297–298, 301
  dependency factor of, 287, 288, 295–296
  and fantasy, 285, 286, 292, 294, 300–301
  focused imagery technique for, 282–305
  self-criticism factor of, 287, 296–297
Desensitization, systematic. *See* Psychotherapy, systematic desensitization
Differential Emotions Scale, 284
Dissociation
  dystonia related to, 80
  repression vs., 78–79

Dreams, 19, 37, 40, 74
  and active imagining therapy, 167–176
  covert conditioning for, 246–248
  and GAI, 141
  hot imagery in, 72–73
  imagery modality of, 8
  logging of, 29–30
  See also Daydreams
Dystonia, 76–83, 85–87

Eidetic Parents Test (EPT), 210, 212–219
Empathy
  conditioned studies of, 318–341
  daydreams related to, 309, 316–317, 333–336
  factor influencing, 341–342
  fantasy related to, 309, 312–317
  therapy for, 342–344
Entrée points in emergent uncovering psychotherapy, 53–58, 65
Epilepsy
  and eidetic therapy, 207
EPT. *See* Eidetic Parents Test
E.S.T. "therapeutic" tongues, 185
Expression. *See* Cognition and expression

Fantasy, 6, 19, 40, 44, 388
  behavior related to, 387
  catathymic imagery in, 125
  and covert conditioning, 244–245
  and depression, 285, 286, 292, 294, 300–301
  and eidetic images, 102
  and empathy, 309, 312–317
Fear Survey Schedule (FSS), 235
Flooding, 228, 270
Forge and the Crucible, The (Eliade), 182
Free association
  Freud's use of, 14
  in GAI, 139–140, 145
  generation of, 69
  purpose of, 57–58, 355–356
  stimuli for, 96–97
FSS. *See* Fear Survey Schedule

GAI. *See* Psychotherapy, GAI (guided affective imagery)
Gestalt therapy, 11, 14, 173, 348n
Glide Foundation films, 182

Hypnosis, 145, 172–173, 186

Imagery
  and biofeedback, 30–31
  covert conditioning factors of, 234–239
    See also Psychotherapy, covert conditioning
  defined, 198
  evaluation of therapeutic uses of, 3–32, 381–393
  interrelated modes of, 8–13, 38–48
  of in-viewing, 96
    See also Psycho-imagination therapy
  percepts vs., 199–200
  and resistance, 40
    in eidetic therapy, 217–219
    in GAI, 141
    in psycho-imagination therapy, 113–115
    See also Security operations
  and structured thought, 186–195
    See also Psychotherapy, active imagining
  types of
    affective, 199. *See also* Psychotherapy, GAI
    after-image, 199, 200
    aggressive, 283
    archetypal, 158, 183–186, 194–195
    body, 105–106, 118
    cathartic, 111
    defiant, 113
    depth, 111–112, 119
    dual, 102–105, 109, 117
    eidetic, 199. *See also* Psychotherapy, eidetic
    free, 283–284
    general, 112, 118–119
    group therapy, 115–119
    hot, 72–73, 88
    imagination, 119, 201
    illusion, 199
    memory, 199–202
    mescaline, 199
    positive, 283
    predicting, 108
    self-image, 101–102, 118
    sexual, 25, 106–108, 118
    socially gratifying, 283
    spontaneous visual, 52–53, 89–90,

Subject Index

Imagery (cont.)
   sexual (cont.)
      99–100. *See also* Psychotherapy, emergent uncovering task, 109–111, 119
Imaginal Processes Inventory, 294
Information processing
   analogic-synthetic, 67, 68, 84–85, 87, 89–91
   and empathy, 317
   semantic-syntactic, 67–68, 86, 87, 89–91
Information sources visual system, 42–43
Inhibitions
   intervention techniques for, 43–48
Initiated symbol projection (ISP), 138
International Society for Guided Affective Imagery, 125
Interventions, 22, 25
   GAI crisis, 143–144, 149, 161
   purposes of, 37, 41
   techniques for inhibition, 43–48
In-viewing, 95–96
ISP. *See* Initiated symbol projection

Law of Visiosomatic Dessociation, 203, 210
Law of Visiosomatic Fixation, 203, 210
Lecture on Jung's Typology (Von Franz), 180

Origin of Consciousness in the Breakdown of the Bicameral Mind, The (Jaynes), 8n

Percepts
   and C-I-G, 218
   concepts vs., 85
   imagery vs., 199–201
   and problem solving, 90
   retrieval of, 84–86
Personality Research Form, 322n
Phobias
   covert conditioning for, 237, 241
   systematic desensitization for, 7, 23, 46
Placebo suggestion, 23, 26, 27
Profile of Nonverbal Sensitivity, 323, 325, 330, 332–333
Projection, mobile. *See* Transformations
Psycheye: Self-Analytic Consciousness (Ahsen), 221–222

Psycho-imagination therapy
   emphasis of, 95–97
   group, 115–119
   resistance in, 113–115
   Shorr Imagery Test, 119–120
   techniques for, 96–119
Psychology and Alchemy (Jung), 182
Psychotherapy
   concepts of, 299–301
   imagery usage related to change in, 381–393
   influence of behavior modification movement on, 225
   interrelated modes of representation in, 8–14, 38–48
   initial phase of, 383
   techniques used in varying methods of, 5–32
Psychotherapy, active imagining
   and archetypal imagery, 183–186, 194–195
   and catastrophy, theory, 193–194
   and dream imagery, 167–176
   realism in, 173–176
   structuralism of, 179–183, 186–195
   techniques for, 168–186
   transformations in, 177–179
Psychotherapy, body-movement
   analytic vs., 351–353, 356–361, 365–367
   basic premise of, 348
   and body-awareness, 353–354
   communication in, 363–366, 370
   and countertransference, 359, 373–375
   and physical contact, 349, 359, 371, 373
   types of, 347–349
   and unconscious factor, 361–363, 365
Psychotherapy, covert conditioning, 44, 45
   behavior catagories in, 228–229, 248–250
   basis and orientation of, 228
   covert modeling
      evaluated, 259–261
      and imagery assessment, 239, 267–270
      parameters of, 261–267
      techniques of, 233, 256–259, 392
   covert vs., overt, 270–272, 274
   overall well-being related to, 243–250, 256
   for phobias, 237, 241

Psychotherapy, covert conditioning (cont.)
  and systematic desensitization, 7, 23–24, 231, 263
  techniques for, 228–250, 255–256
Psychotherapy, eidetic, 123
  Age Projection Test in, 210–212, 216, 220
  Eidetic Parents Test in, 210, 212–219
  and experimentalist, 201
  group, 221
  image classifications in, 198–201
  and ISM, 201–204
  personality structuring in, 204–210
  resistance to, 217–219
  techniques for, 205–207, 210–221
Psychotherapy, emergent uncovering, 17
  directional drive factors in, 51–92
  and information processing, 67–69
  security operations in, 52, 54–59, 75, 80–83, 86
  and spontaneous visual imagery, 51–53, 89
  techniques for, 53–67, 87
Psychotherapy for depression. *See* Depression
Psychotherapy for empathy. *See* Empathy
Psychotherapy, GAI (guided affective imagery)
  motifs of, 132–139
  precursors of, 125–126
  statistical studies of, 149–155
  symbolic psychodynamics of, 143–148, 158, 161–163
  techniques for, 125–157
  transference relationships in, 159–161
  transformations (mobile and synchronic) in, 127–130, 146–147
Psychotherapy, implosive, 28, 52
Psychotherapy, systematic desensitization, 173, 255, 392
  covert conditioning techniques for, 7, 23–24, 231 263
  covert vs., overt, 270–272, 274
  and covert modeling, 263
  effectiveness of, 28
  and phobias, 7, 23, 46

Quinlan-Janis Self-Esteem Scale, 284

Reinforcement Survey Schedule, (RSS), 235, 244

Repression
  define vs., 46
  dissociation vs., 78–79
  factors in, 43, 218
Rêve Éveillé Dirigé, Le (Desoille), 7, 123
RSS. *See* Reinforcement Survey Schedule

Security operations, 52, 54–59, 62–64, 80–83, 86, 95–96
Self-awareness, 21, 29–30, 180
  and behavior change, 384–386
  psyche-imagination therapy techniques for, 95–119
Self-control, 22, 30–31
  cognitive theory of, 300
  triad technique for, 242–243
Self-disclosure factors, 52–67, 87
Self-effacement, 57–58
Self-efficacy, 26–28
Self-esteem factors, 25, 53–59, 63, 64, 75–83
Self-regulation. *See* Self-control
Sex
  and arousal imagery, 25, 106–108, 118
  covert conditioning for deviation, 230
Schizophrenia, 87
  and body-movement therapy, 373
  and eidetic therapy, 206
Shorr Imagery Test, 119–120
Sports
  covert conditioning for, 31, 245
Stimuli
  in eidetic therapy, 201, 205–207, 214
  in free association, 96–97
  and imagery, 199, 200
  interrelated factors in, 41
Stream of consciousness, 3–4
Stress innoculation techniques, 24–25
Structuralism
  in active imagining
    abstracted, 191–195
    of healing, 179–183, 184–185
    of thought, 186–191
  of personality in eidetic therapy, 204, 207–210
  of role-taking in empathy, 314–317, 341
Symbols
  in active imagining, 190
  degeneration of, 181

Symbols (cont.)
   and experience transformation,
     365–366
   and feeling, 352
   in GAI, 123, 133, 143–145, 158,
     161–163
   ISP, 138
Symptomatic Reaction Scale, 65
Syntonia, 76

T.A. rescripting, 173, 185
Tao of Physics, The (Capra), 190–191
TAT. *See* Thematic Apperception Test
Test of Implied Meanings, 323, 325–328, 338
Test of Social Reasoning, 323, 328–329, 331
Thematic Apperception Test (TAT), 128
Thought representations
   defined, 8
   interrelations of, 8–13, 38–48
   therapists' use of, 10–21

Tibetan Book of the Dead (Evans-Wentz), 179
Transference
   in GAI, 159–161
   See also Countertransference
Transformations
   in active imagining, 177–179
   in GAI, 146–147
     mobile projection, 127–129
     synchronic, 130

Visual Thinking (Arnheim), 189–190

Wechsler Adult Intelligence Scale, 5
World Test for Children, 128

Yoga, 180–183, 348, 350

Zen, 182

Milton Keynes UK
Ingram Content Group UK Ltd.
UKHW050708210724
445729UK00019B/415